Proclus on Whole and Part: A Reappraisal of Mereology in
Neoplatonic Metaphysics

Philosophia Antiqua

A SERIES OF STUDIES ON ANCIENT PHILOSOPHY

Series Editors

Frans A.J. de Haas (*Leiden*)
Irmgard Männlein (*Tübingen*)

Advisory Board

Keimpe Algra, *Utrecht University* – George Boys-Stones, *University of Toronto* – Philipp Brüllmann, *University of Heidelberg* – Klaus Corcilius, *University of Tübingen* – George Karamanolis, *University of Vienna* – Inna Kupreeva, *University of Edinburgh* – Mariska Leunissen, *The University of North Carolina at Chapel Hill* – Sara Magrin, *University of Pittsburgh* – Marije Martijn, *Vrije Universiteit Amsterdam* – Christopher Moore, *Pennsylvania State University* – Noburu Notomi, *The University of Tokyo* – Pauliina Remes, *Uppsala University* – David Runia, *University of Melbourne* – Barbara Sattler, *Ruhr University Bochum* – Frisbee Sheffield, *University of Cambridge and Downing College* – Svetla Slaveva-Griffin, *Florida State University* – Carrie Swanson, *University of Iowa* – Katja Vogt, *Columbia University* – Christian Wildberg, *University of Pittsburgh*

Previous Editors

C.J. Rowe (*Durham*)
J.H. Waszink†
W.J. Verdenius†
J.C.M. Van Winden†

VOLUME 172

The titles published in this series are listed at *brill.com/pha*

Proclus on Whole and Part:
A Reappraisal of Mereology in Neoplatonic Metaphysics

By

Arthur Oosthout

BRILL

LEIDEN | BOSTON

The Library of Congress Cataloging-in-Publication Data is available online at https://catalog.loc.gov
LC record available at https://lccn.loc.gov/2024049627

Typeface for the Latin, Greek, and Cyrillic scripts: "Brill". See and download: brill.com/brill-typeface.

ISSN 0079-1687
ISBN 978-90-04-72175-3 (hardback)
ISBN 978-90-04-72176-0 (e-book)
DOI 10.1163/9789004721760

Copyright 2025 by Arthur Oosthout. Published by Koninklijke Brill BV, Leiden, The Netherlands.
Koninklijke Brill BV incorporates the imprints Brill, Brill Nijhoff, Brill Schöningh, Brill Fink, Brill mentis,
Brill Wageningen Academic, Vandenhoeck & Ruprecht, Böhlau and V&R unipress.
Koninklijke Brill BV reserves the right to protect this publication against unauthorized use. Requests for
re-use and/or translations must be addressed to Koninklijke Brill BV via brill.com or copyright.com.
info@brill.com for more information.

This book is printed on acid-free paper and produced in a sustainable manner.

Contents

Acknowledgements IX
Figures and Tables XI

1 **Introduction** 1
   1.1 Status Quaestionis 4
      1.1.1 *Established Scholarship on Proclean Mereology* 5
      1.1.2 *The Author's Own Recent Work on Proclean Mereology* 7
   1.2 A Preview of Proclean Mereology 8
   1.3 Overview of the Study 10
   1.4 Essential Proclean Concepts and Terminology 13
   1.5 Critical Editions and Translations 15

PART 1
The Mereological Question

2 **Mereology 101** 21
   2.1 Classical Extensional Mereology 22
   2.2 David Lewis's Argument for Unrestricted Composition 24
   2.3 Peter Van Inwagen and the Special Composition Question 28
   2.4 The Whole as a Structure in Plato 32
      2.4.1 *Socrates and Theaetetus versus Extensional Mereology* 33
      2.4.2 *The Whole-as-Structure Model* 36
      2.4.3 *Philebus 23c–26d* 38
      2.4.4 *Timaeus 31b–32c* 40
   2.5 Structure as a Part in Aristotle 42
      2.5.1 *Harte versus Koslicki on the Regress Argument* 43
      2.5.2 *Mereological Considerations on Koslicki's Neo-Aristotelian Theory* 46
      2.5.3 *Aristotle versus Van Inwagen* 47
   2.6 The Two Sides of Modern Mereology 47

VI   CONTENTS

PART 2
The Central Tenets of Proclean Mereology

3 Quantity versus Complexity 55
  3.1 Proclus' Rule in the *Elements of Theology* 57
  3.2 'A Being First, Then a Living Being': the Proclean Rule in Action 64
  3.3 Stacking Material Substrates: the Proclean Rule and Demiurgy 70
  3.4 The Compatibility of the *TP*- and *IP*-Passages 77
  3.5 The Double Meaning of Συνθετώτερον 78

4 A Wholesome Trinity 83
  4.1 The Basics of the Threefold Wholeness 87
  4.2 Whole above Part: the Roots of Proclean Mereology 92
  4.3 Two Examples from Proclus' Cosmology 98
  4.4 The Whole in Each Part: a Reappraisal of Previous Readings 105
  4.5 Stronger Apart and Stronger Together 108

PART 3
Part and Whole in Proclus' Theology and Cosmology

5 Dividing the Indivisible 115
  5.1 Balancing the Relativistic Whole and the Determinate Whole 117
  5.2 The Distinctive Character of the Intelligible Whole 122
    5.2.1 *The Eternal Whole* 124
    5.2.2 *The Perfect Composite* 128
  5.3 Unfolding the Heaven 131
  5.4 The Evolution of Whole into Part 135
  5.5 The Division of the Platonic Forms by the Intellective Gods 142
  5.6 The Development of Axiology, Cosmology, and Perfection 150
  5.7 The Indivisible Divided 154
    5.7.1 *The Concepts 'Whole', 'Perfect', 'Part', and 'Division' in*
           Proclean Theology 154
    5.7.2 *Relative or Rigid?* 157
    5.7.3 *The Whole and the Good* 159

6 Uniting the Imperfect 161
  6.1 The Mereological Role of Time 163
  6.2 Between a Systematic and an Exegetical Mereology 168
    6.2.1 *The Introduction to the Third Book of the*
           Timaeus-Commentary 169
    6.2.2 *The Third Gift of the Demiurge: the Whole of Wholes* 171

CONTENTS   VII

6.2.3   *The Tenth Gift of the Demiurge: Resemblance to the*
   Paradigm 172
6.2.4   *The Demiurge's Speech to the Young Gods* 175
6.2.5   *The Mereological Lessons from the Four Passages* 178
6.3 Material Existence and the Partial Wholeness of the Individual 182
6.4 The Question of the Partial Good 195

PART 4
Bringing the Parts Together

7 **The Best Kind of Whole (for a Neoplatonist)** 205
 7.1 Reflecting on the Sum of the Parts 205
  7.1.1 *Formalists versus Naturalists (Aka to Be Fuzzy or Not to*
    Be Fuzzy) 205
  7.1.2 *The Right Kind of Composition* 207
  7.1.3 *Expanding the Concept of Wholeness* 207
  7.1.4 *The Division of the Indivisible Whole* 208
  7.1.5 *(A)Part Alone, Whole Together* 210
 7.2 What Is Proclus' Definition of the Whole(Some)? 211
 7.3 Is Proclus' Mereology Consistent? 219
 7.4 Is the Proclean Whole Fuzzy or Fantastical? 224
 7.5 Are Proclean Compounds Whole in an Ethical Sense? 227
 7.6 Is Proclus' Mereology Actually Any Good? 229

Bibliography 231
Index locorum 245
Index rerum 249

Acknowledgements

This manuscript was developed from the author's doctoral dissertation, 'Proclus and the Mereological Link Between Ethics and Metaphysics. Perfection as Part of Cosmology' (KU Leuven, 2022). The research which formed the basis for both the PhD thesis and this reworked monograph was made possible by C1 (BOF) funding provided by the Internal Funds KU Leuven as part of the interdisciplinary research project 'Longing for Perfection. Living the Perfect Life in Late Antiquity—A Journey Between Ideal and Reality' (grant No. C16/17/001) from 2018 to 2022. From 2022 to 2023, during which time the dissertation was reworked into the present manuscript, the author received PDM-funding (grant No. PDMt2/22/004) from the same KU Leuven Internal Funds. The final revisions were made possible by a brief extension of funding from the aforementioned C1 research project on late ancient perfection in early 2024.

The manuscript builds not only on the PhD thesis, but also on the publications by the author during his doctoral research. Most importantly, the fourth chapter, 'A Wholesome Trinity', reincorporates an article which the author previously published in *Ancient Philosophy*, and for the reuse of which in the present monograph he received the graceful permission of the *Philosophy Documentation Center* (the reused material includes fig. 3; for the full reference to the article, see the first footnote of chapter 4). Other publications by the author are treated as would be any other secondary source: where necessary for the line of argument of the book, select insights from those earlier publications are summarised or paraphrased with the adequate references. For a more detailed overview of the author's previous publications which factor into his arguments in the present study, see chapter 1, section 1.2 below.

The author thanks the members of the aforementioned research project on late ancient perfection for the valuable feedback they provided at the author's presentations of his work in progress. Special thanks go out to the two project members who served as the supervisors for the PhD thesis: Gerd Van Riel and Geert Roskam. They gave astute and comprehensive feedback on the candidate's philosophical interpretations and his translations of the Greek texts, while also granting him ample space in which to develop his own perspective on the material.

The remarks of the doctoral commission, which consisted of the aforementioned supervisors alongside Marije Martijn, Jan Opsomer, and Pieter d'Hoine, were equally important to the development of this monograph. Many of the improvements which turned the PhD thesis into the present manuscript were only made possible by the insightful criticisms and comments which the aforementioned scholars provided during and after defence. The author is likewise grateful to Frans de Haas, editor of *Philosophia antiqua*, and to the anonymous reviewer of Brill for their remarks on the manuscript. It goes without saying that the author is solely responsible for any remaining errors.

The author additionally thanks the many delightful colleagues, both young and old, who serve or have served as members of the De Wulf-Mansion Centre for Ancient, Medieval, and Renaissance Philosophy at the KU Leuven's Institute of Philosophy between 2018 and the present day. His gratitude extends also to five young scholars of the Institute of Philosophy and the Faculty of Arts at KU Leuven: Thibaut Lejeune, Maxime Maleux, Wim Nijs, Reuben Pitts, and Laurens van der Wiel. With them, the author was able to share both the joys and difficulties of starting an academic career over many a glass of wine, most often enjoyed alongside a pizza at a delightful little restaurant in Leuven called *La Piazzetta*.

I must express special gratitude to three people: to Ellen Bloksma, my mother, for her unerring support, love, and sage life advice granted even across the border between Belgium and the Netherlands; to Henri Oosthout, my father, for having the grace to use his enormous philosophical acumen for such lowly tasks as checking my writing and proofreading my translations, and for being available at all times to help me develop my capacities as a philosopher through our extensive discussions; to Louise Dewez, my partner, for being the shining centre of light, warmth, and purpose in my life just as Plato's Good provides those things to the Platonic philosopher.

Leuven, Belgium
2024

Figures and Tables

Figures

1 The transmission of intelligible characters into the sensible by the hypostasis of Soul   68

2 'Proclus' rule' as it applies in the *Parmenides*-commentary (production of the sensible cosmos)   73

3 Proclus' three kinds of wholes as described in the *Elements of Theology*   92

Tables

1 The results of the Proclean rule as described in Proclus, *TP* III.6   65

2 The parallel developments of wholeness and perfection in books three and four of the *Platonic Theology*   141

3 The intellective hebdomad, and the Platonic dialogues from which Proclus distils the primary characteristics of the hebdomad's intellective triads   143

4 The parallel between Proclus' three kinds of wholes and the manifestations of Platonic Forms as described in the primary and secondary sources   149

5 Overview of the development of wholeness, perfection, and division in the Proclean Intellect   160

6 Overview of the mereological properties (ἰδιότητες) of the One, the intelligible realm, and the intelligible-intellective realm as distilled from Plato's *Parmenides*   160

7 Schematic overview of the kinds of wholes and parts enumerated in the passages discussed in chapter 6, section 2   179

8 The intelligible and cosmic beings discussed in the fifth book of the *Timaeus*-commentary, ranked by dissolubility   186

9 The parallel between the different kinds of forms as described in chapter 5 and the different manifestations of the Form of a mortal creature   194

10 The three kinds of divided beings enumerated in the *Platonic Theology*   198

CHAPTER 1

Introduction

The concept of being whole carries some interesting connotations. Although contemporary philosophical discourse often starts from a neutral understanding of the term 'whole', namely as designating a collection of parts, many philosophers find it difficult to let go of the intuition that a whole is something *more* than a simple collection of parts. For example, one cannot claim to be a car manufacturer by simply throwing some car parts on a pile. When the car is correctly manufactured, there is also some structure, arrangement, or interaction between the parts that makes them into a functional car. Similarly, few would claim that a car is still truly whole after thieves have broken the windows to get inside or stolen the wheels. The claim that a thing is whole intuitively implies that it is also *complete*, in the sense that no essential parts are missing.

Such pregnant uses of the term raise issues of identity. In purely material terms, the car built by the manufacturer contains the exact same parts which the amateur would foolishly dump on a heap. What exactly causes the parts assembled in the factory to become a car while the amateur's car parts remain a heap? Furthermore, to what extent can parts of the completed car be removed or replaced until the car is no longer the same as it originally was? How many parts can one remove before the car becomes incomplete? How many parts can one replace before one has a functionally new car? In other words, what exactly is the whole beyond the sum of its parts? This question has vexed philosophers throughout history, and the answers proposed by various thinkers have themselves been subjected to extensive studies. Within the context of ancient philosophy, however, there is one philosopher whose extensive treatment of this topic has yet to receive a complete (pun intended) analysis: the Neoplatonic philosopher Proclus (± 412–485 AD).

Given its name, it should come as no surprise that Proclus' Neoplatonic philosophy was indebted to the writings of Plato. The oeuvre of the influential philosopher provided Proclus with his ultimate divinity, the One or Good, the concept of transcendent Ideas or Forms shaping all that comes to be in our sensible world, and many other metaphysical notions. Naturally, Proclus' views on the relations between parts and wholes are similarly inspired by the philosopher to which his school of thought owed its name. In fact, when Proclus introduces his most distinctive theorem on part-whole relations in the third book of his *Platonic Theology*, namely the idea that there are three distinct

© ARTHUR OOSTHOUT, 2025 | DOI:10.1163/9789004721760_002

ways in which a thing can be whole, he refers immediately to Platonic dialogues such as the *Timaeus*.[1] In that work of Plato's, the titular speaker recounts a grand mythology of the creation of our sensible universe, which is described as the ultimate organism of which each of us is a part. In this mythology, it is revealed that the creator-god or Demiurge contemplates the intelligible paradigm which encompasses the four universal genera of living beings, and then fashions the image of that paradigm, our material cosmos, into the best thing it could possibly be.

> τάδε διανοηθείς, πρῶτον μὲν ἵνα ὅλον ὅτι μάλιστα ζῷον τέλεον ἐκ τελέων τῶν μερῶν εἴη, πρὸς δὲ τούτοις ἕν, ἅτε οὐχ ὑπολελειμμένων ἐξ ὧν ἄλλο τοιοῦτον γένοιτ' ἄν, ἔτι δὲ ἵν' ἀγήρων καὶ ἄνοσον ᾖ.
>
> (...)
>
> διὰ δὴ τὴν αἰτίαν καὶ τὸν λογισμὸν τόνδε ἕνα ὅλον ὅλων ἐξ ἁπάντων τέλεον καὶ ἀγήρων καὶ ἄνοσον αὐτὸν ἐτεκτήνατο.
>
> PLATO, *Tim.* 32c8–33b1

And these were [the Demiurge's] intentions: first, that [the universe] might be a living being as whole as possible, a complete thing composed of complete parts; next, that it might be one, inasmuch as there were no things left over out of which another like it might come into existence; further, that it might be secure from age and ailment.

(...)

For this reason and with this reasoning, he fashioned it to be one whole, composed of all wholes, complete and ageless and without sickness.

> Tr. BURY 1929 (modified)

Since the 'totality' ($\pi\tilde{\alpha}\nu$) contains all that is, it is the ultimate whole that can be conceived, to the extent that it encompasses all other wholes. According to Timaeus, this means that the cosmos is also 'complete' ($\tau\acute{\epsilon}\lambda\epsilon o\nu$). There is, after all, nothing outside of the universe that it could be missing. However, the Greek adjective $\tau\acute{\epsilon}\lambda\epsilon o\nu$ refers to more than simply being complete in the sense of being a full sum of parts. It also means 'fulfilled' or, more pertinently, 'perfect'.[2] In fact, the Platonic passage implies, not that the universe is a complete yet unordered heap of all things, but that all of its parts are arranged in an

---

1 The specific kinds of wholes distinguished by Proclus are discussed in full detail in chapter 4. For the complete set of Platonic dialogues referenced by Proclus in this instance, see chapter 4, section 2 specifically.

2 See *LSJ* s.v. τέλειος; cf. Harte (2002a: 131).

INTRODUCTION

optimal manner. That it is not just full but also perfect is implied by the statement that the Platonic universe does not decay or wither. Furthermore, the sublimity of the universe is such that even its parts are whole in the sense of being perfect. In summary, Plato not only employs the concept of being whole in the pregnant sense described above, i.e., of a whole as something which is complete, but also specifically interprets this completeness as *perfection*. The universe is whole, and thus perfect.

As the systematic philosopher that he is,[3] Proclus takes Plato's link between the concepts of being whole and being perfect and runs with it, incorporating it into the fabric of his deeply complex metaphysical system. As mentioned above, Proclus distinguishes three manners in which a thing can be whole. Inspired by the aforementioned passage from the *Timaeus*, Proclus assigns to the concept of perfection the same threefold distinction in the fourth book of his *Platonic Theology*.[4] If one accepts that wholeness is linked to perfection (through the overlap between completeness and perfection) as Proclus does, then it stands to reason that both wholeness and perfection should be defined in the same way. Dirk Baltzly has picked up on this, remarking that 'the concepts of being perfect or complete (τέλειον) and being whole are treated [by Proclus] as exactly parallel in structure.'[5]

Yet, as mentioned above, conceiving of the whole as something beyond the mere sum of its parts raises a number of difficult philosophical problems. The most pressing of these is the question of how the multitude of parts becomes a singular entity. Given that the concepts of unity and multiplicity lie at the heart of Neoplatonic philosophy, the question of how to define the whole separately from its parts is an essential one for Proclus. In fact, Proclus appears to show an even greater interest in the whole than his fellow Neoplatonic philosophers do, for the database analysis of the *Thesaurus Linguae Graecae* indicates that 'ὅλος' is the tenth most frequently occurring lemma in Proclus' oeuvre, with a whopping 4070 occurrences. Furthermore, the declension 'ὅλον' is the tenth most frequently occurring *wordform* in Proclus' works, popping up no less than 1268 times.[6]

---

3   For this distinctive aspect of Proclus' style of philosophy, see Martijn's and Gerson's (2016) chapter in the introductory volume *All from One: A Guide to Proclus*, edited by Pieter d'Hoine and Marije Martijn. I shall refrain from a lengthy introduction to Proclus' life and thought, since everything an unfamiliar reader might wish to know about Proclus is explained in the pages of the aforementioned volume.

4   See the discussion of Proclus, *TP* IV.25, 74.20–75.20 in chapter 5, section 4.

5   Baltzly (2008: 408 n. 22), my addition between brackets.

6   For comparison, 'ὅλος' is only the 40th most frequently occurring lemma in Plotinus' *Enneads*, and does not even make the top 100 of most frequently occurring lemmata in Plato's writings;

The frequent appearance of the term 'whole' is not the only indication of Proclus' interest in part-whole relations. In fact, one could rightly interject that neither the Greek wordform 'ὅλος' nor the declension 'ὅλον' automatically denote the philosophical concept of the whole. However, Proclus devotes an entire section of the first half of his *Elements of Theology* to the concepts of part and whole. Given that the goal of the *Elements of Theology* is to establish the fundamental tenets of Proclus' philosophy, and that the work's first half introduces the universal concepts underpinning Neoplatonic metaphysics, the relation between whole and part is clearly a fundamental aspect of Proclean thought. Furthermore, the concept of wholeness plays a similarly important role in Proclus' exegesis of the second hypothesis of Plato's *Parmenides*, a dialogue which was considered by the Neoplatonic commentators to be the most important of all Platonic works. Lastly, Proclus defines the relation between whole and part by using the same triadic framework he applies to many other fundamental aspects of Platonic thought, such as the concept of participation. In other words, Proclus not only follows Plato in intuiting some connection between the notion of the whole and the notion of being perfect, but he also deals extensively with the fundamental question of what it means to be whole in the first place.

Unfortunately, procuring information on Proclus' concept of the whole and its close relation to the concept of perfection is a rather complex affair. By this I do not mean to say that no scholarly analyses of Proclean mereology exist. In fact, there are quite a few good insights on Proclean parts and wholes to be found. However, these insights are somewhat scattered.

1.1 Status Quaestionis

Although mereology (from the Greek μέρος, meaning 'part') is now known as a separate field of study which bridges logic and metaphysics, it only came to enjoy such a status in the twentieth century, when the Polish mathematician and philosopher Stanisław Leśniewski conceived of a logical system focused on parts and wholes (it is to this system that the modern discipline owes its name).[7] In antiquity, the study of parts and wholes had no such special status.

---

see *TLG—Statistics* (http://stephanus.tlg.uci.edu/Iris/inst/stat.jsp) s.v. 'Plato', 'Plotinus', and 'Proclus'.

7 The very first occurrences of distinctly mereological theories can be found in the writings of Brentano and Husserl, the latter of which 'may rightly be considered the first attempt at a thorough formulation of a theory, though in a format that makes it difficult to disentangle the analysis of mereological concepts from that of other ontologically relevant notions', as Varzi (2016) notes.

INTRODUCTION

This does not mean that ancient philosophers held no interest in these concepts. On the contrary, the roots of the discipline 'can be traced back to the early days of philosophy'.[8] Yet in ancient philosophy, questions concerning the nature of parthood could arise within almost any topic of discussion, since the terms 'whole' and 'part' have a much wider range of meaning than most contemporary, axiomatised theories allow.[9]

1.1.1 *Established Scholarship on Proclean Mereology*

Within Proclus' philosophy, mereology similarly occurs in a variety of contexts. Unfortunately, the scholarly analyses of this aspect of his thought have yet to be unified. There are a number of articles, edited volumes, and monographs available to the reader aiming to master Proclean mereology. However, the analyses contained in these works often focus primarily on some other aspect of Proclus' philosophy, in which mereology plays a secondary role. For example, Jan Opsomer's papers on Proclus' account of the production of the sensible cosmos by the Demiurge point to interesting passages of Proclus' *Timaeus*-commentary, in which the philosopher distinguishes between cosmic entities which exist 'holistically' (ὁλικῶς) and cosmic entities which exist 'partially' (μερικῶς).[10] Yet one might equally be drawn towards Proclus' description of eternal existence as 'whole at once' (ἅμα ὅλον) and end up reading Emilie Kutash's analysis of the relation between time and eternity.[11] Alternatively, one might be intrigued by the aforementioned distinction between three different kinds of wholeness, and end up lost in a variety of scholarly analyses linking Proclus' mereological triad to different strands of Neoplatonic philosophy, ranging from the theory of the henads to the relations of participation between transcendent hypostases and the question of whether Platonic Ideas of individuals exists according to Proclus.[12]

---

8   Varzi (*ibidem*).

9   The wide applicability of the discipline in ancient discourse was once again revealed at the conference *Part and Whole in Antiquity* (September 23rd through 25th of 2021), organised by myself and three valued colleagues, Sokratis-Athanasios Kiosoglou, Thibaut Lejeune, and Dashan Xu. The topics broached at that conference ranged from Presocratic conceptions of the city-state to Platonic psychology, Aristotelian ethics, and Epicurean physics; cf. Oosthout, Kiosoglou, and Lejeune (2024).

10   Opsomer (2000a, 2003, 2006a, 2016; cf. 2021). For Proclus' distinction between holistic and partial cosmic entities, see chapter 6, section 2.2.

11   Kutash (2009). For the designation of eternal existence as ἅμα ὅλον, see chapter 5, section 2; cf. O'Neill (1962) and Opsomer (2000b: 363 n. 50).

12   The *status quaestionis* concerning specifically the topic of the threefold wholeness is outlined in more detail in the introduction to chapter 4. The topics mentioned here are discussed by Butler (2010), Chlup (2012), and Baltzly (2008) and d'Hoine (2010 and 2021), respectively.

Scholarly inquiries into Proclean mereology itself are unfortunately less common, and often restricted in their focus. Aside from the previously mentioned analyses of the three kinds of wholeness, which differ greatly in their approaches to the material, examples of other studies of Proclean mereology include an analysis by Theo Kobusch of how neither unity nor totality automatically equate to wholeness for Proclus, and a paper by Sarah Klitenic Wear which focuses exclusively on Proclus' exegesis of a single lemma from the *Parmenides*-commentary (though this in no way diminishes the quality of the analysis itself).[13] The link between perfection and wholeness fares even worse in contemporary scholarship, being mostly relegated to brief remarks or footnotes.[14]

Recently, however, interest in Proclean mereology has grown. Aside from Baltzly's aforementioned analysis of the threefold wholeness and Klitenic Wear's inquiry into the *Parmenides*-commentary, Pieter d'Hoine has spoken about Proclean mereology at a number of conferences, and his research has culminated in the publication of a new paper on the three kinds of wholes which also incorporates some elements from the aforementioned production of the sensible cosmos and from Proclus' *Parmenides*-commentary.[15]

Nevertheless, an interested reader might conclude on the basis of the varying scholarly analyses that Proclus' mereological contemplations are themselves scattered. For example, Baltzly suggests in his study of the tripartite whole that 'we might wonder about the extent to which all of Proclus' deployments of the distinction between the three notions of whole are coherent and unified.'[16] Such a suggestion undersells Proclus' systematic philosophy, for his mereological considerations, however much the context of their occurrences may vary, are bound together by a rather solid theoretical framework, which is founded on two basic notions. First, Proclus is both a systematic philosopher and an exegete of Plato, and he thus has to mediate between providing universal truths about the world and its workings and analysing each Platonic theorem within its proper context. Proclus navigates this tension by first distilling from Plato a set of general theoretical notions (such as a distinction between composition in a quantitative sense and composition in a qualitative sense, or the division of wholeness into three kinds), and subsequently by moulding those notions to the exegetical context in which he wishes to apply them. Second, Proclus'

---

13   Kobusch (2000); Klitenic Wear (2017).

14   See, e.g., the reference to Baltzly (2008) above.

15   D'Hoine (2021).

16   Baltzly (2008: 406 n. 21). This sentiment has previously been expressed by Dodds (1963: 237) and Glasner (1992: 197–198).

INTRODUCTION

view on wholeness and parthood are informed by the general Neoplatonic view of unity, which equates the concept of the one from Plato's *Parmenides* with the ultimate Good from the *Republic*. In other words, Proclus' concept of the whole derives not merely from Platonic metaphysics itself, but also from Plato's ruminations on the metaphysical background of his ethics. As I shall argue, this equation of unity with goodness grounds Proclus' aforementioned link between the concepts of being whole and being perfect.

1.1.2   *The Author's Own Recent Work on Proclean Mereology*

In the multiple years of research leading up to the completion of this monograph, I myself published three papers which touched on select aspects of Proclean mereology or on adjacent subject matter. The specific topics treated in these publications were, respectively, Proclus' aforementioned theory of the three kinds of whole,[17] Proclus' reaction against an earlier description of the divisibility of Plotinus' transcendent Intellect by Porphyry,[18] and Proclus' understanding of the concept of perfection and the possibility of transcending it.[19] Since this monograph seeks to provide the reader with a clear overview of Proclus' understanding of the concept of wholeness, select passages of the book necessarily build upon these earlier publications, though in each case to a varying extent.[20]

Proclus' theory of the three kinds of whole is so essential to the topic of this study that it required a detailed analysis in this book as well. For this reason, chapter four, 'A wholesome trinity', is based on the article of the same name which was published in the journal *Ancient Philosophy*,[21] in the sense that the text of the article has been reincorporated into the book with the graceful permission of its original publisher. A full reference to the original publication is included in the first footnote of that chapter, as well as a brief summary of the formal changes in this version of the text and the mostly minor additions to its content, which touch on ideas or sources which had not yet been developed or published when the original article was written.

The subject matter of the other two publications is important to this study to a lesser extent, and thus no reproduction of their original text is required here. Proclus' views on the divisibility of Plotinus' Intellect and his discussion

---

17   Oosthout, A. (2022a).

18   Oosthout, A. (2022b).

19   Oosthout, A. (2023a).

20   Additional publications of mine to which I refer to a lesser extent in this monograph are Oosthout and Van Riel (2023) and Oosthout, A. (2023b) and Oosthout, A. (forthcoming).

21   Oosthout, A. (2022a).

of wholeness and perfection are briefly relevant in the first two sections of chapter five, 'Dividing the indivisible', and there my previous publications on those topics are treated as would be any other established publication. By this I mean that only select insights of mine necessary for understanding the analysis of any given primary passage discussed in those sections of the book are summarily cited or paraphrased from my earlier works with the appropriate references. If the reader wishes to know my full thoughts on those specific topics, I refer them to the relevant publications themselves.

1.2   A Preview of Proclean Mereology

The central question of ancient mereology is the way in which a multiplicity of distinct parts is able to become a single entity. Ancient philosophers were generally fascinated by the issues of reconciling unity and multiplicity,[22] and the whole is a prime example of this issue, both as a concept and as a natural phenomenon (alongside notions such as genera and universals, which in some schools of thought overlap with the concept of being whole). For a Neoplatonic philosopher like Proclus, the importance of wholeness cannot be understated, for it is in a way the primary metaphysical link between our material existence and the divine goodness of the One to which every Neoplatonist strives to return. This is exemplified by a passage from the fifth and final book of Proclus' *Timaeus*-commentary. There Proclus discusses a lemma from the *Timaeus* in which the titular speaker recounts how the Demiurge bound the components of the universe together.[23] In his commentary, Proclus launches into a discussion of what it means for things to be 'bound together'. First, he defines that which is *not* bound together: it is either a pure unity, or a pure plurality. The pure unity contains nothing within itself which could be bound together. The pure plurality, on the other hand, has no determinable constituents or 'units' to speak of, because it is 'an indistinct mixture' (σύγχυσις) born out of elements which have 'perished together' (ἐκ συνεφθαρμένων).[24]

Since Neoplatonic philosophy is at its core henological more so than ontological, the ultimate metaphysical opposition which lies at its heart is not

---

22   Think, for example, of the many attempts by ancient philosophers to impose unity and stability onto the manifold and ever-changing entities in the universe, from Parmenides' concept of being to Platonic Ideas and Aristotelian forms. The most intelligent (if not the most accessible) analysis in all of antiquity of the problems resulting from this imposition of one upon many can, in my personal opinion, be found in the *Parmenides* of Plato.

23   Plato, *Tim.* 41a8–b2.

24   Proclus, *IT* V, 63.15–21 (3.210.9–15 Diehl).

INTRODUCTION

between being and non-being, but between pure unity and absolute multiplicity. The nature of this absolute multiplicity is indeterminate: its parts have lost all of their distinctive characteristics and are melted together into a pure continuum, as Proclus reveals in this passage (this continuum can be understood as the Neoplatonic descendant of the receptacle from Plato's *Timaeus* and as a counterpart to the contested Aristotelian concept of prime matter).[25] In contrast, the unity of the ultimate first principle, the One, is so absolute that it cannot be pluralised, and hence cannot be defined in any way.[26] In between these two extremes stand composite beings, which are one and many at the same time in such a way that both the individual parts and the composite whole possess their own 'distinctive character' (ἰδιότης).[27] In Proclus' words:

> μόνως ἄρα δεσμός ἐστιν, ὅταν καὶ πολλὰ ᾖ καὶ σῳζόμενα μίαν ἔχοντα συνεκτικὴν αὐτῶν καὶ συναγωγὸν δύναμιν εἴτε σωματικὴν εἴτε ἀσώματον. εἰ δὲ τοῦτο, καὶ ἥνωται τὰ δεδεμένα διὰ τὸν δεσμὸν καὶ διακέκριται, διότι σῴζει τὴν οἰκείαν ἕκαστον φύσιν.
>
> PROCLUS, *IT* V, 63.21–25 (3.210.9–19 Diehl)

> So there is only a bond when there are many things which are also preserved, and which possess a single power that maintains them and draws them together, whether corporeal or incorporeal. If this is the case, the things which are bound are both unified because of the bond and distinct, because each preserves its proper nature.
>
> Tr. TARRANT 2017 (modified)

In other words, the concepts of the whole and the part exist in an equilibrium, whereby the parts retain their own substantial nature despite their unification so that the whole is, in the words of Aristotle, 'something other' (ἕτερόν τι) than the parts themselves.[28] The obvious question which then arises is, what is the whole beyond its parts? (Or the inverse, what are the parts outside of the whole?) The answer is not as simple as it might appear from this passage, for Proclus' concept of being whole does not apply without qualification to any unified multiplicity. Proclus instead proposes a more restricted

---

25 On the question of whether Aristotle supported the idea of an entirely indeterminate receptacle, see e.g., Robinson (1974) and Ainsworth (2020). For the receptacle in Plato, see *Tim.* 49–52; cf. Van Riel (2021).

26 Van Riel (2016: 76).

27 For this concept, see chapter 3, section 2.

28 See the discussions of Aristotle's *Met.* Z.17, 1041b11–33 in chapter 2, section 5.

definition of the concept linked to the aforementioned concepts of goodness and perfection.

1.3   Overview of the Study

In this study, I aim to bring together the parts of contemporary scholarship concerning Proclean mereology into a cohesive whole. In order to do so, I pursue three objectives. The first (objective 1) is to establish a theoretical framework with which to approach Proclus' mereology in its own terms. In pursuing this objective, I take inspiration from the approach of two distinguished scholars who have similarly distilled mereological theories from Plato and Aristotle. The second (objective 2) is an analysis of the universal metaphysical concepts underpinning Proclus' mereology, by which I mean the axioms and models which Proclus defines and which subsequently inform his analyses of part-whole relations in their varying contexts. The last (objective 3) is a cohesive overview of the various occurrences of mereological issues within Proclus' metaphysics. In this latter part of the study, special attention is paid to other aspects of Proclus' mereology mentioned in this introduction, e.g., the aforementioned link between wholeness and perfection, and the way in which mereology constitutes a bridge between the metaphysical and axiological sides of Proclus' worldview. Unity is goodness, after all, and as the midpoint between one and many, the concept of being whole is similarly intertwined with the Neoplatonic divide between good and evil.

Having sketched the outlines of the overall topic and the scholarly *status quaestionis*, this first introductory chapter will close with an overview of the contents of the subsequent chapters, make clear knowledge of which aspects of ancient philosophy and the Platonic school on the part of the reader is necessary to follow the arguments of this study, and elucidate the author's methodology in citing from and discussing primary sources.

The rest of the book is divided into four parts, the first three of which deal with the three aforementioned objectives, while the fourth brings together insights from each of the previous parts into a conclusion. The first and fourth parts encompass a single chapter each, while the second and third parts both contain two chapters.

The book's second chapter (Part 1, objective 1) provides the theoretical framework for this study through an analysis of the discipline of mereology as it was defined in the twentieth and twenty-first centuries. This approach is inspired by Verity Harte's study of mereological issues in Plato. Faced with the aforementioned absence of a clearly defined role for mereology in

INTRODUCTION

antiquity, the scholar opens her analysis with a brief discussion of contemporary mereology in order to more clearly define the Platonic concepts which are subsequently introduced.[29] In a similar vein, my own chapter first discusses the origins of contemporary mereology as a logical field of study, and then outlines the specific arguments and theories from mereology which have shaped previous scholarly inquiries into ancient theories of parts and wholes. First, our focus will be placed on what David Lewis calls the axiom of 'unrestricted composition', i.e., the notion that any two objects may compose a fusion or set. I then discuss the alternatives suggested by more naturalistically inclined philosophers such as Peter Van Inwagen.[30] Subsequently, the chapter discusses two analyses of ancient authors, i.e., Harte's aforementioned study of Plato and Kathrin Koslicki's Neo-Aristotelian mereology, both of which specifically drew from the theoretical framework provided by contemporary philosophers.[31] From both the contemporary theories and the assessments of Platonic and Aristotelean mereology, a number of issues are distilled which must also be accounted for in our analysis of Proclean parts and wholes.

The third chapter (Part 2, objective 2) discusses the first aspect of Proclus' general views on mereology, i.e., his conception of composition. It does so by contrasting the universal Neoplatonic notion of increasing multiplicity in the descent from the One to what Olympiodorus calls 'Proclus' rule'.[32] Whereas the universal Neoplatonic rule equates increasing multiplicity with increasing distance from the One, Proclus' rule states that those beings located in the middle of the causal hierarchy of beings are 'more composite' (συνθετώτερα).[33] Analyses of the *Elements of Theology*, in which Proclus outlines this rule, and of the *Platonic Theology* and *Parmenides*-commentary, in which scholars have located two examples of this rule, show that Proclus holds a rather complex view of composition.

The fourth chapter (Part 2, objective 2) discusses the tripartite division of the concept of wholeness. It constitutes a microcosm of this study as a whole, taking a Neoplatonic concept of which various different (and sometimes contradictory) analyses exist and distilling from Proclus' writings the theoretical background which informs each of these analyses. In this case, my source texts are the *Elements of Theology* and the third book of the *Platonic Theology*. Furthermore, two examples of the threefold wholeness in Proclus'

---

29   Harte (2002a: 8–47).
30   Lewis (1991); Van Inwagen (1990).
31   Koslicki (2008).
32   See the introduction to chapter 3.
33   See chapter 3, section 2.

Timaeus-commentary are discussed to illustrate how Proclus adapts his mereological model to the exegetical context in which he employs it. Lastly, the previous scholarly analyses of this theorem are reviewed and, where necessary, amended. This chapter comprises the reincorporated text of my previous publication on this subject matter, as noted above.[34]

The fifth chapter (Part 3, objective 3) discusses the issue of multiplicity and division in the intelligible realm, known as the home of the Platonic Forms, where no spatiotemporal dimensions exist. This chapter discusses the way in which Proclus incorporates the concepts of wholeness and perfection into his complex hierarchy of divine intelligible principles (of which there are many) and how he develops them in tandem with the causal procession of incorporeal principles. Here the third, fourth, and fifth books of the *Platonic Theology*, which treat the Neoplatonic concept of the transcendent Intellect in detail, are the main sources for the analysis. Special attention is paid to Proclus' equation of wholeness with eternity (an equation which follows from his exegeses of the *Timaeus* and *Parmenides*), and the way in which this equating of the whole with the eternal allows Proclus to connect his concept of wholeness to the Neoplatonic good at various levels of the transcendent Intellect. The discussion of the various manifestations of wholeness in Proclean Intellect is preceded by a brief reflection on the two main (and contradictory) ways in which Proclus applies the term 'whole' to the incorporeal hypostases: as a marker for relative universality in comparing superior intelligible principles to inferior ones, and as a marker for a specific intelligible principle whose primary characteristics manifest again and again in its participants.

The sixth chapter (Part 3, objective 3) mirrors the fifth, discussing our sensible material realm instead of the intelligible one. Whereas the fifth chapter revolves around the question of division in the indivisible Intellect, the sixth chapter raises the question of what kind of wholeness and perfection can be ascribed to the mortal and fallible creatures we perceive around us. This question follows from the equation of wholes with eternal beings discussed in the previous chapter, since it implies the rejection of non-eternal beings normally conceived of as wholes (e.g., the individual mortal human as a physical whole) from Proclean mereology. In other words, things with a finite temporal existence would no longer be considered singular wholes. Fortunately for us mortals, the opposite turns out to be true. After a brief discussion of the relation between temporal wholeness and eternal wholeness, which in large part follows Kutash's analysis, four passages from Proclus' *Timaeus*-commentary

---

34   See section 1.1.2 above.

INTRODUCTION

are discussed which all categorise the kinds of wholes and parts in the sensible cosmos in different ways. These passages further exemplify what is suggested in the third chapter, namely the idea that Proclus' mereological theorems constitute theoretical models which are adapted in whatever way the exegetical context in which they are applied requires. Furthermore, each of these passages suggests that Proclus' distinction between eternal wholes and partial mortals is not as strict as it appears, leading into a final discussion of Proclus' analysis of the mortal creature and the way in which it too may have some claim to being whole. Here the Neoplatonic union between unity and the good is again emphasised.

The seventh and final chapter (Part 4, general conclusion) summarises the conclusions reached in the previous ones, and reflects on the overarching characteristics of Proclean mereology. It does so in four respects. First, it is determined, in light of the previous chapters, how exactly Proclus defines the concept of being whole in relation to the concepts of unity and goodness. Second, I review how Proclus' theoretical framework is able to remain consistent across his exegeses of the Platonic works. Third, Proclus' late ancient mereology is compared to the theories of modern philosophers, and the advantages each has over the other are made clear. Lastly, I critically assess the question of whether Proclus' axiological understanding of the concept of wholeness serves as an adequate link between his metaphysics and his ethics.

1.4   Essential Proclean Concepts and Terminology

Given the sheer complexity of Proclus' philosophical system, some matters, concepts, and terms must be made clear at the outset of this study. Although the finer details of Proclean reality are reiterated where necessary,[35] the reader is expected to at least be familiar with the Neoplatonic division of reality into hypostases as established by Plotinus. Familiarity with the broad strokes of Platonic subjects such as the cosmology of the *Timaeus* and the theory of the Forms is also presumed. Given this study's strict focus on Proclus himself, extensive knowledge of the history of the Platonic school of thought between Plato and Plotinus on the part of the reader is not essential. A basic knowledge of its most prominent followers in the centuries following Plotinus' life, on the other

---

35   For example, Proclus' rather complex division of the Plotinian Intellect into multiple hypostases is expounded in schematic form in the fourth chapter for the convenience of the reader, even though the entire Proclean system has already been mapped in other scholarly works, for which see, e.g., d'Hoine and Martijn (2016: 325–326).

hand, is required, since the study makes reference to multiple Neoplatonic philosophers such as Porphyry, Iamblichus, Syrianus, and Damascius.

With respect to the terminology used in this study, it is important to keep in mind that Proclus distinguishes between intelligible Platonic principles *qua* truly transcendent and unparticipated and these same principles *qua* participated by and/or immanent in their participants (primarily in order to avoid the issues that arise out of participation in transcendent Forms as described in Plato's *Parmenides*).[36] In other words, the souls possessed by corporeal entities are not entirely the same as the universal monad of Soul, since the latter remains strictly transcendent at all times. Similarly, the life in which an individual living being partakes is not identical to the transcendent Life, which is the monad of all living things. Following the convention among contemporary scholars, the monadic manifestations of such principles are always capitalised, while participated instances are not, as in the aforementioned examples.

Furthermore, there is some ambiguity to Proclus' cosmological terms, specifically to the concept of τὸ πᾶν. Although the term literally means 'the totality' or 'the universe', Proclus often follows Plato's use of the term in his *Timaeus* to describe the cosmos produced by the Demiurge, i.e., the sensible realm of things which come to be and change over time. In contrast to this cosmos stands the realm of true being in which the aforementioned intelligible principles are located. Since Proclus' version of Neoplatonic metaphysics encompasses a rather complex intelligible realm which flows forth from the supra-essential One yet transcends the works of the Demiurge, τὸ πᾶν is translated as 'the cosmos' whenever Proclus employs it in its restricted sense of 'all that belongs to the sensible realm'. In contrast, I refer to the totality of hypostases produced by the One, i.e., all of the intelligible, supra-cosmic, and cosmic levels of reality, as 'the Neoplatonic universe' or 'Neoplatonic reality' (though neither description includes the One itself, which in Proclus' system transcends any and all forms of reality).

Lastly, given the aforementioned wide applicability of mereological issues across various disciplines in ancient philosophy, I have restricted the scope of this study to Proclus' analysis of the question of what it means to be whole, and the way in which his answer is informed by Plato's metaphysics both in an ontological and in an axiological sense.[37] The concept of the part thus receives

---

36 For which see the footnotes at the start of chapter 4.

37 In terms of the primary sources, this study mainly focuses on Proclus' *Elements of Theology*, *Platonic Theology*, and *Timaeus*-commentary, with the occasional excursus to the *Parmenides*-commentary.

INTRODUCTION

a comparatively smaller amount of attention, resulting in the necessary exclusion of some aspects of Platonic mereology from this study. The tripartite soul from the *Republic* and Proclus' interpretation of that theory, for example, is not essential for my current purposes and, as such, is not included in this study (it has also been sufficiently analysed elsewhere).[38] The focus of this study is also restricted to wholeness as it occurs in nature, since Proclus considers man-made artefacts to be whole in name only due to their lack of participation in any intelligible principle.[39]

1.5 Critical Editions and Translations

Greek citations from Plato's works derive from the OCT texts edited by Burnet. Citations from Aristotle's *Metaphysics* and *Topics* derive from the OCT texts edited by Jaeger and Ross, respectively, while the *History of Animals* and *Parts of Animals* are cited from Tricot's and Louis's *Budé* editions. References to the works of Plato and Aristotle naturally use the Stephanus-pages and Bekker-numbering. For all other primary sources, abbreviated references are used to signify the chapters, pages, and/or line numbers of the following critical editions—the full references to these sources, arranged according to the names of the editors, are incorporated into the bibliography.

Proclus:
- DMS (*De malorum subsistentia*) = *On the Existence of Evils*, tr. Opsomer and Steel 2003.
- ET = *The Elements of Theology*, ed. Dodds 1963.
- ICr = *In Platonis Cratylum Commentaria*, ed. Pasquali 1994.
- *In Eucl.* = *In primum Euclidis elementorum librum commentarii*, ed. Friedlein 1873.
- IRP = *In Platonis rem publicam comentarii*, ed. Kroll 1899–1901.
- IP = *In Platonis Parmenidem Commentaria*, ed. Steel 2007–2009.
- IPh = *Institutio Physica*, ed. Ritzenfeld 1912.
- IT = *In Platonis Timaeum Commentaria*, ed. Van Riel 2022.[40]
- TP = *Théologie platonicienne*, edd. Saffrey and Westerink 1968–1997.

---

38   Perkams (2006); Helmig (2014).
39   For Proclus' views on artefacts, see d'Hoine (2006a and 2006b); cf. Opsomer (2021).
40   For citations from the *Timaeus*-commentary, the corresponding page and line numbers of the previous edition by Diehl (1965) are noted as well.

Other authors:
- *De Corpore* = Thomas Hobbes, *Elementorum philosophiae sectio prima de corpore*, ed. Molesworth 1839.
- *DM* (*De Mixtione*) = Alexander of Aphrodisias, *Praeter commentaria scripta minora*, ed. Bruns 1892.
- *DP* (*De Principiis*) = Damascius, *Traité des premiers principes*, ed. Westerink 1986 and 1989.
- *Enn.* (*Enneades*) = Plotinus, *Opera*, edd. Henry and Schwyzer 1951–1973 (*editio maior*) and 1964–1982 (*editio minor*).
- *Fr.* Dillon = Iamblichus, *In Platonis dialogos commentariorum fragmenta*, ed. Dillon 1973.
- *Fr.* DK = *Die Fragmente der Vorsokratiker*, edd. Diels and Kranz 1952.
- *IA* = Nicomachus of Gerasa, *Introductionis arithmeticae libri II*, ed. Hoche 1866.
- *IH* = Syrianus, *In Hermogenem commentaria*, vol. 1, ed. Rabe 1892.
- *In Alc.* = Olympiodorus, *Commentary on the first Alcibiades of Plato*, ed. Westerink 1956.
- *In IA* = Iamblichus, *In Nicomachi arithmeticam introductionem*, edd. Pistelli and Klein 1975, or John Philoponus, *In Nicomachi arithmeticam introductionem*, ed. Giardina 1999.
- *In Phys.* = Simplicius, *In Aristotelis physicorum libros quattor priores commentaria*, ed. Diels 1882.
- *IP* = Damascius, *Commentaire du Parménide du Platon*, ed. Westerink 1997, or Marsilio Ficino, *Commentaries on Plato. Vol. 2: Parmenides*, ed. Vanhaelen 2012.
- *Isagoge* = Porphyry, *Isagoge et in Aristotelis categorias commentarium*, ed. Busse 1887.
- *PIL* (*Περὶ ἰδεῶν λόγου*) = Hermogenes, *Opera*, ed. Rabe 1985.
- *Ref.* = Nicholas of Methone, *Refutation of Proclus' Elements of Theology*, ed. Angelou 1984.
- *Sent.* = Porphyry, *Sententiae ad intelligibilia ducentes*, ed. Lamberz 1975.
- *Vitae* = Plutarch, *Vitae Parallelae. Vol. 1.1*, edd. Ziegler and Gärtner 2000.

Whenever texts from different authors share the same title (e.g., Proclus', Damascius', and Ficino's *Parmenides*-commentaries), the name of the author precedes the reference to the primary source (e.g., 'Proclus, *IP*' refers to Proclus' *Parmenides*-commentary, 'Damascius, *IP*' refers to Damascius' text of the same name, and 'Ficino, *IP*' refers to Ficino's work).

For the sake of clarity, the *signa critica* have been made uniform in all Greek citations, whereby additions on the part of the editor are written as <...>, while deletions on the part of the editor are written as {...}.[41] All modifications in the Greek on my part are indicated in the footnotes. When a cited passage contains a citation from another ancient work, as is often the case in exegetical texts, the citation within the passage is written as '...'. References to the sources of such citations are given in brackets directly after the citation.[42]

Translations of Greek phrases or lines cited in the running text are my own unless stated otherwise. Block citations of Greek passages are generally accompanied by established English translations. In those cases the name(s) of the translator(s) and the date of publication are noted at the bottom of the citation. Modifications in those translations on my part are always indicated by one of two terms: 'slightly modified' in the case of minute changes or insertions (often of a typographical nature), and 'modified' in the case of changes to the actual interpretation of the original phrases or sentences. If no source is indicated at the bottom of a block citation, the accompanying translation is my own.

---

41   This *signum*, also used in, e.g., Van Riel's new edition, is chosen instead of the more traditional [...] in order to avoid confusion with the latter's use throughout this study to designate insertions in the translations accompanying the Greek passages.

42   For example, a citation from a Platonic work in the Greek text of a commentary by Proclus is written as '*Plato-citation*' (*respective Stephanus-pages and* OCT-*lines*).

PART 1

The Mereological Question

∴

How can we know the world without first knowing all the world's parts? How can we truly know a single thing without first knowing the entire world?

HENRI OOSTHOUT, *The metaphysical circle*, 28-01-2021, https://anhypotheton.eu/en/c95a

CHAPTER 2

Mereology 101

Already in antiquity, philosophers discussed what it meant to be a part of something and struggled with paradoxes of composition and the identity of the whole. A well-known example is the paradox of the Ship of Theseus, which, according to Plutarch, plagued the philosophers of antiquity. The Athenians preserve the famous ship of Theseus. Each time a plank starts to rot, they replace it with a new plank. Eventually, after enough time has passed, every part of the ship will have been replaced. At this point, a dispute arises between philosophers: do the Athenians still have in their possession the same ship as they did originally, or did they inadvertently destroy the old ship and create an entirely new one?[1] From the Pre-Socratics onwards, such discussions of parthood and wholeness appear throughout antiquity, from the Aristotelian question of what a whole is aside from its parts to Stoic discussions of the Sorites paradox and Epicurean reflections on the nature of indivisible atoms.[2]

Nowadays, the study of parts, wholes, and their interrelations constitutes a distinct philosophical discipline called mereology, which overlaps with multiple other fields within philosophy. Scholars of mereology have looked at parts and wholes from both logical and metaphysical perspectives. For example, one may approach the notion 'part' from a mathematical standpoint (which are the members of a given mathematical set?) or from a logical one (how can

---

1   Plutarch, *Vitae* 23.1 (*Theseus*), 20.13–20. Hobbes would later expand the paradox (*De Corpore* 11, 11.7). Suppose one also kept the deteriorated planks and eventually found a way to restore them. If one then collected all of the old planks and rebuilt Theseus' ship out of them, one would have two ships: the one repaired over time through the replacement of its planks, and the one rebuilt out of the restored original planks. Which one of them would be the ship of Theseus?

2   Varzi (2016). For an example of Pre-Socratic mereology, see the paradoxes of Zeno. The paradoxes against plurality—especially the argument from denseness, which is cited in Simplicius, *In Phys.* 1.3, 140.29–33—involve division; cf. Hugget (2019). For Aristotle's theory of parts and wholes, see his *Metaphysics*, specifically Δ.25–26 (the definitions of 'part' and 'whole'), Z.10 (various types or modes of parthood and wholeness), and Z.17 (on the composition of a whole). A passage from the latter chapter is discussed below. Other works of Aristotle in which parts and wholes make an appearance include the *Physics*, *Topics*, *Parts of Animals*, and *On the Soul*. See Mignucci (1993) for an analysis of the Sorites paradox in Stoicism. For Epicurean discussions of the indivisible atoms, see, e.g., Vlastos (1965), Verde (2021), and Martini (2024). Discussions on parts and wholes in Plato's works will be discussed below and throughout the dissertation.

© ARTHUR OOSTHOUT, 2025 | DOI:10.1163/9789004721760_003

the mechanisms of composition be delineated in formal terms?). On the other hand, one may discuss physical beings, such as an artefact or a person, and attempt to describe their physical parts and wholeness. In all cases, the central issue of mereology is the relation between the many parts and the one whole. How can one be a single person and millions of particles at the same time?

Before we dive into the vast complexities of Proclean metaphysics, we must properly define the discipline of philosophy that we are dealing with in this inquiry. Unfortunately, the ancient thinkers did not consider the study of parts and wholes to be a distinct (sub)discipline of philosophy, and for that reason they did not discuss it as such. As a result, if one wants to know what the core issues of mereology are, one needs to look to the works of contemporary philosophers who treat it as a field of philosophy in its own right. This chapter will chart a few examples of the most important mereological theories and discussions of the twentieth and twenty-first centuries, as well as two attempts to place interpretations of ancient metaphysics within the framework of these contemporary theories. From these examples, I shall distil a number of mereological notions, questions, and problems that we should keep in mind once we turn to Proclus' discussions on the nature of wholeness and parthood. Please note also that my goal in this chapter is specifically to illustrate a number of problems and philosophical discussions which will contribute to our inquiry into Proclus, not to chart the entire history of the discipline of mereology for its own sake. I do not pretend to give the reader here a complete overview of all of the approaches to parthood relations and their accompanying arguments from the twentieth and twenty-first centuries.[3]

2.1   Classical Extensional Mereology

As we previously noted,[4] the first modern variant of mereology proper was developed by Leśniewski.[5] He devised three formal systems, 'whose union [he considered] to be one of the possible foundations for the whole of the system

---

3   Informative overviews of mereology proper can be found in Simons (1987: 5–100), Koslicki (2008: 23–90), and Varzi (2016). The first chapter of Harte's (2002: 13–25) study on parts and wholes in Plato also contains a concise overview of some of the issues within modern mereology, though it is not as exhaustive as the other sources. A more technical overview of the axiomatisation of mereology can be found in, e.g., Hovda (2009a).

4   See chapter 1, section 1.

5   The information in this section is mainly derived from the aforementioned surveys of mereology by Simons (1987: 5–100) and Koslicki (2008: 23–90).

of the mathematical science.'[6] The three systems were protothetic, which corresponds to a calculus of equivalent statements, ontology, which must not be understood in the accepted sense but rather as denoting a calculus of names or individuals, and mereology.[7] Mereology, the system of parthood relations, was 'dedicated to the most general problems of the theory of sets'.[8] Leśniewski's definitions of parthood were disseminated in Anglophone circles by Henry Leonard and Nelson Goodman, who felt that the mathematician's idiosyncratic phrasings needed to be restated 'in more useable form, with additional definitions, a practical notation and a transparent English terminology.'[9] Leśniewski's mereology and Leonard and Goodman's Calculus of Individuals, which must not be confused with Leśniewski's ontology, were among the first in a family of logical systems that is now known as *Classical Extensional Mereology*, henceforth abbreviated to CEM.[10] Variants of CEM share their axioms,[11] which include:

> *asymmetry*:
> $x < y \rightarrow \sim(y < x)$
> i.e., if x is part of y, then y is not part of x,

> *transitivity*:
> $(x < y \,\&\, y < z) \rightarrow x < z$
> i.e., if x is part of y and y is part of z, then x is part of z,

> the *Weak Supplementation Principle*:
> $(x < y) \rightarrow (\exists z)\,(z < y \,\&\, z \textupharpoonleft x)$
> i.e., if y has x as a part, then it also has z as a part where z does not overlap x,

---

6   Leśniewski (1927, in Surma et al. 1992: 176).

7   Leśniewski (1927, in Surma *et al.* 1992: 176–77). Interestingly, although mereology depends on ontology and ontology on protothetic, Leśniewski devised the systems in the reverse order, viz. mereology-ontology-protothetic; see Simons (2015).

8   Leśniewski (1916, in Surma *et. al.* 1992: 129).

9   Leonard and Goodman (1940: 46). Leśniewski's axioms and definitions are drawn up without any of the propositional symbols common to logical theories.

10   Other early proponents of extensional mereology included Alfred North Whitehead and Alfred Tarski, as noted by Simons (1987: 101). Modern theories belonging to this family of systems are also categorised under *General Extensional Mereology* in contemporary scholarship. As Varzi (2016) explains, *General Extensional Mereology* 'corresponds to the classical systems of Leśniewski and of Leonard and Goodman, modulo the underlying logic and choice of primitives.'

11   The axioms as presented here are drawn up in the same way as by Koslicki (2008).

and the *General Sum Principle*:

$$(\exists x)(F(x)) \rightarrow (\exists x)(\forall y)((y \circ x) \leftrightarrow (\exists z)(F(z) \ \& \ (y \circ z)))$$

i.e., for any objects that do not overlap, there exists a fusion of those objects.

The *General Sum Principle*, which is also known as the principle of *Unrestricted Composition*, would prove to be a contested axiom in mereology and contribute to what Paul Hovda describes as the divide between 'formalistic' and 'naturalistic' philosophers. In Hovda's view, there are two types of philosophers in the discipline of mereology. On the one hand, there are those who suggest that the world chiefly consists of 'natural mereological structure' which is empirically observable, 'and for which there is no a priori reason to think that it will fit any neat formal pattern.' On the other hand, there are those who claim to possess 'an a priori science of mereology' which reveals the formal patterns of the parthood relations which exist in the world.[12]

2.2   David Lewis's Argument for Unrestricted Composition

Lewis was among the most prominent proponents of CEM and of a formalistic approach to mereology more generally. In fact, within the field of mereology, his *Parts of Classes* (1991) became an influential work. In this study, he reformulates the logical axioms of CEM in more accessible ontological terms,[13] and posits three main axioms of mereology.

> *Transitivity*: If x is part of some part of y, then x is part of y.
> *Unrestricted Composition*: Whenever there are some things, then there exists a fusion of those things.
> *Uniqueness of Composition*: It never happens that the same things have two different fusions.[14]

The ontological assessment of the *General Sum Principle* provoked no small amount of reactions from scholars of mereology. Lewis must have predicted

---

12   Hovda (2014: 141–142).

13   It must be noted that an ontological rewording of the *General Sum Principle* can already be found almost a decade before Lewis's book in an article by Judith Jarvis Thomson (1983: 202). However, although Thomson and Lewis agree on the fact that for every set of objects there exists a fusion of those objects, they do not agree on the question of how those fusions must be situated in time; contrast Thomson (*ibidem*) to Lewis (1986: 202–203).

14   Lewis (1991: 74).

such a response, because after introducing the three axioms, he immediately comes to the defence of his mereological universalism. *Unrestricted Composition* allows me, the White House, and the planet Jupiter to compose a fusion, or the trout and the turkey to compose a trout-turkey (the latter is an example of Lewis's own). Yet the oddity of such fusions is not a sufficient reason for rejecting their existence, according to Lewis: 'Describe the character of the parts, describe their interrelation, and you have *ipso facto* described the fusion.' The logical set which contains a trout and a turkey is perfectly describable as 'part fish and part fowl', Lewis argues, and likewise as 'partly here, partly there.'[15]

This argument revolves around the fact that, within the logical parameters of CEM, it only matters whether parts x and y exist. To state that the trout-turkey exists is simply to affirm that the trout and the turkey exist. Or, in Lewis's words, 'given a prior commitment to cats, say, a commitment to cat-fusions is not a *further* commitment. The fusion is nothing over and above the cats that compose it. It just *is* them.' This argument leads to Lewis's conclusion that mereology is 'ontologically innocent'.[16] The fusion's 'character is exhausted by the character of its parts.'[17] It is no problem to state that any two x'es compose a fusion y within the realm of logic, because in describing y one simply describes the x'es. This is Lewis's thesis of *Composition as Identity*, whereby 'the "are" of composition is, so to speak, the plural form of the "is" of identity.'[18]

As both Lewis himself and other scholars have noted, this ontologically innocent conception of mereology involves a problematic conflation of one and many. The trout and the turkey are two things, but the trout-turkey is (presumably) one thing. If a and b compose a(n ontologically innocent) fusion c, then the fusion is nevertheless *numerically* distinct from its parts. If they were not, if mereology were truly ontologically innocent, there would be no reason to speak of fusions at all. There would be no point in stating 'the trout-turkey exists' as numerically indistinct from its parts, viz. as a unity instead of a plurality, since one could simply state 'the trout and the turkey exist'. The contrast between the oneness of the fusion and the plurality of its parts implies that the whole is at least to some degree distinct from the parts.

To be fair, Lewis does admit that his theory of *Composition as Identity* is limited in his manner, stating that 'what is true of the many is not exactly what's true of the one. After all they are many while it is one.' He nevertheless asserts that his mereology remains innocent in a special sense: even if we describe

---

15   Lewis (1991: 80).
16   Lewis (1991: 81).
17   Lewis (1991: 80).
18   Lewis (1991: 82).

many things as one fusion taken together, 'this one thing is nothing different from the many.'[19] However, Lewis presents this suggestion as an argument which supports his ontologically innocent mereology, rather than as a hypothesis which needs to be proven in its own right. As Harte notes in her analysis of Lewis's mereology, 'there is little here to persuade the detractor.'[20]

For example, Lewis quotes Donald Baxter's discussion of what Baxter calls the 'Non-Identity view', i.e., the notion that a whole is not identical to its parts, and the 'Identity view', i.e., the notion that a whole is identical to its parts.[21] Baxter presents the example of a malicious land-owner who tries to pull off a mereological scam. The owner divides his stretch of land into six parcels, which he individually sells to six different persons. He then proclaims to them that he only sold them ownership of the parts of the land, and so retains ownership of the land as a whole. In response, the six customers argue that *they* jointly own the six parcels rather than the owner, and Baxter notes that this claim is intuitively correct. 'But this suggests', Baxter concludes, 'that the whole was not a seventh thing.'[22]

Lewis presents this example of Baxter's as conclusive proof for the ontological innocence of mereology. 'Specify the present ownership of the six parcels and thereby you specify the ownership of the original block of land.'[23] In a way, he is right. If the original owner sells all six parcels, he does not retain a seventh type of ownership. He no longer owns anything at all. However, Baxter then introduces *joint ownership of the whole*. The problem with this argument is the fact that joint ownership of six parcels does not automatically follow from the fact that six individuals own six parcels of land that happen to be spatially adjacent.[24] If it did, would I not, by analogy, automatically take part in joint authorship of all the research output that happens to originate from my home institution? This seems counterintuitive. The original stretch of land has been divided and legally dissolved into six separately owned stretches of land. Presumably, joint ownership constitutes a *new* type of ownership that must be established separately from the ownership of the six individual parcels. Even if it is going too far to state that the newly introduced joint ownership is

---

19   Lewis (1991: 87).

20   Harte (2002a: 23). This problematic aspect of Lewis's mereology has been criticised by others too; see, e.g., Van Inwagen (1994) and Koslicki (2008: 40–44).

21   Lewis (1991: 83).

22   Baxter (1988: 597). The core of this argument (that the sum total of 'one, two, three, four, five, six' cannot be a seventh thing, but is simply 'six') can be traced back all the way back to Plato's *Theaetetus*, as we shall see in section 4.1 below.

23   Lewis (1991: 83).

24   Harte (2002a: 98) employs this argument in reverse. If one already has ownership of the collective whole, one cannot simply introduce separate ownership of the parts.

ontologically (or in this case, legally) distinct from the ownership of the individual parcels, there is still a clear numerical distinction between the *six* individually owned parcels and the *one* jointly owned whole.[25]

In fact, Harte points out that Baxter's argument only holds if one presumes that the whole is identical to its parts. In that specific case, defining ownership of the whole as a new type of ownership would indeed result in a 'double counting' of the parts, since on that view one first counts the total sum of the parcels jointly owned by the respective buyers, and then counts the collection of the exact same six parcels which the original sellers claims to retain ownership of. In other words, if the whole is nothing more than the sum of its parts, then the statement 'the sum of the parts plus the whole' indeed equates to 'the sum of the parts plus the sum of the parts'.[26] If, on the other hand, one presumes that joint ownership of the land is a distinct type of ownership, as I do here, the accusation Baxter raises against the Non-Identity view turns out to be 'misplaced', as Harte notes, since one is no longer simply enumerating the six patches of land in describing joint ownership of the whole. In this case, within the statement 'the sum of the parts plus the whole', the term 'whole' no longer denotes what was already counted in the first half of the statement, i.e., the sum. In Harte's words, here 'the addition of the whole to our list adds one to the total, and not the number of the parts.'[27]

But if two things cannot just be lumped together into a set, how does one determine which parts actually compose a whole or a fusion? Here Lewis raises a difficult issue for opponents of *Unrestricted Composition*. If one wants to remove 'queer fusions' from their ontology, Lewis explains, one has to reckon with the fact that 'many respects of queerness are matters of degree.' Yet the statement that a trout-turkey exists to a lesser degree than some other fusion is nonsensical: 'once you've said "there is" your game is up.' In summary, Lewis concludes, the dividing line between 'normal' wholes and 'odd' wholes is vague in a way that the ontological distinction between existent things and non-existent things cannot be.[28]

---

25 Elsewhere, Lewis (1991: 85) discusses a fusion between Possum and Magpie. He writes: 'describe Magpie and Possum fully—the character of each, *and also their interrelation*—and thereby you fully describe their fusion' (my emphasis). What exactly is this interrelation?

26 Harte (2002a: 97); cf. Lewis (1991: 81).

27 Harte (2002a: 98). This argument leaves open the question of how to avoid the mereological scam hypothesised by Baxter, however. Harte's answer is that 'the whole is related to its parts, and it is so related to its parts that I cannot sell all of them without selling it, nor sell it without selling them' (*ibidem*).

28 Lewis (1991: 81). For a further defence of this minimalist approach to parts and wholes, see Varzi (2000), who argues against the types of problems raised by those who argue for a more ontologically committed mereology.

In other words, if one were to accept CEM as Lewis does—for the sake of the argument, let us briefly ignore the conflation of one and many—, then the only requirement for the composition of a whole would be the existence of its parts, which is a simple case of A or not-A. If the parts exist, the whole exists. If they do not, the whole does not. If, on the other hand, composition requires something other than the existence of its parts, if the parts must exist in a certain manner or to a certain degree so that only some things actually compose numerically distinct wholes—in other words, if composition is *restricted*—, as the naturalistic philosophers argue, then the exactitude of the either-or-distinction of existence is lost. If the parts exist, the whole exists, but only in certain cases. As a result, a mereological system that only accepts composition to a certain degree will be 'fuzzy'.[29]

Proponents of *Restricted Composition* must inevitably confront this vagueness, as pointed out by Achille Varzi. If one refuses to accept odd or gerrymandered fusions, he explains, then one can no longer describe the world itself as the totality of all that exists. After all, we group the many things within the universe under a wide variety of different categories (e.g., objects versus events), and thus the universe itself as we describe it will inevitably be an odd fusion in some respect. Varzi argues that this fact has no bearing on the feasibility of a Lewisian ontology: 'The question of what figures are salient and what aren't—what sums are natural and what aren't—is an interesting one, but it has no ontological significance.'[30] In contrast, the difficulty of describing part-whole relations in semantic terms is a problem that the proponent of restricted composition must tackle.

2.3   Peter Van Inwagen and the Special Composition Question

There are a number of ways in which a proponent of *Restricted Composition* can approach the problem of vagueness. One may distinguish a mereology of existent parts in the strict Lewesian sense from looser ways of describing unities, e.g., in a causal or functional sense.[31] One may accept vagueness as part of their mereology.[32] Or one may attempt to devise a system that avoids Lewis's

---

29   Lewis (*ibidem*); for the term 'Restricted Composition', see Koslicki (2008).

30   Varzi (2006: 111–113). However, Varzi (*ibidem*: 115–116) does acknowledge that we should not conclude from this that the universe must be described exclusively with the terminology of set theory, since one must accept the problematic claim that the universe is a unique collection of elements in order to call it a set, as Simons (2003: 238) has pointed out.

31   This is the position defended by Varzi (2000, 2006, and 2008).

32   See, for example, Simons (1987), Van Inwagen (1990), and Koslicki (2008).

criticisms entirely, either by taking a strongly holistic approach to parthood or a nihilistic one.[33] In either case, the proponent of *Restricted Composition* must first devise an alternative to CEM. If, in this new mereology, composition is restricted, the creator of the new system must explain *how* composition is restricted. Van Inwagen is a prominent example of a modern philosopher who articulates this challenge, asking: 'When is it true that ∃y the xs compose y?'[34] Van Inwagen calls this question the *Special Composition Question*, henceforth abbreviated to SCQ.

In other words, the creator of an alternative to CEM must define either a principle or a set of circumstances in which the x'es compose a numerically singular whole y. If a satisfactory principle for restriction can be determined, the philosopher may be able to rule out counterintuitive fusions such as Lewis's trout-turkey. The SCQ lays bare the central challenge facing naturalistic philosophers who seek to provide an alternative to the formalistic approach exemplified by CEM.

Van Inwagen's own answer may strike the reader as no less odd than Lewis's trout-turkey. Van Inwagen concludes that '(∃y the xs compose y) if and only if the activity of the xs constitutes a life (or there is only one of the xs).'[35] In this case, 'life' denominates the individual life of a particular organism.[36] As a result, an individual human being is a unified whole, whereas a chair is simply a plurality of material simples arranged in the shape we call 'chair'.[37] Van Inwagen's life-principle for *Restricted Composition* is a rather intriguing proposition, and not without merit.[38] For example, a chair may be disassembled and reassembled, but the same cannot be done to a living being; fully disassembling an organism equates to killing it. Furthermore, the principle of life enables Van Inwagen to make an explicit argument for the acceptance of vagueness within mereology. The boundaries of life, he writes, are inherently vague. He points

---

33   The holistic approach is exemplified by the Plato presented by Harte, for which see section 4 below. An example of mereological nihilism, which does away with the notion of parthood altogether, can be found in Sider (2013).

34   Van Inwagen (1990: 30).

35   Van Inwagen (1990: 82). The final conditional between brackets, i.e., if there is only one of the x'es, is added here by Van Inwagen for the sake of completeness and not discussed elsewhere in his monograph; Van Inwagen (1990: 288 n. 29).

36   Van Inwagen (1990: 83).

37   Van Inwagen (1990: 124–141).

38   Interestingly, Van Inwagen's expulsion of non-living objects and artefacts from the realm of composition (and ontology) enables him to make short work of the paradox of the Ship of Theseus. There is no actual ship, only material simples arranged to form the shape of a ship. Whether they are arranged in the manner of a ship or not makes no difference for the identity of those simple parts, as Van Inwagen (1990: 128–29) points out.

out, for example, that according to his theory the human embryo is 'a mere virtual object' until the point in time at which it is considered to be alive. Yet Van Inwagen considers it to be 'very doubtful' that a mathematically precise moment can be determined at which the unborn human is first alive. Similarly, there is no clear moment at which one can state that a dying person changes from a living whole into a mere mass of material simples.[39] As Van Inwagen summarises, 'individual human lives, therefore, are infected with vagueness at both ends. (Even if a person is "instantly" volatilised by the explosion of a hydrogen bomb, the end of his life is a *bit* vague. Nothing happens instantly in nature.)'[40]

However, Van Inwagen does not entirely succeed in justifying his rejection of all wholes that are not living organisms, which he explains through a thought experiment.[41] Consider a very long and very thin snake. Suppose we weave the snake between two trees in such a way as to create a hammock. If the snake were intelligent, and if it were asked whether the hammock was numerically distinct from it, the snake would answer in the negative, Van Inwagen states. For 'we have not augmented the furniture of the world but only rearranged it.'[42] What strikes me as odd, however, is that this thought experiment does not seem to involve composition at all. The hammock is not made out of multiple entities, but out of a single organism that is already unified. Instead, the metaphor creates an argument that, intriguingly enough, resembles Lewis's argument for ontological innocence. Van Inwagen argues that the hammock is nothing more than the snake (or, analogously, a chair is nothing more than its material particles) not unlike the way Lewis argues that fusions in general are nothing more than their parts.

What Van Inwagen seems to be getting at here is that non-living beings are only composite unities in the eye of the beholder, since the snake looks like a hammock to an observer but is not actually such a thing in any ontological sense. This is confirmed when he asserts that statements such as 'there are chairs in this room' constitute *sentences* rather than *propositions*. 'Therefore, they neither entail nor are entailed and they are not the objects of affirmation and denial.'[43] In the same way that the statement 'the sun has moved behind the trees' does not contradict the Copernican thesis—since the statement merely describes the position of the sun relative to the observer—the

---

39   Van Inwagen (1990: 237–238).
40   Van Inwagen (1990: 238).
41   Van Inwagen (1990: 126–127).
42   Van Inwagen (1990: 127).
43   Van Inwagen (1990: 101).

MEREOLOGY 101

sentence 'there are chairs in this room' does not contradict the metaphysical proposition that only living beings and material simples have true existence, according to Van Inwagen.[44]

In order to prove that artefacts do not exist as unified compounds, Van Inwagen asserts that any sentence involving non-living compounds can be rephrased so as to involve only living beings and material simples.[45] Take, for example, the sentence 'some chairs are heavier than some tables.' Van Inwagen rephrases it as 'there are xs that are arranged chairwise and there are ys that are arranged tablewise and the xs are heavier than the ys.'[46] He admits that the statement still requires the presence of a chairwise arrangement, but claims that it does not require a concept of 'chair'.[47] According to Van Inwagen, the existence of a 'chair-receptacle', i.e., a chair-shaped space R in which material x'es exist in closer relation to each other than to the y's outside R, does not auto-matically lead to the composition of the unity 'chair' within R.[48] 'Our answer to the SCQ entails that there are no material objects but organisms and sim-ples, and our suggested technique of paraphrasis enables us to escape some of the more embarrassing consequences of this position.'[49] Unfortunately, these arguments are not entirely convincing. Van Inwagen's paraphrase of 'some chairs are heavier than some tables' indeed posits only the x'es and the y's as material objects, but even in this rephrasing there is still *something else* beside the matter in the form of chairwise and tablewise arrangements. We may no longer speak of chairs as material unities, but their particles remain bound to a certain structure, even in Van Inwagen's analysis.

It should be noted that Van Inwagen's removal of all non-living compounds from his mereology also flies in the face of knowledge that was, even at the time, empirically attested and widely accepted in physics and chemistry. Without acknowledging the presence of some form of mereological structure in non-living things, Van Inwagen's theory makes even the simple distinctions between well-known molecular compounds impossible. If all non-living things are sim-ply heaps of material simples, how does one account for the obvious difference between the ways water and oxygen, which are both compounds of atoms, interact with their environment on a molecular level?[50]

---

44   Van Inwagen (1990: 101–102).
45   Van Inwagen (1990: 108).
46   Van Inwagen (1990: 109).
47   Van Inwagen (1990: 289 n. 40).
48   Van Inwagen (1990: 105).
49   Van Inwagen (1990: 111).
50   To be fair, the application of unrestricted composition to the realm of physiology is sim-ilarly indefensible in the face of modern empirical science. For example, one could not

32 CHAPTER 2

2.4 The Whole as a Structure in Plato

The challenges of crafting a restricted mereology prompted two scholars to revert their gaze to their predecessors in antiquity. As stated above, the ancients faced challenges similar to those of modern thinkers in deciphering the nature of parthood. As a result of this, some scholars have compared contemporary theories to their ancient counterparts and vice versa. Most notably, Harte assessed Plato's notions of parthood through the lens of modern mereological discourse, while Koslicki looked to Aristotle in the hope of laying the foundations for a solid theory of restricted mereology.

In their readings of Plato and Aristotle, both scholars came to the conclusion that a whole is marked by a dichotomy between its *structure* and its *content*. Unlike Van Inwagen, whose stance on the matter of structure is somewhat vague, both Harte and Koslicki are realists when it comes to structure. The things that compose the whole constitute its content. The trout and the turkey, for example, constitute the content of Lewis's (in)famous 'trout-turkey'. Composition itself happens because onto the content of the whole a certain structure is imposed. Harte explains the dichotomy through the example of a dinner party. Suppose there are eight guests at a dinner party, four men and four women. The guest are seated across the table in a certain arrangement, so that each man is flanked by two women and vice versa. If this specific dinner party forms a whole, the guests make up its content and the seating arrangement constitutes its structure.[51]

For a proponent of *Restricted Composition*, the structure is as essential to the whole as the content is.[52] A proponent of *Unrestricted Composition*, such as Lewis, would of course argue otherwise, but according to Harte Plato himself rejects an unrestricted conception of composition. In the first half of her book, Harte discusses a number of Platonic passages, e.g., *Parmenides* 131a–c (the dilemma of participation) and *Sophist* 244b6–245e2 (discussion of the Monists), wherein paradoxes of parthood are discussed. All of these problems stem from an ontologically innocent conception of composition, according to Harte. Other passages show an alternative, restricted approach to composition on Plato's part, e.g., *Sophist* 251d5–e1 and 252e9–253a2 (only some things compose a whole, just as the letters of the alphabet can only form certain

---

combine two hydrogen atoms and one oxygen atom into a Lewesian compound of H_2O without there being some change in the molecule's natural properties or interactions with other chemicals (in this case, the creation of water and its distinct properties).

51   Harte (2002a: 159–160).
52   Harte (2002a: 160).

MEREOLOGY 101

combinations).[53] However, the starting point of Harte's analysis of Plato's writings is another dialogue of his: the *Theaetetus*.

2.4.1 *Socrates and Theaetetus versus Extensional Mereology*

Towards the end of the *Theaetetus*, Socrates and the titular interlocutor attempt for a third time to define what knowledge (ἐπιστήμη) is. The latest definition under scrutiny is the notion that 'knowledge is a true opinion with an account',[54] a definition inspired by Socrates' recounting of a dreamed conversation in which certain perceptible yet unknowable elements (στοιχεῖα) were said to constitute fully knowable complexes (συλλαβαί).[55] Socrates is not satisfied with the suggestion from the dream, however, and suggests that he and Theaetetus assess the dream critically through the use of the very same examples which it provided: the letters (στοιχεῖα) and the syllables (συλλαβαί).[56]

At first glance, the suggestion from the dream appears to be sound. The syllable is knowable because it is divisible into its letters ($ΣΩ = Σ + Ω$), whereas individual letters are unknowable by virtue of their indivisibility ($Σ = ??? + ???$).[57] However, Socrates suggests to Theaetetus' approval that the syllable $ΣΩ$ is nothing beyond the letters $Σ$ and $Ω$.[58] Here Plato introduces an unspoken mereological assumption, as Harte points out.[59] The syllable constitutes an ontologically innocent compound in the Lewesian mould: describing the letters equates to describing their fusion, the syllable (in other words, a whole is simply all of its parts, and a syllable is a whole; hence, the syllable is simply all of its letters). Yet, if we accept this mereological assumption, we can no longer uphold the epistemological suggestion of the dream, i.e., that the syllable is knowable but the letters are not. To know the syllable $ΣΩ$ is nothing more than to know the set $\{Σ, Ω\}$, and to know the set one must first know the set's members, $Σ$ and $Ω$.[60]

Socrates concludes (again to Theaetetus' approval) that it might be better to do away with the notion that the syllable is simply the collection of the letters and to postulate instead that the syllable is 'one idea' (note the use of the

---

53   Harte (2002a: 48–157).

54   Plato, *Theaet.* 202c7–8: δόξαν ἀληθῆ μετὰ λόγου ἐπιστήμην εἶναι.

55   Plato, *Theaet.* 201d8–202c5.

56   On the synonymity of the distinctions 'element/compound' and 'letter/syllable' in Greek, see Harte (2002a: 33). Note, however, as Harte (*ibidem*) also points out, that Plato does not always equate the letter-syllable relation with the part-whole relation in this passage.

57   Plato, *Theaet.* 203a1–b10.

58   Plato, *Theaet.* 203c4–7.

59   Harte (2002a: 35); cf. Marmodoro (2021: 118–119).

60   Plato, *Theaet.* 203c8–e1.

term ἰδέα) 'which itself contains itself and is different from the letters.'[61] One might conclude from this statement that Socrates aims to define the whole (the syllable) as something which transcends the collection of its parts (the letters), in contrast to the view that would later be supported by Lewis.[62] However, Socrates surprises both Theaetetus and the reader by suggesting that, if the syllable is truly different from the letters, then it is simply *does not have any parts*.[63]

To explain himself, Socrates commences a brief digression on the distinction between the whole (ὅλον), the totality of the parts (πᾶν), and the total number of the parts (ἅπαντα μέρη).[64] First, Socrates convinces Theaetetus of the fact that 'all the parts' (τὰ πάντα) and 'all of the parts' (τὸ πᾶν) are not numerically distinct: for example, saying 'six' is not any different from saying 'one, two, three, four, five, six'. The totality of the parts is simply the full set of the individual parts—again, this is perfectly compatible with Lewis's notion of the 'ontologically innocent' compound.[65] However, Theaetetus postulates that the whole (ὅλον) is something other than the totality of the parts (πᾶν/ ἅπαντα μέρη), and he earns Socrates' praise for his 'brave defence' of his views (Ἀνδρικῶς γε, ὦ Θεαίτητε, μάχῃ). Yet Socrates is undeterred: the whole, he argues, is that from which nothing is missing. The totality is also that from which nothing is missing. Thus, the whole is exactly the same as the totality, and thus exactly the same as the manifold of its parts.[66] Defeated, Theaetetus assents: 'It now seems to me that the total and the whole do not differ at all ...'[67]

---

61   Plato, *Theaet.* 204a1–2: ἰδέαν μίαν αὐτὸ αὑτοῦ ἔχον, ἕτερον δὲ τῶν στοιχείων.

62   This is how Proclus will engage with the part-whole relation, as we shall see in chapters 4 and 5. Marmodoro (2021: 124–128 and 136–137) argues that Plato himself endorses this notion as well, albeit as one of two possible ways of defining the relation between a whole and its parts.

63   Plato, *Theaet.* 204a5–10.

64   Plato, *Theaet.* 204a11–205a10. This digression is only summarily discussed here, since an extensive analysis of these specific lines can already be found in Harte (2002a: 40–44).

65   Harte (2002a: 45).

66   Note the implied connection between the notions of 'whole' and 'complete' in this context. As Marmodoro (2021: 120) points out, neither Socrates nor Theaetetus make any attempt to prove that the term 'whole' should be interpreted in this strict sense, nor to prove that the things which would be missing from an imperfect whole are automatically the same as the things which could hypothetically be missing from a totality. The notion that a whole is something which is complete or perfect also heavily informs Plato's use of the term in the *Timaeus*, as we noted in chapter 1, and it will recur in Proclus' conceptualisation of the whole.

67   Plato, *Theaet.* 205a7: Δοκεῖ μοι νῦν οὐδὲν διαφέρειν πᾶν τε καὶ ὅλον. Theaetetus' somewhat unenthusiastic response is vital for our understanding of the implications of the digression, as Harte (2002a: 39) also indicates.

Having locked himself and his interlocutor into the proto-Lewesian view of part-whole relations, Socrates proposes again that the syllable should simply *not* be considered as the whole which is composed of the letters. There are no other parts to the ontologically innocent whole than the letters, after all, and if the syllable is nevertheless different from the letters, then it is not the whole collection of them. In other words, the syllable is wholly distinct from the whole constituted by the letters (in other words, a whole is all of its parts, hence, the whole is all the letters, but the syllable is not the letters, hence, the syllable is not a whole). This means that the syllable, as an independent entity, is fundamentally indivisible. Yet the suggestion from the dream was that only divisible things are knowable. Thus, this alternative account of the nature of the syllable again blocks the definition of knowledge granted by Socrates' dream—i.e., that the syllable is fully knowable *qua* complex while the letters are solely perceptible *qua* simple things. Whereas before, the problem was that an equation between syllable and letters made both equally knowable, now a distinction between the syllable and the letters makes both equally unknowable.[68]

As Harte points out, the aporetic ending of the discussion, in which both attempts to explain the relation between the syllable and the letters fail to provide a foundation for the desired definition of knowledge, implies either that the argument is faulty, or that its underlying assumptions are problematic.[69] The underlying mereological assumption for the entire discussion is the notion that a whole is nothing more than the sum of its parts, as indicated by Socrates' deconstruction of Theaetetus' suggestion that a whole is something other than the totality of the parts. If we take the aporia of the dilemma to imply that its underlying assumption is problematic, then we would be incited conclude, as Harte suggests, that the proto-Lewesian notion of an ontologically innocent compound is a problematic one. In this respect, the dialogue subtly nudges us to side with Theaetetus and his lack of enthusiasm for the view that the whole is merely the sum of its parts. Unfortunately for someone who supports this reading of the passage, a viable alternative is not given in the dialogue itself (the ultimate ending of the text is again an aporia). Yet Harte distils from other dialogues of Plato a feasible alternative: the whole is something other than the sum of its parts, namely the structure which brings the parts together.[70]

---

68   Plato, *Theaet.* 205a11–e8.

69   Harte (2002a: 35).

70   It should be noted that Marmodoro (2021: 124–128 and 136–137) has recently argued against Harte's interpretation. In her view, Plato instead wants us to conclude that the proto-Lewesian approach to parthood relations is perfectly valid in the realm of sensible beings, while the example of the syllable as one indivisible ἰδέα is meant to provide a positive account of the way in which a Platonic Form constitutes 'a complex that is partless';

2.4.2 The Whole-as-Structure Model

Harte discerns two ways of connecting the structure to the whole. Either the whole *has* the structure besides its parts, so that the structure is essential for the composition of the whole but not for the existence of the parts, or the whole *is* its structure, so that structure is essential for the existence of both the whole and the parts.[71] Harte argues that Plato subscribes to the second model (wholeness as structure). In her reading of Aristotle, Koslicki affirms the first model (structure as something the whole has). Both approaches have their own advantages and drawbacks.

One of the main advantages of Harte's Platonic mereology is the fact that it neatly sidesteps Lewis's argument of vagueness. Lewis's reasoning revolves around a bottom-up approach to composition, which Harte calls an 'atomistic' view, whereby one starts with the existence or non-existence of the parts.[72] One then either accepts the existence of the fusion on the basis that the parts exist, or one is forced to conjure up a separate principle that provides the existence of the fusion.

Harte points out that the major problem of this approach is the fact that the structure or arrangement of a whole (in her own example, the arrangement of a set of dinner guests), becomes 'like something added after the fact of their [scil. the parts] being taken together'. In other words, if one postulates the existence of eight individual dinner guests, the dinner arrangement then exists only if one *adds* the notion that they 'collectively instantiate a certain structural property.'[73]

If, however, one were to take a 'holist conception' of the whole, i.e., a top-down approach to parthood relations,[74] and start with the whole *as* a structure wherein the parts exist, then structure provides existence for both the whole and its parts, given that this structure in now 'built into the identity of both parts and whole.' Instead of asking what collective property we need to add to our parts to make them instantiate a whole, Harte's approach simply requires

---

Marmodoro (2021: 128). I respectfully disagree with this interpretation, because I do not see how Plato's description of the two horns of the dilemma and the aporetic conclusion of this passage support the idea that one horn of the dilemma is only problematic when applied to intelligible principles and the other only problematic when applied to sensible ones. It seems more likely to me that, as Harte concludes, Plato considers the two horns of the dilemma to be problems that flow forth from the equation of a whole with the sum of its parts *in general*.

71   Harte (2002a: 161).
72   Harte (2002a: 276–277).
73   Harte (2002a: 163).
74   Harte (2002a: 277).

that we ask: 'What structures are there?'[75] Harte's conception of Platonic structure, then, functions as both an answer to Van Inwagen's SCQ and as a counterweight to Lewis's arguments for mereological universalism.

The whole-as-structure model creates a difficulty of its own, as Harte herself admits. If the structure is essential for the existence of the parts, then the parts can only exist so long as the structure exists. In the case of the dinner party mentioned above, this would mean that the dinner party does not exist unless the guests are seated in the determined arrangement. However, the guests themselves also would not exist outside of the seating arrangement. To modern metaphysicians, such a conclusion is highly counterintuitive. Harte does 'not have much that is positive to say on this matter; but the problem should certainly be noted.'[76] One could, of course, postulate that the guests only exist *qua* guests while at the dinner party and *qua* human beings of themselves. Yet to do so, one would have to reduce parthood to a relational property of the part and, as Harte herself points out, deal once again with Lewis's challenge of providing some additional criterion to determine when the part has this relational property.[77]

Aside from the problem of parts existing separately from the whole, Harte's structure/content-dichotomy is sound and excludes fewer objects from our ontology than Van Inwagen's life-principle does. But how must we understand Platonic structure? The first example Harte gives, comes from *Sophist* 261d1–262e1, where the Eleatic Stranger and Theaetetus discuss the way in which names and verbs fit together in sentences. In this instance, according to Harte, the syntactic structure of a sentence is shown to determine not only the meaning of the sentence but also the meaning of the words themselves. 'Central to Plato's syntactic intuition is the thought that names and verbs are not, as such, separable; they are separable in the sense that a name could occur with other verbs or a verb with other names.'[78]

---

75   Harte (2002a: 164).

76   Harte (2002a: 165). Whereas Harte accepts this difficulty as an unavoidable consequence of her Platonic model of parthood, Koslicki (2008: 112–117) finds the problem to be sufficient reason for rejecting a Platonic whole-as-structure model of composition in favour of an Aristotelian one where the whole has structure.

77   Harte (2002a: 191 n. 51 and 278). Despite her reservations, Proclus' approach to the concept of the part as separated from its whole will turn out to be quite similar to what I suggest here.

78   Harte (2002a: 173). Note that I here restrict myself to discussing Harte's interpretation of the *Sophist* as an illustration of her whole-as-structure view. One could put her interpretation of Plato's views on the meaning of names as such and the meaning of accounts (λόγοι) in contrast to, e.g., De Rijk's (1986: 199, 272–273, 313–316 *et al.*).

38   CHAPTER 2

The two Platonic passages Harte discusses in most detail are *Philebus* 23c–26d and *Timaeus* 31b–32c. In the former, Socrates and Protarchus discuss certain mixtures and their composition out of limit and the unlimited. In the latter, Timaeus discusses the unity of the cosmos brought about by the harmony between the four basic elements. From her reading of both passages, Harte develops a concept of structure that is heavily mathematical in nature.

2.4.3   *Philebus 23c–26d*

Let us consider Harte's reading of the *Philebus* first.[79] In this dialogue, Socrates, Philebus, and Protarchus discuss whether the contemplative life is superior to the pleasurable life or vice versa. In 23c–26d, after concluding that the ideal life is a mixture of knowledge and pleasure, Socrates delves into a digression on the nature of such mixtures. He distinguishes four classes: unlimited (ἄπει-ρον), limit (πέρας), the mixture (μικτόν) of limit and unlimited, and that which causes the mixture to come into existence.[80] To the class of the unlimited belong those opposites that stand on a scale, e.g., hotter and colder, greater and smaller, more and less. So long as these qualities are limitless (ἄπειρα), they are undefined. It is not clear *how much* hotter the hotter is on its own, for example.[81] Limit is the proportion, or number (ἀριθμός), which is imposed onto the scale of the undefined opposites in order to delineate the ratio between them and create a determinate quality.[82] A ratio between hotter and colder, for example, creates a determinate temperature. This is the mixture of limit and limitlessness.[83]

Harte interprets this Phileban mixture as a kind of composition in the abstract.[84] Limit becomes the structure of this abstract whole, while the unlimited stands for its content. Harte reworks Socrates' examples of hotter and colder for the unlimited and the hot-to-cold ratio for limit into a new metaphor. Suppose one is preparing a bath. There are two taps, one of which dispenses hotter water, and the other of which dispenses colder water. These streams of hotter and colder water constitute the unlimited, since simply running the taps by themselves does not imply that one always ends up with a bath of the same temperature. As Harte explains, 'for so long as I am simply running water—and not thinking about the kind of bath I would like to result—it is to

---

79   I will specifically discuss Harte's reading in terms of its implications for modern mereology here.
80   Plato, *Phil.* 23c9–d8.
81   Plato, *Phil.* 24a6–25a4.
82   Plato, *Phil.* 25a6–11.
83   Plato, *Phil.* 25b5–e5.
84   Harte (2002a: 182 and 208).

all intents and purposes irrelevant which of the indefinite number of ways in which they might differ in temperature I have produced.'[85]

The two taps, then, represent opposite ends of a spectrum (hot versus cold). In order to create what Harte calls a 'perfect bath', a certain ratio needs to be imposed on the indeterminate temperatures of the hotter and colder streams, creating water of a determinate temperature. This ratio imposed upon the hotter and colder tabs constitutes the limit of which Socrates speaks in the *Philebus*.[86]

In other words, only after a ratio has been imposed upon the hotter and colder taps does the resulting bath acquire a determinable temperature. Whereas the unlimited is an abstract conception of the parts of something, i.e., of its content, limit is an abstract conception of the structure of a whole. As befits the top-down model Harte has presented, in the absence of any limit, the unlimited is only vaguely defined. The imposition of limit onto the unlimited not only defines the mixture (the whole) but also the unlimited itself.[87] Harte again admits that, within this model, the content of a whole is unintelligible on its own. However, her reading of the *Philebus* presents other difficulties.

First, if the mixture of limit and unlimited is meant to be an abstract conception of the composition of a whole, does that make Phileban mixtures of all wholes? It is not entirely certain that the Platonic text points towards such an interpretation of its concepts.[88] In fact, one might wonder if limit, unlimited, and mixture must be seen as an abstract conceptualisation of composition at all. Do these terms not describe the demarcation of *qualities*, such as large and small, or hot and cold, rather than the composition of wholes?[89] Socrates uses a mode of description wherein two essential aspects of a quality, limit and unlimited, are distinguished, but does this confirm that the two aspects of the determinate quality are actual parts of it? It does not necessarily do so.

Suppose we fully accept this mereological interpretation of limit, unlimited, and mixture. Equating all wholes with Phileban mixtures creates its own issues for modern philosophers. First, Socrates conceives of mixture,

---

85   Harte (2002a: 187).

86   Harte (2002a: 187–188).

87   Harte (2002a: 189–190).

88   Socrates gives only three specific examples of Phileban mixtures, viz. health, music, and the weather (*Phil.* 25e7–26a4), none of which imply that this discussion revolves specifically around composition.

89   Julius Moravcsik has already shown that the division of abstract wholes into parts is just one of the approaches Plato takes towards the central questions of the *Philebus*. Another approach, which is the one used in 23c–26d, is that of 'Forms as systems of abstract elements the comprehension of which allows us to formulate abstract theories' (Moravcsik 1979: 101).

limit, and unlimited as *three* separate concepts. This casts doubt on Harte's whole-as-structure model, wherein limit and mixture should logically be identified as *one* concept.[90] Furthermore, a theory of composition based on Phileban mixtures seems to be purely mathematical or, as we shall see below, geometrical. But, as Koslicki has rightly noted, 'structure, in the sense of what is mathematically expressible (number, measure, ratio, proportion), cannot be all there is to a whole, otherwise the bathwater Harte considers as an example of a perfect Phileban mixture of hot and cold water will literally turn out to be a mathematical ratio, such as 2:1.'[91]

2.4.4 *Timaeus 31b–32c*

Whereas the supposed mereological undertones of *Philebus* 23c–26d are somewhat difficult to discern, Harte's next example is more clearly related to parthood. In *Timaeus* 31b–32c, the titular character describes how the Demiurge, in creating the universe, sought to make it one whole. Since the universe is corporeal, it consists of at least the elements fire, which makes it visible, and earth, which makes it tangible.[92] In order to create a unified body out of these two elements, fire and earth must be bound together in harmony. Mathematical proportion (ἀναλογία), Timaeus states, is the most harmonious of bonds.[93] In a mathematical proportion, the terms may be switched around without the loss of the proportion itself. If, for example, 2, 4, and 8 stand in a proportional sequence of 2:4 :: 4:8, one may switch the terms around and the proportion will remain the same, viz. 4:2 :: 8:4.[94] Both simple and squared numbers need only one middle term to create a proportion. Yet the elements of the universe are three-dimensional solids.[95] In the case of cubed numbers, two middle terms are needed to create a mathematical proportion. For example, if $a = 2$ and $b = 3$, the proportional sequence between a^3 and b^3 is $a^3{:}a^2b :: a^2b{:}ab^2 :: ab^2{:}b^3$, or 8:12 :: 12:18 :: 18:27. Thus, between the two three-dimensional elements fire and earth, the Demiurge placed two other elements, air and water, in order to create universal harmony and unity.[96]

---

90   Koslicki (2008: 106).

91   Koslicki (2004; cf. 2008: 107).

92   Plato, *Tim.* 31b4–9.

93   Plato, *Tim.* 31c1–4.

94   Plato, *Tim.* 31c4–32a7; the numerical example is Taylor's (1928: 93–96).

95   Plato, *Tim.* 32a7–b3.

96   Plato, *Tim.* 32b3–c4; the example given is again Taylor's (*ibidem*). For an extensive analysis of Proclus' interpretation of this mathematical bond between the elements, see Martijn (2010: 173–191).

Here Harte's model of composition through structure is discernible from the Platonic text. The harmony between the four elements of the Timaean cosmos clearly forms a mathematical structure. One could then ask whether the elements themselves make up the content of the universal whole. Harte, however, rightly points out that, in the *Timaeus*, Platonic structure goes 'all the way down'.[97] This becomes clear in *Tim.* 53c–61c, where Timaeus discusses the composition of the four elements themselves. There he reveals that the structure of the three-dimensional solids is actually composed of two-dimensional triangles. Even the elements themselves are structured mathematically. But if all layers of the Timaean cosmos are structure, what is the content that is structured?

The issue of the Platonic 'receptacle', i.e., the thing on which the order of the cosmos and the structure of the elements are imposed, remains pertinent.[98] In fact, as Gerd Van Riel recently argued, 'many centuries later, it still is not clear if the receptacle has anything to do with matter in Plato's worldview; it might also be referring to his concept of "place" in ways that are not yet fully understood, or to neither matter nor place.'[99] Harte's spin on this issue is informed by her reading of Plato's mereology. Since, according to Harte, the whole *is* its structure in Platonic mereology, the receptacle has no positive characteristics of its own. It must not be seen as matter in the sense of 'bodily stuff', but rather as empty space which is a type of matter akin to Aristotle's 'intelligible matter' (ὕλη νοητή).[100] 'In the Timaean cosmos there is nothing that can be characterised positively that is not in some way the product of structure.'[101]

This interpretation of the Timaean elements and their structure is less problematic than the interpretation of the Phileban mixtures as abstract models for composition. However, there is one issue with Harte's reading. In his aforementioned paper, Van Riel proposes that *Tim.* 31b–32c and 53c–61c do not imply that matter has some sort of negative existence in the cosmos. Instead, Van Riel argues that Timaeus simply does not discuss matter at all in his monologue.[102]

---

97   Harte (2002a: 247); cf. *Tim.* 33a7, where Timaeus calls the universe a 'whole of wholes' (ὅλον ὅλων). However, Marmodoro (2021: 199–201) argues that the *Timaeus* describes the cosmos as something composed *both* in a top-bottom way *and* in a bottom-up way: 'The *paradeigma* provides *teleological structure* too, by embodying the Good, which the Demiurge copies into the world, bottom-up.' This double approach to the composition of the cosmos is very similar to the one ultimately taken by Proclus, as we shall see.

98   See Plato, *Tim.* 52d.

99   Van Riel (2021: 171).

100   Harte (2002a: 250–251); cf. Aristotle, *Met.* H.6, 1045a33–35.

101   Harte (2002a: 265).

102   Van Riel (2021).

This reading weakens Harte's argument. If we suppose that the *Timaeus* does not provide any implicit insight on the nature of matter, we cannot state with certainty, as Harte does, that there even is any material content which requires the mathematical structure of the universe for its existence, unless we bring in Aristotle's intelligible matter to smooth over the gaps.

2.5   Structure as a Part in Aristotle

Lastly, our attention must be drawn to Koslicki's interesting and expansive neo-Aristotelian mereology, which constitutes an alternative to Harte's whole-as-structure model. Let us first discuss Koslicki's reading of Aristotle. As is well known, Aristotle distinguishes the matter (ὕλη) of a thing from its form (εἶδος). In the case of wholes, the material elements of a thing do not automatically compose a unity, something they would likely do in Lewis's mereology. In Aristotle's view, there must actually be *something else* (ἕτερόν τι) which unifies the material parts, since the dissolution of a whole does not automatically result in the dissolution of its parts. Per Aristotle's own example, it is possible to divide the syllable into separate letters without also destroying those letters. What is actually dissolved in such a case, then, must be something other than the parts themselves.[103] Although Aristotle does not explicitly define the other thing as the being's form, this can be inferred from his statement that the undefined 'other thing' is the substance (οὐσία) of a thing, its principle (ἀρχή), and the primary cause of its being (αἴτιον πρῶτον τοῦ εἶναι).[104]

In *Metaphysics* Z.17, Aristotle argues for the existence of this other aspect of the whole and its status as a thing's essence through a twofold regress argument. First, if the two elements (στοιχεῖα) of a compound are bound together by a third element, then a fourth element is needed to bind the third to the first two, and so on. Thus, a whole cannot be merely the sum of its parts. Secondly, if some 'other thing' which unites the elements does exist, but is itself already composed of parts, a second 'other thing' is needed to ensure the internal unity of the first, and a third 'other thing' is needed to ensure the unity of the second, and so on. In other words, the cause which unites the parts will, in this case, always be a collection of parts which is itself in need of unification. In

---

103   Aristotle, *Met.* Z.17, 1041b11–19. Aristotle's argument is markedly similar to Plato's in the *Theaetetus*, insofar as both philosophers ostensibly aim to prove that a whole cannot just be the sum of its parts, though Aristotle's *modus ponens*-approach to the issue obviously differs from Plato's aporetic one.

104   Aristotle, *Met.* Z.17, 1041b25–33.

summary, the 'other thing' which brings together parts into a whole cannot be one of the elements that compose the whole, nor can it be composed of elements in and of itself.[105]

2.5.1   *Harte versus Koslicki on the Regress Argument*

This passage is informative for those who wish to discern the differences between Harte's and Koslicki's theories of restricted composition, since both researchers propose different interpretations of this particular passage. Harte's rejection of the whole-having-structure model is based in part on this regress argument from Aristotle's *Metaphysics*. In fact, Koslicki suggests that this Aristotelian passage, rather than any of Plato's writings, provides the primary motivation for Harte's choice in favour of the whole-as-structure model.[106]

The difference between Harte and Koslicki lies in their interpretation of the word 'στοιχεῖον'. Harte seems to interpret the term as 'element' or 'part' in a general sense of the term.[107] Thus, the regress argument shows that structure cannot be one of the parts of the whole. In this respect, I agree with Harte. However, this argument does not necessarily support Harte's model wherein the whole *is* its structure. Aristotle does not state here that the compound is identical to its structure (i.e., the 'other thing', its essence). He instead states that, in order for the compound to exist, it must *not only* (οὐ μόνον) be the elements that compose it, *but also* (ἀλλὰ καί) something else.[108]

In contrast to Harte, Koslicki concludes both that the whole *has* its structure and that structure is a part of the whole. She interprets 'στοιχεῖον' in the more restricted sense of 'material element'. Although Aristotle employs both senses of 'element' in his writings, the final lines of this passage clearly imply that 'στοιχεῖον' here denotes matter, e.g., the material elements in flesh or the letters in a syllable. If one accepts this restricted reading of 'στοιχεῖον', as Koslicki does,[109] the regress no longer forces one to choose Harte's model. Instead, it simply demands that the structure of a whole is not (one of) its material elements.

Here too I agree with Koslicki's initial reading. However, I do not fully agree with Koslicki's subsequent conclusions. She states that the regress argument does not exclude the option that the 'other thing' is a part of the compound,

---

105   Aristotle, *Met.* Z.17, 1041b19–25.

106   Koslicki (2008: 108). This suggestion is not entirely unlikely. We have already seen that an Aristotelian conception of matter influenced Harte's reading of the *Timaeus*.

107   Harte (2002a: 133).

108   Aristotle, *Met.* Z.17, 1041b16–17: ἔστιν ἄρα τι ἡ συλλαβή, οὐ μόνον τὰ στοιχεῖα τὸ φωνῆεν καὶ ἄφωνον ἀλλὰ καὶ ἕτερόν τι ....

109   Koslicki (2008: 109–110).

only that it excludes parts that are *ontologically indistinct* from the elements, i.e., parts that are just more matter.[110] Thus the structure can be part of the whole, just not in the same way its content is. This is reflected in Koslicki's own neo-Aristotelian mereology.

> (NAT) *Neo-Aristotelian Thesis*: The material and formal components of a mereologically complex object are *proper parts* of the whole they compose.[111]
>
> (MAC) *Mereological Analysis of Constitution*: Some objects, m_1, ..., m_n, *constitute* an object, O, just in case m_1, ..., m_n are O's *material components*, i.e., m_1, ..., m_n are those among O's *proper parts* which satisfy the constraints dictated by O's *formal components*, f_1, ..., f_n.[112]

It is not clear how this neo-Aristotelian thesis is supposed to avoid the very same regress delineated above. If the material components m_1, ..., m_n are brought together by *further* parts, viz. the formal components f_1, ..., f_n, what other thing brings the material components and the formal components together?[113] Indeed, Koslicki herself seems to admit that her original interpretation of *Metaphysics* Z.17 is not entirely impervious when she states: 'we should thus stick with the mereological interpretation of the hylomorphic approach, *despite the regress*, and deal with the problem of unity as best as we can.'[114]

Koslicki brings forward a passage from *Metaphysics* Δ.25 as proof of the fact that Aristotle considers both form and matter to be parts.[115]

> ἔτι εἰς ἃ διαιρεῖται ἢ ἐξ ὧν σύγκειται τὸ ὅλον, ἢ τὸ εἶδος ἢ τὸ ἔχον {τὸ} εἶδος, οἷον τῆς σφαίρας τῆς χαλκῆς ἢ τοῦ κύβου τοῦ χαλκοῦ καὶ ὁ χαλκὸς μέρος (τοῦτο δ' ἐστὶν ἡ ὕλη ἐν ᾗ τὸ εἶδος) καὶ ἡ γωνία μέρος.
>
> ARISTOTLE, *Met.* Δ.25, 1023b19–22

---

110   Koslicki (2006: 722–723).

111   Koslicki (2008: 181).

112   Koslicki (2008: 185).

113   Note that in this neo-Aristotelian mereology, each compound also potentially has multiple formal components instead of a single form.

114   Koslicki (2006: 727), my emphasis.

115   Koslicki (2006: 724–725). She also cites *Met.* Δ.18, 1022a32, *Met.* Z.7, 1032b32–33, and *Met.* Z.8, 1033b13–19 as examples of passages where Aristotle seems to ascribe to both matter and form the status of a part.

Then there are the things into which the whole is divided or of which it consists, either the form or that which has a form—for example, of the bronze sphere or the bronze cube both the bronze (that is, the matter in which the form is) is a part and the angle is a part.

Tr. REEVE 2016 (modified)

This passage makes a strong case for Koslicki's general argument, although Aristotle's examples are somewhat ambiguous. Why does he indicate the angle or corner (γωνία) of the cubic shape rather than the shape itself? Is the angle a part of the shape, and does this mean that the cubic form has parts of its own? This would contradict both the regress argument of Z.17 (in which the unifying principle is stated to have no elements of its own) and Koslicki's own interpretation of Aristotelian hylomorphism, whereby she takes the form to be a mereological atom.[116] What further complicates the matter is the sheer complexity of Aristotle's metaphysics and the fact that his writings do not always allow for one clear-cut interpretation of his concepts. For example, in *Metaphysics* Δ.25 and Δ.26, Aristotle compiles multiple types of parts and wholes. Koslicki herself states that the complexity of Aristotle's mereological reflections requires him 'to incur certain costs: definitions, matter/form compounds, species, and genera cannot be straightforwardly understood as being ordered by means of a *single* asymmetric and transitive relation of proper parthood.'[117]

As the passage from *Metaphysics* Δ.25 shows, Koslicki's proposition is certainly not spurious. Yet the text from Z.17 simply does not explicate the division between ontologically and mereologically distinct parts that she distils from it.[118] Just as the passage supports Harte's conclusion that the structure of a whole is not one of its parts, but not her proposition that this prevents the whole from *having* its structure, so is Koslicki supported by Aristotle in stating that the στοιχεῖα of a whole are its material elements, but not in her assumption

---

116   Koslicki (2006: 728–732 and 2008: 159–162).

117   Koslicki (2008: 158–159), my emphasis.

118   For a more elaborate counterargument to Koslikci's reading of Aristotle based on this specific criticism, see Marmodoro (2013) and Rotkale (2018). Marmodoro's (2013: 18–19) alternative to Koslicki's thesis, namely that the structure is not another part of the whole but rather constitutes the reidentification of individual things as parts of a whole—in the sense that, e.g., a finger is only a finger *qua* part of a body, whereas it is simply flesh if severed—comes closest to the mereological approach we shall distill from Proclus' writings as well. Yet another argument against Koslicki's form-as-part can be found in Donnelly (2011), who does not discuss Koslikci's reading of Aristotle specifically. Instead, her criticism of Koslicki's theses is informed by contemporary mereology.

that the unifying principle (the 'other thing') is defined as another type of part. Ultimately, what Aristotle affirms with his regress argument is no more than the fact that a compound has parts or elements which are material and that for these parts to form a unity, there must be something else to the compound. Aristotle does not explicate whether the compound *is* or *has* this other thing, nor whether this other thing is also a type of part.

2.5.2 *Mereological Considerations on Koslicki's Neo-Aristotelian Theory*
Koslicki's hylomorphic mereology has a number of advantages over Harte's Platonic model. First of all, like Harte's mereology, Koslicki's theory allows for the inclusion of artificial and non-living wholes in our ontology, in contrast to Van Inwagen's theory of composition through life-activity. Unlike Harte's theory, Koslicki's model of composition makes structure essential only for the existence of the whole, not for the existence of the parts. Thus, the parts are capable of existing independently from their whole.

In exchange, the neo-Aristotelian model loses an advantage Harte's theory had. Because Koslicki takes a bottom-up approach to composition, as Lewis and Van Inwagen did, the neo-Aristotelian mereology cannot leapfrog Lewis's arguments against *Restricted Composition* in the same way Harte's top-down mereology did. This is apparent from Koslicki's own criterion for *Restricted Composition*: 'some objects m_1, ..., m_n, compose an object, O, of kind, K, just in case m_1, ..., m_n, satisfy the constraints dictated by some formal components, f_1, ..., f_n, associated with objects of kind, K.'[119] The composition of an object O of kind K requires that there are certain formal elements f_1, ..., f_n, yet those formal objects can only be defined in relation to their associated kind K. Depending on the kind to which a whole belongs, the constraints dictated by its formal components could be strict or lenient, precise or vague. Indeed, the formal components can even be ontologically distinct between different kinds of wholes.[120] Which structures the specific forms of each kind of object actually constitute is not a matter for mereology, according to Koslicki. Mereology 'does not settle matters of ontological commitment; rather, it presupposes them to be resolved elsewhere within metaphysics or outside of philosophy altogether.'[121] As a result, however, Koslicki's formal components are only really defined as being

---

119   Koslicki (2008: 173).
120   Koslicki (2008: 172–174).
121   Koslicki (2008: 170–171). When she states that ontology can be discussed 'outside of philosophy altogether', she refers of other fields of science, such as mathematics, chemistry, or linguistics (2008: 199–254).

structural parts of the whole which exist besides the parts, which in turn make up the content of the whole.[122]

2.5.3   *Aristotle versus Van Inwagen*

Van Inwagen stated that 'there are no material objects but organisms and simples.'[123] Interestingly, Van Inwagen's view of parthood implies that there is *something else* to compounds besides the material objects, not unlike Aristotle's does. In the case of living beings, this distinction is relatively obvious. The material parts or x'es of a living being have a life-activity, and it is this activity which enables the composition of the unified living being.[124] Compare this to the 'other thing' of Aristotle, which is the principle of the compound's existence. Van Inwagen excludes artefacts from his ontology of unified wholes but, as I have argued, even in those cases his theory implies that there is at least *something* more to a supposed chair than the material simples. Even in his new paraphrase of the sentence 'some chairs are heavier than some tables', he cannot avoid talking about chairwise arrangements and chair-receptacles. Here too, we have some other thing besides the material elements. The difference between a chairwise arrangement and life-activity, according to Van Inwagen's theory, is that only the latter actually unifies its material elements.

On this point, Aristotle and Van Inwagen would most likely disagree. Aristotle leaves the nature of the unifying principle largely undefined. He does not introduce any sort of distinction between one principle which leads to true compounds and another principle which only leads to compounds in our perception. Indeed, neither of the examples given by Aristotle involve life-activity, but the syllable and the flesh are still compounds (σύνθετα). As a result, Aristotle's ontology of composition (and, by extension, Koslicki's) is less restrictive than Van Inwagen's.

2.6   The Two Sides of Modern Mereology

The development of modern mereology was markedly shaped by its heritage from logic. Within the confines of formal logic and set theory, a whole is the full sum of the singular elements included within it. After all, a logical set of A and B has no existence or identity beyond A and B. As a result, formalistic philosophers working within this logical framework, such as Lewis, tend to posit

---

122   Cf. Hovda (2009b).

123   Van Inwagen (1990: 111).

124   Van Inwagen (1990: 82).

an axiom of unrestricted composition, i.e., the notion that any two things can fuse and form a whole. Yet when one applies this logical axiom to real phenomena in nature, one runs into problems.

The simplest problem of a Lewesian mereology is the fact that it does not adequately account for the numerical distinction between a separated A and B and a set of AB. The former is two in number, the latter one. This problem is made clear by Baxter's example of the divided land. Baxter claims that the six owners of the adjacent parcels of land also own the combined stretch simply by virtue of their individual ownerships, which is a completely logical conclusion within the confines of set theory. When we speak of real tracts of land, however, it seems more intuitive to say that a singularly owned stretch of land is different from six individually owned parcels, even if the difference is only a numerical one. Already in antiquity, Aristotle argued for such an approach to mereology, stating that a compound is not just its material elements, but also 'something else' (ἕτερόν τι). This other thing is not a further element, but the essence or principle (ἀρχή) of the thing created from those elements. Without such a principle, the elements simply constitute a heap.

The problem runs deeper than a numerical distinction, however. From Lewis's perspective, a trout-turkey is just as valid a fusion of trout and turkey as the trout is of eyes, gills, fins, and the like. To the naturalistic philosopher (or the layman), however, it seems counterintuitive to argue that the trout-turkey is a real unity just as the trout is. The latter is capable of uniting its elements in the real world in a way that the trout and the turkey together are not. A proponent of a logical form of mereology might wonder what exactly distinguishes the trout from the trout-turkey, and rightly so. As Lewis argued, the distinction between a possible fusion and an impossible fusion runs a significant risk of becoming fuzzy. The greatest issue faced by philosophers who argue for restricted composition, i.e., the notion that only certain things can form truly unified wholes, is the lack of a self-evident criterion for distinguishing true compounds from mere collections.

One could argue that proponents of the naturalistic approach to mereology struggle with the trout-turkey in part because they view composite things from a materialistic perspective.[125] As Aristotle and Koslicki's analysis of him showed, the claim that a collection of material elements constitutes a compound requires the addition of some structuring formal element or elements, the presence and mereological character of which then needs to be explained (is it the whole itself, or a further element of it?). Similarly, Van Inwagen takes

---

125   I thank Jan Opsomer for this suggestion.

recourse to the formal element of 'life' to explain why certain material simples constitute an ontologically distinct whole, whereas others do not. In contrast, as Varzi noted, the question of whether the elements of an ontologically innocent fusion are material or formal in nature has no bearing on their being counted within the sum total of the fusion, and thus it is not a problematic question for the formalistic student of mereology. For these philosophers, there is no fusion too odd to be included.

A proponent of a naturalistic mereology can in turn deal with the vagueness caused by the addition of formal or structural elements in two ways. The first solution is to posit a criterion for restricted composition in the hopes that it will withstand accusations of fuzziness from logicians. The most notable example discussed in this chapter is Van Inwagens life-criterion. As counterintuitive as it seems to deny wholeness to all inanimate compounds, from rocks to cars, life is nevertheless an attractive criterion for wholeness because it is very clearly the unifying principle of an organism in the Aristotelian mould, distinct from any specific part of the living creature's body. Its removal causes an irrevocable change in the compound, for once destroyed the living being cannot be brought back to life, whereas inanimate objects can be disassembled and reassembled any number of times. Indeed, the only fuzziness left in this mereology is the gradual change from life to lifelessness and vice versa, a fuzziness which Van Inwagen candidly accepts.

The removal of inanimate wholes from our ontology is a sticking point, however, especially in the age of modern chemistry and physics. Even if Van Inwagen refused to acknowledge that the collection of material simples in which his writings are collected is a truly unified book, there is some 'bookwise' arrangement that makes it so that the material simples in which his ideas can be read form a book and not a chair. In this regard, Koslicki's Neo-Aristotelian mereology appears to be a superior alternative, for her criterion is a formula of wholeness comprised of the formal and material components determined by whatever ontological kind one considers at that moment. This formula for composition is far less strict than Van Inwagen's life-principle and, as such, grants inanimate wholes a place in our ontology.

However, Koslicki's formula is infected by vagueness to a greater extent than Van Inwagen's distinction between life and lifelessness, and for two reasons. First, the Aristotelian distinction between a thing's elements and its unifying principle, which equate to a being's matter and form, respectively, is muddled because of the fact that Koslicki considers both the material and formal components of a being to be proper parts of it, as per her *Neo-Aristotelian Thesis*. Indeed, her *Mereological Analysis of Constitution* allows for a multitude of formal parts within a compound, which is potentially equal to or even greater than the number of material components. The singular Aristotelian cause which makes the compound a whole is missing here. Second, Koslicki's unifying principle is not only mereologically complex, but also lacks a clear identity of its own, unlike Van Inwagen's life-principle. Although the specific meaning of the concept of life can be a subject of controversy, it is undoubtedly a clearer criterion for distinguishing true compositions from false ones than the statement that 'm_1, ..., m_n, compose an object, O, of kind, K, just in case m_1, ..., m_n, satisfy the constraints dictated by some formal components, f_1, ..., f_n, associated with objects of kind, K.'[126] As we noted, Koslicki leaves the question of what kinds of beings belong in our ontology to other areas of philosophy or to other sciences altogether. Within the confines of mereology, however, we are left with only a set of as yet undetermined logical variables. In this sense, one could argue that Koslicki's view on composition is somewhat of a hybrid between the mereology of the formalists and Van Inwagen's metaphysical mereology.

In contrast to Van Inwagen and Koslicki, Harte's Platonic analysis avoids the issue raised by Lewis entirely. If one postulates that the whole is ontologically prior to the parts (or, analogously, that the logical set is prior to its components), one does not have to determine a criterion for determining when parts can compose a whole. The whole is logically prior to the parts, and as such it creates the parts rather than vice versa. Unfortunately, this mereological theory has its own problem. As Harte herself admitted, her version of Platonic mereology robs the parts of independent existence. If the existence of the guests at a dinner party depends on the seating arrangement of the dinner party itself, then it stands to reason that the guests would cease to exist once they became disconnected from the structure offered by the dinner party. Van Inwagen and Koslicki sought to determine which wholes can or cannot be composed out of any given set of parts. In contrast, Harte needs to determine which parts can or cannot be separated from any given set of wholes.

Until now, then, the definitive theory of composition has remained out of our reach. Various approaches to the nature of wholeness have been pitted against one another without a clear victory on any side. Varzi goes so far as to suggest that 'disputes on these matters are deadlocked', despite his own preference for a minimalist definition of the whole in a Lewesian vein. As he explains, 'there are no obvious reasons to take mereological extensionality for granted (except perhaps considerations of ontological simplicity and nominalistic parsimony), but nor is there a knockdown argument against it, and it appears that we have an ontological question which can be settled only by looking at its tenability vis à vis linguistic intuitions.'[127]

---

126   See section 5.2 above.

127   Varzi (2008: 114).

As we move on to Proclus' views on composition in the next chapter and the chapters beyond, using the problems raised here to inform the inquiry into Proclean mereology, we should keep a few things in mind. First, although it would not be wise to impose any of the aforementioned theories and arguments onto Proclus' writings haphazardly, there are a number of notions made clear by these modern students of mereology that will apply also when we face the complexities of Proclean mereology. Since Plato and Aristotle both favoured restricted composition over its unrestricted counterpart, we can reasonably expect Proclus to do so as well. This means that Proclus likely answers or at least discusses the two questions raised in the last paragraph: what is a whole beyond the collection of its parts, and what is left of the parts when they are separated from their whole? Second, we should be mindful of the difference between the logical and ontological forms of mereology, i.e., the difference between a formula like Lewis's or Koslicki's, which contains abstract variables, and a metaphysical theory like Van Inwagen's, which takes the really existent phenomenon of life as its criterion for restricted composition. If Proclus turns out to be Van Inwagen's predecessor rather than Koslicki's, then it will be improper to attempt to reformulate his mereology in more formal terms, and vice versa. In summary, like the contemporary philosophers, Proclus will need to face this ultimate choice: the chaos of complete mereological freedom, or the potential imperfections of an ordered set of wholes and non-wholes. Fantastical wholes or fuzzy wholes. The trout-turkey or '$f_1 \ldots f_n$ of kind K'.

PART 2

The Central Tenets of Proclean Mereology

∵

Τὸ μέρος που ὅλου μέρος ἐστίν.
—Ναί.
Τί δὲ τὸ ὅλον; οὐχὶ οὗ ἂν μέρος μηδὲν ἀπῇ ὅλον ἂν εἴη;
—Πάνυ γε.

PLATO, *Parmenides* 137c6–8, ed. J. Burnet, Oxford: Clarendon Press, 1901
(repr. 1967)

CHAPTER 3

Quantity versus Complexity

The central thread running through the entirety of Neoplatonic metaphysics is the procession from absolute unity towards increasing multiplicity (and the reversion in the opposite direction). This is as true for Proclus' metaphysics as it is for Plotinus' or, indeed, for any member of the Neoplatonic school. As Plotinus explains in the first essay of the fifth *Ennead*, Intellect revolves around the One as a circle revolves around its midpoint. The difference between the circle and the point is the fact that the former is divisible, and thus internally multitudinous, whereas the latter is not.[1] This metaphor is not exclusively applicable to the Intellect and the One, for Plotinus also describes the spawn of Intellect, Soul, as 'that which revolves around Intellect'.[2] In this case, Intellect is the more unitary principle, and Soul the more divisible one. In other words, Plotinus describes Neoplatonic reality through the metaphor of concentric circles flowing forth from the same midpoint, each wider and thus more divisible than the last.

In his *Elements of Theology*, Proclus presents his own version of the Plotinian metaphor through a proposition which states that, the closer any multiplicity stands to the first principle that is the One, the smaller its number is and the greater its power.[3] The various levels of Proclean reality conform to this notion just as they do in Plotinus' thought: the hypostasis of Intellect is less divisible or multitudinous than the totality of Soul, which in turn is less multitudinous than the full collection of corporeal things.

Yet Proclus adds a rather interesting theorem to Neoplatonic metaphysics. Each of the many intelligible beings distinguished by Proclus constitutes a generative principle, and all corporeal and sensible things derive their being and characteristics from these intelligible causes. However, not all sensible things are caused by all intelligible things. Proclus rejected Iamblichus' belief that the generative powers (δυνάμεις) of principles such as Soul, Intellect, and the One extend equally far down into physical reality—at least, that is what Olympiodorus tells us.[4] The 'rule of Proclus', as Olympiodorus calls it, states

---

1 Plotinus, *Enn.* V.1 [10], 7.6–9.

2 Plotinus, *Enn.* V.1 [10], 7.43: τοῦτο δ' ἐστὶ τὸ περὶ νοῦν κινούμενον.

3 Proclus, *ET* 62, 58.22–23: Πᾶν πλῆθος ἐγγυτέρω τοῦ ἑνὸς ὂν ποσῷ μέν ἐστι τῶν πορρωτέρω ἔλαττον, τῇ δυνάμει δὲ μεῖζον.

4 Olympiodorus, *In Alc.* 109.18–111.2. Although Olympiodorus explicitly links this theorem to our philosopher, Dodds (1963: 231) has argued that the doctrine 'is older than Proclus'. Nevertheless, the idea was not yet accepted by Iamblichus, who according to Olympiodorus

---

© ARTHUR OOSTHOUT, 2025 | DOI:10.1163/9789004721760_004

that the generative power of a higher intelligible principle extends further down than that of a lower intelligible being. In other words, a lesser generative principle cannot produce or inform as many beings as its superior peers do. As a result, the lowest sensible beings mirror the highest intelligible beings, since those superior intelligible principles are the only causes with a power great enough to reach the lowly products. This theorem makes for a clever move on the part of Proclus. It allows him to explain why lesser objects such as rocks are simpler than supposedly superior beings such as human beings, which have more parts.[5] It has also been suggested that the rule of Proclus bolsters the Neoplatonic tradition of theurgy, since the latter included divination through the use of seemingly lowly objects.[6]

However, the mirror between the intelligible and the sensible is not a perfect one. Because the Neoplatonic system still intrinsically revolves around increasing multiplicity in the descent from the One, the sensible things cannot truly mirror the intelligible principles. This tension between the mirrored complexity of superior intelligible principles and inferior sensible beings on the one hand and the steadily increasing multiplicity on the other becomes especially clear when one studies the mereological consequences of Proclus' unique perspective on causality. Unfortunately, these mereological consequences have not been explored in much detail by modern scholars, despite the valuable contributions that have been made in charting a number of other aspects of the 'Proclean rule'. I shall give the necessary overview of Proclus' rule in the next section, but I am certainly not the first to do so. E.R. Dodds already explained the basics in his commentary on Proclus' *Elements of Theology*, as did Ernst-Otto Onnasch and Ben Schomakers in theirs.[7] Radek Chlup discusses this theory of causality in more detail in his introduction to Proclean metaphysics.[8] Furthermore, Opsomer and Van Riel have looked more deeply

---

(*ibidem*) conceived of the generative power of all principles as capable of reaching the lowest substrate. It is important to note also that the later Neoplatonists do not employ δύναμις solely in the Aristotelian sense of a receptivity to actualisation. The term can also denote a power to generate other beings (cf. Proclus, *ET* 78). For an account of the difference between active and receptive δύναμις as Proclus sees it, see Steel (1996).

5   Dodds (1963: 232).

6   See, e.g., Chlup (2012: 90). For a more exhaustive bibliography of this specific claim, see Siorvanes (1996: 206 n. 130). However, Siorvanes (1996: 187; cf. 189–199) cautions against simply concluding that Proclus saw lowly material objects as direct links to the divine, stating that such a suggestion '[rests] on a fundamental misunderstanding of Proclus' metaphysics of participation and causation, and of the aim of theurgy' (cf. the footnotes to section 2 below). An analysis of the role of material objects in theurgy which avoids such a problem can be found in, e.g., Van den Berg (2000: 429–431 and 435–436).

7   See Dodds (1963: 232) and Onnasch and Schomakers (2015: 272).

8   Chlup (2012: 97–99).

into specific instances where Proclus applies his rule of causality. Opsomer discusses a passage from book three of the *Platonic Theology*, where Proclus enumerates various kinds of corporeal beings and their inheritance from various intelligible principles.[9] Van Riel explains how Proclus' rule informs the process of demiurgy.[10] I shall discuss the same passages as these two scholars have done, since those texts contain clear examples of Proclus' rule. However, I shall approach these texts from a mereological angle, whereas their interest lay in studying other aspects of Proclus' rule: the nature of irrational souls and the various layers of the material substrate(s), respectively.

3.1   Proclus' Rule in the *Elements of Theology*

In propositions 57 through 60 of his *Elements of Theology*, Proclus explains the basic mechanics of causality as he sees it. Proposition 57 establishes the thrust of the Proclean rule: 'every cause both operates before the thing it causes and establishes more things after this effect.'[11] The higher intelligible being is superior to the lower beings it causes. For example, Intellect is superior to Soul.[12] This means that it is not only more perfect (τελειότερον) than its consequent, but also possesses greater generative power (δυνατώτερον).[13] 'The more powerful a cause is, the more things it produces.'[14]

From this, Proclus concludes that every product of Soul is also the product of Intellect, but not *vice versa*, since Intellect's generation of products is prior to that of Soul (πρὸ ψυχῆς ἐνεργεῖ). At the same time, Intellect's generation of products continues after the generative power of Soul has been depleted. For example, ensouled things participate in both Soul and Intellect due to their being both ensouled and given form, whereas soulless things only participate in a given form, which they obtain through their participation in Intellect. Thus some things no longer participate in Soul, but still participate in Intellect. Likewise, that which is beyond the reach of Intellect still participates in the Good, since 'all things come from it' (πάντα γὰρ ἐκεῖθεν), and thus even the absence of form is caused by the Good.[15]

---

9   Opsomer (2006b: 137–140; cf. 2016: 156).

10   Van Riel (2009: 256–57).

11   Proclus, *ET* 57, 54.34–35: πᾶν αἴτιον καὶ πρὸ τοῦ αἰτιατοῦ ἐνεργεῖ καὶ μετ᾽ αὐτὸ πλειόνων ἐστὶν ὑποστατικόν.

12   Cf. Proclus, *ET* 7, 8.1–2.

13   Proclus, *ET* 57, 54.25–26: εἰ γάρ ἐστιν αἴτιον, τελειότερόν ἐστι καὶ δυνατώτερον τοῦ μετ᾽ αὐτό.

14   Proclus, *ET* 57, 54.30–31: εἰ οὖν δυνατώτερον τὸ αἴτιον, πλειόνων ἐστὶ παρακτικόν.

15   Proclus, *ET* 57, 56.8–16.

As stated before, this means that the generative power of a higher cause extends further down through reality than the power of a lower cause. As a result, the lowest entities of our universe (from lifeless beings to simple formed matter to unformed substrates) derive from fewer intelligible principles than higher beings such as animals or people. The lowest level of all reality is touched only by the productive power of the One.

In contrast, the higher beings of the sensible world, such as human beings, are caused by a greater number of intelligible principles. These multiple principles all contribute to the existence of their shared product. For, as Proclus explains, any given principle is itself caused by some higher principle which possesses yet greater productive power. Hence, a principle such as Intellect is just as capable of producing the products of Soul as Soul itself is. Thus, a superior principle like the Intellect contributes to the generation of everything which is produced by its inferior brethren, such as Soul.[16] There are no ensouled beings which lack a form, after all.

In creating a human being, for example, the One, Intellect, and Soul are all co-producers.[17] The result is highly interesting from a mereological perspective: 'all that is produced by a greater number of causes is *more composite* than that which is produced by fewer.'[18] Proclus then explains what this 'compositeness' means.

εἰ γὰρ πᾶν αἴτιον δίδωσί τι τῷ ἀπ' αὐτοῦ προϊόντι, τὰ μὲν πλείονα αἴτια πλείονας ποιήσεται τὰς δόσεις, τὰ δὲ ἐλάττονα ἐλάττους. ὥστε καὶ τῶν μετασχόντων τὰ μὲν ἐκ πλειόνων ἔσται, τὰ δὲ ἐξ ἐλαττόνων, ὧν ἑκάτερα μετέσχε, τὰ μὲν διὰ τὴν ἐκ πλειόνων αἰτίων πρόοδον, τὰ δὲ διὰ τὴν ἐκ τῶν ἐλαττόνων. τὰ δὲ ἐκ πλειόνων συνθετώτερα, τὰ δὲ ἐξ ἐλαττόνων τῶν αὐτῶν ἁπλούστερα.

PROCLUS, ET 58, 56.19–25

If every cause gives something to that which proceeds from it, more causes will bestow more gifts, less causes fewer. As a result, some of the participants will be composed of more [gifts], others of fewer, in virtue of their respective procession from more or fewer causes. But things made up of more elements are more composite; things made up of fewer of the same elements are less so.

Tr. DODDS 1963 (modified)

---

16   Proclus, *ET* 57, 54.32–56.3.

17   Cf. Chlup (2012: 89) and Onnasch and Schomakers (2015: 272).

18   Proclus, *ET* 58, 56.18–19: πᾶν τὸ ὑπὸ πλειόνων αἰτίων παραγόμενον συνθετώτερόν ἐστι τοῦ ὑπὸ ἐλαττόνων παραγομένου.

Proclus emphasises that the more composite being 'will consist of more things' (ἐκ πλειόνων ἔσται), these things being the 'gifts' (δόσεις) of the intelligible principles. Thus, these recipients of the intelligible gifts are composite. What these gifts that make up the parts of the composite recipients actually are remains to be determined, as does the way in which they are structured within the whole. Onnasch and Schomakers suggest that Proclus is thinking of 'eine Anhäufung von Abbildern und Abbildern von Abbildern usw. der metaphysischen Ursachen',[19] but they do not reveal whether they consider this Anhäufung of gifts from the intelligible causes to be mereological in nature.

In proposition 60, Proclus provides valuable insight on this matter. He states that 'all that is the cause of more things is stronger than that whose power is confined to fewer things and which [i.e., the lesser cause] produces the parts of the wholes which the former [i.e., the greater cause] produces.'[20] In other words: the higher intelligible principle produces more effects and thus 'has a greater and more universal generative power.'[21] As a result, the higher principle gives rise to the product as a whole, while its lesser co-producers create the parts of that whole.

Yet this whole is not a composition in the most common sense of the word, i.e., an aggregate of distinct proper parts.[22] Instead, the parts created by the causes have a relation of transitivity, i.e., within whole x, part a is part of x, while part b is part of a.[23] In other words, the gifts of the intelligible principles stack on top of one another. Proclus explains as much in propositions 70 through 72 of the *Elements of Theology*, where he once again compares the gifts of superior causes to those of inferior causes.

> Πάντα τὰ ἐν τοῖς ἀρχηγικοῖς αἰτίοις ὁλικωτέραν καὶ ὑπερτέραν τάξιν ἔχοντα ἐν τοῖς ἀποτελέσμασι κατὰ τὰς ἀπ' αὐτῶν ἐλλάμψεις ὑποκείμενά πως γίνεται ταῖς τῶν μερικωτέρων μεταδόσεσι·
>
> PROCLUS, *ET* 71, 66.31–68.2

---

19   Onnasch and Schomakers (2015: 271).

20   Proclus, *ET* 60, 58.3–5: πᾶν τὸ πλειόνων αἴτιον κρεῖττόν ἐστι τοῦ πρὸς ἐλάττονα τὴν δύναμιν λαχόντος καὶ μέρη παράγοντος ὧν θάτερον ὅλων ὑποστατικόν ἐστιν.

21   Proclus, *ET* 60, 58.12: μείζονα δύναμιν ἔχει καὶ ὁλικωτέραν.

22   For example, my arm and my leg are both part of my body, but not part of each other.

23   For the axioms of modern mereology, including the axiom of transitivity, see chapter 2, section 1. For example, my finger is part of my hand, and my hand is part of my body. Hence, my finger is also part of my body. In this case, my finger and my hand are not distinct from one another in the same way my arm and my leg are.

> All things which in the principal causes have a higher and more universal (ὁλικωτέραν) rank become in the resultant beings, through the irradiations which proceed from them, a kind of substratum for the gifts of the more specific (μερικωτέρων) principles.
>
> Tr. DODDS 1963 (slightly modified)

Proclus goes on to explain that the various gifts in which a product of intelligible principles participates are placed ·in an order of priority, whereby the 'more whole' or 'more universal' (ὁλικώτερα) causes put their stamp on the product before the 'more particular' (μερικώτερα) causes get to shape it.[24] In short, the gift of each causal principle is seated in the gifts from its superior co-producers. Conversely, the new gift serves as a substrate for the subsequent gifts from inferior co-producers.[25]

How must we distinguish intelligible principles which constitute wholes from intelligible principles which constitute parts? In ET 60, Proclus merely states that the 'cause of more' creates the composite product as a whole, while the 'cause of fewer' creates the parts. Yet the notion that each gift serves as a substrate for its successor applies to the entire procession of causes which inform a product.[26] Should we conclude, then, that every gift bestowed upon the product constitutes both a part of the preceding gift and the whole of which the succeeding gift is a part?[27] Or should we draw a line somewhere in the procession between those causes that establish a whole and those that establish parts? This issue is exacerbated by the fact that Proclus seemingly does not distinguish the terms 'whole' and 'part' from the terms 'universal' and 'particular'. Baltzly picks up on this, stating that 'Proclus seems to intuit some intimate connection between the two distinctions, though the exact nature of

---

24   Proclus, *ET* 71, 68.2–8.

25   Proclus, *ET* 72, 68.17–18; cf. Lloyd (1998: 106–107).

26   For example, matter serves as a substrate for the formed body, which subsequently serves a as substrate for the soul; cf. Proclus, *ET* 72, 68.24–27.

27   This implies that the compound is only composed of parts that stack on top of each other. Interestingly, most modern scholars in the field of mereology would not accept this. Many modern theories of mereology adhere to the *Weak Supplementation Principle*, which states that $(x < y) \to (\exists z)\,(z < y\, \&\, z \nmid x)$, i.e., every whole y with part x must have at least one other part z which does not overlap with x; cf. Koslicki (2008: 17–20). In contrast, the product of Proclus' multiple intelligible causes will not have two truly distinct parts, for they are all ordered in a single procession. Note, however, that Proclus does allow for multiple distinct parts within a single step of the procession, as is explained below. For a more detailed discussion of the relativity of the concept of wholeness in Proclus' metaphysics, see Oosthout, A. (2022b)—this subject matter is touched upon briefly in chapter 5, section 1 of this book as well.

this connection is not easy to fathom.'[28] For example, Proclus uses the terminology of part and whole to describe the distinction between particular and universal souls in this *Timaeus*-commentary, despite the fact that a particular soul is not a literal part of the universal soul, expect if one describes it as a part of its definition, as Baltzly notes.[29]

The notion that the concepts of the whole and the concepts of the genus or the universal overlap in some sense is not unique to Proclus. Already in his book of definitions in the *Metaphysics*, Aristotle notes that genera and species can be considered as parts of each other's definitions, and that the universal is a whole because it 'encompasses many things' (ὡς πολλὰ περιέχον).[30] When Plotinus reintroduces the five greatest genera from Plato's *Sophist* in his sixth *Ennead*, he prefaces his description with a brief argument against the idea that the genera, *qua* wholes, should be composed in an atomistic sense, for otherwise they cannot also function as productive principles.[31] The implication of that argument is not that the greatest genera are not wholes, but rather that *qua* principle each of them is whole in the holistic sense which Harte also distilled from Plato's writings.[32]

The clearest expression of the notion that the genus and the species are related to one another as whole and part can be found in Porphyry's *Isagoge*, as Anthony Lloyd has pointed out.[33] More specifically, Porphyry ends a passage in which he describes the ways in which genera, species, and individuals are predicated of one another with the following argument: 'The genus is some kind of whole, the individual a part, and the species is both whole and part. But the species is part *of* another, whereas it is whole not of another but *in* others: it is the whole in the parts.'[34] The genus or universal is here envisioned as an extensional whole, i.e., as a set which includes each of the species and each of the individuals, though without any distinction between class membership and class inclusion, as Lloyd notes.[35]

Proclus incorporates this notion of the genus-as-extensional-set into the *Elements of Theology*. In propositions 73 and 74, he ranks the concepts of being, wholeness, and universal in terms of their generality. Being is a more universal

---

28   Baltzly (2008: 206 n. 492).

29   Proclus, *IT* IV, 149.2–10 (3.115.19–27 Diehl); Baltzly (2013: 206 n. 492 and 207 n. 494).

30   Aristotle, *Met.* Δ.26, 1023b29–32.

31   Plotinus, *Enn.* VI.2 [43], 2.14–26.

32   See chapter 2, section 4.2.

33   Lloyd (1998: 44).

34   Porphyry, *Isagoge* 8.1–3: ὅλον γάρ τι τὸ γένος, τὸ δὲ ἄτομον μέρος, τὸ δὲ εἶδος καὶ ὅλον καὶ μέρος, ἀλλὰ μέρος μὲν ἄλλου, ὅλον δὲ οὐκ ἄλλου ἀλλ᾽ ἐν ἄλλοις· ἐν γὰρ τοῖς μέρεσι τὸ ὅλον.

35   Lloyd (1998: 44).

notion than the whole, Proclus argues, for there exist things in the universe which are parts and only parts, and if there existed a transcendent principle of wholeness before a principle of being, then every existent thing would automatically be a whole (per the Proclean rule).[36] In contrast, the whole must be a more universal notion than the Platonic Form, because the Form is divided in one specific manner, whereas any kind of divisible thing is called 'whole'. The specific manner in which the Form is divided is the division of a universal *qua* extensional set into its particular members, as is revealed by Proclus' statement that 'the Form is something which is already cut up into multiple *individuals.*'[37]

This confirms that Proclus, like Porphyry, envisions the universal which encompasses its respective individuals as a certain kind of whole. Yet this knowledge does not answer our question about the distinction between principles which produce things as wholes and principles which produce their parts. In fact, it introduces another difficulty: if universality is merely a specific kind of wholeness, represented by the Platonic Forms, then how can we speak of a distinction between 'more universal' and 'more particular' causes which is applicable even to principles such as Being, which according to propositions 73 and 74 should transcend the very notion of universality?[38]

Leaving aside for now this issue terminology,[39] we can nevertheless conclude that the distinction 'universal/particular' is here conceptualised as a particular kind of 'whole/part'-distinction. When the superior cause is described as being 'more holistic' (ὁλικωτέραν) and its gift as a whole (ὅλον), one can interpret these terms in this specific manner and thus conclude from *ET* 70–72 that the gift is not whole in the common sense of the word, but rather more universal, because it serves as a substrate for the more specific gift of a successive cause.[40]

The Proclean rule also has interesting consequences for the lowest levels of reality, as is confirmed in proposition 59. There Proclus writes that 'all that is simple in its essence is either greater than the compounds or lesser.'[41] Proclus argues for this proposition by pointing out that the products at the extreme

---

36 Proclus, *ET* 73, 70.5–9.

37 Proclus, *ET* 74, 70.17–21: πᾶν γὰρ ὅλον ἐστὶ τὸ ἐκ μερῶν ὑφεστός, εἶδος δὲ τὸ εἰς πλείω τὰ καθέκαστα ἤδη τεμνόμενον. Cf. Plato, *Pol.* 263b8–10.

38 This criticism was voiced already by Nicholas of Methone, for which see chapter 5, section 1.

39 For a more extensive discussion of the consistency of Proclus' use of mereological terminology, see chapter 5, section 1, and chapter 7, section 3.

40 In his other writings, Proclus gives examples of such substrates. We shall turn to the relevant passages in the next section.

41 Proclus, *ET* 59, 56.28–29: πᾶν τὸ ἁπλοῦν κατ᾽ οὐσίαν ἢ κρεῖττόν ἐστι τῶν συνθέτων ἢ χεῖρον.

QUANTITY VERSUS COMPLEXITY

end of the causal hierarchy will be informed by fewer principles, since lower principles do not have the same causal reach as their superior predecessors. Thus, these later products will be simpler than their more composite predecessors. The same notion holds for the principles themselves, but in reverse, since those principles which stand higher above the middle of the causal scale will have less superior principles in which they themselves participate and thus will not yet be composite.[42] This means that the lowest level of reality, which derives solely from the One, mirrors the first principle in its absolute simplicity.

> διὰ γὰρ τοῦτο καὶ τὸ ἔσχατον τῶν ὄντων ἁπλούστατον, ὥσπερ τὸ πρῶτον, ὅτι
> ἀπὸ μόνου πρόεισι τοῦ πρώτου· ἀλλ' ἡ ἁπλότης ἡ μὲν κατὰ τὸ κρεῖττόν ἐστι
> πάσης συνθέσεως, ἡ δὲ κατὰ τὸ χεῖρον. καὶ ἐπὶ πάντων ὁ αὐτός ἐστι λόγος.
>
> PROCLUS, *ET* 59, 56.36–58.2

> Because of this, the last being is the simplest, like the first, for the reason that it proceeds from the first alone. But the one is simple as being above all composition, the other as being beneath it, and the same reasoning applies to all other things.
>
> Tr. DODDS 1963 (modified)

Here the aforementioned tension between Proclus' new perspective on causality and the old Neoplatonic theorem of increasing multiplicity becomes apparent. According to the Proclean rule, the ultimate material substrate must be absolutely simple (ἁπλούστατον), just as the One is. Yet this perfectly simple matter is also the end-point in a procession towards minimal unity. Proclus himself implies as much in propositions 80 and 86, where he not only reveals that body as such has no character save divisibility, but also that the unqualified body, because of its great distance from the One, is quantitatively *infinite*.[43] How are we to reconcile the utter simplicity of the unqualified body, which would logically involve a lack of composition, as per *ET* 58 above, with its infinite divisibility? In order to answer this question, we must discover what exactly the more composite beings above matter are composed of. Luckily,

---

42   Proclus, *ET* 59, 56.30–36.

43   Lang (2017: 79–80); see specifically Proclus, *ET* 80, 74.31–32 and *ET* 86, 80.5–8; cf. Proclus, *IP* VI, 1119.8–10. The unqualified body discussed here is one of the final levels in the procession from the One, but not the ultimate level itself. True matter is so lacking in quality that it cannot even be characterised as a body. For a discussion of the various types of material substrates, see Van Riel (2009); see also Siorvanes (1996: 183–189) and Opsomer (2016: 156–159).

Proclus reveals the nature of the mysterious gifts from the intelligible principles in his other texts, to which we must now turn.

3.2 'A Being First, Then a Living Being': the Proclean Rule in Action

The clarification we seek can be found in the sixth chapter of the third book of the *Platonic Theology*.[44] There Proclus delineates the same principles from *ET* 57–59, this time with examples of principles and products within the procession towards complexity and back again to simplicity. Above body (τὸ σωματικόν) stand, in ascending order, the principles of Soul (ψυχή), Intellect (νοῦς), Life (ζωή), and Being (τὸ ὄν).[45] The latter three principles equate to Plotinus' Intellect, while Soul is the link between the intelligible and the sensible.[46]

As established in *ET* 57, Soul produces the least amount of things in the sensible world due to its low status relative to the other principles. Proclus reveals that, of all things in the sensible world, 'only the rational living beings participate in Soul.'[47] After all, the gift bestowed by Soul is reason (λόγος), something in which only human beings share. Of course, we rational animals also participate in the gifts given by the superior principles of Intellect, Life, and Being, for these three causes co-produce whatever is produced by Soul.[48] Intellect provides a more universal gift, namely any kind of cognitive ability (γνωστικὴ δύναμις).[49] In this gift, not only humans participate, but irrational animals as well. Life provides a yet more universal gift, which is movement or change (κίνησις).[50] In this gift, even plants participate.[51] Finally, lifeless things, e.g., rocks or elements, participate only in the most universal of these principles,

---

44 Dodds, Chlup, and Onnasch and Schomakers also look to this chapter in order to fill out their overview of the Proclean rule.

45 Proclus, *TP* III.6, 23.11–13.

46 Cf. Proclus, *IT* III, 206.10–207.7 (2.151.30–152.24 Diehl) and 222.18–223.10 (2.163.33–164.19 Diehl). For Proclus' division of Plotinus' Intellect into the triad of Being-Life-Intellect, see *ET* 103. For an overview of this post-Iamblichean triad and its many applications in Proclean metaphysics, see d'Hoine (2016).

47 Proclus, *TP* III.6, 23.16–17: ψυχῆς μὲν γὰρ τὰ λογικὰ μετέχει ζῷα μόνον.

48 Proclus, *TP* III.6, 23.13–14.

49 Proclus, *TP* III.6, 23.27.

50 Proclus, *TP* III.6, 25.5.

51 Proclus, *TP* III.6, 24.9–11. Note, however, that Proclus does ascribe to plants the capacity for 'awareness' (συναίθησις). As Opsomer (2006b: 140) points out, this actually implies that 'es keine Lebensform auf der Welt gibt, die nicht, sei es im Fall der Pflanzen nur sehr schwach, am Geist teilhat.'

namely Being.[52] Its gift is form, which can be deduced from Proclus' statement that *privation* of form is inherent to that which no longer participates in Being.[53] Above Being stands the One, which is not only the first principle of all determinable beings (from rocks to plants to animals to human beings) but also the sole cause of the last level of reality.[54]

The complete theorem of causation as it applies to these principles and products can be pictured either schematically, or through a figure.[55] My own understanding of this manifestation of the Proclean rule is visualised in table 1.

However, Proclus' theory of causation is even more nuanced than the current models imply. In describing the products, Proclus is quite clear: some participate in more intelligible principles, others in less. Yet when Proclus rearticulates the theory from the point of view of the productive principles,

TABLE 1   The results of the Proclean rule as described in Proclus, *TP* III.6

Being	Life	Intellect	Soul	Rational human beings	Irrational animals	Plants	Lifeless objects
BEING/FORM	Formed	Formed	Formed	Formed	Formed	Formed	Formed
	LIFE	Alive	Alive	Alive	Alive	Alive	
		INTELLECT	Intellectual	Intellectual	Intellectual		
			SOUL	Ensouled			
	INTELLIGIBILIA				*SENSIBILIA*		

---

52   Proclus, *TP* III.6, 24.20–24.
53   Proclus, *TP* III.6, 26.10–11.
54   Proclus, *TP* III.6, 26.6–11.
55   For the former, see Dodds (1963: 232), Opsomer (2006b: 138), or Onnasch and Schomakers (2015: 271–262). For the latter, see Chlup (2012: 89 and 98). Chlup not only draws up a double pyramid, but also presents an alternative schema of causation in which each principle is placed next to the product of which it is the highest cause (i.e., 'One next to Matter', 'Intellect next to Soulless things', and 'Soul next to Ensouled Beings'; Chlup (2012: 89)). Such a schema further emphasises the parallel between the One and the lowest level of reality, which Chlup designates as matter, for which cf. Van Riel (2009) and Opsomer (2016). However, it somewhat undersells the distance between the One and 'matter'. One may look at this scheme and deduce that the One produces the lowest level of reality before all other things. Yet Proclus clearly states that matter is caused directly by the One not because it is prior to other sensible things, but because its absolute inferiority makes it unreachable for the productive power of any other intelligible principle (Proclus, *ET* 59, 56.34–36). Logically speaking, the lowest level of reality is the *last* thing the One produces (Proclus, *ET* 25, especially 30.5–6).

the picture becomes a bit more complex. In his description of the productive power of Soul, he states:

ψυχὴ μὲν ἀπάντων μετέχει τῶν πρὸ αὐτῆς, τὸν μὲν λόγον κατὰ τὴν ἑαυτῆς ἰδιότητα λαχοῦσα, τὸν δὲ νοῦν καὶ τὴν ζωὴν καὶ τὸ ὂν ἀπὸ τῶν πρεσβυτέρων αἰτίων·
διὸ δὴ καὶ τὰ μετ᾽ αὐτὴν ὑφίστησι τετραχῶς, κατὰ μὲν τὸ ὂν τὸ ἑαυτῆς τὰ πάντα
καὶ μέχρι σωμάτων, κατὰ δὲ τὴν ζωὴν πάντα τὰ λεγόμενα ζῆν καὶ μέχρι τῶν
φυτῶν, κατὰ δὲ τὸν νοῦν πάντα τὰ γνωστικὴν ἔχοντα δύναμιν καὶ μέχρι τῶν
ἀλογωτάτων, κατὰ δὲ τὸν λόγον τὰ πρώτιστα τῶν μετέχειν αὐτῆς δυναμένων.

PROCLUS, *TP* III.6, 25.12–21

Soul participates in all of the principles before it, obtaining reason in virtue of its own unique character, but deriving its mind, life, and being from the higher causes. Because of this, it bestows existence upon the things after it in a fourfold way. In virtue of its being, it produces all things even up to bodies; in virtue of its life, all things said to be alive even up to plants; in virtue of its mind, all things which possess a cognitive ability even up to irrational animals; in virtue of its reason, it produces the first of the things capable of participating in it.

Paradoxically, this implies that a rock is in some way co-produced by Soul, even though it cannot logically participate in Soul. Chlup picks up on this, remarking that 'all bodies receive their being from soul (whether an individual or the cosmic one).'[56] Given that a rock is part of the cosmos, it is still bound to the World Soul. Yet how can a rock be produced by Soul without receiving a share in the distinctive character transmitted by Soul, i.e., discursive reason? Inversely, how can Soul reach the level of lifeless bodies if it is an inferior, and therefore weaker, principle than Intellect, Life, and Being?

As Proclus reveals in the passage above, the answer to these questions lies in differentiating the gift provided by Soul itself from the gifts it receives from superior principles. Soul derives its intellect, life, and being from the eponymous principles, and it in turn passes these gifts down to corporeal things, acting as a sort of metaphysical transmitter.[57] In contrast, Soul owes its possessing reason to its own *distinctive character* (κατὰ τὴν ἑαυτῆς ἰδιότητα). This distinctive character is not strong enough for Soul to bestow it upon all sensible beings. It only reaches a limited number of things in the material realm. Although Proclus does not state as much in *ET* 57–59, later propositions—specifically *ET* 97 (and

---

56 Chlup (2012: 97); cf. Proclus, *TP* III.6, 21.20–21.

57 Chlup (2012: 99).

QUANTITY VERSUS COMPLEXITY   67

ET 99)—confirm that the gift each principle bestows upon its products from itself is (a diminished version of) its own distinctive character.[58]

With this information, we can attempt to answer the issue that was raised above. As a productive principle, Soul has two modes of production. The first mode consists of the transmission of Soul's own distinctive character to sensible beings. It seems that this mode of production depends on the strength of Soul's own productive power as described in *ET* 57–59.[59] Hence, the distinctive character of Soul only reaches down as far as rational beings. The second mode of production consists of the transmission of the distinctive characteristics of a higher principle. In transmitting these superior characteristics, Soul relies not upon its own power but upon the power of the productive principle in which it partakes. Hence, it reaches irrational animals only because it is given being (οὐσιωμένη), life (ἐζωωμένη), and intellection (νενοωμένη) by the combined powers of Being, Life, and Intellect which come into it from above.[60] It produces plants as a participant of being (οὐσιωμένη) and of life (ἐζωωμένη), and its productive power even reaches lifeless bodies, but only insofar as it is a participant of being (οὐσιωμένη).

It is important to note that this twofold process of transmitting both a thing's own distinctive character and the characteristics of superior principles is not unique to Soul. It is the same for Intellect, Life, and Being. Intellect can only project its own unique character downwards as far as the irrational animals, but it nevertheless contributes to the transmission of Life up to plants and of Being up to lifeless things.[61] Likewise, Life transmits its unique character downwards up to plants but still assists in transmitting the gift of Being to lifeless objects.[62]

We can now infer in what way exactly some products of multiple intelligible principles can be 'more composite' than others. Each product is composed of more or fewer distinctive characters (ἰδιότητες), depending on the generative powers of its respective principles. As Proclus states in *ET* 60, the highest

---

58   Proclus, *ET* 97, 86.8–9: πᾶν τὸ καθ' ἑκάστην σειρὰν ἀρχικὸν αἴτιον τῇ σειρᾷ πάσῃ τῆς ἑαυτοῦ μεταδίδωσιν ἰδιότητος·.

59   Proclus, *IT* III, 394.7–10 (2.291.28–32 Diehl).

60   Proclus, *IT* III, 392.21–25 (2.290.26–30 Diehl). This would also explain why animals can have an irrational soul, despite Proclus' insistence that 'in general it is clear in many places that Plato suggests that Soul is the *rational* soul, and that the other [types of soul] are only images of souls' (*TP* III.6, 23.21–25: ὅλως πολλαχοῦ δῆλός ἐστι καὶ ὁ Πλάτων ψυχὴν τὴν λογικὴν εἶναι τιθέμενος, τὰς δὲ ἄλλας εἴδωλα ψυχῶν). See Opsomer (2006b) for a more detailed analysis of Proclus' views on the irrational soul.

61   Proclus, *TP* III.6, 25.21–26.

62   Proclus, *TP* III.6, 25.26–26.2.

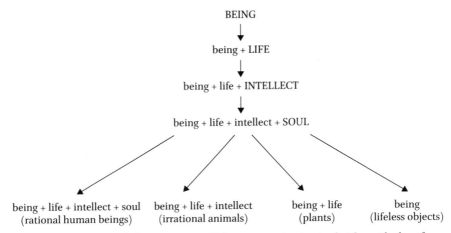

FIGURE 1   Soul not only bestows its own ἰδιότης upon rational animals (alongside the gifts of its superior brethren), but also instantiates irrational living beings, plants, and lifeless objects through the powers of the superior principles in which Soul itself partakes

principles constitute the whole, and further principles add parts to the product. Take a human being, for example. He or she derives his or her form as a whole from Being, which Proclus designates as the principle of all wholes here.[63] Life, Intellect, and Soul subsequently bestow a number of unique characteristics upon the human being, which are his or her life-powers, cognitive abilities, and capacity for reason, respectively. Of course, these 'parts' of the human being are not material elements like the στοιχεῖα of Aristotelian compounds.[64] Instead, they are more akin to conceptual parts.

Proclus establishes in the *Elements of Theology* that the gifts of successive causes stack on top of one another, whereby the gift of the primary cause serves as a substrate for the gift of the secondary cause. The example of the human being helps us to understand exactly what this stacking of gifts entails. In the *Elements of Theology*, Proclus himself presents the human being as an example.

δεῖ γὰρ (εἰ τύχοι) γενέσθαι πρῶτον ὄν, εἶτα ζῷον, εἶτα ἄνθρωπον. καὶ ἄνθρωπος οὐκέτι ἔστιν ἀπολιπούσης τῆς λογικῆς δυνάμεως, ζῷον δέ ἐστιν ἐμπνέον καὶ

---

[63]   Proclus, *TP* III.6, 26.1–6. More specifically, the second intelligible triad, Eternity, which is situated in the level of intellect that corresponds to Being, i.e., the intelligible intellect, is the αὐτοολότης or principle of all wholes; cf. Proclus, *ET* 52, 69, and 103, Opsomer (2000b), d'Hoine (2016), and Oosthout, A. (2023a). See also chapter 5, section 2.1.

[64]   See Aristotle, *Met.* Z.17, 1041b11–33, as discussed in chapter 2, section 5.

αἰσθανόμενον· καὶ τοῦ ζῆν πάλιν ἀπολιπόντος μένει τὸ ὄν (καὶ γὰρ ὅταν μὴ ζῇ τὸ εἶναι πάρεστι).

> PROCLUS, *ET* 70, 66.18–22

Thus, for example, a thing must become a being first, then a living being, and then a human being. And again, when the logical faculty has failed it is no longer human, but it is still a living being, since it breathes and feels. And when life in turn has abandoned it being remains to it (for even when it no longer lives it still has being).

> Tr. DODDS 1963 (modified)

As the human being is born and grows up, it receives the various gifts from the intelligible principles in order. One turns from a formed but lifeless thing into a living being, then develops cognitive abilities, and finally begins to think rationally. At the end of one's life, this process is reversed. This example aligns neatly with the human being as we have sketched above. With the addition of Intellect to the procession, the makeup of human beings in conceptual terms is as follows. Their forms are created by Being and serve as the substrate for their life-powers, granted to them by Life. These life-powers serve as the substrate for cognitive activity (perception, imagination, and the like) bestowed upon them by Intellect. Finally, their cognitive abilities serve as the substrate for their capacity to reason, which they derive from Soul.

We can also take our first steps in dealing with the tension between Proclus' mirrored increase of complexity and the more generally Neoplatonic increase of multiplicity. Although matter is quantitatively infinite, it does not contain multiple *distinct* characters. A human being, on the other hand, is conceptually more complex due to its heap of distinctive characters, despite the fact that he or she is more limited in a purely quantitative sense.

My model of this instance of the Proclean rule differs from the standard reading as proposed by Dodds and reinforced by Chlup and Onnasch and Schomakers.[65] Dodds added two terms to the procession from Being to lifeless bodies: the One at the top and matter at the bottom. Such a schema is attractive, because it seems to offer a complete overview of Proclean causality from the first principle all the way to the last product. Yet there are two reasons not to follow their lead. First, Proclus reveals very little about the exact nature of the gift of the One in this passage (although both Dodds and Onnasch and Schomakers come to the evident conclusion that it is unity). He only tells us

---

65   Dodds (1963: 232) and Onnasch and Schomakers (2015: 272).

70   CHAPTER 3

that, unlike the other principles mentioned here, the One transmits its distinctive character to *all* things. More importantly, however, there is at least one other instance of Proclus' rule that does not fit easily in this supposedly complete model. Proclus also filters the process of demiurgy through the lens of mirrored causes and products, and the principles and created beings enumerated in that discussion are different from those mentioned here. The process of demiurgy also provides further insight in our current inquiry into the mereological consequences of Proclean causality. Therefore, we must now turn to Proclus' *Commentary on Plato's Parmenides*.

3.3   Stacking Material Substrates: the Proclean Rule and Demiurgy

In Plato's *Timaeus*, the titular character explains how the creator-god or Demiurge structured the cosmos as a perpetually becoming (γιγνόμενον) and ever-moving image of an intelligible paradigm.[66] This paradigm is a perfectly complete living being, which contains the Forms of all living beings within itself.[67] After bestowing upon the universe both a spherical body and a universal soul, and after creating the four elements and structuring the heavenly spheres within the cosmic body, the Demiurge turns to the new gods (one of the species he has created in the image of the Forms within the paradigm) and implores them to fill in the parts of the cosmic structure, such as the shapes of individual human beings and animals.[68]

By Proclus' time, the elements of the Platonic creation story naturally had been integrated into the Neoplatonic framework of metaphysical principles. More specifically, the various divine beings from the *Timaeus*, e.g., the Demiurge, the paradigm, the young gods, and others, have taken up position in the procession from superior causal principles to inferior ones. Both the Paradigm and the Demiurge are counted among the intelligible principles, each having been granted its own rank.[69] Proclus divides the Plotinian Intellect into three hypostases, viz. the intelligible (νοητόν = Being), the intelligible-intellective (νοητὸν καὶ νοερόν = Life), and the intellective (νοερόν = Intellect).[70] The

---

66   Plato, *Tim.* 28a–c.

67   Plato, *Tim.* 30c7–d1.

68   Plato, *Tim.* 41c ff.

69   As we head into Proclus' discussion of these concepts I switch to the capitalised term (Paradigm), since Proclus distinguishes between the universal Paradigm and more specific transcendent paradigms (for the latter, see, e.g., Proclus, *IP* IV, 912.30–914.9). He also distinguishes the one Demiurge from the younger gods as demiurges.

70   For the distinction between Being, Life, and Intellect, see section 2 above.

Paradigm of the cosmos, which Proclus calls the 'Living Being itself' (αὐτοζῷον), is one of the intelligible gods.[71] The Demiurge, whom Proclus identifies as Zeus, is a cause of a lower rank, being an intellective god.[72] The young gods who complete the cosmos at the Demiurge's behest are causative principles of an even lower calibre, belonging to the realm of becoming and generation (γιγνόμενα) rather than the realm of eternal principles (ὄντα) like the Demiurge and the Paradigm.[73]

As we have seen, Proclus states that the higher cause produces more things in the sensible world than its inferior co-producers. Thus, the Paradigm or Living Being itself produces more than the Demiurge does, who in turn produces more than the young gods do. As before, the product of all of these causes will be more composite (συνθετώτερον) than the product of fewer of them. But what exactly are the gifts each cause bestows upon its product in this case? And where exactly does the causal reach of each divine principle end? In the fourth book of his *Commentary on Plato's Parmenides*, Proclus explains what the ultimate product of each cause is.

First, Proclus distinguishes four paternal and generative divinities who together produce the material cosmos in all its forms: the Father who produces the substrate of dermiurgy, the Father and Maker who casts his reflections upon this substrate, the Maker and Father who imposes an overall structure upon the partially informed substrate, and the Maker who fills the structured whole

---

71   See Proclus, *IT* II, 310.14–313.3 (1.418.30–420.19 Diehl), *TP* III.14 and III.18, *et al.*; cf. Opsomer (2000a: 131 and 2000b).

72   Proclus, *TP* V.3, 16.5–7; cf. *TP* V.1 and V.12, and Opsomer (2000a: 131).

73   Proclus, *IT* V, 195.14–20 (3.311.9–16 Diehl). In actuality, the process of demiurgic creation is even more complex than it is made to appear here. As Proclus explains, 'of the entire demiurgic structuring [of the cosmos], one aspect is the demiurgic cause of the wholes in a universal manner, another of the parts in a universal manner, a third of the wholes in a particular manner, and the fourth of the parts in a particular manner' (*IT* II, 153.14–17 (1.310.15–18 Diehl): τῆς γὰρ δημιουργικῆς ἁπάσης διακοσμήσεως τὸ μέν ἐστι τῶν ὅλων ὁλικῶς δημιουργικὸν αἴτιον, τὸ δὲ τῶν μερῶν ὁλικῶς, τὸ δὲ τῶν ὅλων μερικῶς, τὸ δὲ τῶν μερῶν μερικῶς). Zeus, the primal Demiurge, creates the universal whole or unitary cosmos (τῶν ὅλων ὁλικῶς) and subsequently cooperates with his brothers Poseidon and Hades in creating the universal and everlasting parts of the cosmos, such as the four elements and the heavenly spheres (τῶν μερῶν ὁλικῶς). The young gods create individual wholes such as human beings (τῶν ὅλων μερικῶς) and subsequently produce the parts of the aforementioned individual beings (τῶν μερῶν μερικῶς), such as limbs. See, for example, *IT* III, 85.16–86.7 and *IT* V, 105.2–11; cf. *TP* V.12 and *TP* VI.9. Opsomer (2000a: 131–132 and 2003: 48–49) has devised a detailed schema which elucidates the entire process of demiurgy in all its aspects. A number of the passages cited here are discussed in more detail in chapter 6, section 2.

72   CHAPTER 3

with particular inhabitants.[74] Although the identities of these four gods are not specified here, from the fifth book of Proclus' *Platonic Theology*, we learn that the Father equates to the very first intelligible principle, also known as the One Being,[75] the Father and Maker equates to the Paradigm of the universe or Living Being itself,[76] the Maker and Father equates to the Demiurge of the cosmos,[77] and the Maker equates to the young gods.[78] Returning to the *Parmenides*-commentary, we find a detailed explanation of the gifts these four divine producers bestow upon the sensible cosmos.

> καὶ διὰ ταύτας τὰς τέτταρας αἰτίας, ἄλλη μὲν ἡ πρὸ πάσης εἰδοποιΐας ὕλη, 'πανδεχές' τι οὖσα καὶ 'ἄμορφον εἶδος' κατὰ τὸν Τίμαιον (*Tim.* 51a7), ἄλλο δὲ τὸ 'δεξάμενον τὰ ἴχνη' (*Tim.* 53b2–3) τῶν εἰδῶν καὶ 'πλημμελὲς καὶ ἄτακτον' (*Tim.* 30a4–5), ἄλλος δὲ ὁ ὅλος κόσμος καὶ ἐξ ὅλων ὑποστὰς πρὸς τὸ 'παντελὲς παράδειγμα' καὶ 'μονογενές' (*Tim.* 31b3), ἄλλος δὲ ὁ ἐκ 'πάντων συμπεπληρωμένος' τῶν ἐν αὐτῷ ζώων, 'καὶ πάντα ⟨ἀθάνατά⟩ τε' καὶ 'θνητὰ λαβών' (*Tim.* 92c5–6), διαφόρων ὑποστησάντων ταῦτα πρὸ τοῦ κόσμου παντὸς αἰτίων.
>
> PROCLUS, *IP* IV, 844.18–26

From these four causes appears first the matter which is prior to all form-giving activity, described in the *Timaeus* (51a7) as something that is 'all-receiving' and 'form without shape'; second, something that 'has received traces' (*Tim.* 53b2–3) of the Forms but is 'disordered and inharmonious' (*Tim.* 30a4–5); third, the cosmos as a whole, composed of wholes in accordance with the 'wholly perfect and unique Paradigm' (*Tim.* 31b3); and last the cosmos 'filled completely with all' the living beings within it and 'which grasped all immortal creatures as well as all mortal creatures' (*Tim.* 92c5–6), whereby different causes establish these creatures prior to the entire cosmos.

> Tr. MORROW and DILLON 1987 (modified)

As Van Riel has already shown, Proclus applies his rule of causality also to the process of demiurgy when he states that 'things which appear to be more imperfect here [i.e., in the sensible world] are products of the prior potencies

---

74   Proclus, *IP* IV, 844.11–18.
75   Proclus, *TP* V.16, 55.3–7. For a more extensive analysis of this chapter of the *Platonic Theology*, see Van Riel (2009: 248–49).
76   Proclus, *TP* V.16, 55.14–19.
77   Proclus, *TP* V.16, 57.15–16.
78   Proclus, *TP* V.16, 53.8–10.

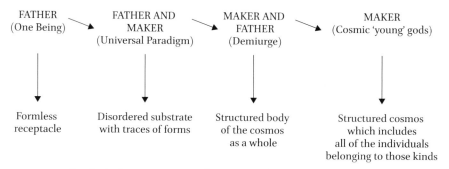

FIGURE 2   Proclus' rule as it pertains to the creation of the cosmos

among the things there [i.e., in the intelligible world], potencies which because of their indescribable effluence are capable of reaching up to the last things [in our world].'[79] Like the various kinds of beings in the third book of the *Platonic Theology*, the various causes and products mentioned in our current passage can be arranged schematically as in fig. 2. This schema is in part based on the one in Van Riel's article, which emphasises a number of other points regarding each cause's mode of production.[80]

The aforementioned passage from the *Commentary on Plato's Parmenides* reveals what each product receives from its cause(s). The lowest product in this schema, the abstract material substrate of creation, is caused only by the Father or One Being. The gift it receives is absolute receptivity (πανδεχές), which allows it to be shaped by the lower gods, and the faintest hint of form or identity (i.e., being an ἄμορφον εἶδος). The immediately superior product is a disordered and discordant mass, informed by both the One Being and the Living Being itself. Together these principles give it not only a single almost-form, but actual traces of forms within it. It is this disordered substrate with traces of formed things which the Demiurge subsequently fashions into

---

79   Proclus, *IP* IV, 845.3–6: τὰ γὰρ ἐνταῦθα δοκοῦντα εἶναι ἀτελέστερα τῶν ἀρχικωτέρων ἐστὶ δυνάμεων ἐν ἐκείνοις ἀποτελέσματα, διὰ τὴν ἐκείνων ἀπερίγραφον περιουσίαν ἄχρι καὶ τῶν τελευταίων προϊέναι δυναμένων. Van Riel (2009: 250).

80   Van Riel (2009: 251); cf. Opsomer (2016). Note, however, that my version of the schema falls short in one aspect. Although it neatly emphasises how each product mirrors its lowest intelligible cause, it may lead the reader to believe that demiurgy is a temporal process, and that the formless receptacle is produced earlier than the structured cosmic body is. This is not the case, for demiurgy is not a temporal process, as Opsomer (2016: 143–44) has noted. Instead, the formless receptacle is the lowest level of the cosmic body in this schema, and as such only the irradiations of the One Being can reach it. This distance between the first principle and the ultimate substrate is more pronounced in Van Riel's (*ibidem*) version of the schema.

74 CHAPTER 3

a structured body, i.e., the cosmos as a corporeal whole. Indeed, the product immediately superior to the disordered mass is the actual sensible cosmos. On top of the first hint and traces of form, which the cosmic body received from the One Being and the Living Being, the Demiurge now adds the structure of the cosmos as a whole.[81] There is a yet more complex product, namely the cosmos which encompasses all of the individual beings within it; not just the universal and everlasting components, but even mortal beings such as individual persons or animals.[82] As Van Riel states, the young gods bestow 'divided being' upon the cosmos on top of the undivided structure of the whole granted by the Demiurge, the traces of forms granted by the Paradigm, and the initial receptivity to form granted by the One Being.[83] At this stage, the cosmos is more complex than at any other stage of its creation, since now it is informed by various causes (διαφόρων ὑποστησάντων ταῦτα).

Once again, the tension between Proclus' mirrored complexity and the Neoplatonic procession towards multiplicity rears its head. The entirety of 'divided being', which is the complete collection of all of the various individual corporeal beings, is compressed into a single rank within the procession. Fittingly, their seemingly singular mirrored cause, the Maker, is itself a collection of young gods. At the levels above and below the Maker and its products, the same dichotomy occurs. For example, the entire cosmic structure as bestowed upon the disordered mass by the Demiurge is merely *one* conceptual part (since it is *one* new distinctive character), yet this one conceptual

---

81   In Van Riel's schema, the construction of the μέρη ὁλικῶς or universal parts is allocated to the domain of the young gods; Van Riel (2009: 251); cf. Proclus, *IT* II, 349.10–13 (1.446.5–8 Diehl) and Opsomer (2003: 39–40). However, it is not entirely certain that this placement is correct. The structure of the entire cosmos as bestowed upon it by the Demiurge would logically already include the universal parts of the cosmos, i.e., the four elements, the heavenly spheres, and so on. In our current passage, Proclus characterises the whole cosmos as a 'whole of wholes' (ἄλλος δὲ ὁ ὅλος κόσμος καὶ ἐξ ὅλων ὑποστὰς πρὸς τὸ παντελὲς παράδειγμα καὶ μονογενές) even before the intervention of the young gods. Proclus also implies elsewhere that the young gods are not the ones to create the universal parts. Rather, the creation of the universal parts constitutes the second step of universal demiurgy, wherein Zeus cooperates with his brothers, Poseidon and Hades. The creation of τῶν μερῶν ὁλικῶς should perhaps be placed under the Maker and Father; cf. Proclus, *IT* V, 105.2–11 (discussed in chapter 6, section 2.4).

82   The main difference between the particular (μερικῶς) and universal (ὁλικῶς) components of the cosmos lies in the fact that only the latter are required at all time for the cosmos itself to exist (see Proclus, *IP* VI, 1112.27–1113.10). Each heavenly sphere, for example, is an essential component (συμπληρωτικόν τινος), the loss of which would fundamentally alter or diminish the cosmos. In contrast, the cosmos does not become imperfect (ἀτελές) upon the death of a mortal being; cf. Oosthout, A. (2023a: 130).

83   Van Riel (2009: 252); cf. Opsomer (2003: 19).

part involves multiplicity in a quantitative sense, for at least four universal elements and a number of heavenly spheres are included in the package.

Although Proclus does not discuss this discrepancy between complexity and quantity, we can infer that the difference between various products is similar to the difference between the kinds of beings from the *Platonic Theology*. Just as a human being is more complex yet less divisible than lifeless bodies, so is the material cosmos more complex once it includes divided being, but more unlimited in divisibility when it is merely a shapeless receptacle. Yet whereas our earlier passage revealed why complexity decreases during the procession towards matter (namely because of the continual loss of distinctive characteristics), our current passage illuminates why the divisibility of the products increases during the procession. In our current passage, the material cosmos with individual creatures within it stands at the highest level of sensible being, the cosmic matter as a shapeless receptacle at the lowest. Both constitute the same thing, namely the entire material substrate of the cosmos. The difference between the two is the degree to which they have been restricted by formal influences from the intelligible realm. On to the shapeless receptacle, increasing gradations of complexity are imposed, starting with simple form-traces and ending with a cosmos wherein even individual heaps of matter are formed.

Indeed, Proclus links form and matter quite explicitly to quantitative limitedness and quantitative limitlessness, respectively.[84] In the sixth book of his *Commentary on Plato's Parmenides*, Proclus discusses how limitedness (πέρας) and limitlessness (ἄπειρον) come into play at every level of reality.[85] Since Socrates suggests in the *Philebus* 'that although those things which are always said to exist are composed of one and many, they innately possess within themselves limit and limitlessness', Proclus concludes that '*everything* that truly is, consists of limit and limitlessness.'[86] As a consequence, both concepts are allotted the highest honours in Proclus' metaphysics, taking up position right beneath the One as the very first henads. Because of this, their images are broadcast through all reality, which means that every level of reality is in some

---

84 Cf. Opsomer (2016: 157).

85 Specifically, Proclus, *IP* VI, 1119.5–1123.14; Siorvanes (1996: 177). The duality of πέρας and ἄπειρον was originally employed by Plato in his *Philebus* to discern ideal proportions, e.g., of health, heat, and, most importantly, the balance between a life of knowledge and a life of pleasure, for which see Moravcsik (1979) and chapter 2, section 4.3. For a more detailed discussion of the role πέρας and ἄπειρον play in shaping the Proclean universe, and of their relation to the other henads, see Van Riel (2000, 2001, and 2016).

86 Plato, *Phil.* 16c9–10: ὡς ἐξ ἑνὸς μὲν καὶ πολλῶν ὄντων τῶν ἀεὶ λεγομένων εἶναι, πέρας δὲ καὶ ἀπειρίαν ἐν αὑτοῖς σύμφυτον ἐχόντων, and Proclus, *ET* 89, 82.1: πᾶν τὸ ὄντως ὂν ἐκ πέρατός ἐστι καὶ ἀπείρου.

way both limited and limitless. In the case of transcendent principles, limit usually manifests itself in a being's unity while limitlessness manifests itself in its generative power. In the case of material existence, on the other hand, Proclus notes that the body of the cosmos *qua* body is shapeless and infinitely divisible, as we have seen before.[87] This unqualified body is subsequently qualified by the 'material form (ἔνυλον εἶδος), which holds fast the matter and sets a limit on its indefiniteness and shapelessness'.[88] The material form is functionally identical to the Aristotelian form, in the sense that it denotes the essence of a species, e.g. the human being, but does not transcend matter. However, in Proclus' eyes these material forms are not independent principles, but instead irradiations from the transcendent Platonic Forms.[89] When these images of the Platonic Forms shape the shapeless matter, they set boundaries on its divisibility. Compare the shapeless receptacle, which is infinitely divisible, to the cosmos with individual beings within it. Quantitatively speaking, the cosmos is less divisible in the latter stage because it can only be divided into so many formed individuals. In contrast, the shapeless receptacle lacks the many distinct characters of the structured cosmos, but in return it gains infinite quantity through unlimited division.[90] It seems that, just as the decrease in complexity during the procession through material products is caused by the loss of distinctive characteristics bestowed upon sensible beings by their intelligible forebearers, so is the increase in quantity and divisibility during the procession caused by this same continual loss of form.

---

87   See section 1 above.

88   Proclus, *IP* VI, 1123.11–13: δέκατον αὐτὸ τὸ ἔνυλον εἶδος, ὃ κατέχει τὴν ὕλην καὶ περιορίζει τὸ ἀόριστον αὐτῆς καὶ ἄμορφον ...

89   For this reason, the adjective 'ἔνυλον' is also often translated as 'enmattered' in modern scholarship. I employ the adjective 'material' in the same sense here. Proclus distances himself from the Aristotelian approach, warning his reader of the fact that 'since some only have eyes for these [material forms], they reduce limit and limitlessness to matter and form' (*IP* VI, 1123.13–14: ... εἰς ὃ καὶ ἀπιδόντες τινὲς μόνον εἰς ὕλην καὶ εἶδος ἀνάγουσι τό τε πέρας καὶ τὸ ἄπειρον). For another brief discussion of the role limit and limitlessness play in the relation between forms and matter, see Opsomer (2016: 159).

90   In Aristotelian terms, the structured cosmos would be called ἀνοιομερής ('composed of distinct parts'), while the shapeless receptacle would be ὁμοιομερές ('composed of like parts'). For this distinction between types of division in Aristotle, see his *His. an.* I, 486a5–14 and *De part. an.* II, 646a11–647b28; cf. Oosthout, A. (2022b: 7).

3.4 The Compatibility of the *TP*- and *IP*-Passages

Before we conclude this chapter of our inquiry, we must reflect briefly on the model of Proclean causality sketched by Dodds, Chlup, and Onnasch and Schomakers. These scholars fill their schema with the principles and products discussed by Proclus in his *Platonic Theology* (Being, Life, Intellect, and so on) and complete it by adding the One and matter at the extreme ends.[91] Although Proclus would undoubtedly claim that his rule informs the entire Neoplatonic universe in a uniform manner, one cannot build a complete schematic overview of Proclean causality as this standard reading seems to imply. The amount of causes and products in the Proclean universe is so great that, at a micro-level, such a schema will never fully add up.

Take, for example, the two instances of the Proclean rule discussed here. If one wanted to combine the various kinds of corporeal species from the *Platonic Theology* with phases undergone by the cosmic substrate in the *Commentary on the Parmenides*, one would encounter a number of problems. For example, the standard reading names matter as the next product after lifeless bodies, which only participate in Being (and in the One). However, we now know that cosmic matter takes multiple shapes, from a structured and formed whole to a shapeless receptacle. At what level must the kinds of corporeal beings from the *Platonic Theology* be placed? Should we see products such as 'irrational animal' and 'plant' as denoting individual creatures, i.e., at the level of divided being, or as the material forms (ἔνυλα εἴδη) or kinds, i.e., at the level of the cosmic whole with its universal parts?[92]

Similar problems arise for the intelligible principles. How exactly should we combine the Fathers and Makers into the procession from Being to Soul as given in the standard reading of Proclean causality? As Proclus explains in the *Elements of Theology*, the triad of Being-Life-Intellect recurs at each subdivision of the intelligible realm.[93] It can be seen in the distinction of the three main levels of the intelligible realm, viz. the intelligible (Being), intelligible-intellective

---

91 Dodds (1963: 232); Chlup (2012: 97–99); Onnasch and Schomakers (2015: 272).

92 The latter seems more likely; see also d'Hoine (2010: 235–36 and 243). In his study of Proclean answers to the criticism of the theory of Forms in Plato's *Parmenides*, d'Hoine remarks on the distinction made by Syrianus and Proclus between the κοινῶς ποιόν of a being, which corresponds to its material form, e.g., the human being as a material species, and the ἰδίως ποιόν of a being, which denotes its form as a specific individual, e.g., Socrates' specific shape; cf. Longo (2005: 386–87), and see also chapter 4, section 4, and chapter 6, section 3.

93 See Proclus, *ET* 103.

(Life), and intellective (Intellect). Yet within the intelligible level, the same division occurs: the One Being or Father (Being), Eternity (Life), and the Living Being or Father and Maker (Intellect). This subdivision is also present within the intellective level, where the Demiurge takes up the role of Intellect, for example.[94] Hence, the term 'Intellect' from the standard reading may just as well apply to the universal Paradigm as to the Demiurge. These issues provide just a few examples of the fact that drafting an all-inclusive schema of Proclean causality will always lead to some kind of difficulty.

All of this indicates that no all-inclusive schema could perfectly mirror the divisions and subdivisions of the sensible beings to those of the intelligible realm. The intelligible realm is more unified and less multitudinous than the sensible realm, owing to its greater proximity to the One.[95] This Neoplatonic tenet makes it so that any mirror-schema can only incorporate a select number of sensible causes (as many as the relevant intelligible principles). For example, the schema devised by Van Riel (as well as my own) is limited to the bodily substrates which mirror the Fathers and Makers, just as Opsomer's schema (and, again, my own) is limited to the individual species which mirror the intelligible principles mentioned in that particular passage.[96] I believe this to be the more prudent approach to charting Proclus' rule than the one employed in the standard reading. A single rhombic schema can never elucidate the full extent of Proclean causality, simply because there will always be a greater number of distinct sensible products than there are distinct intelligible causes. It would also go beyond the boundaries of what Neoplatonic philosophers consider to be epistemologically feasible. After all, how would a mere schema suffice to incorporate the ultimate One which transcends all reality and hence all cognition?[97]

3.5   The Double Meaning of Συνθετώτερον

The rule of Proclus manifests itself in various ways in various aspects of Neoplatonic metaphysics. Yet in every case, it remains true that the distinctive

---

94 See, e.g., Proclus, *IT* II, 311.10–16 (1.419.16–23 Diehl).

95 See Proclus, *ET* 62.

96 Van Riel (2009: 251); Opsomer (2006b: 138).

97 Opsomer (2003: 6 n. 2) has speculated that the Neoplatonic philosophers would not be particularly fond of the schemata modern scholars like to devise. Likewise, the schemata on display in this text, as well-suited as they might be for elucidating parts or aspects of the Neoplatonic universe, cannot hope to cover the full scope of Proclean causality in a unitary manner.

QUANTITY VERSUS COMPLEXITY

characteristics (ἰδιότητες) bestowed upon a product by higher causes serve as substrates for the characteristics bestowed upon the product by lower causes. No distinctive characteristic of a human being can exist unless the more universal ones do. One cannot think rationally without any cognitive abilities nor have cognitive abilities if one is not alive. The same notion of one unique character forming the basis for further characteristics holds true for the Fathers and Makers and their products. The 'all-receiving' receptacle produced by the One Being serves as the substrate for the traces of the forms bestowed upon matter by the intelligible Paradigm, the disordered mass with traces of forms serves as the substrate for the universal structure designed by the Demiurge, and so on.

As we have seen, Proclus designates the products with a greater number of received characteristics as more *composite* (συνθετώτερον), which in this case equates to them being more *complex*. Proclus characterised the various causes as more universal (ὁλικώτερον) and more particular (μερικώτερον), respectively. The products themselves were defined in terms of parts and wholes.[98] In general, it is easy to see how a product of multiple causes is composite. It contains multiple distinct characteristics—in the case of a human being, for example, not only a whole form, but also life-powers, cognition, and a capacity for reason.

At the same time, the distinction between part and whole is blurred by the fact that none of the conceptual parts are equivalent to one another. For example, one cannot say that form and reason are distinct enough within the composite human being as to be independent parts, for reason presupposes cognition, which presupposes life, which presupposes form. In other words, one cannot characterise reason and form as parts of the human being in the manner of $x > z$ & $y > z$.[99] Instead, this division of the human being into distinctive characters comes far closer to the modern mereological axiom of *transitivity*, which establishes that $(x > y$ & $y > z) \rightarrow x > z$. This also makes it difficult to discern in any instance exactly which principles create wholes and which principles create parts. In the case of the kinds of corporeal beings, the dividing line seemingly lies between Being, whose gift is form, and the other principles. Yet in the case of demiurgy, such a line is harder to draw. After all, even the individuated creatures that arise in the final phase of the process are wholes in some way. In other words, wholeness appears to be relative, at least to a certain extent.

Additionally, the examples discussed by Proclus in the *TP*-passage show that each additional gift from the intelligible principles functions more as a

98   Specifically in Proclus, *ET* 60 (cited in section 1 above).
99   Where, for example, $x = reason; y = form; z = the\ human\ being$.

particularisation of the product than as a distinct new part. The kinds of corporeal beings are continuously specified, for example, starting from the most universal gift, namely form, to the maximally specific gift of reason that only human beings participate in. In other words, Proclus does not seem to distinguish between division and particularisation here. This makes sense, given that the Greek terms for 'more universal' (ὁλικώτερον) and 'whole' (ὅλον) share their root, just as the terms for 'more particular' (μερικώτερον) and 'part' (μέρος) share theirs. As such, every gift in the procession (e.g., cognition) is both more particular than its predecessor (e.g., life-powers) and more universal than its successor (e.g., reason), which implies that every gift can also be characterised as a part in relation to its predecessor and as a whole in relation to it successor.

This does not mean that Proclus abolishes all compositions or collections of the kind of $x > z \,\&\, y > z$, i.e., an aggregate of distinct proper parts. Within the realm of the intelligible principles, complexity runs parallel to quantity. Just as the higher intelligible principles are simpler than their inferior brethren, so are they less multitudinous.[100] The problems arise when we discuss the corporeal realm. There too products differ from one another in both complexity and in quantity. In the *IP*-passage we discussed, the structured cosmic body not only gains a new distinctive character, but this new character also involves a composition out of multiple wholes (ὁ ὅλος κόσμος καὶ ἐξ ὅλων ὑποστάς). Furthermore, the gift of the young gods comprises the creation of individual mortal beings, at which point the quantity of cosmic parts skyrockets. However, divisibility into distinct proper parts no longer runs parallel to the particularisation of the product through additional gifts from the intelligible causes. In fact, both run counter to one another. The more particularised or complex a product is, the less multitudinous. After all, the human being owes its high status compared to a lifeless heap of bodily material not only to the fact that he or she inherited more formal characteristics from the intelligible principles, but also to the fact that an unqualified heap of body is far more divisible quantitatively than the human being is. After all, the human being stands closer to the One.

The interplay between the formal principles which descend from the intelligible realm and the matter on which they impose order may provide an answer to this issue or, at the very least, an explanation for its occurrence. Proclus links divisibility and endless quantity explicitly to material nature, which explains why quantity and divisibility increase as the procession continues through the sensible creatures. Furthermore, the passage which dealt with the Fathers and Makers strongly implied that it is the introduction of any kind of form included

---

100   Proclus, *ET* 62, 58.30–32.

QUANTITY VERSUS COMPLEXITY

in the gifting of distinctive characteristics by the intelligible principles which limits this divisibility. The greater the measure in which a body is delimited by distinctive characters, the more restricted is its divisibility. Furthermore, our passage from the *Platonic Theology* made it clear that form is the gift from Being which serves as a substrate for further distinctive characteristics.

Although the interrelation between form and matter explains the opposition between complexity and multiplicity on the level of corporeal beings, there remains the fundamental difference between the intelligible realm, where complexity and multiplicity are linked, and the sensible realm, where complexity and multiplicity are opposed. This difference is underscored by Proclus in his *Commentary on Plato's Timaeus*. When he comments on the union between soul and body,[101] Proclus notes:

> αὕτη δὲ ἡ ἀρχὴ θεία πάντως ἐστίν, ἡ δὲ ἀπὸ τῶν ἀτελῶν ὁρμωμένη δῆλον ὡς ἔνυλός ἐστι· καὶ γὰρ ἐν θεοῖς μὲν τὰ τελειότερα πρὸ τῶν ἀτελεστέρων ἐστίν, ἐν δὲ τοῖς ἐνύλοις ἔμπαλιν· ἀπὸ γὰρ τῶν ἀτελῶν ἡ γένεσις ἄρχεται καὶ πρόεισιν ἐπὶ τὸ τέλειον.

> PROCLUS, *IT* III, 389.5–9 (2.287.24–28 Diehl)

> The starting point [of the soul's life][102] itself is entirely divine, whereas the soul that starts from imperfect things is clearly in matter. Indeed, among the gods the more perfect beings precede the less perfect, yet among material things the opposite is true. After all, becoming starts from imperfect things and proceeds to that which is perfect.[103]

> Tr. BALTZLY 2009 (modified)

As a result, the term 'συνθετώτερον' gains two distinct connotations. To be more composite is to be less perfect for the gods, but for corporeal beings it means greater perfection. In other words, the term 'συνθετώτερον' can be understood as 'more pluralised' in matters concerning the realm of being, yet in matters concerning the realm of becoming its meaning is closer to 'more well-defined'.[104]

In conclusion, it would seem that Proclus' metaphysics incorporates at least *two* kinds of composition. One concerns the number of distinctive characters that make up a being. These characteristics are bestowed upon it by different

---

101   I.e., Plato, *Tim.* 36e2–5.
102   Proclus refers to Timaeus' statement in this lemma (see the previous note) that the soul has a θείαν ἀρχὴν ἀπαύστου καὶ ἔμφρονος βίου πρὸς τὸν σύμπαντα χρόνον.
103   Cf. Proclus, *ET* 45, 46.15–17.
104   I thank Gerd Van Riel for suggesting to me this idea of a double meaning.

intelligible principles, but just as those principles stand together in a single procession from the One, so do the distinctive characters stack on top of each other in a single procession of substrates and superstrates. This is composition in terms of *complexity*, and in the case of corporeal beings, it is expressed by their material form. These sensible beings mirror the intelligible beings. In this regard, the beings at the extreme ends of the spectrum are simpler, whereas beings closer to the centre are more complex. In Aristotelian terms, these compositions always consist of heterogenous parts (ἀνομοιομερῆ).[105]

The second kind of composition concerns the divisibility of beings in terms of *quantity*. In this case, the sensible beings do not mirror the intelligible principles, for they continue the procession from unity to multiplicity as it was in the intelligible realm, progressing from heterogenous compounds to homogenous ones (ὁμοιομερῆ).[106] This latter type of divisibility is explicitly linked to material nature, as illustrated by the fact that the ultimate quantity is found in the infinitely divisible essence of the unqualified body. Proclus' concept of perfection is bound to this second type of divisibility, as we have seen. The complexity of a being has no direct bearing on its perfection, since the more complex human being outshines the simpler stone whereas a simpler god transcends a more complex one. Instead, a being's level of perfection is linked to its rank in the order of *quantitative* divisibility. Clearly, Proclus' mereology lacks neither quantity nor complexity.

---

105   Cf. the footnotes to section 3 above. These conceptual parts are comparable to what Harte (2002a: 70) calls 'property-parts' in her discussion of the dilemma of participation from Plato, *Parm.* 131a–c, e.g., the *F*-ness which is a property of object *a*.

106   These quantitative parts are comparable to what Harte (*ibidem*) calls 'instance-parts', e.g., the *F*-ness of object *a* as a manifestation of the Platonic Form *F*. Note that this comparison is applicable mainly in the case of the intelligible principles, where one can distinguish, e.g., the Intellect's complexity in terms of property-parts (unity, being, life, and intellect) from its quantitative divisibility in terms of instance-parts (the multiplicity of participated intellects). The material substrate of the cosmos, on the other hand, is not an *F*-ness *stricto sensu* and thus cannot be said to possess Harte's instance-parts.

CHAPTER 4

A Wholesome Trinity

Most ancient philosophers believed that the whole is more than just the sum of its parts.[1] Proclus stands out, however, since he is known for distinguishing not one, but *three* wholes from each collection of parts. In his *Elements of Theology*, Proclus argues that 'every wholeness exists either before the parts, or is composed of the parts, or exists in the part.'[2] Proclus outlines these three types of whole as follows:

1. The whole before the parts (ὅλον πρὸ τῶν μερῶν) is the whole 'which pre-exists in its cause.'[3]

2. The whole composed of the parts (ὅλον ἐκ τῶν μερῶν) is the whole 'in all of the parts at once.'[4]

3. The whole in the part (ὅλον ἐν τῷ μέρει) is the whole 'in each of the parts.'[5]

---

1 See, for example, the mereological views of Plato and Aristotle, as discussed by Harte and Koslicki (for which see chapter 2, sections 4 and 5). The text of this chapter was previously published as an article titled 'A Wholesome Trinity. Proclus on the transcendence of whole over part' in *Ancient Philosophy*, volume 42, issue 2 (2022), pp. 515–536 (https://doi.org/10.5840/ancientphil202242235). The arguments I presented there are so essential to this study that it was necessary to include them in this monograph as well. I am grateful to the journal's publisher, the *Philosophy Documentation Center*, for granting me permission to reincorporate the text into this book. The additions made to this reworked version of the text are: the extended response to Butler's reading in section 4, the references to d'Hoine's (2021) study throughout the chapter, a slightly more detailed discussion of the translation of the technical term 'ὕπαρξις' in section 4.2 (wherein Proclus' use of the *Philebus* is also noted in the running text in this version, instead of in a footnote), and the brief reflection on Siorvanes's (1996) interpretation of Proclean wholes as universals in the final section of the chapter. Additionally, the response to Baltzly in section 4 was part of a footnote in the original article, but has been expanded and moved into the running text here so as to form a separate section alongside the aforementioned response to Butler's analysis. For the sake of consistency within the monograph as a whole, the translations accompanying block citations have been changed from my own to (modified versions of) existing ones where applicable, and a few of the longer block citations from the article have been replaced by paraphrases of the relevant passages. Outside of these additions and some corrected writing errors throughout, the text and figure of this chapter are the same as those of the original publication in *Ancient Philosophy*.

2 Proclus, *ET* 67, 64.1–2: πᾶσα ὁλότης ἢ πρὸ τῶν μερῶν ἐστιν ἢ ἐκ τῶν μερῶν ἢ ἐν τῷ μέρει. For a brief overview of the history of this doctrine in Neoplatonic thought, see Dodds (1963: 236–37).

3 Proclus, *ET* 67, 64.4: ἐν τῷ αἰτίῳ προϋποστάν.

4 Proclus, *ET* 67, 64.5–6: ἐν ἅπασιν ὁμοῦ τοῖς μέρεσι.

5 Proclus, *ET* 67, 64.7: ἐν ἑκάστῳ τῶν μερῶν.

© ARTHUR OOSTHOUT, 2025 | DOI:10.1163/9789004721760_005

In his seminal commentary on the *Elements of Theology*, Dodds has suggested that this threefold wholeness mirrors another triad of Proclus', namely the unparticipated, the participated, and the participant.[6] In other words, Dodds suggests that Proclus distinguishes between a whole that transcends its parts, a whole that is immanent in its parts, and a whole in which each part shares individually. However, Dodds felt that Proclus betrayed 'a certain looseness in his application of these formulae'.[7] Nevertheless, later scholars have taken this parallel to heart, for a link between wholeness and participation returns in the writings of Robert Brumbaugh, Lucas Siorvanes, Baltzly, and Chlup.[8] However, most scholars read Proclus' propositions in light of a specific aspect of his thought, resulting in a diverse set of readings which do not readily align with one another.

For example, Brumbaugh and Baltzly link the three wholes to the various instances of a Platonic Form. Baltzly takes the whole before the parts (the first kind) to be the equivalent of a transcendent Form, and sees the whole composed of parts (the second kind) as a participated form which is immanent in this or that thing; Baltzly likens this second kind of form to an Aristotelian genus.[9] In comparing Proclus' mereology to Georg Cantor's set theory, Brumbaugh takes a similar approach. He compares the Form to the criterion which determines the unity of a Cantorian set and the Form's participated derivation to the extensional set itself.[10] Since their readings align at their core, both Brumbaugh and Baltzly run into the same problem: their approach only accounts for two of the three kinds of whole. What are we to make of the third kind, the whole in the part? Brumbaugh candidly admits that this third kind of whole does not match anything in Cantorian set theory.[11] Baltzly also admits that he can

---

6   Dodds (1963: 237). The distinction between the unparticipated (ἀμέθεκτον) and the participated (μετεχόμενον) is employed by Proclus in order to combat the criticisms raised against the theory of Forms in Plato's *Parmenides*. More specifically, distinguishing between the unparticipated Form as transcendent principle and the participated form as immanent in its participant allows Proclus to best the famous 'third man'-argument (see Plato, *Parm*. 132a1–b2 and Proclus, *IP* IV, 890.1–14; cf. *ET* 23). See Gerson (2011) for a more detailed overview of Proclus' answer to the 'third man'.

7   Dodds (1963: 237); this sentiment is echoed by Ruth Glasner (1992: 197–198).

8   See Brumbaugh (1982), Siorvanes (1998a), Baltzly (2008), and Chlup (2012). Recently, however, d'Hoine (2021) has critically reassessed the relation between these two concepts. For a brief summary of the most prominent issue resulting from this parallel, as pointed out by d'Hoine, see the footnotes to section 5 below.

9   Baltzly (2008: 404).

10   Brumbaugh (1982: 112). Interestingly, Baltzly (2008: 404) feels that 'this rush to assimilate the whole-of-parts to a class is too hasty.'

11   Brumbaugh (*ibidem*).

only offer an 'admittedly speculative answer'.[12] If the first two kinds of wholes designate the transcendent Form and the immanent characteristic in its participants, then the third kind of whole could be an 'atomic form' (ἄτομον εἶδος) which is only present in one individual, e.g., the specific characteristics of a kangaroo named 'Skippy'.[13]

Chlup, on the other hand, suggests that the three wholes are linked to relations of participation between different hypostases. He refers to proposition 108 of the *Elements of Theology*, where Proclus discusses how the particular members of any hypostasis are linked to the originating principle of that hypostasis. In short, Proclus claims that the particular members of a given hypostasis can participate in a superior hypostasis either through their own monadic principle, or through a parallel particular member in the superior hypostasis.[14] In other words, a particular soul can participate in the hypostasis of intellect either through the complete unitary hypostasis of soul, which derives from intellect, or through a particular intellect which parallels the particular soul. According to Chlup, the whole before the parts equates to an intelligible principle as participated by its particulars.[15] The whole composed of parts is the collection of particulars which participate in their hypostasis's originating principle, 'being able to participate in all of its aspects at once.'[16] In defining the whole in the part, Chlup states that 'each of [the products] can only relate to the superior plane through one of this plane's own particular members that mirrors the monad in itself.'[17] As such, the whole composed of parts seems to refer to participation through one's monad, while the whole in the part seems to refer to the participation through the parallel particular in the superior hypostasis.

Edward Butler places the three kinds of whole in an entirely different context.[18] Reading Proclus' *Platonic Theology*,[19] Butler finds a link between the three kinds of wholes and Proclus' theory of the henads. According to Butler, the three kinds of wholes constitute products of different classes of henads. The whole before the parts derives from the class of henads which produces unparticipated monads or transcendent universals, the whole composed of parts constitutes the class of henads which coexist with beings in order to form

---

12   Baltzly (2008: 404–405).
13   Baltzly (2008: 405).
14   Proclus, *ET* 108, 96.9–12.
15   Chlup (2012: 103).
16   Chlup (*ibidem*).
17   Chlup (*ibidem*), my addition between brackets.
18   Butler (2010: 142–143).
19   Specifically *TP* III.27, 94.26–95.4.

immanent universals, and the whole in the part equates to any being which participates in 'ontic principles as a result of divine activity'.[20] Butler is correct in concluding that, for Proclus, mereology transcends the Platonic Forms,[21] and the passage from the *Platonic Theology* to which he refers explicitly confirms that the three kinds of wholes are related to the henads in some way. However, Butler's reading of Proclean mereology is grounded in his own vision of Proclean henadology, which stands in stark contrast to other scholarly readings of the henads.[22] In order to adopt Butler's reading, one must accept, for example, that beings participate in classes of henads instead of individual gods, a notion which Proclus both confirms and rejects, even within the same treatise.[23] I am also not entirely convinced by Butler's rejection of the notion of the One as a singular first principle and his subsequent suggestion that *each* henad is the One.[24]

Baltzly comes to the same conclusion as Dodds did, suggesting that 'we might wonder about the extent to which all of Proclus' deployments of the distinction between the three notions of whole are coherent and unified.'[25] Given the disparity of the available readings of Proclus' mereology, one might be inclined to agree with this assessment. However, Proclus' various deployments of the three wholes *can* be seen as coherent. My primary issue with the readings presented here is that they are restricted by the fact that the three kinds of wholes end up tied to a specific aspect of Neoplatonic thought. By this I do not mean to say that Baltzly's or Chlup's reading or any other is wrong on its own, but rather that such readings only reveal how the three wholes function within a specific part of Proclus' metaphysics. One reading shows us a link between the three wholes and Platonic Forms, while the other shows us a link between the three wholes and participatory relations, and a third reveals a connection between wholes and henads. None of these readings reveal the function of the three wholes in their own right. Proclus does not distinguish three kinds of

---

20   Butler (2010: 143).

21   Butler (*ibidem*); cf. Proclus, *ET* 74, 70.15–16.

22   The most notable alternative is found in Van Riel (2001 and 2016). Recently, Jonathan Greig (2020) has attempted to mediate between the various opposing interpretations of Proclean henadology and offered his own view on Proclus' elusive divine unities.

23   Compare, for example, Proclus, *ET* 135 and 162–165. The former proposition establishes that each henad can only be participated by one genus of beings, whereas the latter propositions posit that each genus of being is preceded by a class of henads. See Dodds (1963: 282–283) for a discussion of this discrepancy in Proclus' metaphysics.

24   Butler (2008a: 98–99). For an analysis of the problematic elements of this specific suggestion of Butler's, see Greig (2020: 41–42). Chlup (2012: 118–119) reappraises Butler's position by ironing out some of its more contentious aspects.

25   Baltzly (2008: 406 n. 21).

A WHOLESOME TRINITY

wholeness solely in order to reinforce other theorems, but rather to establish a mereological basis which informs each and every whole in the Neoplatonic universe. We shall see how Proclus uses the three kinds of wholes to devise a blueprint for his mereology, in which the whole is an independent existence above and beyond its parts without becoming wholly disconnected from them.

4.1   The Basics of the Threefold Wholeness

As stated above, Proclus establishes the three kinds of wholes in his *Elements of Theology*, specifically in propositions 67 through 69. We shall not comb through every line of these passages, for they have been studied extensively in the past.[26] Instead, our focus lies on the main arguments of the propositions, so that we may re-establish the basics of Proclus' three wholes. Proclus introduces the three kinds of wholes by emphasising that, when we consider the form of 'each thing' (τὸ ἑκάστου εἶδος), we think either of the thing's cause or the thing's parts, which participate in the aforementioned cause. The manifestation of a thing's form in its cause is called the whole before the parts. Furthermore, the form of a thing might be seen in its parts in one of two ways, namely in the total collection of all of the parts, or in an individual part. In the first case, we speak of the whole composed of parts, whereas we refer to the whole in the part in the second case.[27] In summary, Proclus separates the principle of the whole from its parts, and in doing so conforms to the general attitude towards parts and wholes among the ancients.[28] He subsequently looks at the parts themselves and distinguishes two other kinds of wholeness within them: the whole composed of parts in the complete aggregate, and the whole in the part within individual parts.

Having delineated the three kinds of wholes, Proclus reveals in what way each of them can be called 'whole'.

> καθ' ὕπαρξιν μὲν οὖν ὅλον τὸ ἐκ τῶν μερῶν· κατ' αἰτίαν δὲ τὸ πρὸ τῶν μερῶν· κατὰ μέθεξιν δὲ τὸ ἐν τῷ μέρει.
>
> PROCLUS, *ET* 67, 64.9–11

---

26   For example, see Lang (2017: 73–74) for a complete outline of the arguments presented by Proclus in his *ET* 67–69.

27   Proclus, *ET* 67, 64.3–9.

28   Compare this, for example, to Aristotle's argument that the principle of a composite thing is 'something other' than its material constituents, as discussed at the start of chapter 2, section 5.

Thus, the whole composed of parts is whole according to ὕπαρξις,[29] the whole before the parts is whole according to a cause, and the whole in the part is whole according to participation.

Tr. DODDS 1963 (modified)

Given their central roles in Proclus' metaphysics, the terms 1) 'according to a cause', 2) 'according to ὕπαρξις', and 3) 'according to participation' require some explanation. Proclus introduces these concepts in the 65th proposition of the *Elements of Theology*, where he states that 'all that subsists in any manner exists either 1) according to a cause, [i.e.,] as an originating principle, or 2) according to ὕπαρξις, or 3) according to participation, [i.e.,] as an image [of something].'[30] The outer terms, 'according to a cause' and 'according to participation', denote the relation between a cause and its product. The cause produces the product, and the product participates in its cause.[31] This idea is rooted in two notions which, for Proclus, are essential aspects of causality. First, 'all that produces something else is superior to what it creates.'[32] Second, 'every productive principle establishes things that are like it rather than things that are unlike it.'[33] Thus, if a principle A creates a product B, then A must be superior to B and B must resemble A. For Proclus, this means that the producer already in some way contains the characteristics of its product within itself 'as pre-existent seminal potentialities'.[34] This notion of product B pre-existing in cause A is referred to by the term 'according to a cause'. The product B, in turn, exists as an image (εἰκονικῶς) of A. The characteristics of A are present in B 'as persistent echoes or reflexions'.[35] This image of cause A in product B is referred to by the term 'according to participation'.

---

29 As is explained below, the term 'καθ' ὕπαρξιν' is not easily converted into English. In order to avoid weakening the meaning of the term, I leave ὕπαρξις untranslated for now.

30 Proclus, *ET* 65, 62.13–14: πᾶν τὸ ὁπωσοῦν ὑφεστὸς ἢ κατ' αἰτίαν ἔστιν ἀρχοειδῶς ἢ καθ' ὕπαρξιν ἢ κατὰ μέθεξιν εἰκονικῶς.

31 For a more in-depth discussion of causation and the relation between cause and product, see Proclus, *ET* 7, 18, 26, 31, *et al.*

32 Proclus, *ET* 7, 8.1–2: πᾶν τὸ παρακτικὸν ἄλλου κρεῖττόν ἐστι τῆς τοῦ παραγομένου φύσεως.

33 Proclus, *ET* 28, 32.10–11: πᾶν τὸ παράγον τὰ ὅμοια πρὸς ἑαυτὸ πρὸ τῶν ἀνομοίων ὑφίστησιν. According to the originally accepted reading of this sentence, e.g., Dodds (1963: 33), 'πρό' is to be translated as 'before', implying that any cause produces similar products first and dissimilar products thereafter. However, Opsomer (2015) has convincingly argued that the preposition should be read as 'rather than'.

34 Dodds (1963: 235).

35 Dodds (*ibidem*).

The middle term, 'ὕπαρξις,' is more difficult to translate.[36] It refers to a being which exists in such a manner that it reveals its own distinctive character, as Carlos Steel has shown. 'En fait, l'ὕπαρξις ne désigne pas l'être ou l'essence en général, mais toujours le mode *propre* qui détermine chaque être dans son caractère distinctif. Le terme est d'ailleurs souvent accompagné de l'adjectif οἰκεῖος ou ἴδιος.'[37] In other words, 'on their own level of reality',[38] all things manifest their distinctive character. In this sense, they exist 'according to ὕπαρξις'.

What does this mean for the three kinds of whole? The whole composed of parts (#2) is the whole as ὕπαρξις or whole as distinctive character. In other words, it is an *actual* composition of parts. Yet its wholeness also in some way pre-exists in its cause and in some way persists in its individual parts. The whole before the parts (#1) is the cause which produces the whole, and in this cause the resulting composition is already seminally present. In contrast, the individual part is whole only in a secondary manner, namely according to participation. This concurs with a central Neoplatonic creed, which states that 'all things are in all things, but in a mode proper to the essence of each.'[39] Thus, the same wholeness manifests itself not just in the actual collection of parts, but also in the cause of the whole and in the individual parts. In each instance, this wholeness takes a different shape.

Proclus subsequently fills in the details of the three wholes, discussing them in ascending order. Thus, he starts with the whole according to participation, the whole in the part. This lowest whole is said by some to be the most difficult part (pun intended) of Proclus' mereology.[40] Indeed, Proclus' definition of the whole in the part appears to be exceptionally vague.

---

36 As a philosophical term, 'ὕπαρξις' has a rich history; Glucker (1994). Even within Proclus' writings it is allotted different meanings in different instances, for an overview of which see Steel (1994). *Pace* Dodds, who clearly grasped the meanings of κατ' αἰτίαν and κατὰ μέθεξιν. In contrast, he read too much of Aristotle into Proclus when he (1963: 63) translated καθ' ὕπαρξιν as 'as a substantial predicate'. Also *pace* Onnasch and Schomakers (2015: 115), who translate 'as selbständiges Dasein'. Unfortunately, this translation misses the fact that, as Steel (1994: 84) notes, 'l'ὕπαρξις ne désigne pas l'être ou l'essence en général'.

37 Steel (*ibidem*).

38 Proclus, *ET* 65, 62.19–20: κατὰ τὴν ἑαυτοῦ τάξιν.

39 Porphyry, *Sent.* 10, 4.7: πάντα μὲν ἐν πᾶσιν, ἀλλὰ οἰκείως τῇ ἑκάστου οὐσίᾳ; cf. Plotinus, *Enn.* v.8 [31], 4.6–8. Proclus cites Porphyry's proclamation almost verbatim in *ET* 103, 92.13. In a more general sense, the idea that all things are present in all things can be traced all the way back to Anaxagoras in the fifth century BC; see specifically *Fr.* B6 DK.

40 See, e.g., Baltzly (2008: 404–405).

90 CHAPTER 4

καὶ γὰρ τοῦτο κατ' ἐσχάτην ὕφεσιν ὅλον, ᾗ μιμεῖται τὸ ἐκ τῶν μερῶν ὅλον, ὅταν μὴ τὸ τυχὸν ᾖ μέρος, ἀλλὰ τῷ ὅλῳ δυνάμενον ἀφομοιοῦσθαι οὗ καὶ τὰ μέρη ὅλα ἐστίν.

PROCLUS, ET 67, 64.11–14

For this [whole in the part] is still the whole, though in its extreme declension, in so far as it imitates the whole composed of parts when it is not just any part, but one that can assimilate itself to a whole whose parts are also wholes.

Tr. DODDS 1963 (modified)

We already know that a whole in the part is an individual part of something, but Proclus does not reveal which kind of part it could be. Hence, various interpretations have been raised, ranging from the more general (Brumbaugh's members of Cantorian sets) to the more specific (Chlup's particulars participating in the monads of superior orders or Baltzly's individual beings). However, Proclus' description of the whole in the part is not so much vague as intentionally generalised. As we shall see, there are different kinds of wholes in parts, but the one thing that is true for all of them is that they share a likeness to the compounds to which they belong. This feature distinguishes them from things which are just parts and nothing else. Exactly how the whole in the part imitates its compound varies, depending on which whole it belongs to.[41] What is important to take away from our current description of the whole in the part is the fact that parts which are also whole form an image of their compound and thus share in its wholeness. In other words, 'chaque partie est non pas une totalité en elle-même, mais contient le *logos* du tout dont elle est une partie.'[42] Indeed, Proclus is quick to emphasise that 'every whole in the part is a part of the whole composed of parts' in some way, for otherwise they would have no wholeness to participate in.[43]

What about the whole composed of parts itself? Given that this is the type of whole which manifests the distinctive character of being a compound, one might expect it to get the bulk of Proclus' attention. Surprisingly, Proclus only really discusses how this whole relates to its parts and to its cause. In fact, of the three propositions devoted to this topic, Proclus spends the first on the general theorem, the second on the whole in the part, and the third on the whole before the parts. What little Proclus does reveal about the compound

---

41 As discussed in further detail in section 3 below.
42 Saffrey and Westerink (1978: 145).
43 Proclus, *ET* 68, 64.15: πᾶν τὸ ἐν τῷ μέρει ὅλον μέρος ἐστὶ τοῦ ἐκ τῶν μερῶν ὅλου.

itself is the fact that no part can contribute to a whole until it is actually unified with other parts within a compound, regardless of whether it is an image of its whole or simply a part.[44]

Conversely, the compound derives its own wholeness from the causal power of the whole before the parts. Per Neoplatonic doctrine, all of the many compounds in the cosmos must derive their wholeness from a singular transcendent source: Wholeness itself. Hence, if there exist a whole as a compound and a whole as a part, there must certainly be a transcendent causal whole as well.

> τὸ ἄρα τοῦ ὅλοις εἶναι τοῖς ὅλοις ἅπασιν αἴτιον πρὸ τῶν μερῶν ἐστιν. εἰ γὰρ καὶ τοῦτο ἐκ τῶν μερῶν, τὶ ὅλον ἔσται καὶ οὐχ ἁπλῶς ὅλον, καὶ πάλιν τοῦτο ἐξ ἄλλου, καὶ ἢ εἰς ἄπειρον ἢ ἔσται τὸ πρώτως ὅλον, οὐκ ἐκ μερῶν ὅλον, ἀλλ' ὅ ἐστιν ὁλότης ὄν.
>
> PROCLUS, *ET* 69, 66.6–10

> Accordingly that which makes all wholes to be wholes is prior to the parts. For if this too be composed of parts, it will be *a* whole, and not *simply* whole; thus it in turn will be derived from another, and either there will be infinite regress or there will exist a term which is primitively whole, being not a whole composed of parts but wholeness as such.
>
> Tr. DODDS 1963 (modified)

The whole before the parts, then, is simply whole (ἁπλῶς ὅλον) and free from the multiplicity inherent in the actual compounds to which it gives rise.[45] Furthermore, it is not one of many wholes, but a unique principle. In summary, the three kinds of wholes of propositions 67–69 are arranged as in fig. 3.

The effect this theorem has on the relation between wholes and parts is interesting. Proclus has taken the idea that a whole is distinct from its parts to heart. Proclean wholes are not just something beyond their aggregated parts, they transcend them entirely. According to Proclus, the whole exists transcendently on its own before the parts even come into play. At the same time, Proclus takes great care to ensure that whole and part remain closely intertwined. For example, the parts themselves are only unified when the transcendent whole turns into a participated whole by descending into them, bringing them together. That the whole composed of parts functions as the link between the transcendent whole and the multitude of parts is obvious from the fact that Proclus mostly discusses this kind of whole in relation to the

---

44 Proclus, *ET* 69, 64.26–28.

45 Cf. Proclus, *TP* IV.19, 56.16–19.

#1: The **whole before the parts**:
- Whole κατ' αἰτίαν (cause)
- Transcends the parts as one-over-many, and is simply whole (ἁπλῶς ὅλον)

#2: The **whole composed of parts**:
- Whole καθ' ὕπαρξιν (distinctive character)
- Brings the many parts together in one composition, thereby manifesting the character of wholeness which pre-existed in its cause

#3: The **whole in the part**:
- Whole κατὰ μέθεξιν (imitation)
- Imitates the wholeness of the compound of which it is a part
- (NB: not all parts can participate in wholeness)

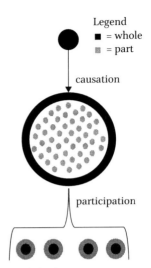

FIGURE 3   The three kinds of wholes as described in the *Elements of Theology*

ones above and below it. In this second kind of whole, one and many meet. Yet Proclus does not stop there. The relationship between whole and part is so strong that the character of wholeness can descend even into those parts capable of imitating their compound in some way.

Now, the main question scholars have struggled with is what we must make of these three kinds of wholes. What constitutes an example of a whole in the part? Are these three wholes linked to Platonic Forms, to relations between different orders of reality, or to something else? In order to fully understand Proclus' mereology, we must do two things. First, we must turn to the *Platonic Theology*, in which the various levels of Neoplatonic reality are discussed in great detail, in order to understand where these three kinds of wholes come from according to Proclus. Second, in order to gain a clearer understanding of each kind of whole, we must study actual examples of each within the Neoplatonic universe.

4.2   Whole above Part: the Roots of Proclean Mereology

In analysing Proclean mereology, most scholars focus on propositions 67–69 from the *Elements of Theology*. However, the *Platonic Theology*, specifically its third book, is equally useful for understanding Proclus' stance on parts and wholes.[46] In the third book, Proclus enumerates and describes in great detail

---

46   Cf. Butler (2010: 142–143), as discussed at the start of this chapter.

the higher hypostases of the intelligible realm.[47] His discussion of the concept of wholeness during this outline is essential for our current study, because it reveals the (Neo)Platonic theorems on which Proclean mereology rests.

For example, the *Platonic Theology* is the work in which Proclus reveals his supposed Platonic sources for the tripartite nature of the whole. In the twenty-fifth chapter of the third book, Proclus names two specific dialogues which inspired his triad of wholeness. From the *Statesman*, Proclus distils the notion of a whole which transcends its parts, since Plato there calls the species a part of the genus, even though the genus is logically prior to its species rather than coordinate with them. From the *Timaeus*, Proclus distils the idea of composite wholes nested within a larger composite whole, since the individual inhabitants of the cosmos are each whole in their own right despite being mere parts on a universal scale.[48]

Here Proclus draws from two different strands of Plato's philosophy, although he himself did not see it that way. For in the Neoplatonic curriculum, the *Statesman*, along with the *Sophist*, was actually regarded as a dialogue about physics.[49] Plato's discussion of species as parts of genera fits neatly into his general cosmology, at least according to Proclus. However, Proclus introduces this division of wholeness intro three types already in the third book of his *Platonic Theology*, at a point where his focus still lies on the utterly transcendent *intelligibilia*. As such, the origin of the tripartite wholeness cannot be ascribed to Plato's (supposed) physiological writings alone.

Some context is needed in order to understand the general line of the argument in which the three kinds of wholes appear here. Proclus' outline of the intelligible hypostases is based on his exegeses of the *Philebus* and the second part of Plato's *Parmenides*, where the titular character presents a number of hypotheses concerning the one. According to the general Neoplatonic reading of the *Parmenides*, the first hypothesis, which supposes that the one is unitary (εἰ ἕν ἐστιν), describes the divine One which transcends even being.[50] The second hypothesis, which supposes that the one *is* (ἓν εἰ ἔστιν), is taken to refer to the intelligible realm.[51]

---

47 Specifically those triads belonging to the νοητά, which occupy the highest ranks within the divine Intellect.

48 Proclus, *TP* III.25, 87.26–88.6. The specific Platonic passages from which these ideas are derived are Plato, *Pol.* 262a8–263b10 and *Tim.* 33a7, respectively. The latter passage was discussed in chapter 1.

49 Chiaradonna and Lecerf (2019); cf. Proclus, *TP* I.5, 25.14–18.

50 For the hypothesis itself, see Plato, *Parm.* 137c4–142a8.

51 For the hypothesis itself, see Plato, *Parm.* 142b1–155e3. For a general overview of the Neoplatonic readings of the second hypothesis of the *Parmenides*, see Beierwaltes (1985: 193ff.). For a more detailed analysis of Proclus' interpretation of this hypothesis from the

Proclus makes this reading yet more complex, for he not only believes that every single characteristic Parmenides ascribes to the one-that-is in the second hypothesis (e.g., that the one is whole, that it is a multitude, that it is both like and unlike, etcetera) demarcates a *separate* level in the procession of being, but he also reinterprets the *Parmenides* through the lens of the triadic structure of limit, limitlessness, and their mixture as described in the *Philebus*.[52] Each 'new' one being constitutes a trinity of principality (ὕπαρξις), power, and being, whereby the principality denotes the triad's supra-essential unity, i.e., its henad or ἕν-aspect. In this context, the adjective 'principal' and its derivation 'principality' are more suitable terms to describe the supra-essential unity of the One and the henads than the more commonly used translation of 'ὕπαρξις' as 'existence'. In English, the latter term is intrinsically linked to the concepts of being and reality (the link to the concept of reality is especially difficult, since as a descendant from the Latin 'realitas', itself derived from 'res', the English term denotes the thing-ness of something). The term 'principality', on the other hand, signifies the One's causal role without making any reference to the verb 'to be' or to a specific character, which would muddle the concept of the supra-essential and indeterminable first principle of the Neoplatonic philosophers.[53] In contrast to the supra-essential one, being equates to the triad's ὄν-aspect (obviously), while the power serves as a middle term connecting these two extremes.[54] Of these triads, the three most divine ones are based on Parmenides' assertions that (1) the one is, that (2) the one-that-is is a whole, and that (3) the one-that-is is a multitude.

Plato's Parmenides posits the first assertion and subsequently argues for the second and third in two steps. First, if the one is, it is supposed that the resulting one being has two distinct characteristics, viz. unity and being, making it a whole with two parts. Secondly, Parmenides suggests that each part requires the other, or in other words, that the one-part must have being and that the

---

    Parmenides, see Steel (2000) and Van Riel (2001: 419–22); cf. Dodds (1928) and Jackson (1967) for an overview of this doctrine in Plotinus, but contrast Gerson (2016).

52   For the Phileban mixture, see chapter 2, section 4.3; for its role in Proclean mereology, see chapter 3, section 3.

53   In this sense, each henad imitates the true One, which transcends being yet still possesses the ὕπαρξις of being the first principle; see, e.g., Proclus, *TP* II.3, 25.19–22.

54   See, e.g., Proclus, *TP* III.25, 86.20–24. These three aspects of the triad, unity, power, and being, mirror the limit, unlimited, and their mixture from Plato's *Philebus* (see Plato, *Phil.* 23c1–27c2, Proclus *TP* III.24, 84.9–14, and Van Riel (2000)). For an overview of the entire procession of hypostases and the divine henads participated by them, see Van Riel (2001 and 2016). For Butler's understanding of the intelligible and intellective triads, see Butler (2008b, 2010, and 2012).

being-part must be one. Hence, even the one-part can be divided individually into one and being, and the same applies to the being-part. Plato's Parmenides then generalises this statement by suggesting that any part is likewise composed of one and being, which means that there is an infinite number of one beings (one for every part which exists). This creates a potentially infinite multitude of one-parts and being-parts.[55] As stated, Proclus takes each step of this argument to designate a separate level in the procession of the intelligible beings. The former one-that-is, with its two parts (step one), constitutes the second intelligible triad and the principle of wholeness (τὴν ὁλότητα τὴν νοητήν).[56] The latter one-that-is, with its infinite number of parts (step two), constitutes the third triad and principle of multiplicity (τὸ νοητὸν πλῆθος).[57] Proclus also reveals that the second triad is not only the principle of wholeness but also of eternity, and that the third triad equates to the intelligible Paradigm of the cosmos from Plato's *Timaeus*.[58]

Let us focus on the second intelligible triad, since it constitutes the divine principle of all wholes. The most notable aspect of Proclus' characterisation of this principle is his effort to simultaneously distinguish and connect the unity of the whole and the multiplicity of the parts. Proclus accepts, per Parmenides' arguments, that the second intelligible triad and first Whole has the one and being as its parts. As such, the one-aspect and being-aspect of this triad are not completely unified like those of the very first triad are.

> διακρίσεως γὰρ οὔσης καὶ μέρη ἐστὶ καὶ τὸ ἐκ τούτων ὅλον. Καλεῖται τοίνυν ἡ Δευτέρα τριὰς ὁλότης νοητή, μέρη δὲ αὐτῆς τὸ ἓν καὶ τὸ ὄν—ἄκρα λέγω—μέση δὲ ἡ δύναμις οὖσα κἀνταῦθα συνάπτει, καὶ οὐχ ἑνοῖ, καθάπερ ἐν τῇ πρὸ αὐτῆς, τὸ ἓν καὶ τὸ ὄν.
>
> PROCLUS, *TP* III.25, 87.7–11

---

55 Plato, *Parm.* 142c7–143a3. In what follows, I focus exclusively on Proclus' interpretation of these arguments. For a thorough analysis of the mereological implications of these arguments within the context of the *Parmenides* itself and Plato's thought as a whole, see Harte (2002a: 73–100).

56 Proclus, *TP* III.25, 86.18–19.

57 Proclus, *TP* III.25, 89.5. Note that Proclus separates the first whole from the first multiplicity by placing both in different triads. Here we have another sign of Proclus' desire to distinguish the unity of the whole from the multiplicity of the parts.

58 See Proclus, *TP* III.27. Proclus' description of the three intelligible triads is based not only on his exegesis of Plato's *Parmenides*, but also on the *Timaeus*. See Opsomer (2000b) for an analysis of the role the latter work plays in Proclus' study of the intelligible triads. For a detailed analysis of the mereological roles of these triads, see Oosthout, A. (2023a); a more succinct analysis can be found in chapter 5, section 2 of this book.

For whenever there is a separation, there are parts and there is the whole which they compose. Now, the second triad is called the intelligible wholeness, and its parts are the one and being—I mean the outer terms—and the power, which is the middle term, connects the one and being in this triad as well, *but it does not make them one*, as it does in the triad before this one.

Yet immediately after admitting to this division within the second triad, Proclus attempts to tie one and being back together through the triad's power. As a middle term, the power of the second intelligible triad reveals the 'kinship' (κοινωνία) between the triad's one- and being-aspects, a notion which Proclus presumably distils from Parmenides' argument that, even when the one and being are considered separately from one another, the one is still an existent *thing* and the being is still *one* thing. In this respect, the triad's power reunites its two parts.[59] Paradoxically, the power itself does not function as a part of the triad, for Proclus insists that 'the one being is composed of *two* parts, namely the one being and the existent one, as Parmenides himself says.'[60] Here Proclus appears to be somewhat constrained by his wish to remain faithful to his Platonic source. Even though it would stand to reason that a triad has three members, and that the power should thus be a part alongside the one and being, Plato's Parmenides only specifies two parts in his argument, and Proclus acknowledges as much.

Leaving aside the somewhat uncertain mereological status of the triad's power, Proclus emphasises the continued kinship of the triad's two definite parts, despite the fact that these parts are no longer truly unified.[61] Unity and being may have been distinguished from one another, but the power of the triad acts as a bridge and ensures that the extreme terms remain closely connected. This hybrid relation of distinctiveness and kinship between the one and being (with power serving as the connective tissue) further illustrates Proclus' goal in distinguishing three kinds of wholes. This becomes clear when he connects each kind of whole to one aspect of the second intelligible triad. As the principle of all wholes, the second triad creates every other whole before the part, every whole composed of parts, and every whole in the part. It creates the first kind through its unity, the second through its power, and the third through its

---

59   Proclus, *TP* III.25, 87.12–14.

60   Proclus, *TP* III.25 87.14–16: τὸ ἓν ὂν ἐκ μερῶν ἐστι δυοῖν, τοῦ τε ἑνὸς ὄντος καὶ τοῦ ὄντος ἑνός, ὥσπερ αὐτὸς ὁ Παρμενίδης φησίν.

61   Proclus, *TP* III.25, 86.20–24.

A WHOLESOME TRINITY

being.[62] Proclus then explains how each of the three kinds of wholes mirrors the member of the second intelligible triad which creates it.

Τὸ μὲν γὰρ ἓν πρὸ παντός ἐστι πλήθους, ἡ δὲ δύναμις ἐπικοινωνεῖ πως ἀμφοτέροις τοῖς ἄκροις καὶ τὰς ἰδιότητας αὐτῶν ἐν ἑαυτῇ συνείληφε, τὸ δὲ ὂν πῃ μετέχει τοῦ ἑνός. Διόπερ ἐκ μὲν τῆς ἑνιαίας ὑπάρξεως ἡ πρωτίστη τῶν ὁλοτήτων, ἡ πρὸ τῶν μερῶν (μονὰς γάρ ἐστι καὶ αὕτη τῶν μερῶν ὑποστατικὴ καὶ τοῦ ἐν αὐτοῖς πλήθους)· ἐκ δὲ τῆς δυνάμεως ἡ δευτέρα (συμπληροῦται γὰρ ἀπὸ τῶν μερῶν, ὡς ἐν τῇ συναγωγῷ δυνάμει τοῦ ἑνὸς καὶ τοῦ ὄντος ἐκφαίνεταί πως τὰ ἄκρα)· ἐκ δὲ τοῦ ὄντος ἡ τρίτη (μέρος γάρ ἐστι τὸ ὂν καὶ γέννημα ἀμφοῖν, τῆς τε δυνάμεως καὶ τοῦ ἑνός, καὶ ἔχει μερικῶς ἑκάτερον).

> PROCLUS, *TP* III.25, 88.12–23

For the one is prior to every multitude, but the power shares in both extremes in some way and keeps their distinctive characters together within itself, and being participates in the one in some way. Because of this, the first of the kinds of wholeness, the whole before the parts, derives from the unitary principality [of the second triad], for this whole before the part is a monad and the thing which gives existence to the parts and to the multiplicity within them. The second kind of wholeness [i.e., the whole composed of parts] derives from the power, for this whole is filled up by the parts, just as in the unifying power of the one and being the extremes are in some way revealed. The third kind of wholeness [i.e., the whole in the part] derives from the being, for being is part as well as offspring of both the power and the one, and it possesses both in a partial manner.

Through the very abstract workings of this intelligible triad, Proclus reveals how the three kinds of wholes interact with one another, and in doing so, he confirms what we deduced from the *Elements of Theology*. Each of the three kinds of wholeness is the same whole in a different manner of existence,[63] just as principality, power, and being are aspects of one and the same triad. The principal unity of the triad of wholeness is the whole as a cause, for it hypostasises the other two wholes while retaining its unity. The power of the triad

---

62   Proclus, *TP* III.25, 88.7–12. Opsomer (2000b: 363) already noted that Proclus' second intelligible triad is 'the first Whole before the parts', but it turns out that Proclus has gone one step further. The second intelligible triad is *all three* kinds of wholes in one.

63   Cf. Proclus, *ET* 67, 64.9–11 (cited in section 1 above).

is the whole as ὕπαρξις, which is to say that it shows the whole's distinctive character of unifying a multiplicity; just as a composition connects the parts to the unity inherited from the whole before the parts, so does the power connect the one and being. Finally, the being of the triad is the whole by participation, for it is whole only by sharing in the wholeness of the one through the power, just as the parts share in the character of the transcendent whole through their compound.

This means that the three kinds of wholes are exclusively applicable neither to the unparticipated and participated instances of Platonic Forms suggested by Baltzly, nor to the relations of participation between different hypostases suggested by Chlup. For here we have a single hypostasis which transcends the Platonic Forms entirely, yet still contains all *three* kinds of wholeness within itself. Both of those earlier suggestions showcase only specific instances of a much more widely applicable theorem, since they cannot account for the three types of wholeness as they appear in our intelligible triad. Even outside of this specific metaphysical principle, the three kinds of wholes appear in other places than those posited by our scholars. After all, Proclus states that, from the second intelligible triad, 'the three kinds of wholes are distributed across the various orders of beings.'[64]

This means that propositions 67 through 69 of the *Elements of Theology* are not (primarily) meant to elaborate a Proclean doctrine on Platonic Forms or on the workings of hypostases. Instead, Proclus there introduces three universal concepts which find their origin in the higher echelons of reality, i.e., within the second intelligible triad. Subsequently, images of this second triad appear throughout reality in the form of the three different kinds of wholes. Thus, the established readings discussed in the introduction need not be wrong. The various kinds of Platonic Forms mentioned by Baltzly could indeed correspond to the various kinds of wholes. However, the origin of the three kinds of wholes transcends the scope of the previous readings (literally and figuratively).

4.3   Two Examples from Proclus' Cosmology

We have a general idea of the nature of each kind of whole from the *Elements of Theology*, and we are aware of the wide applicability of Proclus' mereology thanks to the *Platonic Theology*. However, it is still unclear which forms the wholes before parts, the wholes composed of parts, and the wholes in parts

---

64   Proclus, *TP* III.25, 88.24–25: Μετὰ μὲν οὖν τὸ νοητὸν αἱ τρεῖς ὁλότητες διήρηνται κατὰ τὰς διαφόρους τῶν ὄντων τάξεις.

A WHOLESOME TRINITY   99

can actually take. As stated, other scholars have already presented a number of examples, and since these studies are valid in their own right, I shall not regurgitate all of them here. Instead, our focus will be placed on just two illuminating examples of the threefold wholeness from Proclus' cosmology. In the passages that are discussed below, Proclus explicitly points to manifestations of the three kinds of wholes both in the material cosmos and in its universal soul. Because of this, these two examples give us a clear picture of the characteristics of each kind of whole.

First, we turn to the World Soul. As described by the titular character of Plato's *Timaeus*, the Demiurge creates the World Soul out of a mixture of metaphysical elements, viz. Being, Sameness, and Otherness.[65] He then divides this mixture into a number of portions, each of which contains all three metaphysical ingredients and stands in mathematical proportion to the other portions.[66] With these portions, the Demiurge fashions two circles which together constitute the World Soul.[67] In his commentary on the *Timaeus*, Proclus argues that the triad of wholeness is represented by this process of creating the World Soul. Specifically, the various steps of the production of the World Soul correspond to each type of whole.[68] Proclus starts with the transcendent whole.

Before the World Soul is composed of portions, it exists as one mixture of Being, Sameness, and Difference. For Proclus, this unitary soul-essence constitutes a whole before the parts, since in this state, the soul is prior to division (πρὸ παντὸς μερισμοῦ). Furthermore, the transcendent nature of the whole before the parts is once again emphasised, as Proclus adamantly tells us that the unitary essence of the soul, i.e., the mixture of Being, Sameness, and Difference as it is before the portions are taken out, remains untouched even after the portions have been removed from the mixture and fashioned into the two circles. In Proclus' words, the soul-mixture is never 'depleted' (οὐ δαπανωμένη) while the Demiurge scoops out all of the portions.[69] At first glance,

---

65   Plato, *Tim.* 35a1–4. Interestingly, the commonly accepted reading of this passage in modern scholarship concurs with Proclus' interpretation of Plato's enumeration of these metaphysical elements of the World Soul—cf. Baltzly (2009: 27–29)—although there were other readings of the passage in antiquity, such as that of Plutarch. See Opsomer (2004: 140–41) for a reappraisal of Plutarch's reading.

66   Plato, *Tim.* 34b10–36b6. For further analysis of the Proclean exegesis of this mathematical aspect of the Soul's creation, see, e.g., Martijn (2010: 192–202).

67   Plato, *Tim.* 36b6–c5.

68   The threefold wholeness of the World Soul is also discussed by Baltzly (2013: 28–29) within the context of his own reading of the three kinds of wholes, for which see the introduction to this chapter.

69   Proclus, *IT* III, 264.4–9 (2.195.28–196.1 Diehl).

this is a paradoxical statement, but it makes sense once one remembers that according to Proclus, demiurgic production is *not* a temporal process.[70] Hence, the steps of the soul's creation are ordered according to logical priority, but not spread out across time.

After the soul's unitary essence comes the whole composed of parts. In the second step of the Demiurge's mixing of the soul-essence, he divides all of the soul-mixture across the aforementioned portions, depleting it (ὅλον τὸ μῖγμα δαπανῶν) and subsequently reconstructing the World Soul 'anew' (ἐκ νέας) out of the portions of the mixture.[71]

As in the *Elements of Theology* and *Platonic Theology*, the whole composed of parts forms the link between the unity of the whole and the multiplicity of the parts. In this reconstructed World Soul, the separated portions of the soul-mixture are harmonised and brought together as one again. This reconstructed soul is a multitude brought together into a unity, whereas the original soul-mixture was *simply* one, just as the whole composed of parts is both one and many, whereas the whole before the parts is just one.

Lastly, Proclus discusses the whole in the part. Here Proclus emphasises the ingredients of the original soul-mixture, Being, Sameness, and Difference. Since the ingredients were totally mixed up in one another to create the desired soul-essence, each portion has at least some of the Being-ingredient, some of Sameness-ingredient, and some of the Difference-ingredient. Thus, each portion of the World Soul is a whole in the part, since its elemental composition is the same as that of the mixture in its entirety.[72]

This is perhaps the most interesting aspect of Proclus' exegesis, as it reveals what Proclus means when he states that the whole in the part imitates its compound. Each of the portions of the soul-mixture is a diminished version of the entire soul, for it is merely a part in a quantitative sense, yet each mimics

---

70   Opsomer (2016: 143–144).

71   Proclus, *IT* III, 264.9–13 (2.196.1–5 Diehl). Note the contradictory use of 'δαπανῶν' in this passage. In the preceding lines, Proclus argued that the Demiurge would never completely use up the soul-mixture which represented the whole before the parts so as not to succumb to the evil of destroying something well-fashioned. Yet here he declares that the Demiurge *does* use up the entire soul-mixture in order to create the whole composed of parts. Proclus would, of course, argue that the creation of the soul is an atemporal process, so that the soul simultaneously remains transcendent and is divided into a composite being. Nevertheless, the fact that he does not at all acknowledge the paradox of stating 'οὐ δαπανωμένην' and 'ὅλον τὸ μῖγμα δαπανῶν' in the same passage is somewhat surprising for a philosopher as meticulously systematic as he.

72   Proclus, *IT* III, 264.13–18 (2.196.5–11 Diehl).

A WHOLESOME TRINITY

the complete soul in the sense that it contains a portion of all three ingredients of the World Soul.

The World Soul also contains each of the three kinds of wholes for another reason. Proclus points out that it animates the sensible cosmos, which is a 'whole of wholes' (ὅλον ἐξ ὅλων) according to Plato.[73] Thus, the World Soul animates both the composite cosmos and the wholes contained within, of which 'each is as a whole in a part' (ὧν ἕκαστόν ἐστιν ὡς ἐν μέρει ὅλον). Additionally, Plato also declares the soul to be 'external' (ἔξωθεν) to the cosmos insofar is it 'envelops' it (ὡς περικαλύπτειν τὸ πᾶν).[74] Insofar as the World Soul fulfils these three functions, it manifests the three kinds of wholeness: it is a whole before the parts as transcendent over the cosmos, a whole composed of parts as animating the composite cosmos, and a whole in the part as animating each of the cosmos's parts.[75]

In summary, the essence of the whole soul, i.e., the mixture of Being, Sameness, and Difference, exists in three ways. Preceding the division of the mixture, the three form a unitary essence (before the parts). The unitary mixture is subsequently divided, and the mixture of ingredients is both fully present in the structured compound of these portions (composed of parts) and partially present in each individual portion (in the part). These three instances of the soul's wholeness also inform its relation to the material cosmos. As a unitary mixture before division, the soul eclipses the material cosmos. As a compound, it animates the entire cosmos, which is itself a compound. Through the wholeness of its parts, it animates those parts of the cosmos which are also wholes.

What about the cosmos itself? Given that Proclus cites Timaeus' characterisation of the cosmos as a 'whole composed of wholes' as one of the main sources of inspiration for his mereology, it is to be assumed that the three kinds of wholes appear within the cosmos as well. They do indeed, but in this instance the function of each kind of whole is a bit more complex. For in his commentary on Plato's *Timaeus*, Proclus distinguishes the whole cosmos from the kinds of wholes and parts within it in a variety of ways.[76] Since my

---

73   Cf. Plato, *Tim.* 33a7.

74   Cf. Plato, *Tim.* 34b3–4.

75   Proclus, *IT* III, 264.18–265.5 (2.196.11–19 Diehl).

76   To give an idea of the sheer number of possible classifications of parts and wholes within the sensible cosmos, Proclus, *IT* III, 2.13–3.13 (2.2.9–3.8 Diehl), III, 85.16–86.7 (2.61.26–62.8 Diehl), IV, 125.12–127.1 (3.97.12–98.11 Diehl), and V, 105.2–11 (3.242.9–19 Diehl) all contain overlapping but (subtly) different categorisations of cosmic parts and wholes. A number of these categorisations by Proclus are discussed by Opsomer (2003 and 2016) and Baltzly (2008 and 2013). For analyses of all of these passages, see chapter 6, section 2.

102   CHAPTER 4

aim in this chapter is to illustrate the function of the three kinds of wholes
through examples rather than give an exhaustive overview of all of their possible instantiations, only one example of the applied threefold wholeness is
discussed here.

One of the essential aspects of the cosmos, according to Platonists, is the
fact that it is the ultimate living being which contains all other living beings,
just as the intelligible Paradigm on which it was based contains all intelligible
living beings. For this reason, it is not only called heaven (οὐρανός) or cosmos
(κόσμος) but often also 'the all' (τὸ πᾶν). 'For,' in Timaeus' words, 'that intelligible living being encompasses within itself all intelligible living beings, just as
this cosmos contains us and all other visible creatures.'[77] In this case, the first
kind of wholeness is to be found not in the cosmos itself but in its intelligible Paradigm.[78] In his commentary on this passage from the *Timaeus*, Proclus
writes that the Paradigm encompasses the living beings not as the full sum of
them nor as their shared predicate, but as their primary principle (ὡς πρωτουρ-
γὸς ἀρχή). 'After all', Proclus notes, 'it is a whole *before the parts*, not a whole
composed of parts' (πρὸ γὰρ τῶν μερῶν ἐστιν ὅλον καὶ οὐκ ἐκ τῶν μερῶν). More
specifically, the Paradigm is a principle which 'encompasses in a unified manner all that the [principles] after it encompass in a divided manner' (ἡνωμένως
περιέχουσα πάντα ὅσα διῃρημένως τὰ μετ' αὐτήν). Its so-called 'parts' (τὰ καλού-
μενα μόρια) are the many genera and species which it transcends.[79]

Unlike the material cosmos, the intelligible Paradigm does not literally contain all intelligible forms of living beings. As we noted in our analysis of the
Platonic Theology, the Paradigm of the cosmos is one of the highest intelligible
principles, taking its place as the third intelligible triad after the One Being and
the first Whole. Just as the former is the principle of all beings and the latter
is the principle of all wholes, so is the Paradigm the principle of all multiplicities. Thus, it does not literally contain all intelligible Forms within itself as
its parts, but rather transcends them as their cause. After all, the Forms are
distributed across the procession of hypostases.[80] In this sense, the intelligible

---

77   Plato, *Tim.* 30c7–d1: τὰ γὰρ δὴ νοητὰ ζῷα πάντα ἐκεῖνο ἐν ἑαυτῷ περιλαβὸν ἔχει, καθάπερ ὅδε
      ὁ κόσμος ἡμᾶς ὅσα τε ἄλλα θρέμματα συνέστηκεν ὁρατά.

78   Cf. Kobusch (2000: 316 and 316 n. 21). Note, however, that the current argument does not
      prevent the sensible cosmos from being itself a whole before the parts; see, e.g., Proclus,
      IT IV, 125.12–127.1 (cited in chapter 6, section 2.3).

79   Proclus, *IT* II, 321.17–322.3 (1.426.12–20 Diehl); cf. Baltzly (2020: 293–294) for his reading of
      this passage, which once again takes the Platonic Forms as its point of reference.

80   For a discussion of the role allotted to the Platonic Forms in Proclean metaphysics, see
      d'Hoine (2016: 107–117). For a schematic overview of the various types of Platonic Forms
      according to Proclus, see Steel (1987: 124). For discussions of the various kinds of things

A WHOLESOME TRINITY

Paradigm is the cosmos *qua* simply whole, for it encompasses in a causal manner all intelligible Forms and, by extension, their material images.

Whereas the Paradigm encompasses all things in a transcendent way, the material cosmos encompasses all things in the sense that it actually contains them.

> ἔστι μὲν οὖν καὶ οὗτος ὁ κόσμος ζῷον ποικίλον κατ' ἄλλο ἑαυτοῦ φωνὴν ἄλλην ἀφιεὶς καὶ ἐκ πάντων τῶν μορίων μίαν—ἔστι γὰρ καὶ εἷς πολύς—, πολὺ δὲ πρότερον ὁ νοητὸς κόσμος καὶ ἓν ζῷόν ἐστι καὶ πλῆθος, ἐν τῷ ἑνὶ τὸ πλῆθος συνῃρηκώς, ὥσπερ αὖ οὗτος ἐν τῷ πλήθει δεικνύει τὸ ἕν· καὶ ὁ μὲν ὅλον ἐστὶν ἐκ τῶν μερῶν, ὁ δὲ ὅλον πρὸ τῶν μερῶν, ἐξῃρημένως τὰ νοητὰ ζῷα περιέχων καὶ κατ' αἰτίαν καὶ μονοειδῶς·
>
> PROCLUS, *IT* II, 326.10–17 (1.429.18–25 Diehl)

Thus, this cosmos too is a multifaceted living thing, emitting different sounds from different parts of itself and a single sound from all of its parts [together]—after all, it is also a manifold one—and much sooner is the intelligible cosmos both a single living thing and a multiplicity, having brought the multiplicity together in the one, just as this cosmos for its part manifests the one in the multiplicity. And the one is a whole composed of parts, the other a whole before the parts, transcendently embracing the intelligible living beings both causally and uniformly.

> Tr. SHARE in Runia and Share 2008 (slightly modified)

Whereas the intelligible Paradigm is a unity that leads to multiplicity (ἐν τῷ ἑνὶ τὸ πλῆθος συνῃρηκώς), the material cosmos is a collection of parts, both immortal and mortal, that come together to form one spherical universe (ἐν τῷ πλήθει δεικνύει τὸ ἕν). Hence, it possesses the distinctive character of an actual composition in contrast to the simpler wholeness of the intelligible Paradigm.

What about the whole in the part? We know that the cosmos is a whole composed of wholes in parts, but Proclus does not give any examples of these in our current passage, so we must look elsewhere. Baltzly has pointed to one example which is rather illustrative.[81] In his commentary on the *Parmenides*, Proclus takes the time to briefly define the notion 'part' after Parmenides

---

in the sensible realm that do not have corresponding Platonic Forms, such as artefacts, individuals, accidental properties, and evils, see d'Hoine (2006a, 2006b, 2010, 2011a, and 2011b).

81   Baltzly (2008: 407).

104　　　　　　　　　　　　　　　　　　　　　　　　　　　　　　　　　　CHAPTER 4

introduces it into his discussion of the one.[82] Among the multiple possible
definitions of the term, Proclus reveals that 'part' may indicate 'that which is in
some way the same as the whole' (τὸ ταὐτόν πως τῷ ὅλῳ).

> καὶ γὰρ τὸ ταὐτόν πως τῷ ὅλῳ καὶ πάντα ἔχον μερικῶς, ὅσα τὸ ὅλον ὁλικῶς,
> μέρος καλοῦμεν, οἷον τοῦ ὅλου νοῦ μέρος εἶναι τῶν πολλῶν ἕκαστον, καίτοι
> πάντων ὄντων ἐν ἑκάστῳ τῶν εἰδῶν, καὶ τὴν ἀπλανῆ μέρος τοῦ παντός, καίτοι
> καὶ ταύτης τὰ πάντα περιεχούσης, ἀλλ᾽ ἕτερον τρόπον ἢ ὡς ὁ κόσμος.
>
> PROCLUS, *IP* VI, 1112.22–27

> Indeed, that which is in some way the same as the whole and has all things
> partially which the whole has holistically, we call 'part', as for example
> [we say that] each of the many intellects is part of the whole Intellect,
> and yet all intellects are in each of the Forms, and the sphere of the fixed
> stars is a part of the cosmos, and yet it too encompasses all things, but in
> a different manner from the cosmos.
>
> Tr. MORROW and DILLON 1987 (modified)

The second example in this passage is relevant for our current discussion.[83] The
sphere of the fixed stars fits the criteria for a whole in the part as described
in the *Elements of Theology*.[84] The material cosmos contains all sensible
things in a general sense. As its part, the outermost celestial sphere contains
everything in a stricter sense: it forms a perimeter around all other things in
the cosmos.[85] As such, it imitates the all-encompassing nature of its whole.

Here too, we see a specific type of wholeness, namely the whole that
encompasses all other wholes, manifesting itself in three ways. The intelligible
Paradigm is the primary and unitary cause of all living beings, and it stands
above them as a transcendent whole before the parts. The cosmos actually
contains all living beings as its parts, giving it the distinctive character of a compound, making it a whole composed of parts. Lastly, the sphere of fixed stars is
primarily a part, yet it shares in the distinctive character of the Paradigm and
the cosmos, albeit to a lesser extent. Whereas the Paradigm pre-includes all

---

82　　For the full overview, see Oosthout, A. (2023a).

83　　For the first example, i.e., the many intellects within the divine Intellect, see Baltzly (2008:
　　　402 and 409) and Oosthout, A. (2022b).

84　　In the *Elements of Theology*, Proclus established that a whole in the part constitutes a part
　　　which can become like its whole. Here Proclus characterises the current type of part once
　　　again as something that is like its whole.

85　　Baltzly (2008: 407) compares the manner in which the fixed sphere contains the other
　　　cosmic elements to the way in which a cup contains tea.

things in its unity, and the cosmos literally consists of all things, the sphere of fixed stars merely encircles all things. One might wonder whether this argument is strong enough to justify labelling the outermost sphere a whole in the part. Its resemblance to the cosmos is, after all, merely a metaphorical one, in contrast to the portions of the soul-mixture which literally contain the same ingredients as the whole mixture.[86] Yet Proclus' basic definition of the whole in the part in the *Elements of Theology* as something which imitates its whole is broad (or vague) enough that it applies both to the portions of the soul-mixture and to the outermost celestial sphere. It should also be noted that the cosmos does not manifest the three kinds of wholes only in these specific ways. As we noted previously, in passages from his *Commentary on Plato's Timaeus* besides the one cited above, Proclus applies the three kinds of wholes to the cosmos in other ways.

4.4   The Whole in Each Part: a Reappraisal of Previous Readings

It should be kept in mind that the examples discussed above, illuminating as they might be, should not be taken to fully define the three kinds of wholes. After all, if one were to conclude that the three kinds of wholes function solely as they do in the World Soul, one would be left with yet another reading of Proclus' mereology that does not align with the previous ones. Such an approach would only leave one with the unsatisfying conclusion that Proclus' mereology is fundamentally inconsistent.

In contrast, each example of the three kinds of wholes in Proclus' writings must be understood in light of the mereological blueprint which Proclus established in the *Platonic Theology*. Since all wholes are images of the second intelligible triad, which is the first Whole, all of the examples of the three kinds of wholes discussed either by others or by myself are merely specific instances of a universal theorem. No single example, whether that be the relation between henads and beings, the various guises of the Platonic Forms, the essence of the World Soul, or the all-encompassing natures of the Paradigm and the cosmos, can ever tell the full story. After all, the wholeness in each of these examples is an offshoot of the first Whole, and likewise each example is itself a specification of Proclus' universally applicable mereology. This interpretation of the triad of wholeness as a recurring image of the intelligible

---

86   In contrast to Proclus, Damascius does distinguish the likeness between the elements of a mixture and the mixture as a whole from the relation between part and whole in other kinds of compositions; see, e.g., Damascius, *DP* II, 175.7–176.7.

wholeness concurs with d'Hoine's recent suggestion that the threefold wholeness constitutes one of the 'triades transversales', which 'ne sont pas restreintes à un niveau déterminé du réel, mais traversent un grand nombre d'échelons.'[87] Although the readings proposed by previous scholars remain valid in this way, they do require some small adjustments, with the exception of Chlup's connection between the three kinds of wholes and the relations of participation between hypostases.[88] Firstly, Baltzly argued that the three kinds of wholes correspond to three different manifestations of a Platonic Form: the transcendent Form, the Form as immanent in its many participants, and the specific characteristics of one individual, such as Socrates. This third type of Form is designated as an 'atomic form' (ἄτομον εἶδος), according to Baltzly. The terminology Baltzly employs here actually derives from Porphyry rather than Proclus, as Baltzly himself admits.[89] Proclus has his own conception of the individual *qua* individual, which he calls the 'individually qualified' (ἰδίως ποιόν), just as the Stoic philosophers did.[90] However, Baltzly's mixing of Porphyrian and Proclean terminology is somewhat problematic, because Proclus also presents his own notion of the atomic form, one which does not seem to equate to his personal qualities or Porphyry's specific individual. On multiple occasions, d'Hoine has convincingly argued that Proclus distinguishes between the visible or material forms (ἔνυλα εἴδη), which are the Platonic Forms as they appear across the material universe, and the individual qualities of an individual.[91] Indeed, Proclus uses the terminology of the 'atomic form' in a passage in which he describes the characteristics of the material forms rather than the characteristics of individuals,[92] a passage which Baltzly erroneously cites as proof for his combination of the Porphyrian and Proclean concepts of atomic forms.[93] Furthermore, Proclus argues against the existence of transcendent principles of individual characteristics in his *Parmenides*-commentary.[94] Therefore, the whole in the part is, in this case, not the Porphyrian form of a specific individual,

---

87 D'Hoine (2021: 178).

88 Proclus rephrases the twofold manner in which a lower participated being participates in a superior hypostasis in mereological terms in his *Commentary on Plato's Timaeus*—specifically Proclus, *IT* IV, 149.7–10 (3.115.21–27 Diehl)—indirectly confirming Chlup's link between the three wholes and participatory relations between hypostases. However, the link between this specific theorem of participation and the three kinds of wholes does raise an issue within Proclus' thought itself, for which see Oosthout, A. (2022b: 12–16).

89 Baltzly (2008: 405); Porphyry, *Isagoge* 7.19–21.

90 See Proclus, *IP* III, 824.11 and v, 981.8–9; cf. Helmig (2006: 260–261).

91 E.g., d'Hoine (2010: 242–43); cf. Helmig (2006) for a more general discussion of the ἔνυλον εἶδος and Proclus' use of the term.

92 See Proclus, *IP* IV, 970.10–31; cf. d'Hoine (2021: 207–210).

93 Baltzly (2008: 405 n. 20).

94 E.g., Proclus, *IP* III, 824.9–825.7; d'Hoine (2010).

A WHOLESOME TRINITY

but rather the sensible material form as it appears within each of the individuals. In other words, the whole before the parts is the transcendent Form, e.g., the Form of the Human Being. The whole composed of parts then becomes akin to the Aristotelian form of the human being, a 'forme participée en tant que forme commune'.[95] Lastly, the whole in the part is this Aristotelian form as it appears in each of us individually, or the 'forme participée en tant que particularisée par le participant matériel' (we should here take 'particularised' in a quantitative rather than an ontological sense).[96] In other words, the whole in the part is not the Form of Socrates, but the form 'human being' as it manifests in Socrates' body.[97]

Butler's reading of the three kinds of wholes as classes of henads which transcend or coexist with beings similarly requires some adjustment if one accepts the reading I propose. Butler suggests that the three kinds of wholes delineate the relation between the henads and the whole of Being, stating that 'beings experience their own relative divinity as virtual parts of the henads, not in the sense that henads have parts, but in the sense that each henad is generative of the whole of Being, that is, the *wholeness* of Being or Being's subsistence *as a whole*.'[98] Perhaps, however, we should read Proclus' application of the three kinds of wholes to the relations between henads and beings slightly differently. In the third book of the *Platonic Theology*, where Proclus defines the three kinds of wholes as aspects and offshoots of the second intelligible triad as discussed above, he briefly elaborates on the relationship between the second intelligible triad and the henads.

> Τριῶν δὲ τῶν ὁλοτήτων οὐσῶν, τῆς μὲν πρὸ τῶν μερῶν, τῆς δὲ ἐκ τῶν μερῶν, τῆς δὲ ἐν τῷ μέρει, διὰ μὲν τῆς πρὸ τῶν μερῶν ὁλότητος ὁ αἰὼν τὰς ἑνάδας μετρεῖ τῶν θείων τὰς ἐξῃρημένας τῶν ὄντων, διὰ δὲ τῆς ἐκ τῶν μερῶν τὰς ἑνάδας τὰς συντεταγμένας τοῖς οὖσιν, διὰ δὲ τῆς ἐν τῷ μέρει τὰ ὄντα πάντα καὶ τὰς οὐσίας ὅλας· μέρη γὰρ αὗται τῶν θείων ἑνάδων μεριστῶς ἔχουσαι τὰ ἑνιαίως ἐν ἐκείναις προϋπάρχοντα.
>
> PROCLUS, *TP* III.27, 94.24–95.4

Since there are three kinds of wholeness, the wholeness before the parts, the wholeness composed of parts, and the wholeness in the part, Eternity measures the henads of the divine beings, henads which transcend their beings, through the wholeness before the parts; it measures the henads

---

95   D'Hoine (2021: 218).
96   D'Hoine (*ibidem*).
97   See chapter 6, section 3.
98   Butler (2010: 143).

which are made coordinate with their beings through the wholeness composed of parts, and it measures all beings and whole essences through the whole in the part. After all, these beings are parts of the divine henads, since they contain in a divided manner what pre-exists in a unitary manner in those henads.

We have seen before that Proclus links the three kinds of wholeness to the three aspects of the second intelligible triad, viz., unity, power, and being, and that these three wholes subsequently reappear at the various levels of reality below the second intelligible triad. In light of this, Proclus is not talking about the relation between the henads in general and the whole of Being in our current passage. Instead, he alludes to the reoccurrence of the one-, power-, and being-aspects within each specific triad. In other words, the second intelligible triad measures the specific transcendent henad of each subsequent triad with the wholeness before the parts, each union of one and being through power with the wholeness composed of parts, and each subsequent being which participates in its own henad with the wholeness in the part.[99] After all, Proclus' aim in this chapter of the *Platonic Theology* is not to provide a generalised discussion of henads and Being, but rather to perform an exegesis of Plato's *Parmenides* (and *Timaeus*) and to describe in detail the development of a One Being which continually remanifests itself in a progressively more divided manner. If the three kinds of wholeness derive from the relation between the unity-, power-, and being-aspects of the second triad, and if they reoccur within subsequent hypostases, it makes sense to suppose that the unity-, power-, and being-aspects of those subsequent triads should be counted among the many manifestations of the three kinds of wholeness.

4.5   Stronger Apart and Stronger Together

Now that the origin of Proclus' three wholes is determined and the previous readings are united, the final question remains: what are we to make of this mereology in general? By dividing the whole intro three kinds, Proclus

---

99   Note that Proclus equates the notion of 'being a part of' with 'participating in' here. In our earlier passages from the *Platonic Theology*, Proclus established that each ὄν-aspect of a triad *participates* in the henad of that triad. Proclus' characterisation of a being as a *part* of a henad here cannot be taken literally, since that would imply that henads themselves have parts. This would be absurd, for of themselves the henads are direct irradiations from the One and so cannot be internally pluralised (see, for example Proclus, ET 103).

incorporates into his part-whole relations the most fundamental notion of Neoplatonic thought: the procession of unity towards plurality. In Neoplatonic metaphysics, the many depends on the one, but that is not all. The one itself transcends the many. It stands on its own as an independent entity. Most philosophers who suggest that the whole is something beyond the sum of its parts will affirm the first point, but not necessarily the second one. Aristotle, for example, agrees that a compound owes its existence not to its elements, but to the essence that binds those elements together. The essence of the syllable binds the letters α and β in order to create βα. Furthermore, certain parts only truly exist within the compound; a separated finger is a finger in name only.[100] Yet Aristotle's forms do not transcend their matter, and the syllable does not exist apart from its letters.

For Proclus, the whole *qua* unity must in some way transcend its many parts, just as every other unity within the Proclean universe transcends the multiplicities that depend on it.[101] For this reason, he posits the existence of the whole *simpliciter*, which functions as the principle of the parts coming together without descending into them like an Aristotelian form does. This transcendent unity is called the whole *before* the parts. It remains undiminished by the multiplicity of the parts, as we saw when Proclus emphasised that the essence of the World Soul was not exhausted when the Demiurge scooped the portions out of the mixing-bowl, or when he located the cause of the cosmos's property of being all-encompassing within the intelligible Paradigm, above and beyond the divided nature of the material cosmos. The second intelligible triad in turn functions as the ultimate whole before the parts, or more accurately as the whole before the wholes, given that it constitutes the Wholeness itself (αὐτοολότης) which Proclus raised as an example of the highest form of wholeness in the *Elements of Theology*. Thus, there exists both one ultimate whole before the parts (the intelligible Wholeness) and more specific wholes before parts for specific types of wholeness, such as the all-encompassing whole or the World Soul.

Despite all his efforts to elevate the whole, Proclus does not separate part from whole entirely. On the contrary, the parts are linked so closely to the whole that even they share in the whole's distinctive character, albeit in a greatly diminished way compared to the transcendent whole itself. For

---

100 Aristotle, *Met.* Z.10, 1035b23–25; cf. Z.17, 1041b11–31. The latter passage is cited in chapter 2, section 5.

101 Compare, for example, the Form as one over its many participants, or the henad of each hypostasis as one over its many images in lower levels of reality. As is written in the very first lines of the *Elements of Theology*: πᾶν πλῆθος μετέχει πῃ τοῦ ἑνός (Proclus, *ET* 1, 2.1).

example, each portion taken out of the original essence of the World Soul by the Demiurge contains all three ingredients of the soul-essence, albeit only a fraction of each. Similarly, the sphere of the fixed stars is similar to the intelligible Paradigm in its all-encompassing nature, but not equal to it. Whereas the Paradigm pre-includes everything in a transcendent causal manner, the outer sphere of the cosmos only contains everything in the strictest sense of the word. Nevertheless, such parts still participate in the wholeness that originates from the transcendent whole, even if their share of wholeness is of a highly diminished kind. Each of these is a whole *in* the part. In this sense, Proclus goes even further than Aristotle. Not only do certain parts derive their existence from their compound (compare Aristotle's finger), they even borrow some of its distinctive characteristics.

It is, of course, paradoxical to claim that the same transcendent whole utterly transcends its parts and is simultaneously present within them. It is equally absurd to claim that the sphere of fixed stars participates directly in the nature of the intelligible Paradigm. If Proclus wishes to fashion a mereology in which the whole fully transcends its parts yet is still intrinsically present in them, he needs a point where the one and the many meet. In the *Platonic Theology*, Proclus revealed that the two divided aspects of the intelligible triads, i.e., their unity and their being, were kept together by each triad's power. Since Proclus' concept of the whole is grounded in the second of these intelligible triads, his mereology has a similar middle term between the transcendent whole and the parts. This middle kind of whole is less unified than the transcendent whole, but not as greatly diminished as the wholeness in the individual parts. It is the complete aggregate of all the parts, combined into a single entity which resembles its creator, the transcendent whole, being one and many at the same time. For example, the cosmos brings together the many material beings within into a single structured entity (hence the name κόσμος),[102] mirroring the transcendent Paradigm, while the reconstructed World Soul unites all of the portions of the soul-mixture into a single entity that mirrors the unitary soul-essence as it is before the Demiurge fashions the two circles. This middle term is the whole in the ordinary sense of the word, i.e., the one which Proclus describes as existing καθ' ὕπαρξιν. In other words, this middle whole is the one that is actually *composed of* parts.

The generalised manner in which the three kinds of wholes are described in this section resembles Siorvanes's reading of the same triad—although he does not incorporate the theory's exegetical background as expounded in the

---

102   Cf. Baltzly (2008: 407–408).

A WHOLESOME TRINITY

Platonic Theology.[103] However, an important difference between our interpretations lies in the fact that Siorvanes appears to conceive of Proclean wholes as straight synonyms for universals.[104] At first glance, Proclus does in fact seem to confirm this interpretation, offering up a triad of universals which would run parallel to the triad of wholes in his other works. To start, there are:

1. the universal (τὸ καθόλου) whose nature it is 'to exist before the many and to generate the multiplicity' (πρὸ τῶν πολλῶν ὑφεστάναι καὶ γεννητικὸν εἶναι τοῦ πλήθους), i.e., the universal *ante rem*, and

2. the universal whose nature it is 'to become visible in the individuals' (ἐν τοῖς καθ' ἕκαστα φαντάζεσθαι), i.e., the universal *in re*.

So far, so good. The universal *ante rem* is clearly analogous to the whole before the parts, and the universal *in re* can be seen as analogous to the whole in the part. However, the third type of universal is:

3. the universal whose nature it is 'to subsist alongside the many in a later-born manner' (ὑστερογενῶς ἐπισυνίστασθαι τοῖς πολλοῖς), i.e., the Aristotelian universal *post rem*.[105]

This final type of universal cannot be directly linked to any of the three types of wholes, since it has a different ontological status from those three wholes and the other two types of universals. All of those things exist in their own right, whereas the later-born universal is purely a product of our thinking (κατὰ ἐπίνοιαν).[106] For this reason, I do not follow Siorvanes in taking together Proclean wholes and universals without qualification.[107]

In contrast, Dodds was correct in suggesting that the three kinds of wholes mirror the three steps of participation. Not necessarily, as Baltzly suggested, because each whole is a type of Platonic Form, but because each kind whole mirrors a step in the process of participation. In every relation of participation,

---

103   Siorvanes (1996: 69–71; cf. 1998a).

104   Siorvanes (1996: 71).

105   The summary of the three types of universals given here is based on Proclus, *In Eucl.* 50.16–51.9. However, the triad of universals is also discussed in, e.g., his *IRP* I, 260.22–25 and *IP* III, 833.26–834.20; cf. Lernould (2011) and d'Hoine (2011b: 38–39) for further analysis of the triad of universals and its development in the Neoplatonic tradition before Proclus.

106   Proclus, *In Eucl.* 51.4. Cf. Granieri (2022: 239–241) for the distinction between purely conceptual *post rem*-universals and really existent *ante rem-/in re*-universals in the writings of Proclus' teacher Syrianus.

107   The discrepancy between Proclus' three kinds of wholes and his three kinds of universals has recently been discussed by d'Hoine (2021: 205 n. 41) as well. In fact, the strenuous relationship between both sets of concepts plagued also the Byzantine commentators of Proclus. A notable example of these commentators who struggle to reconcile the three wholes with the three universals is Eustratius of Nicaea, as discussed in Gersh (2021).

the unparticipated principle gives rise to the participant, but only through the participated character which links the two outer terms.[108] Likewise, the parts which imitate wholes take after the transcendent whole, but only through the wholeness of the compound in which they come together.

A modern student of mereology might wonder whether Proclus' theory of parts and whole is needlessly complex, with new instances of wholeness at every turn, and the odd fact that the actual compound becomes less like the essence of the whole and more like a link between the parts and the true unity above. Such arguments would not fly for Proclus, however. Whereas modern students of mereology tend to focus on the unity within the multiplicity (an approach more akin to an Aristotelian mereology than a Platonic one) a devout follower of Neoplatonic philosophy knows that the one ultimately stands above the many. The composition itself remains critically important even within this worldview, since it bridges the gap between the transcendent whole and the partial whole. Clearly, for someone who loves triads as much as Proclus does, this tripartite mereology could not be more wholesome.

---

108   However, the parallel is not a perfect one. As d'Hoine (2021: 219) points out, the concept of a whole in the part necessarily implies an internal distinction between the part (which participates) and its wholeness (which is participated), which is 'la raison pour laquelle sa correspondance avec un terme précis de la triade de la participation pose problème'. This internal distinction within the whole in the part is not as evident in the case of incorporeal principles, but it shows itself quite clearly in sensible individuals, as d'Hoine (2021: 203–204) shows.

PART 3

Part and Whole in Proclus' Theology and Cosmology

∵

Everything on this earth, everything in the universe shall pass, but the world as a whole, all that is, with all its dynamics, shall not pass. We are mortal and every moment of our consciousness is fleeting, but as part of all that is, embedded in the dynamics of time, we are eternal, albeit eternal in our temporality.

HENRI OOSTHOUT, *The passage of time and the mathematical universe,* 9-12-2021, https://anhypotheton.eu/passtimemathuniv.php

CHAPTER 5

Dividing the Indivisible

One of the most fundamental distinctions in Proclean metaphysics is the Platonic distinction between intelligible being and sensible becoming (arguably second in importance only to the distinction between unity and plurality). In the previous chapters, we focused primarily on Proclus' overall approach to the concepts of composition and wholeness. Even there, however, the distinction between the intelligible and the sensible was crucial for our understanding of the philosopher's arguments and theoretical models, most obviously in our analysis of the Proclean rule. These next two chapters focus on the intelligible and the sensible aspects of the Neoplatonic universe in more detail. For even as we analysed the internal structure of the second intelligible principle, i.e., of the monad of Wholeness, and distilled from it the inner workings of Proclus' threefold whole, the philosopher implored us that the causal influence of this monad flowed downward into many lower levels of reality (a few of which we discussed by way of examples).

This third part of the book, then, maps in more detail the ways in which Proclus develops his concepts of whole and part as the influence of the intelligible principle of Wholeness flows downward all the way from the highest echelons of the transcendent Intellect to the utterly material and sensible creatures which are granted only a finite amount of time in the cosmos. In this chapter, we trace the development of the concept of wholeness which runs parallel to the development of the hypostases which are present in Intellect. In the subsequent chapter, we turn our attention to the wholeness, or lack thereof, of the things which come to be within the sensible cosmos.

What does an inquiry into the types of wholes Proclus links to intelligible being and sensible becoming, respectively, teach us that the more general study of wholeness in the previous chapters does not? It has already become clear that Proclus uses the philosophical term 'whole' in a variety of ways. Most notable is the distinction between a purely extensional understanding of what a whole is, namely as the total sum of its parts, and the less 'ontologically innocent' understanding of the whole as a certain unity which is essentially distinct from and transcendent over its parts.[1] In the previous chapters, we described primarily how Proclus accounts for this distinction between the extensional

---

1 See chapter 2, section 2.

© ARTHUR OOSTHOUT, 2025 | DOI:10.1163/9789004721760_006

whole and the ontological whole, noting that the latter is represented by the way in which the three kinds of whole (before the parts, composed of parts, and in the part) continually remanifest in different essences, such as the unity or compositeness of the World Soul or that of the sensible cosmos itself.[2] Yet we also noted that the ultimate Whole-itself was itself a determinate intelligible principle in Proclus' metaphysical hierarchy, one that also served as the principle of eternity. The Proclean whole, then, is not only more than just the sum of any set of parts, but also bears a specific distinctive character (ἰδιότης) which arises in Proclus' procession of being, and which is subsequently refracted by inferior principles. In other words, the Proclean term 'whole' has in ontological terms a much stricter meaning than we previously noted.

An especially important part of Proclus' ontological development of the notion of wholeness is the overall (Neo)platonic tendency to ascribe, in Lloyd's words, 'values or perfections' to intelligible principles, best exemplified by the manner in which the Platonic Idea of something is also the *ideal* version of that thing (e.g., per Lloyd, 'the Idea of Beauty being what is perfectly or completely beautiful'),[3] or by Plotinus' equation of the ultimate One with the utterly transcendent Good from Plato's *Republic* VI.[4] Such an axiological conceptualisation of the intelligible principle of Wholeness fits rather well with Plato's own equation of wholeness with completeness or perfection, and indeed we already noted that Baltzly pointed briefly to the fact that 'the concepts of being perfect or complete (τέλειον) and being a whole are treated [by Proclus] as exactly parallel in structure.'[5]

In this chapter, then, we fill in the colours of Proclus' concept of wholeness after having sketched its contours in the previous chapters. To this end, we will start from a closer look at Proclus' characterisation of the second intelligible triad as not only the principle of wholeness but also of eternity. Subsequently we shall descend along with our philosopher through the various intelligible triads in order to reconstruct the role Proclus allots to wholeness and parthood,

---

2   See chapter 4, sections 2 and 3. The adjective 'extensional' is used throughout this chapter in the broad sense defined above, and should not be confused with the more specific 'extensionality of parthood'-principle discussed by Varzi (2006)—in this more precise sense, 'extensionality' refers to fact that there can be no two composites with exactly the same proper parts, and is roughly equal to the principle of uniqueness of composition which was defined by Lewis and cited in chapter 2, section 2 of our inquiry.

3   Lloyd (1998: 105).

4   As noted also by Lloyd (1990: 121). Proclus' own interpretation of *Republic* VI is informed not only by Plato's *Parmenides*, but also by the *Philebus*, as described in Oosthout and Van Riel (2023).

5   Baltzly (2008: 408 n. 22), my addition between brackets; see chapter 1.

DIVIDING THE INDIVISIBLE

respectively, in the causal procession of intelligible beings from the One, on the basis of which we may unearth the exact nature of the correlation between wholeness and perfection, which Baltzly indicated but did not expand upon.

5.1   Balancing the Relativistic Whole and the Determinate Whole

Applying the concept of parthood to the Neoplatonic notion of Intellect is a complex affair. The primary difficulty lies in the Intellect's status as a nonextended thing, a status it owes to its transcendence over the time and space in which sensible things exist. In fact, Proclus explicitly distinguishes the intelligible from the sensible in his *Timaeus*-commentary by the fact that the former kind of existence belongs to things which are 'in every way simple and allow for no composition nor for dissolution.'[6] How can something which has no spatiotemporal dimensions be divisible into parts? Furthermore, the indivisibility of the transcendent Intellect is an essential part of Proclus' explanation for one of its most famous characteristics: the fact that the Intellect knows itself.

In the *Elements of Theology*, Proclus bases his explanation of the Intellect's self-knowledge on its previously proven capacity for self-reversion.[7] To give some context, the three processes of remaining (μονή), procession (πρόοδος), and reversion (ἐπιστροφή) constitute a fundamental part of Proclean metaphysics. In short, the distinctive character of a productive principle proceeds downwards through reality while the principle itself remains at its own level, but at the same time every principle also continuously strives to return to its own producer(s).[8] However, any particular intellect which reverts upon the one Intellect is at the same time inseparable from that Intellect. In other words, the incorporeal substances can revert *upon themselves* because of their indivisibility.

Proclus establishes this general rule early on in his treatise. In the fifteenth proposition of the *Elements of Theology*, he argues that bodies, and divisible substances in general, cannot revert upon themselves because of their spatial extension. The parts of an extended body exist separately from one another (ὁ τῶν μερῶν χωρισμός), and thus an extended body is not capable of reverting

---

6   Proclus, *IT* v, 65.9–10 (3.211.15–16 Diehl): ἐκεῖνα [i.e., τὰ νοητά] γὰρ ἄλυτά ἐστιν ὡς ἁπλᾶ πάντῃ καὶ οὐδεμίαν ἐνδεχόμενα σύνθεσιν ἢ λύσιν. We analyse this passage in more detail in chapter 6, section 3.

7   Proclus, *ET* 82, 83, and 167, 76.22–78.4, 144.22–146.16.

8   See especially Proclus, *ET* 25–39 and 28.21–42.7. For the procession of distinctive characters through Neoplatonic reality, see figs. 1 and 2 in chapter 3.

upon itself 'as a whole is reverted upon a whole' (ὡς ὅλον ἐπεστράφθαι πρὸς ὅλον). Proclus concludes, *modus tollens*, that only a nonextended and indivisible thing is capable of reverting upon itself as a whole.[9]

Proclus employs this general rule again in the one hundred seventy-first proposition as a foundation for the claim that every form of intellect is *indivisible*.[10] It should be noted, however, that Proclus also immediately links this particular kind of indivisibility to spatiotemporal dimensions, i.e., to the aforementioned extended nature of bodily substances, and that he confirms the existence of a 'unified manifold' (ἡνωμένον πλῆθος) within the incorporeal Intellect.[11]

The notion of a nonextended multiplicity within the Intellect is not an invention of Proclus'. Already in Plotinus, we find the notion of Intellect as 'a manifold which is undivided and yet again divided' (πλῆθος ἀδιάκριτον καὶ αὖ διακεκριμένον, Armstrong's translation), which is to say that the many beings within Intellect are pressed together into a nonextended unity without being mixed up with one another.[12] Elsewhere, Plotinus describes how the intelligible principles are only truly considered to be separable parts when we grasp them in our discursive thinking; as soon as we let these principles slip through the fingers of our mind, they hasten back to their natural state of nonextended unity.[13] It is nevertheless interesting to reflect briefly on the way in which Proclus rephrases the manifold-in-one of Intellect in mereological terms, as he does both in the second half of his *Elements of Theology* and in his commentaries on the Platonic dialogues.

A mereological rephrasing of the Plotinian divided yet undivided Intellect can be found already in the writings of Plotinus' faithful student, Porphyry.

---

9   Proclus, *ET* 15, 18.1–6.
10 Proclus, *ET* 171, 150.1.
11 Proclus, *ET* 171, 150.2–6 and 12–14. This has not stopped some commentators, both modern and premodern, from taking Proclus' statement that intellect is indivisible for a universal quantification, and subsequently from concluding that Proclus must contradict himself in placing any kind of multiplicity within intellect. Two notable proponents of this view are Nicholas of Methone (*Ref.* 180, 157.7–9) and Dodds (1963: 293–294), the latter of whom specifically emended his edition of the Greek text of the *Elements of Theology* to solve this supposed difficulty. As I and other scholars have argued, however, such an emendation is not only unnecessary, but also introduces *new* problems into the internal structure of Proclus' *Elements of Theology*. For my analysis of Nicholas' and Dodds' objections, see Oosthout, A. (2022b: 3–10). Other criticisms of this position, which I cite in that paper as well, can be found in Trouillard (1965: 169 n. 2), Onnasch and Schomakers (2015: 333), and d'Hoine (2021: 189–190).
12 Plotinus, *Enn.* VI.9 [9], 5.13–20; cf. Oosthout, A. (2022b: 1).
13 Plotinus, *Enn.* VI.2 [43], 3.20–30.

DIVIDING THE INDIVISIBLE 119

As I have shown previously, Porphyry employs Aristotelean terminology to describe the relation between the Intellect as a whole and the 'parts' it contains.[14] More specifically, Porphyry employs the term 'composed of homogenous parts' (ὁμοιομερής) to describe the way in which every part of Intellect reflects the Intellect as a whole. The full argument, which Porphyry gives in his *Sentences*, goes as follows.

> Ἡ νοερὰ οὐσία ὁμοιομερής ἐστιν, ὡς καὶ ἐν τῷ μερικῷ νῷ εἶναι τὰ ὄντα καὶ ἐν τῷ παντελείῳ· ἀλλ' ἐν μὲν τῷ καθόλου καὶ τὰ μερικὰ καθολικῶς, ἐν δὲ τῷ μερικῷ καὶ τὰ καθόλου {καὶ μερικὰ} μερικῶς.
>
> PORPHYRY, *Sent.* 22, 13.13–16

> The intellectual essence is homogenous in its parts (ὁμοιομερής), in the sense that the beings are both in the partial intellect and in the wholly perfect intellect. Yet in the universal intellect the partial intellects are also present universally, whereas in the partial intellect the universal intellect is also present partially.

With this argument, Porphyry creates a fluid notion of wholeness for the Intellect. A particular intellect constitutes not only a specific part of the one Intellect (e.g., one of the highest genera from the *Sophist*, or any given Platonic Idea) but also the whole of Intellect, a fact that is made possible by Intellect's nonextended nature. This idea fits well with the Porphyrian and Proclean approaches to the genus-species relations between subsequent intelligible principles within Intellect, whereby the mereological status of any given principle is relative rather than fixed. Recall that both Porphyry and Proclus underscored the principle that 'all things are in all things', that Porphyry proclaimed the species to be both whole and part by virtue of its relations to its genus and its individuals, respectively, and that Proclus emphasised the fact that the many intelligible principles of his Intellect as ordered in a hierarchy of 'more universal' (ὁλικώτερον) and 'more particular' (μερικώτερον) causes.[15] In fact, Proclus explicitly incorporates Porphyry's aforementioned distinction between the 'whole' Intellect and the 'partial' intellect into his *Elements of Theology*.[16]

In this respect, one might claim that wholeness is a relative concept for Porphyry and Proclus, in the sense that the extent to which any given intelligible

---

14   Oosthout, A. (2022b: 6–7).
15   See chapter 3, section 1, and chapter 4, section 1.
16   Proclus, *ET* 180, 158.11–18; cf. Dodds (1963: 293) and Oosthout, A. (2022b: 6).

principle is called 'whole' or 'part' depends on whether one describes its relation to a superior principle or an inferior one.[17] For example, in my previous work, I pointed towards passages from Proclus' *Platonic Theology* and the *Timaeus*-commentary which describe the intelligible Paradigm of Plato's cosmogony in different mereological terms depending on whether one describes its relation to its own causal principles (to which it is a 'part' or 'more particular') or to the cosmic beings that it itself causes (to which is a 'whole' or 'more universal').[18]

And yet Proclus is uneasy about committing to this relative notion of wholeness. Most notable in this regard is his response to Porphyry's description of intellect as 'composed of homogenous parts' (ὁμοιομερής). Proclus considers the Aristotelean term to be a marker for the melding together of material substances (think of Aristotle's example of flesh which, when cut up, reveals smaller pieces of flesh), and he subsequently accuses Porphyry of describing the transcendent Intellect in a wrongfully materialist manner.[19] In Proclus' view, the result of Porphyry's argument would be that the various principles and Platonic Forms within the Intellect are mixed up with one another in precisely the way that the Neoplatonic thinkers wished to avoid.[20]

The notion of relative wholeness is problematic for Proclus' metaphysics in a broader sense as well. Although blurring the lines between wholes and parts works within an extensional framework of sets whose members are further

---

17 A yet more radical notion of relative wholeness can be found in Nicholas of Methone's response to the *Elements of Theology*. Eager to rob Proclus' many intelligible principles of their status as separately existent divinities and to affirm the sole existence of the Christian Trinity, the Byzantine bishop states that calling anything in the universe 'whole' or 'part' (with the exception of the ultimate whole, the Trinity itself) involves not an essential predication but merely an accidental one, specifically one belonging to Aristotle's category of the πρός τι. See Oosthout, A. (forthcoming) for the full analysis of Nicholas' version of relative wholeness and parthood.

18 Oosthout, A. (2022b: 36); cf. chapter 4, section 5, and section 4 below.

19 Proclus, *IT* III, 344.10–24 (2.253.26–254.10 Diehl) and 345.16–17 (2.254.26–27 Diehl). I have already discussed these passages in Oosthout, A. (2022b: 19–23) and so will not repeat a detailed analysis of them here. For Aristotle's materialist use of the term 'ὁμοιομερής,' see, e.g., his *History of Animals* I, 486a and *Parts of Animals* II, 646a ff.

20 Note, however, that Proclus' criticism of Porphyry is not entirely honest. Aristotle himself does not employ the term 'ὁμοιομερής' only to describe material parts which are utterly blended together. He also reflects on the fact that 'homogenous parts' considered more broadly cannot always carry the same predicates as their whole in his *Topics* V.5, 135a20–b6. This means that Porphry's borrowing of the Aristotelean term does not immediately indicate that the Intellect's parts blend together as Proclus seems to think; this important nuance was unfortunately lacking in my earlier discussion of Porphyry's use of the term in Oosthout, A. (2022b: 7), and I thank Jan Opsomer for pointing this out to me.

sets, as exemplified by the Neoplatonic stacking of genera and species on top of each other, it does not work in a metaphysical system built from intelligible principles with their own distinctive characters. One could, for example, describe the relations between the successive intelligible principles of Being, Life, and Intellect as successive part/whole- or universal/particular-relations, whereby the mereological status assigned to Life is solely dependent on whether one considers its participation in Being or its status as a causal principle of Intellect. Yet, as we saw previously, Proclus does not stick to a notion of wholeness which is universally applicable in this broad sense.

In contrast to, e.g., the threefold process of participation or the three modes of being (as a cause, as a distinctive character, or by participation), the notion of wholeness is tied to a specific triad in the procession of transcendent principles, namely the second intelligible triad.[21] This means that both the Neoplatonic principle of Wholeness itself and its subsequent manifestations as the three kinds of wholes are linked to specific substantial characters. In other words, every whole in the Proclean universe is specifically a *particular kind of thing*. In the case of Wholeness itself, this is the whole with the distinctive character of being eternal;[22] further manifestations of the three kinds of wholes also always revolve around a specific essence, such as the three kinds of wholeness of the cosmos or the three kinds of wholeness of the World Soul.[23]

From this perspective, we can see more clearly why Proclus responds unfavourably to Porphyry's positing of a homogenous Intellect. Whereas the notion that wholeness and parthood are merely relations allows for the creation of a scale of universality and particularity on which one can posit any given genus or species, it does not allow for the positing of clearly delineated essences within the Intellect. If each principle within the Intellect is a distinct thing, and Wholeness itself is one of those distinct principles, then the notion of the whole cannot be simply some abstract term which is applicable anywhere in the procession of being.

In the end, then, we have two approaches to understanding what a whole is in Proclus' writings: the whole as both an extensional and a relative term, i.e., as that which contains any given set of participants or functions as a genus to any given species, on the one hand, and the whole as an ontologically fixed term, i.e., as that which denotes the manifestation of a particular essence such as the three kinds of the whole World Soul or the three manifestations of the whole Intellect, on the other hand. These two approaches to the concept of

---

21 See chapter 4, section 2.
22 See section 2 below.
23 See chapter 4, section 3.

122 CHAPTER 5

wholeness are not easily unified.[24] For example, the heavily (and often unfairly) critical Nicholas of Methone points out a real problem of Proclus' mereology when he notes that the term 'whole' is linked to a specific intelligible principle, namely the second intelligible triad, but is then also used by Proclus to describe any given universal-particular relation in the intelligible realm, which would logically include also the relation between the second intelligible principle, Wholeness itself, and the first, Being itself. This results in the paradoxical notion, per Nicholas' criticism, 'that Being is "more whole" (ὁλικώτερον) than the Whole'.[25] The gap between the purely extensional whole and the ontologically determinate whole in Proclus' philosophy is further widened by the fact that Proclus adds an axiological layer to the latter kind of whole as well. We shall return to the issue of these two approaches to mereology at the end of the chapter, and again in the last chapter. First, however, we must discuss in detail Proclus' ontologically determinate definition of wholeness and in particular the axiological connotations that this definition contains.

5.2 The Distinctive Character of the Intelligible Whole

Proclus' ultimate ontological definition of what wholeness entails not only goes further than the extensional and relativistic notion which he applied to the relations between intelligible principles as one another's genera and species, but

---

24 It is difficult to see, for example, how Proclus could combine Porphyry's fluid distinction between a universal Intellect and any given particular intellect which remains homogenous with the former, on the one hand, with his own insistence on there being three strictly delineated manifestations of 'the whole intellect' per his schema of the threefold wholeness, on the other hand (the aforementioned proposition of the *Elements of Theology* in which Porphyry's argument is incorporated *also* refers explicitly to the three kinds of wholes). D'Hoine (2021: 190–191 and 204) provides a possible solution to this issue, to which I have suggested an alternative, though without being absolutely sure of the superiority of my suggestion over d'Hoine's, for which see Oosthout, A. (2022b: 26–27).

25 Nicholas of Methone, *Ref.* 73, 75.32–76.5: ταῦτα περὶ τοῦ ἐκ μερῶν ὅλου καλῶς λεγόμενα οὗτος κοινὰ καὶ περὶ τοῦ πρὸ τῶν μερῶν παραλαμβάνει καὶ δεικνύειν οὕτω νομίζει τὸ ὅλον ἕτερον εἶναι τοῦ ὄντος καὶ τὸ ὂν ὁλικώτερον τοῦ ὅλου καὶ οὕτω φανερῶς ἀτοπολογῶν ἐν τῷ λέγειν ὁλικώτερόν τι τοῦ ὅλου ἀναισθητεῖ. See Oosthout, A. (forthcoming), for a more extensive discussion of Nicholas' grievances regarding this issue. It should be noted that Proclus himself attempts to avoid this issue by describing Being as 'transcendent over the Whole' (Proclus, *ET* 73, 70.10–11: τὸ πρώτως ὂν ἐπέκεινα τῆς ὁλότητος ἐστιν) rather than 'more universal than the Whole' (ὁλικώτερον τοῦ ὅλου), though his more general description the relativity of universal and particular causes in *ET* 70 does not explicitly mention Being-itself as an exception from the sliding scale of universals and particulars.

DIVIDING THE INDIVISIBLE

also specifies the concept beyond the abstract model of three kinds of wholes which we discussed before. In the third, fourth, and fifth books of the *Platonic Theology*, Proclus weaves together his exegeses of various Platonic dialogues to create his (in)famous system of over a dozen intelligible hypostases which constitute the Plotinian Intellect. During the construction of this metaphysical skyscraper, Proclus returns multiple times to the concept of wholeness. Each time he does so, he applies the notion of the whole to a new hypostasis of the procession of beings. As a result, the concept of wholeness gains progressively more essential properties as Proclus' journey through the layers of the Intellect continues. To fully understand the Proclean whole, then, we must retrace the philosopher's steps and discuss the application of the notion of wholeness in the third, fourth, and fifth books of the *Platonic Theology*.[26]

We start our journey through the many hypostases of the Intellect in the third book of the *Platonic Theology*, at the level of the second intelligible triad or principle of Wholeness itself. Previously we discussed Proclus' use of passages and arguments from Plato's *Parmenides* and *Philebus* in order to fashion the second intelligible triad into the blueprint for his model of threefold wholeness.[27] To study the second intelligible triad in all its aspects, however, we must also discuss its role as the principle of Eternity. In this capacity, the triad is informed mainly by Proclus' exegesis of the *Timaeus*.

Particularly important to Proclus' envisioning of the intelligible triads is the passage in which Timaeus develops his previous distinction between true being and coming-to-be into a distinction between existing eternally and existing in time, whereby the former existence 'remains in one' (μένοντος αἰῶνος ἐν ἑνί), whereas the latter existence proceeds according to number.[28] Timaeus then reveals that the universal Paradigm is a true being and thus eternal, but that the cosmos is a generated thing and thus required the fashioning of time by the demiurge for it to exist in.[29] In Proclus' view, Timaeus here reveals the existence of three intelligible principles, namely the universal Paradigm, the principle of the eternity in which the Paradigm exists, Eternity itself, and 'the one' in which

---

26   The discussion of the third book of the *Platonic Theology* in this chapter of the monograph will be rather more concise than those of the fourth and fifth books, since in an earlier paper I have already discussed Proclus' axiological assessment of the second and third intelligible triads, specifically their roles in defining the concept of perfection; see Oosthout, A. (2023a). In this book, I shall only summarily discuss the specific insights from that earlier paper which are relevant to the current inquiry.

27   See chapter 4, section 3.

28   Plato, *Tim.* 37d5–7. The earlier distinction can be found in *Tim.* 27d5–29d3.

29   Cf. Oosthout, A. (2023b).

Eternity itself is said to remain.[30] Combining these three concepts with the aforementioned three intelligible triads distilled from the *Parmenides* and the *Philebus*, Proclus defines the first intelligible triad as the One Being, the second intelligible triad as both Eternity and Wholeness itself and the third intelligible triad as both the Universal Paradigm and Multiplicity-itself.[31]

5.2.1 *The Eternal Whole*

The equation of the *Timaeus*-derived Eternity with the *Parmenides*-derived Whole-itself has two important (and connected) consequences for Proclus' definition of what it means for a thing to be whole. The first is the fact that wholeness comes to be intrinsically associated with eternity, and vice versa.[32] In the *Elements of Theology*, for example, we find the argument that truly eternal things are eternal because they are the whole of themselves 'at once' (ἅμα ὅλον).[33] Taken on its own, this argument does not define all wholes as whole-at-once, and so does not exclude the possibility of a thing being whole in a temporal sense, i.e., insofar as it changes over time in regard to its parts while remaining the same in its essence.[34] Such a temporal type of wholeness would be comparable to the theory of four-dimensionalism as proposed by modern mereological scholars. Proponents of this theory of four-dimensionalism or perdurantism suggest that any being has temporal parts as well as spatial ones in order to account for change over time. This stands in contrast to proponents of three-dimensionalism or endurantism, who claim that a compound of parts exists in its entirety *at a specific moment in time*.[35] However, Proclus does not restrict himself to either approach: he notes in the same proposition of the *Elements of Theology* that Eternity is the principle of *all* wholes.[36]

Similarly, Proclus establishes in the twenty-seventh chapter of book three of the *Platonic Theology* that Eternity and Wholeness are interchangeable as principles. Just as every eternal being is whole because it possesses all of itself at once, so is the whole eternal because it never gives up 'either its essence or

---

30 For a more detailed analysis of Proclus' arguments for positing these three separate principles, see Opsomer (2000b).

31 Cf. chapter 4, section 2 above. For a schematic overview of these triads, see Oosthout, A. (2023a: 120).

32 Oosthout, A. (2023a: 120–123).

33 Proclus, *ET* 52, 50.15–20; cf. Opsomer (2000b: 363 n. 50).

34 Cf. Oosthout, A. (2023a: 121).

35 Koslicki (2008) discusses both sides of the debate extensively. Sider (1997) also provides a comprehensive overview, albeit with a clear preference for the theory of four-dimensionalism.

36 Proclus, *ET* 52, 50.21; Oosthout, A. (2023a: 121).

DIVIDING THE INDIVISIBLE

its proper completeness' (οὐδὲν γὰρ τῶν ὅλων ἢ τὴν οὐσίαν ἢ τὴν τελειότητα τὴν οἰκείαν ἀφίησιν). Proclus raises the sensible cosmos with its heavenly spheres and four elements from the *Timaeus* as an example of a true whole since it is everlasting (ἀίδιος) and thus never loses its proper nature and essential constituents. In contrast, that which does not partake of eternity is not a whole but a 'divided being' or 'partial being' (μερικόν), which exists for a finite amount of time and whose primary characteristic is its susceptibility to decay and corruption.[37]

The second consequence of equation Eternity with Wholeness itself is that the whole becomes an axiologically loaded concept in Proclus' metaphysics. The aforementioned distinction between eternal wholes and finitely existing partial beings in book three of the *Platonic Theology* links back to an important passage in the first book of that same work. More specifically, when Proclus discusses the nature of evil in the eighteenth chapter of book one, he explains its appearance in the sensible world through a distinction between two types of participants in the goodness bestowed upon all things by the One Good. The first type of participant is able to keep its participation in the good 'pure' (τὰ μὲν ἀκήρατον φυλάττει τὴν μέθεξιν), whereas the second type is unable to preserve the goodness it receives stably (μονίμως) and keep it good forever (ἀεὶ ὡσαύτως), since it is 'partial' (μερικόν) and material (ἔνυλον). This changeable nature causes the latter type of participant to be susceptible to evil.[38]

The two types of participants can be linked to the two manifestations of participated goodness Proclus distils from Plato's *Republic*: the intelligible Form of the Good as present in intelligible principles, and 'our good' (τὸ ἀγαθὸν ἡμῶν), i.e., the good as present among sensible beings.[39] Furthermore, Proclus' designation of the fallible participants of the good as 'partial things' (μερικά) in this same passage shows that the distinction between stable intelligible participants of the good and changeable material participants of the good is the same as the distinction between eternal wholes and temporal 'divided beings'. The axiological connotation, then, which is attached to the term 'whole' in Proclus' metaphysics is that of something which possesses its proper goodness in a stable manner; in contrast, the term 'partial' gains the added connotation of being something which is not stably good.[40]

---

37   Proclus, *TP* III. 27, 94.13–24; Oosthout, A. (*ibidem*).

38   Proclus, *TP* I.18, 83.21–84.9.

39   Oosthout and Van Riel (2023: 379–381); cf. Proclus, *IRP* I, 269.14–270.12.

40   Oosthout, A. (2023a: 123–125). Within the procession of intelligible principles, Eternity constitutes the first hypostasis where the concepts of stability and changeability apply. The One Being is nothing but being, and as such it cannot also have the character of being stable; Proclus, *TP* III.16, 56.10–16.

Aside from these two main consequences for our understanding of the Proclean whole, the concept of Eternity has other distinctive characteristics which colour the term 'whole' in Proclus' philosophy. First, Eternity is repeatedly characterised as the principle of permanence (διαμονή) in Proclus' *Timaeus*-commentary, most notably in the long (over thirty pages!) discussion of *Tim.* 37d3–7.[41] However, this permanence is not one of a temporal kind.[42] Proclus' statement that no proper whole ever relinquishes its natural state of completeness implies that he envisions a whole as something timeless. In this regard, he would certainly object to the suggestion of modern four-dimensionalists that a whole is a changeable entity whose parts vary over time. Yet to group him with the opposing faction of the three-dimensionalists would be equally rash. Although modern three-dimensionalism supposes that an object is always 'wholly present', the theory does not necessarily provide an escape from the boundaries of temporal existence.[43] What is unique about Proclean wholes is specifically their timelessness. Recall that Proclus' mereology presumes that every form of wholeness begins as a transcendently existing unity, a whole *simpliciter* (ἁπλῶς ὅλον). In its simplicity, such a whole cannot exist in time, since that would require its division across the past and the future.[44] Instead, beings which are simply whole know only an eternal present.

Eternity's role as the principle of immortality likewise has interesting consequences for Proclean mereology. As noted by Opsomer, Proclus uses citations from Aristotle's *De Caelo* and from Plato's *Phaedo* in order to support his claim that 'the intelligible Life and the god who primarily holds this life together will possess immortality and is the source of the whole of everlastingness; this is

---

41   Proclus, *IT* IV, 10.10–44.9 (3.8.12–34.13 Diehl). See, e.g., *loc. cit.* 20.19–21 (15.31–16.1 Diehl): καὶ τὸ μὲν ἓν ὂν τοῦ εἶναι μόνως αἴτιον πᾶσι τοῖς ὁπωσοῦν ⟨οὖσιν⟩ εἴτε ὄντως εἴτε οὐκ ὄντως, ὁ δὲ αἰὼν τῆς ἐν τῷ εἶναι διαμονῆς.

42   As I pointed out in my previous paper, the property of being everlasting (ἀΐδιος), which Proclus ascribes to the sensible cosmos, is not quite equal to the status of being eternal (αἰώνιος), since the former denotes existence for all time whereas the latter denotes simply *being* without any reference to time; see Oosthout, A. (2023a: 122 n. 34), and cf. *IT* II, 49.21–50.8 (1.239.2–13 Diehl), 235.3–9 (1.366.20–27 Diehl), and Kutash (2009: 45–46).

43   Sider (1997: 11–12). As Sider points out, three-dimensionalism defines the composite as being wholly present 'at time t'. The latter predicate obviously cannot be applied to Proclus' atemporal eternity. For another discussion of three-dimensionalism, see Thomson (1983).

44   The existence of temporal beings which are also whole, such as the beings within the sensible cosmos, is ensured by the other two kinds of wholeness, the whole composed of parts and the whole in the parts. These types of wholes reveal actual multiplicity and division within themselves, whereas the whole before the parts only prefigures such things.

DIVIDING THE INDIVISIBLE

Eternity.'[45] In other words, within the realm of the intelligible gods, Eternity takes up the position of life below being (i.e., obviously, the One Being) and above intellect (i.e., the universal Paradigm from the *Timaeus*).[46] If Eternity is equal to intelligible Life, then every eternal being must also be a living being. Since these beings are timeless, they are by necessity immortal. This equation of eternity with immortality also concurs with Proclus' rule, since the two subsequent incorporeal genera, intellect, and soul, are logically posterior to life.

However, the fact that Proclus equates wholeness with eternity implies that all true wholes must also be immortal living beings. The passage in which Proclus contrasts the eternal whole to the individual being (μερικόν) already implied as much. Mortal creatures or lifeless things, such as rocks, are not true wholes. It is an implication that at first glance constitutes an even more restrictive alternative to Van Inwagen's suggestion that only living beings are wholes while all other things are mere collections of matter. Yet Proclus' stance on the (lack of) wholeness of mortal creatures is more nuanced than it appears here, as we shall see later.[47] Furthermore, Proclus makes a subtle distinction within the second intelligible triad. Damascius tells us that, according to Proclus, 'eternity transcends life; for it is the father of the second triad [i.e., its one-aspect], whereas life is its fatherly intellect [i.e., its being-aspect], just as the wholeness is its power.'[48] According to the rule of Proclus, then, there exist things in the sensible realm which are beyond the causal reach of life, but which nevertheless participate in wholeness because of their perpetuity.[49]

---

45 Proclus, *TP* III.16, 56.3–6: Ἡ τοίνυν ζωὴ ἡ νοητὴ καὶ ὁ θεὸς ὁ τῆς ζωῆς ταύτης συνεκτικὸς πρώτως ἕξει τὸ ἀθάνατον καὶ ἔστι πηγὴ τῆς ὅλης ἀιδιότητος· τοῦτο δέ ἐστιν ὁ αἰών. Opsomer (2000b: 365–366); cf. *De Caelo* 279a22–28 and *Phaedo* 106d2–9. Proclus specifically cites Aristotle's application of the terms 'ἀθάνατος' and 'θεῖος' to the concept of eternity in *TP* III.16, 55.20–22. Socrates' statement in the *Phaedo* that the Form of Life is an immortal being is cited in *TP* III.16, 56.1–3.

46 For Proclus' distinction between being, life, and intellect, see his *ET* 103; cf. d'Hoine (2016).

47 We discuss the consequences Proclus' distinction between wholes and μερικά has for mortal creatures in more detail when we turn our attention to the sensible cosmos, for which see chapter 6, section 3.

48 Damascius, *IP* I, 24.23–25.2: ἐπέκεινα τῆς ζωῆς ὁ αἰών· αὐτὸς μὲν γὰρ ὁ πατὴρ τῆς δευτέρας τριάδος, ἡ δὲ ζωὴ ὁ πατρικὸς νοῦς, ὥσπερ δύναμις ⟨ἡ⟩ ὁλότης—cf. Proclus, *ET* 105, 94.17–20. Keep in mind that the distinction between being and life in this case refers to the *internal* distinction between the ἕν-, δύναμις-, and ὄν-aspects of the second intelligible triad. It does not imply that Eternity is the same as the One Being. For Damascius' own version of the hierarchy between these three concepts, see his *IP* I, 34.18–37.20.

49 Damascius (*IP* I, 24.21–22) raises the example of unqualified body, which is whole despite its lifelessness.

128

5.2.2 *The Perfect Composite*

Having fully delineated the distinctive characteristics of the Proclean whole, we move on to the first principle which participates in Wholeness itself: the third intelligible triad, which is both the *Parmenides*-derived intelligible Multiplicity and the *Timaeus*-derived universal Paradigm. In combining these two notions, Proclus refers to the suggestion made by Plato's Timaeus that the Paradigm used by the Demiurge contained four Forms on which the godly craftsman based the four kinds of living beings: the gods of the heavens, the winged creatures of the skies, the aquatic inhabitants of the oceans and rivers, and the creatures which walk the earth. The Paradigm prefigures these four kinds of living beings, and thus possesses an internal manifold of four.[50]

In his commentary on this *Timaeus*-passage, Proclus develops this tetrad in more detail. After recounting the three intelligible triads,[51] Proclus emphasises that the first is a monad, the second is a dyad of one and being, and the third is a tetrad. However, the universal Paradigm is not just a tetrad. Since it proceeds from and reverts upon the triads above it, it also exists monadically and dyadically. The name 'Living Being itself', Proclus explains, refers to its status as the transcendent monad of all living beings, whether they be intellective, life-giving (ζωτικά, i.e., souls), or corporeal living beings. At the same time, it encompasses within itself manifestations of the first henads, these manifestations being the two genders, masculine and feminine, which appear in some form or another throughout the various levels of reality but are 'started' by the first henads 'in their one containment of the living being' (δεῖ προάρχειν αὐτῶν τὰς πρώτας ἑνάδας ἐν τῇ μιᾷ τοῦ ζῴου περιοχῇ). From these two genders, the Paradigm has established within itself the four kinds of living beings, and in this manner, it is tetradic as well.[52]

---

50 Plato, *Tim.* 39e7–40a2; Oosthout, A. (2023a: 125–127)—as I explain in more detail in that paper, the suggestion from the *Parmenides* that there is an infinite manifold within the one being is reworked by Proclus into an infinity of productive power within the one being (see Proclus, *TP* III.26, 92.15–21).

51 Proclus, *IT* IV, 136.13–20 (3.105.20–28 Diehl). In contrast to what I suggest here, Baltzly (2013: 190 n. 439) proposes that 'the subjects in this three-step process are never specified … it seems best to me to treat them as phases or moments in a continuous process of emanation. We could, of course, treat them as separate objects or levels of being, but note the use of adverbs in what follows. This suggests we should think of these stages of phases in terms of activities or modes.' I respectfully disagree with this suggestion, since Proclus clearly refers to the τῶν θεῶν νοητῆς οὐσίας and explicitly mentions the characteristics of the intelligible triads, such as the fact that the first being is a father while the third is both maker and father (on the fathers and makers, see chapter 3, section 3).

52 Proclus, *IT* IV, 137.3–17 (3.106.4–19 Diehl).

DIVIDING THE INDIVISIBLE

Like any other metaphysical principle, the Paradigm inherits essential characteristics from its superiors, which are in this case the unity of an unparticipated principle, granting it the status of the Living Being itself, and the duality of the two genders derived from the Limit and the Unlimited.[53] However, it also manifests its own distinctive character, which it subsequently transmits across the lower orders.[54] Taken together, Proclus' readings of the *Timaeus* and the *Parmenides* suggest that the distinctive character of the Paradigm is being a fourfold multiplicity by virtue of the fact that it contains the four Forms of living beings.

However, the Paradigm does not contain merely four Forms out of the myriad of Forms in the Platonic universe. As Proclus explains in his *Timaeus*-commentary, the number of Forms contained by any given intelligible principle is conversely linked to the universality of those Forms: the more universal Forms are lesser in number than the more specific ones. Thus, the four kinds of living beings within the Paradigm manifest again in more pluralised forms in lower levels of reality.[55] Compared to the cosmos, for example, the Paradigm is *one* whole before the parts.[56]

As a result, the Paradigm encompasses in a transcendent manner all the Forms of living beings which will manifest themselves in a partial manner (μερικῶς) as particular intellects within the intellective realm.[57] This shows that the wholeness of such metaphysical principles is to an extent relative, despite Proclus' apprehension on this matter. Whereas the universal Paradigm is a transcendent unity *qua* intelligible Intellect compared to particular intellects, or *qua* Living Being itself compared to the individual kinds of living beings, it is at the same time a multiplicity in comparison to the more unified Eternity and One Being because of its tetradic nature. If we take the liberty of applying Proclus' own mereological terms in contexts where he does not do so himself, we might claim that the Paradigm is at once a whole *before* the parts when compared to the realms below it and a whole *composed* of parts when compared to the second intelligible triad before it.

---

53   The first henads after the One itself are Limit and the Unlimited, for which see, e.g., Van Riel (2001: 427–428). Since the two genders Proclus mentions here derive from the first henads, it makes sense to presume that, in Proclus' eyes, they are linked to the concepts from Plato's *Philebus*.

54   For the distinction between inherited ἰδιότητες and a principle's own unique ἰδιότης, see chapter 3, section 2.

55   Proclus, *IT* IV, 137.27–138.14 (3.106.28–10 Diehl); Oosthout, A. (2023a: 126–127).

56   See chapter 4, section 3, and especially the citation from Proclus, *IT* II, 326.10–17 there.

57   Cf. the citation from Porphyry's *Sentences* in section 1 above.

In fact, Proclus points out in book three of the *Platonic Theology* that the Paradigm contains the first true internal multiplicity, since the One Being transcends any form of divisibility and the dyadic Eternity is 'not yet a multitude of beings' (πλῆθος δὲ οὔπω τῶν ὄντων ἐστίν). This also explains, Proclus tells us, why it is the universal Paradigm which is called 'all-complete' or 'wholly perfect' (παντελές) in Plato's *Timaeus*,[58] since only a multiplicity can be complete insofar as it contains all of its essential constituents (συμπληρωτικά).[59] Through these arguments, Proclus bestows an axiological property upon the Paradigm as well: the property of being perfect or complete, insofar as it is not missing any of its essential parts.[60] In this respect, the Paradigm is truly the intelligible Totality (τὸ πᾶν) on which the sensible totality is based.[61]

This notion of the totality as that which is complete can be traced back not only to Plato's *Timaeus*, but also to other dialogues of his. A notable example is the *Theaetetus*, from which we previously discussed a vital passage. There Socrates defined the totality as that from which nothing is missing, and, despite Theaetetus' hesitations, he argued that this same property belonged to the whole as well. However, the *Theaetetus* only suggested that perhaps the whole should not simply be equated with the sum total of its parts (as indicated by Theaetetus' struggle against Socrates' position, and the overall aporetic end of the discussion).[62] In contrast, Proclus takes a much more assured stance in the debate: for him the whole (ὅλον) is undoubtedly something over and beyond the totality (πᾶν) of the parts, and the fact that this stance might be a reaction on the Neoplatonic thinker's part to the discussion from the *Theaetetus* has not gone unnoticed.[63] The distinction between whole and totality is reflected in their placements in the intelligible realm: the first Whole occupies the second rank among the three intelligible principles, whereas the first Totality occupies the third.[64]

---

58   See Plato, *Tim.* 31a4–b3 *et al.*

59   Proclus, *TP* III.15, 53.24–54.9; for the term 'συμπληρωτικόν,' see Proclus, *IP* VI, 1112.22–1113.4, and cf. *ET* 67, 64.6–7, Kobusch (2000: 316–317), Baltzly (2008: 408), and d'Hoine (2021: 212).

60   Oosthout, A. (2023a: 127–131).

61   Cf. Plato, *Tim.* 28b.

62   See chapter 2, section 4.1.

63   Klitenic Wear (2017: 222). Note that Proclus himself does not cite the *Theaetetus* as a source of inspiration for his three kinds of wholes, but rather the *Statesman* and the *Timaeus* (for which see Proclus, *TP* III.25, 87.26–88.6, cited in chapter 4, section 2). Nevertheless, Klitenic Wear's suggestion that Proclus was (at least partially) inspired by this passage seems logical. For a discussion of Proclus' interpretation of the distinction between ὅλον and πᾶν in more general terms, see Charles-Saget (1982: 84–88) and Kobusch (2000: 318–319).

64   Cf. Butler (2010: 141–142 and 2012: 138) and Oosthout, A. (2023a: 136).

DIVIDING THE INDIVISIBLE   131

Within the intelligible hypostasis, then, the notion of wholeness manifests in two ways. In its most primal form, the whole is that which possesses all of itself at once and in a stable manner. Its unchanging unity ensures that the goodness bestowed upon it by the ultimate Good is never tarnished, and in this way, it is whole in an axiological sense. This stable goodness then evolves into an actual compound which retains within itself all of its essential constituents. The goodness of this composite whole is represented by its completeness. Just as the primal Compound manifests a lesser form of wholeness compared to the primal Whole, so the primal Whole and the primal Compound each manifest the good in their own way: the first as being a transcendent and stable unity, the second as being a manifold which encompasses all the parts that it should encompass.[65] Thus, in the third book of the *Platonic Theology*, wholeness and perfection are not coordinate with one another (as one might erroneously infer from Baltzly's remark that they are 'exactly parallel in structure'); instead, perfection is subordinate to wholeness, insofar as it manifests not in the transcendent whole but only in the composite whole.[66]

5.3   Unfolding the Heaven

Although I warned against reading Baltzly's equation of wholeness with perfection into the third book of the *Platonic Theology*, it must be noted that Baltzly himself refers to a passage in Proclus' *fourth* book, instead of the previously discussed third one.[67] As such, we must also investigate whether Proclus' concepts of wholeness and perfection do actually coalesce later on in the procession of beings, after their separate introduction among the intelligible triads. The next stop in our journey through Proclus' theological mereology is the so-called intelligible-intellective realm. To recap, the first triads in the procession of beings within the incorporeal intellect were the One Being, Eternity or Wholeness itself, and the universal Paradigm or the Living Being itself. Together, these constituted the intelligible (νοητόν) hypostasis. However, Proclus' incorporeal intellect has more than one aspect. In fact, Proclus distinguishes within the incorporeal and self-reverting intellect three aspects: the

---

65   As I noted in Oosthout, A. (2023a: 131–137), perfection is therefore not equal to the ultimate goodness according to Proclus, but a more specific form of it. This also means that the ultimate Wholeness of Eternity is 'beyond perfection' (ὑπερτέλειος). Proclus' arguments for this claim are discussed in detail in that paper as well, and so need not be restated here.

66   Baltzly (2008: 408 n. 22); cf. Oosthout, A. (2023a: 136).

67   The specific reference given by Baltzly (2008: 408 n. 22) is '*Theol. Plat.* iv 74.28–75.20'.

object of thought, the thinking principle, and the act of thinking itself. Within the intellect as a whole, these three aspects coincide because intellect knows *itself* and is thus its own object of thought, which means that it is also aware of its own activity.[68] Yet, as we have seen, the incorporeality of intellect does not stop Proclus from distinguishing aspects or parts within it. Just as each triad in the procession of beings encompasses a transcendent henad, a being which participates in that henad, and a power between the two which links them, so does the intellect in its entirety contain a transcendent intelligible aspect (νοητόν), an intellective aspect (νοερόν) which contemplates the intelligible, and an intermediate aspect which links the two. Proclus coins this intermediate level of intellect 'intelligible-intellective' (νοητὸν καὶ νοερόν), because the triads within it are illuminated by the intelligible ones and create the intellective ones at the same time.[69]

Proclus discusses this intelligible-intellective realm in detail in the fourth book of his *Platonic Theology*. Whereas the third book, in which Proclus enumerated the intelligible triads, was built in large part on his exegesis of Plato's *Parmenides, Timaeus,* and *Philebus,* the main source of inspiration of the fourth book is Plato's *Phaedrus*. Indeed, the overwhelming majority of chapters in this book (four through twenty-six!) focus on Plato's description of the journey of the gods through heaven in lines 246d6 through 247e6 of the *Phaedrus,* while the remaining chapters (twenty-seven through thirty-nine) return to the second hypothesis on the one in Plato's *Parmenides,* albeit only in a condensed manner.[70]

In the *Phaedrus,* Socrates discusses the journey of the gods through heaven just after he uses his famous metaphor of the charioteer and the pair of horses to describe the human soul. In contrast to the human soul, which is weighed down by the unruly horse of its pair, the divine charioteers, led by Zeus himself, easily guide their chariots to the top of the celestial arch (ἄκραν ἐπὶ τὴν

---

68 Proclus, *ET* 168, 146.18–23.

69 Proclus, *TP* IV.1, 8.27–9.9. Butler (2010: 155 and 2012: 132) rightly emphasises the fact that the intelligible-intellective realm should not be thought of merely as connective tissue in between the intelligible and intellective realms. Proclus treats the intelligible-intellective realm as a level of reality in its own right, with its own intelligible-intellective triads and its own distinctive characteristics.

70 Saffrey and Westerink (1981: 173 n. 4): 'les chapitres 27 à 39 n'offrent qu'un aperçu très condensé et très incomplet du commentaire de Proclus sur cette partie du *Parménide,* si l'on en juge par l'exposé et la critique que Damascius en a donnés dans son propre commentaire.' For an overview of Damascius' testimony and criticism of Proclus' full thoughts on the second hypothesis of the *Parmenides,* see Saffrey and Westerink (1981: xlvi–lxiii).

DIVIDING THE INDIVISIBLE 133

ὑπουράνιον ἀψῖδα πορεύονται).[71] There they are able to peer into the realms *above* heaven (ὁ ὑπερουράνιος τόπος), where true being (οὐσία ὄντως οὖσα) is revealed to them, after which they complete their circular journey through the heavens by returning to their starting point.[72]

In the *Parmenides*, the titular philosopher continues his hypothesis that the one exists (ἓν εἰ ἔστιν).[73] Having established that an existent one must be a whole with one and being as its parts and must thus have an internal multiplicity, Parmenides continues by suggesting that, since the one- and being-parts of the one being are distinct from one another, they can be conceived of either individually or as a pair and, hence, as a *dyad*. The numbers two (one and being taken together) and one (the one or being taken individually) together make three, and so on, leading to the creation of number within the one being.[74] Furthermore, Parmenides argues that being is distributed to all things (since all things exist), which means that it is scattered across all these beings into parts great and small.[75] Since the one is equal to being, it too is scattered across all beings into infinite parts. Thirdly, since the one being is now a whole composed of parts, it must have a beginning, middle, and end, which means that it has a determinable shape.[76]

Just as he does in the third book of his *Platonic Theology*, Proclus distinguishes three intelligible-intellective triads which correspond to various aspects of the mythology from the *Phaedrus* and to the three new dialectical steps in Parmenides' hypothesis. First, Proclus emphasises that the heaven described in Plato's *Phaedrus* is not the sensible heaven of the cosmos (*TP* IV.5), since among other things this would mean that Plato's gods contemplate earthly things rather than intelligible ones.[77] Instead, the myth of the *Phaedrus* describes an *intelligible* heaven (νοητὸς οὐρανός), according to Proclus.[78] It is important to keep

---

71   Plato, *Phaedr.* 247a8–b2.

72   Plato, *Phaedr.* 247c3–d1.

73   Plato, *Parm.* 142b1–155e3.

74   Plato, *Parm.* 143d1–7. For the preceding arguments, see chapter 4, section 2.

75   Plato, *Parm.* 144b1–c1. As before, see Harte (2002a: 73–100) for an analysis of the implications of this argument for Plato's mereology.

76   Plato, *Parm.* 144d5–145b5.

77   Proclus, *TP* IV.5, 20.5–14.

78   Note that the adjective νοητός is employed here as an opposition to αἰσθητός, not as a signifier of the intelligible aspect of intellect specifically. This association between the myth of the *Phaedrus* and the intelligible realm in general can be traced back to Plotinus, for which see Saffrey and Westerink (1981: xviii-xxv); see also Saffrey and Westerink (*ibidem*: xxix–xlv) for a more detailed overview of Syrianus' and Proclus' own engagement with the *Phaedrus*. For another discussion of Proclus' approach to the dialogue, see Sheppard (2000).

134   CHAPTER 5

in mind that, as Butler points out, the heaven of the *Phaedrus* 'is for Proclus not a discrete place, but the connecting, synthesizing continuum of intelligibility'.[79] Thus, even though Proclus distils three celestial 'regions' from the *Phaedrus*, these should not be understood as actual locations in the sky.

The first celestial 'region' Proclus distinguishes is the realm above heaven (ὑπερουράνιος), also called Adrastia, in which the gods are able to see true being. The triad situated here is most closely linked to the intelligible triads (*TP* IV.11), and represents participated being in contrast to the unparticipated being of the intelligible One Being (*TP* IV.10). It spawns three virtues: science, temperance, and justice (ἐπιστήμη, σωφροσύνη, and δικαιοσύνη; *TP* IV.14), and is also the origin of number, as described in the *Parmenides* (*TP* IV.28–34).[80] The second celestial level is the heavenly arch itself (ἡ ἐντὸς οὐρανοῦ περιωπή), a circular hypostasis that constitutes the connective order (συνεκτικὴ τάξις) and is the cause of continuity and concord (*TP* IV.19).[81] It also incorporates the one *qua* whole composed of parts as described in the *Parmenides*. The final level is an interesting one. Proclus takes Plato's remark at *Phaedrus* 247a8–b2, i.e., that the gods reach the 'ἄκραν ἐπὶ τὴν ὑπουράνιον ἁψῖδα', quite literally and postulates the existence of a *sub*celestial triad below the heavenly circumference, which equates to the principle of shape in the *Parmenides*.[82] Interestingly, this subcelestial hypostasis possesses a *perfective* character (τελεσιουργὸς ἰδιότης; *TP* IV.24).

As he did for the intelligible hypostasis, Proclus uses his exegesis of the Platonic dialogues to structure the intelligible-intellective realm: the first intelligible-intellective triad is the supra-heavenly realm of being from the *Phaedrus* as well as the intelligible Number derived from the *Parmenides*; the second intelligible-intellective triad is both the heavenly arch from the *Phaedrus* and the whole divided into scattered one- and being-parts; the third intelligible-intellective

---

79   Butler (2010: 147).
80   For further analysis both of the role of number in this triad and of the three virtues, see Butler (2010: 147–154).
81   A fitting role for the hypostasis that stands at the very centre of Proclean intellect.
82   Within the context of the *Phaedrus* itself, it makes more sense to interpret 'ἄκραν ἐπὶ τὴν ὑπουράνιον ἁψῖδα' as expressing the idea that the gods reach the highest point of the celestial *ceiling*. Proclus himself seems to have been aware of the fact that the subcelestial realm could easily be considered a Neoplatonic invention, even if the Neoplatonic thinkers themselves believed it to be a veritable part of Plato's doctrine; see Proclus, *TP* IV.23, 68.23–69.8; cf. Oosthout, A. (2023b). As Saffrey and Westerink (1981: xxv) have noted, there are indeed no signs of a proper (Neo)platonic commentary on the *Phaedrus* until Iamblichus. However, since our current objective is to discuss Proclus' reading of the *Phaedrus* specifically, the veracity of his exegesis is not an issue that needs to concern us within the confines of this inquiry.

triad is the subcelestial realm Proclus takes to be indicated in the *Phaedrus* and the intelligible Shape he takes from the *Parmenides*.[83]

Each intelligible-intellective triad mirrors the corresponding intelligible triad. More specifically, Proclus notes in the twenty-seventh chapter of book four that the *Parmenides*-derived distinctive characters of the intelligible-intellective triads each mirror the distinctive character of the corresponding intelligible triad: Number is derived from the One Being; the intelligible-itellective whole is derived from the intelligible whole; from the intelligible Multiplicity, the third intelligible-intellective triad inherits its perfection (τὸ τέλειον).[84]

Elsewhere, Proclus is even more explicit. Each intelligible-intellective triad unfolds (ἐστιν ἀνέλιξις) the multiplicity that was either minimally present or only implicit in its corresponding intelligible triad. The unity of the One Being is unfolded into the 'uniting triad' (συναγωγὸς τριάς). The continuity (συνοχή) of Eternity is unfolded into the aforementioned connective order (συνεκτικὴ τάξις). Lastly, the wholly perfect nature of the Paradigm is unfolded into the 'perfecting' (τελεσιουργός) triad.[85]

Previously, Proclus described the multiplicity of the intelligible triads relative to one another by designating the One Being a monad, Eternity a dyad, and the Paradigm a tetrad. In a similar vein, each intelligible-intellective hypostasis is triadic when compared to the monadic nature of the intelligible hypostases. When discussing these triads, Proclus occasionally refers to each as a set of three gods.[86] Thus, although these triads constitute their own hypostases independently from the intelligible ones, they simultaneously develop the distinctive characters of those triads. It is this aspect of the intelligible-intellective triads that is relevant to our current enquiry: how are the concepts of wholeness and perfection, which originated from Eternity and the Paradigm, developed in this next stage of Proclean causality?

5.4 The Evolution of Whole into Part

Proclus once again situates the concept of wholeness in the second triad. One might wonder what distinguishes the intelligible-intellective whole from the intelligible whole. In contrasting the intelligible triads to the intelligible-intellective ones, Proclus assigns to both triads the exact same signifier, 'τὸ ὅλον',

---

83   Cf. the schematic overview in d'Hoine and Martijn (2016: 325).
84   Proclus, *TP* IV.27, 78.18–79.6.
85   Proclus, *TP* IV.25, 76.3–8.
86   Cf. Proclus, *TP* IV.1, 9.10–21.

whereas the first and third intelligible-intellective triads are made distinct from their intelligible counterparts (number versus one being and perfection versus multiplicity).[87] Nevertheless, the intelligible-intellective wholeness is not equal to the primal intelligible Wholeness of Eternity. In one of the chapters which resumes his exegesis of the *Parmenides*, Proclus writes that the second intelligible-intellective triad is whole in a different sense from the second intelligible triad. The intelligible triad, he notes, is whole in the sense that it unifies its two parts, i.e., the one- and being-aspects of the triad. The intelligible-intellective triad, in contrast, is whole in the sense that it is composed out of 'unitary parts' (τῶν μερῶν τῶν ἑνιαίων) and 'the many beings' (τῶν πολλῶν ὄντων). The intelligible wholeness is thus prior with respect to its unity (καθ' ἕνωσιν προηγουμένη).[88]

As was noted previously, Proclus considers each new proposition about Plato's one being in the *Parmenides* to be a *new* one being and thus a new hypostasis.[89] Since Plato's Parmenides argues for the wholeness of the one being at two different instances, Proclus' metaphysical system must include two separate hypostases which are characterised by wholeness. As a result, Proclus distinguishes between two one-beings-as-wholes based on these two distinct arguments presented by Parmenides, the first of which defines the one being as a whole because of the internal distinction between one and being,[90] and the second of which argues that both the one and being are scattered across the many beings which participate in them.[91] Since Proclus' intelligible wholeness is based on the former argument, its wholeness comprises its two internal parts: one and being. The intelligible-intellective wholeness, on the other hand, is linked to a one being which has been scattered across the many participating unities and beings, and as such its one is composed of one-parts (τῶν μερῶν τῶν ἑνιαίων) and its being is composed of all beings (τῶν πολλῶν ὄντων). As Steel notes, 'au degré intelligible-intellectif, il faut distinguer la totalité de l'un et celle de l'être.'[92] In this way, the heavenly arch or second intelligible-intellective triad unfolds the unitary wholeness of Eternity or the second intelligible triad into a whole composed of many parts.[93]

---

87   Proclus, *TP* IV.27, 78.18–79.6 (as discussed in the antepenultimate paragraph of the previous section).

88   Proclus, *TP* IV.27, 79.8–15.

89   See chapter 4, section 2; cf. Ficino, *IP* XCV.2, 244.13–18.

90   Plato, *Parm.* 142c7–143a3.

91   Plato, *Parm.* 144b1–e7.

92   Steel (2000: 390).

93   The intelligible-intellective whole is inferior to the intelligible principle of Number, whereas the intelligible whole is superior to it. As Steel (2000: 389) states, 'en effet, cette

DIVIDING THE INDIVISIBLE

This implies that Eternity and the heavenly arch can be categorised as a whole before the parts and a whole composed of parts, respectively. Although Proclus does not explicitly classify both triads as such, he does reveal that the heavenly arch constitutes the hypostasis where the contrast between whole and part materialises. In the thirty-fifth chapter of the fourth book, he develops his exegesis of Parmenides' argument of the divided one being further. After comparing the heavenly arch to the realm above heaven, which equates to the one being-as-number in the *Parmenides*, Proclus writes:

> Ὥστε ἐκεῖ μὲν ἐξῄρητο τῶν πολλῶν ἡ ἑνάς, ἐνταῦθα δὲ συντάττεται τῷ πλήθει. Διὸ καὶ ἡ πρώτη σύνταξις ἀπογεννᾷ τὸ ὅλον ὁμοῦ τοῖς μέρεσιν, ἡ δὲ τοῦ ὅλου καὶ τῶν μερῶν ὑπόστασις παράγει τὸ πεπερασμένον ἅμα καὶ ἄπειρον. Ἑξῆς γάρ ἐστιν ἀλλήλοις τὸ ἕν, τὸ ὅλον, τὸ πεπερασμένον, καὶ τὰ τούτοις οἷον ἀντίστοιχα, τὰ πολλά, τὰ μέρη, τὰ ἄπειρα. Καὶ ἔστι τὸ μὲν ἓν αὐτὸ ἡ ἀρχὴ τῶν λοιπῶν, τὸ δὲ ὅλον ἤδη σχέσιν ἔχει πρὸς τὰ μέρη καὶ δυάδος ἔμφασιν καὶ πρόεισιν εἰς τὴν πρὸς τὰ μέρη σύνταξιν, τὸ δὲ πεπερασμένον ἤδη πλῆθός ἐστι πέρατος καὶ ἑνὸς μετέχον, καὶ οἷον τριάς ἐστιν.
>
> PROCLUS, *TP* IV.35, 104.5–15

As such, there [i.e., in the realm above heaven] the henad transcended the many, but here [in this second intelligible-intellective triad] it is drawn up beside the multiplicity. Because of this, the first co-arrangement generates the whole together with the parts, and the hypostasis of the whole and the parts brings forth the limited at the same time as the unlimited.[94] For the one, the whole, and the limited follow each other, as do their counterparts, as it were: the many, the parts, and the unlimited. And the one [i.e., the henad of this triad] is itself the principle of the others, whereas the whole already has an inclination towards its parts, the appearance of a dyad, and a procession towards the co-arrangement with the parts. The limited, on the other hand, is already a multiplicity which participates in limit and the one, and it is as it were a triad.

In sum, Proclus ascribes to the heavenly arch three oppositions: one versus many, whole versus part, and limit versus unlimited. The realm above heaven,

---

seconde multiplicité est déjà « distinguée » (πλῆθος διακεκριμένον) en unités différentes par l'altérité; c'est la multiplicité du nombre.'

94 Proclus seems to refer to an internal distinction within the second intelligible-intellective triad. Perhaps he is thinking of the three essential aspects of every hypostasis, i.e., the henad, the power, and being?

138 CHAPTER 5

and by extension the intelligible triads above that, did not yet reveal this distinction between these three sets of counterparts, for there the one still transcended the many. In contrast, the second intelligible-intellective triad is the point where the ontological concept of the part is distinguished from the ontological concept of the whole.[95] This would concur with Proclus' statements elsewhere that there are things which are no longer whole but just parts, such as the parts of corporeal beings.[96] Recall that the highest beings are simple by virtue of their proximity to the One, and that various ontological concepts or distinctive characters (ἰδιότητες), such as the concept of being a part, only come to be as the procession of one beings continues. As such, the distinctive character of being a part must have some point of origin in the procession of beings, and this second intelligible-intellective triad seems to be it.

However, this triad does not instantiate parts which exist separately from their wholes. Given the rule of Proclus, the character of parthood which is instantiated by this triad must have a shorter causal reach than the superior character of wholeness. In other words, the ontological concept which is defined here is the part *qua* member of a composite whole. Parts which have become separated from their wholes are simply beings, participating only in the causal irradiations from the One and the One Being.[97]

Below the heavenly arch lies the subcelestial realm, which Proclus characterises as the *perfecting* triad. The passage which Baltzly cites in order to support his assertion that wholeness and perfection are exactly parallel according to Proclus stems from the twenty-fifth chapter of the fourth book of the *Platonic Theology*, where Proclus discusses this third intelligible-intellective triad. After introducing the concept of a subcelestial realm, Proclus emphasises that this perfective triad has three main aspects, just as the previous triad did, i.e., the oppositions between one and many, whole and part, and limited and unlimited, respectively. He then reveals what the three aspects of the perfective triad are.

The perfective triad, from which all lesser forms of perfections flow forth regardless of the degree to which they are indeed perfect, has three aspects. First, the henad of the triad represents what Proclus calls the perfection before

---

95 This reading has been suggested to me by Gerd Van Riel. Since truly distinct kinds of beings and Platonic Forms will not be revealed to us until we reach the intellective realms (see the next section), it makes sense to presume that the opposition ὅλον-μέρος in this triad refers to the ontological concepts of whole and part in the abstract sense rather than to any specific kind of whole or any specific kind of part.

96 Cf. Proclus, *El Theol.* 73, 70.10–12 and *IT* III, 86.4–7 (2.62.6–8 Diehl); see also chapter 6, section 3.

97 See Proclus, *ET* 73, 70.10–14, chapter 6, section 3, and chapter 7, section 2.

DIVIDING THE INDIVISIBLE

the parts (ἡ πρὸ τῶν μερῶν τελειότης).[98] Like all divine henads, this one exists in a 'self-perfect' manner (αὐτοτελῶς). That is to say, Proclus explains, that the henad entirely transcends the pluriform essence of which it is the unifying principle, whereas lesser unifying principles like the unifying principle of a pluriform soul or the unifying principle of a pluriform body are inherently mixed up in their pluriform participants. Second, the perfection out of parts (ἡ ἐκ τῶν μερῶν τελειότης) exists together with its parts rather than before them, and is completed (συμπληροῦται) by those parts. Proclus points to the sensible cosmos as described in Plato's *Timaeus* as an example of this kind of perfection, since the sensible cosmos is complete or perfect insofar as no essential component is missing from it.[99] Third is the perfection in the parts (τελειότης ἡ ἐν τοῖς μέρεσιν), a notion which Proclus again derives from Plato's *Timaeus*, specifically by citing Timaeus' statements that the material cosmos is a 'perfect thing composed of perfect things' and a 'wholes composed of wholes'.[100] Together, these three concepts constitute the threefold perfection (τριττὴ τελειότης).[101]

The connection between wholeness and perfection is obvious: just as Proclus distinguished three kinds of wholeness, so does he distinguish three kinds of perfection here that mirror the kinds of wholeness, a fact he himself explicates in this passage. This is the 'parallel in structure' mentioned by Baltzly.[102] However, this passage reveals a number of interesting aspects of the relation between wholeness and perfection beyond the fact that both are divided in the exact same threefold manner. Firstly, Proclus affirms once again that the *Timaeus* constitutes his main source of inspiration for the

---

98 Note that Proclus' language in this passage is somewhat ambiguous: he refers only to 'the henads' or 'the gods' in plural, and one might thus attempt to read the passage in light of Butler's vision on the henads, i.e., as reflecting the way in which this intelligible-intellective triad participates in the henads in general. I argue below, however, that this multiplicity of gods refers to the henads as participated by the beings coming after this perfective triad.

99 Cf. the *Timaeus*-passage discussed in chapter 1.

100 Plato, *Tim.* 32d1 and 33a7, respectively.

101 Proclus, *TP* IV.25, 74.20–75.20.

102 Baltzly (2008: 408 n. 22). There is, however, no direct line of analogy between the second intelligible triad and third intelligible-intellective triad. Instead, the wholeness of Eternity is passed on to the subcelestial realm by the intelligible-intellective wholeness of the heavenly arch; cf. Saffrey and Westerink (1981: 171): 'il s'agit de procéder par analogie et de construire cette troisième triade intelligible-intellective, cause de perfection, sur le modèle de la deuxième triade, la classe mainteneuse, qui sera elle-même appelée totalité dans le chap. 27.' Proclus himself points out in the current passage that wholeness and perfection are connected 'because the perfective genus [i.e., the third intelligible-intellective triad] grows together with the connective genus [i.e., the second intelligible-intellective triad] and because the perfective monad is placed after all of the connective ones' (*TP* IV.25, 75.18–20: διότι δὴ καὶ τὸ τελεσιουργὸν γένος τῷ συνεκτικῷ συμφύεται καὶ πᾶσι τοῖς συνεκτικοῖς ὑποτέτακται τελεσιουργὸς μονάς).

140 CHAPTER 5

before-the-parts/composed-of-parts/in-the-part-distinction.[103] Indeed, the fact that Proclus connects perfection to wholeness stems, by his own admission, directly from the fact that Plato's Timaeus uses both terms interchangeably to describe the idea of a unified cosmos composed of individually unified beings.

Secondly, the three kinds of perfection might not imitate the three kinds of wholeness merely by copying their relation to parts. Previously, we discussed how Proclus defined the relations between the three kinds of wholes by referring to the three essential aspects of every intelligible triad: a transcendent henad (before the parts), a participating being (in the part), and a unifying power between them (composed of parts).[104] Here Proclus links the first kind of perfection, the perfection before the parts, to the henads that prefigure beings and multiplicities, just as he linked the whole before the parts to the henad of the second intelligible triad. Further on, Proclus adds that 'if I must say my piece, all kinds of perfection come from all leaders [within the third intelligible-intellective triad]; but the perfection before the parts belongs more so to the first, whereas the perfection composed of parts belongs to the middle one and the perfection in the part to the third.'[105] If we accept the idea that Proclus' henads exist parallel to the procession of being (per Van Riel's suggestion but in opposition to Butler's thesis),[106] we may argue that the three kinds of perfection mirror the relation between henad, power, and being within each triad starting from the third intelligible-intellective one, just as the three kinds of wholes mirrored those aspects within each triad starting from the second intelligible one.

Lastly, the subcelestial triad unfolds the unity of the Paradigm into greater multiplicity, just as the heavenly arch unfolded the primal wholeness of Eternity into a distinction between whole and part.

Πρὸ δὲ τῆς τριάδος ταύτης ἡ μονοειδὴς τελειότης καὶ ἡ παντελὴς ὕπαρξίς ἐστιν ἡ νοητὴ τριάς, ἣν καὶ ὁ Τίμαιος 'κατὰ πάντα τελείαν' (*Tim.* 31b1) προσείρηκεν. Ἀλλ' ἐκεῖ μὲν ἡνωμένως αἱ τρεῖς προϋπῆρχον τελειότητες, μᾶλλον δὲ μία πηγὴ πάσης ἦν τελειότητος ἡ τριὰς ἐκείνη, ***

PROCLUS, *TP* IV.25, 75.26–76.3

Before this triad [i.e., the perfective subcelestial one], the intelligible triad, which Timaeus also denominated as 'perfect in every respect' (*Tim.* 31b1),

---

103 Previously, he named the *Timaeus* alongside the *Statesman* as his main source for distinguishing the three kinds of wholes within the second intelligible triad, for which see Proclus, *TP* III.25, 87.26–88.6 (also discussed in chapter 4, section 2).

104 See chapter 4, section 2.

105 Proclus, *TP* IV.25, 75.23–26: Καὶ εἴ με δεῖ τοὐμὸν εἰπεῖν, πᾶσαι μὲν ἐκ πάντων εἰσὶ τῶν ἡγεμόνων αἱ τελειότητες· ἀλλ' ἡ μὲν πρὸ τῶν μερῶν τῷ πρώτῳ προσήκει μᾶλλον, ἡ δὲ ἐκ τῶν μερῶν τῷ μέσῳ, ἡ δὲ ἐν τῷ μέρει τῷ τρίτῳ.

106 See chapter 4, section 4; Van Riel (2001: 426–428 and 2016: 89–94).

DIVIDING THE INDIVISIBLE   141

forms the uniform perfection and wholly perfect principality [i.e., the Paradigm]. But there the three kinds of perfection pre-existed in a unified manner, and that triad was more so a singular source of all perfection.***

Eternity contained all three kinds of wholeness in one, and they only became separate upon their subsequent descent across the hypostases.[107] Now, Proclus reveals to us that the Paradigm too was the source of the three kinds of perfection all along. These three kinds existed as one, and it once again falls upon the corresponding intelligible-intellective triad to unfold this unity into a multiplicity. In this regard, the subcelestial triad is not so much the primal source of perfection, but rather the metaphysical principle which divides that primal Perfection into multiple kinds.

Although wholeness and perfection are indeed parallel in structure, as Baltzly indicated, they are not truly equal. If they were, Proclus' distinction between Eternity as the supra-perfect whole and the Paradigm as the wholly perfect totality would not hold, and neither would the allocations of the distinction between whole and part and the division of the three kinds of perfection to different intelligible-intellective triads. The relation between the concepts of wholeness and perfection remains the same in the intelligible-intellective realm as in the intelligible one.

However, there is one other mereological concept that has not yet been fully developed at this point in the procession of beings: division. Its time to shine comes when Proclus moves on to the final level of the incorporeal intellect.

TABLE 2   The parallel developments of wholeness and perfection in books three and four of the *Platonic Theology*

Eternity: Intelligible Wholeness (ἁπλῶς ὅλον)	
	The Paradigm: Intelligible perfection (μία πηγὴ πάσης τελειότητος)
The heavenly arch: Distinguishes the ontological concepts of 'whole' and 'part' (ἕν, ὅλον, πεπερασμένον versus πολλά, μέρη, ἄπειρα)	
	The subcelestial realm: Divides perfection into three kinds, corresponding to the three kinds of wholeness

107   Proclus, *TP* III.25, 88.24–89.2 (as discussed in chapter 4, section 2).

142   CHAPTER 5

5.5   The Division of the Platonic Forms by the Intellective Gods

As the name implies, the intelligible-intellective realm is not the last stage in the unfolding of Proclean intellect. That honour belongs to the intellective gods. Here the procession towards multiplicity switches to a higher gear, for Proclus no longer distinguishes just three triads. Instead, the intellective realm comprises *seven* hypostases. The primary gods on this level are Cronus, Rhea, and Zeus, who make their first of many appearances here. Although these gods are still called 'wholly perfect' by Proclus (more on this later), they are not as uniform and transcendent as the intelligible gods were.

In the first chapter of book five of the *Platonic Theology*, Proclus explains the primary difference between the highest and lowest levels of Intellect. The superior intelligible hypostasis is a transcendent unity, encompassing all of the Intellect's principles not as a complete set (οὐχ ὡς πλήρωμα τοῦ νοῦ), but as their prior cause and the thing to which their centripetal movement is directed. In contrast, the intellective hypostasis represents the Intellect as a pluriform thing within which all of the principles are distinguished from one another (ἐν ἑαυτῷ τὰς αἰτίας διελόμενος).[108]

This means that the intellective hypostasis contains more specific causal principles than the intelligible triads did—recall the distinction between four universal kinds of living beings within the Paradigm and more specific kinds of Platonic Forms which appear in larger numbers. For example, whereas Eternity formed the intelligible principle of all wholes and the heavenly arch only distinguished wholes from parts, the intellective realm constitutes the point of origin of *every* kind of division (ἀπάσης ἐξάρχει διαιρέσεως), sees the rise of the 'hypostasis of partial natures' (ἡ τῶν μερικῶν ὑπόστασις) and is the cause of 'all the Forms' (τῶν εἰδῶν πάντων αἰτία), i.e., all specific formal natures.[109]

The intellective gods continue to unfold the intelligible multiplicities just as the intelligible-intellective triads did, and they do so to an even greater extent. For example, because the intellective gods are yet more divided than their forebearers, their so-called immaculate godhood (ἄχραντος θεότης) becomes separated from their fatherly godhood. This results in a second trinity of gods, each member of which accompanies the respective members of the first.[110] These six gods are joined by a final monad, which is, according to Proclus,

---

108   Proclus, *TP* V.1, 8.13–20.
109   Proclus, *TP* V.12, 41.10–18.
110   Proclus, *TP* V.1, 10.7–18.

DIVIDING THE INDIVISIBLE

TABLE 3   The intellective hebdomad, and the Platonic dialogues from which Proclus distils the primary characteristics of the hebdomad's intellective triads

Platonic Theology v			*Platonic sources*
Being	*Life*	*Intellect*	
Cronus			*Cratylus* 396b6–7, *Parmenides* 145b6–e6, *Statesman* 268d–274e
	Rhea/Hecate		*Cratylus* 402b1–d3, *Parmenides* 145e7–146a8
		Zeus/Demiurge	*Cratylus* 396a2–b5, *Critias* 121b7–c5, *Parmenides* 146a9–147b8, *Philebus* 30d1–4, *Protagoras* 320c–322d, *Statesman* 145e7–146a8, *Timaeus*
Athena			*Cratylus* 396b6–7, *Protagoras* 322d7, *Parmenides* 145b6–147b8
	Korè		
		The Curetes	
	Final monad of intellect		*Parmenides* 146a9–147b8

the cause of the separation between the intellective gods.[111] Together, these monads constitute the intellective hebdomad, which can be mapped as in table 3.[112]

These seven principles each give rise to an intellective hebdomad *of their own*—in other words, Cronus gives rise to his own hebdomad, as do Rhea, Zeus, and the other gods—, which extends down into the sensible cosmos.[113] This means that the intellective realm in total comprises seven *times seven* gods.

As can be grasped from the schema, Proclus no longer grants a central role to his exegesis of the *Parmenides*. Only the final three chapters of the fifth book of the *Platonic Theology* (v.37–39) are devoted to the continuation

---

111   Proclus, *TP* v.2, 10.20–23.

112   Steel (2000: 398), Chlup (2012: 126), and d'Hoine and Martijn (2016: 325–326). A much more extensive discussion of the hebdomadic nature of intellective intellect can be found in Saffrey and Westerink (1987: ix–xxxvii).

113   Proclus, *TP* v.2, 11.25–12.3. This specific idea is derived from the *Timaeus*, where the titular speaker reveals that the Demiurge leaves the first circle of the World Soul, the circle of Sameness, as it is, but divides the circle of the Different into seven circles (Plato, *Tim.* 36d1–3); cf. Proclus, *TP* v.4, 19.5–12.

144   CHAPTER 5

of Parmenides' revelations about the one being. In the thirty-plus chapters
before these, Proclus devotes most of his attention to mythological passages
both from various works of Plato and from other sources, such as the *Chaldean
Oracles* and the Orphic tradition.[114] In his exegesis of Plato, he also starts to
focus more and more on citing small passages or even merely a sentence or
two in order to support the theology presented in the fifth book of the *Platonic
Theology*. Nevertheless, special mention should be made of the *Timaeus* and
Cratylus. The former remains vitally important for Proclus' theology because
Proclus equates Zeus with the Demiurge. The latter is used throughout the fifth
book because the Socrates of that dialogue offers etymologies for the names of
the gods. It should come as no surprise that, in Proclus' eyes, these etymologies
contain vital clues to the gods' true natures.[115]

Proclus' description of the intellective realm as the locus of the division of
causes obviously warrants some attention in our mereological enquiry. More
specifically, the way in which the three highest gods (Cronus, Rhea, and Zeus)
develop the concept of division itself (διάκρισις) corresponds with Proclus' mis-
sion to place the one above the many. In the twelfth chapter of the fifth book,
Proclus introduces Zeus by retracing the process of the division of causes and
Forms through the intellective realm.

Proclus starts with the first intellective god, i.e., Cronus,[116] who is the
'founder of all division' (τῆς διακρίσεως ἦν ἀρχηγὸς πάσης). Cronus reveals himself to be 'one intelligible cosmos among the intellective ones' (εἷς ἀπεφαίνετο
κόσμος νοητὸς ἐν τοῖς νοεροῖς), which means not that he is an intelligible principle in disguise, but that he encompasses all of the distinguished principles 'of
the wholes' (τὰς διῃρημένας τῶν ὅλων ἀρχάς) within the intellective realm in a
unitary and transcendent manner, as exemplified by the fact that after bringing forth the intellective principles he reverts them to himself again (πάλιν εἰς
ἑαυτὸν ἐπέστρεφε τὰ γεννώμενα) and subsequently retains them within himself.

---

114   For example, both the myth of the two ages from the *Statesman* and the myth of
      Prometheus from the *Protagoras* are presented by Proclus as revelations about the intel-
      lective gods. It should be noted that Proclus does not use the Chaldean writings only in the
      fifth book: they are referenced throughout the *Platonic Theology*. However, 'les références
      aux *Oracles* se multiplient à partir du livre IV'; Brisson (2000: 121). For a detailed discus-
      sion of the many references to the *Chaldean Oracles* in Proclus' *Platonic Theology*, see
      Brisson (2000); cf. Chlup (2012: 125–127) and d'Hoine and Martijn (2016: 323–328) for a
      more concise schematic overview of which Chaldean and Orphic concepts are located in
      which Proclean hypostasis.
115   In fact, Proclus devoted an entire commentary on the *Cratylus*. Van den Berg (2008) pro-
      vides a full analysis of this work and of Proclus' interpretations of Plato's etymologies in
      general.
116   Cf. Saffrey and Westerink (1987: 170).

DIVIDING THE INDIVISIBLE   145

The second intellective divinity, the goddess Rhea,[117] brings forth the same plurality of intellective principles together with Cronus, but unlike her husband she is unable to retain the indivisible unification (ἀδιάκριτον ἕνωσιν) within which Cronus placed the principles, and thus she brings forth a manifold of intellective gods and reason-principles (λόγοι). In doing so, she also distinguishes her husband from the demiurgic monad: Zeus.[118]

In other words, although Cronus sets the division of Platonic Forms in motion, he does not reveal their actual multiplicity. Instead, it remains hidden within him, similarly to the way in which a whole before the parts contains the multiplicity of parts only as a cause. Note that Proclus refers to Cronus' products as 'the wholes' (τὰ ὅλα), presumably to emphasise their eternal nature. The wholes to which Proclus refers here appear to be particular kinds of wholes as they appear among the Platonic Forms and in our world, in contrast to the concepts of wholeness and parthood themselves, which were established in superior hypostases.

Unlike her husband, Rhea is unable to keep the division of Forms hidden. Already in the preceding chapter, Proclus emphasised that Rhea 'at the same time transcends her fulfilments and is coordinate with them; thus, she is both uniform and pluriform,'[119] implying that she forms the middle term between the unitary monad of division and the actual division of causes as performed by Zeus. In this regard, Rhea plays a similar role to the whole composed of parts or the second intelligible-intellective triad, which were both whole and part at the same time.

As the third intellective god, Zeus does not (partially) hide the division of the Forms, but reveals it in full, since he is an intellect first and foremost. Proclus explains that it is typical of an intellect (νοῦ ἴδιον), i.e., of a third triad, to divide principles and reveal multiplicity, but that the three primary manifestations of this kind of intellect (the third intelligible triad, the third intelligible-intellective triad, and the third intellective triad) each divide their allotted multiplicity to a different extent. Within the Paradigm, the many Platonic Forms are encompassed uniformly (ἑνοειδῶς, through the four most universal Forms of living beings). Although the intelligible-intellective triad of perfection possesses a lesser measure of unity, it nevertheless transcends 'absolute division' (τῆς παντελοῦς διακρίσεως ἐξήρητο), revealing only a

---

117   Cf. Saffrey and Westerink (1987: 170).
118   Proclus, *TP* V.12, 40.10–24.
119   Proclus, *TP* V.11, 38.9–16: ἡ τούτων ἁπάντων ἕνωσις καὶ ἡ ὅλη θεὸς ὁμοῦ μὲν ἐξήρηται τῶν ἑαυτῆς πληρωμάτων, ὁμοῦ δὲ συντέτακται αὐτοῖς, καὶ οὕτω δὴ μονοειδής τε καὶ πολυειδής ἐστι, καὶ μία καὶ ἁπλῆ καὶ αὐτοτελὴς ὑπάρχουσα κόσμος ἐστὶ ζωογονικός.

146   CHAPTER 5

manifold of 'the primary principles of the wholes' (πρώτισται τῶν ὅλων ἀρχαί).
In contrast to the preceding divinities, Zeus sets all division in motion, creating
the 'hypostasis of partial things' (τῶν μερικῶν ὑπόστασις). Unlike his forebears,
he does not encompass, say, a mere four Forms of living beings. He 'possesses
the one wholly perfect intellective cause of *all* forms' (τὴν μίαν παντελῆ τῶν
εἰδῶν πάντων αἰτίαν ἔχει νοεράν).[120]

In other words, Zeus is the principle of the actual division of the particular
Platonic Forms. Whereas the Paradigm contained all Forms in a transcendent
way through its tetrad, Zeus is the one cause of each particular Form.[121] Since
Zeus is one of the lower principles within the intellect as a whole, he stands
close to the edge of true wholeness, as indicated by Proclus' statement that the
intellective intellect is directly responsible for the creation of the previously
discussed partial beings (μερικά). The intellective intellect in general is characterised by Proclus as the intelligible level immediately preceding the transition
into the realm of becoming. For example, when discussing the problems concerning participation from the *Parmenides*,[122] Proclus orders the various types
of Platonic Forms in the Neoplatonic universe according to their role as paradigms or images.

The types of forms one can distinguish, Proclus tells us, are the natural forms
(φυσικὰ εἴδη) which are linked to sensible things, the psychic forms (ψυχικά)
in the realm of soul, the intellective Forms at the lower end of Intellect, 'and
no others prior to these' (καὶ οὐκέτι πρὸ τούτων ἄλλα). Proclus also emphasises the role the intellective Forms play as the starting point of the various
formal natures which exist in lower hypostases, characterising them as pure
paradigms at the top of a scale of things which are alternatively paradigms
or images, depending on whether one considers their relation to superior or
inferior things, respectively.[123]

In short, the intellective Forms distinguished by Zeus are characterised as
the transcendent monads prior to the various types of forms present in the
intermediate realm of souls and in the material realm of nature. However, both

---

120   Proclus, *TP* V.12, 41.7–18.
121   This is my interpretation of μίαν παντελῆ τῶν εἰδῶν πάντων αἰτίαν from the passage cited
       above. Note the use of παντελής to describe Zeus rather than the Paradigm here, which
       will be discussed in more detail in the next section. The distinction between the four uni-
       versal kinds of living beings and the distinguished Forms here is comparable to Proclus'
       distinction in the *Parmenides*-commentary between the participated intellect which is
       ὁλικός and the participated intellect which is μερικός, for which see Proclus, *IP* I, 628.1–21
       and Oosthout, A. (2022b: 14).
122   Specifically, Plato, *Parm.* 132d5–e5.
123   Proclus, *IP* IV, 913.1–7.

DIVIDING THE INDIVISIBLE

unity and wholeness can be interpreted as relative concepts in the Proclean procession from more universal to more particular principles,[124] and thus the unity immediately preceding the realm of souls and the realm of nature is at the same time more pluralised than any of its superior intelligible brethren. Since Zeus creates Forms which designate more specific principles (the Human Being or the Dog, for example)[125] than the whole-part-distinction from the intelligible-intellective realm, the division performed at this level of reality allows Proclus' mereology to transition from basic concepts such as Wholeness itself to the kinds of wholes which are found in the sensible cosmos, such as people and dogs.

In contrast to his son, Cronus is the unitary monad of division itself, while Rhea bridges the gap between the single principle of division and the actual process of distinguishing the Forms. In this regard, the three divine principles of division, like the three kinds of wholeness and perfection before them, obey the Neoplatonic edict that unity precedes plurality. One might even argue that the three gods correspond to the three kinds of wholes or perfection to some extent. Cronus and Rhea mirror the whole before the parts and the whole composed of parts, respectively, by virtue of the fact that Cronus is the transcendent unitary principle of a multiplicity while Rhea connects this transcendent unity to the actual division of the Forms as performed by Zeus. Of course, Zeus is explicitly not characterised in terms that are directly applicable to the final kind of wholeness, the whole in the part, since he remains a transcendent monad. However, as the most pluralised of these three intellective gods and the final monad prior to the actual distinguished Platonic Forms, he does play the role of the whole in the part considered relative to his parents.

The distinguished Forms themselves admit of a similar parallel. In the thirtieth chapter of the fifth book, Proclus returns to the division of the Forms by Zeus.

> Ἐν δὴ ταύτῃ τῇ τάξει πρῶτον μὲν ἐκλάμπει τὰ γένη πάντα καὶ τὰ εἴδη, διότι κατὰ τὴν ἑτερότητα μάλιστα χαρακτηρίζεται, τῶν ὁλικῶν πασῶν ὑποστάσεων τὸ πέρας κληρωσαμένη, καὶ ἀπὸ ταύτης ἐπὶ πάντα πρόεισι, τόν τε μετεχόμενον νοῦν καὶ τὰς πολυειδεῖς τῶν ψυχῶν διακοσμήσεις καὶ τὴν σωματικὴν ἅπασαν φύσιν. Τριττὰ γὰρ ὑφίστησι γένη τῶν μετ' αὐτήν, ὡς τὸ ὅλον εἰπεῖν, τὰ μὲν ἀμέριστα καὶ πρῶτα, τὰ δὲ μέσα τῶν ἀμερίστων καὶ μεριστῶν, τὰ δὲ μεριζόμενα περὶ τοῖς σώμασι· καὶ διὰ τούτων ἀπογεννᾷ πάντα τὰ μερικώτερα γένη τῶν ὄντων.

> PROCLUS, *TP* V.30, III.18–26

---

124 See chapter 3, section 1, and section 1 above.
125 Cf. Proclus, *IP* II, 734.15–735.17 and III, 823.12–824.8.

148   CHAPTER 5

In this order [of Zeus], all of the genera and Forms shine forth for the first time, because they are characterised by difference most of all,[126] since it [i.e., difference] was allotted the limit of all the universal hypostases, and from this order they [i.e., the genera and Forms] proceed to all beings,[127] to the participated intellect, to the pluriform orders of souls, and to the entire nature of bodies. For it [i.e, the order of Zeus] gives rise to three genera [of Forms] beyond it. In summary, some are the first indivisible Forms, some are intermediate between the indivisible and divisible beings, and some are divided across the bodies. And through these three genera, it creates all of the more specific genera of beings.

These three genera of Forms recall those d'Hoine distilled from Proclus' *Elements of Theology* and *Parmenides*-commentary: the unitary unparticipated Form, the participated Form 'en tant que forme commune', and the participated Form 'en tant que particularisée par le participant matériel'.[128] Those three manifestations of the Forms corresponded to the three kinds of wholes, and the three genera in this passage seem to do so as well, since the Forms in intellect are undivided (ἀμέριστα), the Forms in souls are both undivided and divided at the same time (μέσα τῶν ἀμερίστων καὶ μεριστῶν), and the Forms spread across bodies are divided (μεριζόμενα).[129] If these three genera do indeed equate to d'Hoine's three manifestations of the Forms, then this passage would also show us in which hypostasis each manifestation can be found.

Like the parallel between the three kinds of wholes and the three intellective fathers, this equation of d'Hoine's manifestations of the Forms with their genera in our current passage is not entirely perfect. The third genus fits quite well with the concept of the form *qua* particularised in an individual

---

126   In the preceding lines (*TP* V.30, 111.6–18), Proclus explains that Cronus is characterised by true being (ὄντως ὄν), Rhea by movement and rest (κίνησις καὶ στάσις; cf. Plato, *Parm.* 145e7–146a8), and Zeus by sameness and difference (τὸ ταὐτὸν ἅμα καὶ ἕτερον; cf. Plato, *Parm.* 146a9–147b8). The two oppositions inherent in Rhea and Zeus are derived from the second hypothesis on the one in Plato's *Parmenides*; see Van Riel (2001: 421–422 and 2016: 87–88).

127   The subject of this phrase appears to jump back and forth between the genera of Forms and difference. There is no other way to read κληρωσαμένη than as congruent with τὴν ἑτερότητα, yet the subsequent πρόεισι seems to refer back to τὰ γένη πάντα καὶ τὰ εἴδη. I have chosen to follow the French translation of Westerink in Saffrey and Westerink (1987: 111), in which the subject changes between the different parts of the sentence.

128   See chapter 4, section 4.

129   The distinction between ἀμέριστον and μεριστόν in this passage refers to the opposition between the spatiotemporal divisibility of corporeal things and the incorporeal timelessness of intelligible beings, which is discussed in the introduction to this chapter.

DIVIDING THE INDIVISIBLE 149

TABLE 4 The parallel between the three kinds of wholes and the manifestations of Platonic Forms as described in the primary and secondary sources

Kinds of wholeness	Manifestations of the Forms as described by d'Hoine (2021: 218)	Genera of Forms (TP V.30)	Hypostasis of origin (TP V.30)
Whole before the parts	Unparticipated Form	Undivided and primary	Intellective intellect
Whole composed of parts	Participated Form$_1$ ('forme commune')	Both undivided and divided at the same time	The order of souls
Whole in the part	Participated Form$_2$ ('forme particularisée')	Divided across bodies	Corporeal nature (φύσις)

hylomorphic compound (ἔνυλον εἶδος), and the soul forms a logical home for the form *qua* composed of parts since it occupies the space in between incorporeal intellect and material existence. However, although equating the unparticipated Form with the genus of the undivided primal Forms (ἀμέριστα καὶ πρῶτα) sounds logical, Proclus implies in our passage that this genus of Forms proceeds to *participated* intellect. This problem can be avoided if we suppose that the unparticipated Forms distinguished by Cronus, Rhea, and Zeus are not equal to their creators.[130] As a result, the intellect in which they make their home is not an unparticipated manifestation of intellect—neither unparticipated Intellect *stricto sensu*, i.e., the Paradigm, nor a more specific monad such as Cronus, Rhea, or Zeus. Instead, the intellect which houses the Forms is a participated one, even if the Forms themselves are not yet participated at this stage. In other words, just as Zeus was the monad of all the Forms but the least whole of the three intellective gods, so are the Platonic Forms themselves unparticipated monads, even if they make their home in a manifestation of intellect which is already participated insofar as it constitutes the inferior manifestation of previous intelligible principles. In any case, it is certain that the division of ontological kinds starts as a unitary process in Cronus and subsequently proceeds to multiplicity, just as the principles of perfection and wholeness did before it.

---

130   Cf. Proclus, *ET* 7, 8.1–2.

5.6 The Development of Axiology, Cosmology, and Perfection

Unfortunately, by this point in Plato's *Parmenides*, the titular speaker has moved on from ascribing mereological characteristics to the one being. Coupled with the fact that Proclus devotes relatively few chapters to Parmenides' second hypothesis in the fifth book, this means that the interplay between the concepts of perfection and wholeness is less pronounced in book five than it was in books three and four. Nevertheless, the three kinds of wholes and the three corresponding kinds of perfection inform Proclus' discussion of the intellective realm. Furthermore, Proclus anticipates the composition of the sensible cosmos. For this reason, a few relevant passages need to be addressed here.

First, in the ninth chapter of book five of the *Platonic Theology*, Proclus once again adds an axiological connotation to the division of causes that characterises the intellective realm, just as he did when he discussed the wholeness of eternal beings. When he describes the nature of the god Cronus, Proclus notes that Plato often alludes to Cronus as the overseer of divine Law. Plato even links the concepts of law and intellect, according to Proclus, since the name 'Cronus' supposedly refers to the Greek word for 'intellect' (νοῦς).[131]

Proclus goes on to explain that Cronus sets the true division (διαίρεσις) of beings in motion, whereas Adrastia constitutes the transcendently uniform principle of this division—recall that Adrastia equates to the first intelligible-intellective triad and the monadic principle of Number, according to Proclus. However, Cronus does not divide beings at random. As the locus of divine Law, he distinguishes the Platonic Forms in a well-ordered procession (κατὰ τὴν εὔτακτον πρόοδον), acts as a measure of the principality (ὕπαρξις) of each Form, and through his divine Law preserves 'the dignity in the kingdom of Cronus' (τὴν ἀξίαν ἐν τῇ Κρόνου βασιλείᾳ).[132] In other words, Zeus' father ensures that every divided Form is granted a share in its proper goodness.[133] This mirrors Proclus' earlier suggestions that Eternity made its products whole and that

---

131 Proclus, *TP* V.9, 32.3–8. The suggestion of an etymological link between 'Cronus' and 'νοῦς' derives from Plato's *Cratylus*, specifically 396b6–7; cf. Proclus, *ICr* 107, 56.24–59. For a more detailed analysis of the exegesis Proclus performs on this passage of the *Cratylus*, see Van den Berg (2008: 156–159).

132 Proclus, *TP* V.9, 32.8–26.

133 Furthermore, Cronus' influence extends into the realms below Zeus, making it so that even the mortal inhabitants of the material cosmos are allotted their proper share in justice; cf. Proclus, *IRP* II, 307.10–13 and Saffrey and Westerink (1987: 166): 'la Loi est donc une divinité qui se retrouve à tous les degrés de la hiérarchie, sa function est celle de la justice distributive.'

DIVIDING THE INDIVISIBLE

eternal beings never lost their proper goodness as a result.[134] In rephrasing the intellective division of Platonic Forms in axiological terms, Proclus ensures that no individualised Form, nor any corporeal being participating in it, is left without a proper goodness.[135]

Second, Proclus refers to his cosmological mereology in the thirteenth chapter, when he discusses the nature of Zeus, also known as the Demiurge. When he wonders in which hypostasis the Demiurge must be situated, Proclus writes:

> Ἔτι τοίνυν τῆς δημιουργίας τετραπλῆς οὔσης, καὶ τῆς μὲν τὰ ὅλα διακοσμούσης ὁλικῶς, τῆς δὲ τὰ ὅλα μέν, ἀλλὰ μερικῶς, τῆς δὲ κατὰ μέρη μὲν διῃρημένης, ἀλλ᾽ ὁλικῶς, τῆς δὲ τὰ μέρη μερικῶς συνυφαινούσης τοῖς ὅλοις, δῆλον ὅτι πρεσβυτάτη μέν ἐστι πασῶν ἡ τῶν ὅλων αἰτία μονοειδῶς καὶ ἀδιαιρέτως· ταύτην δὲ ἀναγκαῖον ἢ πρὸ τῶν νοερῶν εἶναι θεῶν ἢ ἐν τοῖς νοεροῖς ἢ μετὰ τοὺς νοερούς.
>
> PROCLUS, *TP* V.13, 42.6–13

> Now then, since the process of demiurgy is fourfold, whereby one phase orders the whole in a universal manner, while a second one orders the wholes, but in a partial manner, and whereby a third divides them into parts, albeit universally, while a fourth weaves the parts together with the wholes in a partial manner, it is clear that the most important of all is the cause of the wholes in a uniform and undivided manner. But this cause must exist either before the intellective gods, among the intellective gods, or after the intellective gods.

The fourfold division of demiurgic creation to which Proclus refers here, comprising the creation of a universal whole, universal parts, partial wholes, and partial parts, stems from his *Timaeus*-commentary.[136] However, Baltzly has suggested that the current passage does not refer to the subject matter of the

---

134   It also concurs with Proclus' dissatisfaction with Porphyry's homogenous intellect, rooted in the idea that every particular intellect must be clearly distinguishable from its peers; cf. the allusion to this matter and the corresponding reference to Oosthout, A. (2022b: 19–23) in section 1 above. Within a homogenous intellect (like the one implied by Porphyry), any division is hypothetically possible, which makes it impossible to clearly delineate beings with a proper and distinct share in goodness. Since Proclus' intellect contains a discrete multiplicity that can only be divided into a pre-set number of beings, this problem is avoided.

135   This will be relevant again when we discuss the wholeness of mortal creatures, for which see chapter 6, section 4. Note that this link between the first intellective monad and divine Law also ensures that every Platonic ἰδέα is not just an idea, but also an *ideal*.

136   See the discussion of Proclus, *IT* III, 85.16–86.7 in chapter 6, section 2.2.

152   CHAPTER 5

Timaeus directly, stating that 'the "parts and wholes" that are discussed in the *Platonic Theology* passage are not concrete sensible particulars, such as those in the example from the *Timaeus*-commentary. Rather, they are what we moderns would class as universals—Proclus' εἴδη νοερά or, equivalently, νοεροὶ θεοί.'[137] However, Proclus does not elaborate on this fourfold distinction any further, instead launching into an argument for situating the Demiurge in the intellective realm rather than any realm above or below it.[138] Thus, although there is no strong argument for rejecting Baltzly's suggestion, one could, for the sake of parsimony, just as plausibly suggest that Proclus simply refers to the fourfold creation of wholes and parts in the material cosmos from the *Timaeus*-commentary here in order to strengthen his claim that the Demiurge belongs in the intellective realm.[139] Regardless of whose reading one choses to accept, this passage provides a clear link to Proclus' cosmological writings and emphasises Zeus's double role as both the final divider of the intellective Forms and the primary creator of all that exists in the sensible cosmos.

Lastly, Proclus starts to apply the term 'wholly perfect' in passages that do not focus on Paradigm. Although many of the more than fifty occurrences of 'παντελής' and variations thereof in the fifth book revolve around the Paradigm, Proclus also uses the adjective to describe triads of a lower rank. For example, he describes the intellective intellect, i.e., the Demiurge, as the locus of 'wholly perfect separation' (παντελὴς διάκρισις).[140] To give another example, in the previously discussed passage on divine Law, Proclus writes: 'hence, the Law, which distinguishes the divine Forms and delineates the things which belong to each, is a certain god who exists together with the order of Cronus by the fulfilment from the one uniform cause, [and this order is the one] where the distinctions of beings and *the wholly perfect procession of Forms* (ἡ παντελὴς τῶν εἰδῶν πρόοδος) exist for the first time.'[141] These passages suggest that the predicate 'wholly perfect' is applicable to the monadic principle of any distinctive character. For example, the monad of division contains in a causal manner *every* particular form of division, similarly to how the Paradigm contains every kind of living being as a whole before the parts. Indeed, Proclus makes it clear

---

137 Baltzly (2008: 401).
138 Proclus, *TP* V.13, 42.14f.
139 Saffrey and Westerink (1987: 170) do not allude to any intellective εἴδη either and simply refer to the *Timaeus*-commentary.
140 See the footnotes to section 5 above.
141 Proclus, *TP* V.9, 32.26–33.2: Θεὸς οὖν τις ὁ νόμος διαιρετικὸς τῶν θείων εἰδῶν καὶ ἀφοριστικὸς τῶν ἑκάστοις προσηκόντων, κατὰ τὴν ἀπὸ τῆς μιᾶς καὶ ἑνοειδοῦς αἰτίας ἀποπλήρωσιν τῷ Κρονίῳ διακόσμῳ συνυπάρχων, ἐν ᾧ καὶ πρῶτον αἱ τῶν ὄντων διακρίσεις καὶ ἡ παντελὴς τῶν εἰδῶν πρόοδος.

DIVIDING THE INDIVISIBLE

that being wholly perfect precedes division into particulars when he discusses the immaculate gods who accompany Cronus, Rhea, and Zeus. Faced with a passage from Plato's *Laws* in which the Athenian Stranger describes Athena as a goddess who dances in full armour (πανοπλία δὲ παντελεῖ κοσμηθεῖσα),[142] Proclus explains that Athena owes the perfection of her armour to her status as a monad above the Curetes which participate in her.

The philosopher appeals to the protective nature of the Curetes, who protect and preserve inferior essences from their transcendent position within the Intellect. Plato's reference to arms (ὅπλα), Proclus tells us, is meant to bring before our mind's eye the protection granted to the armed individual and the preservation of the city-state through its arms. In the same vein, the myths describe the Curetes as wearing an armed attire to emphasise their protective nature. That Plato grants Athena a 'wholly perfect' suit of armour (παντελεῖ πανοπλίᾳ) is due to the fact that the myths establish Athena as the one henad of the Curetes (αὐτὴν δὲ ἄρα τὴν μίαν αὐτῶν ἑνάδα ... ὑπερίδρυσαν ἐκείνων). The full suit of armour, Proclus concludes, precedes the more divided forms of protection just as 'the wholly perfect precedes the things which are divided into parts' (προηγεῖται ... τὸ παντελὲς τῶν κατὰ μέρη διῃρημένων).[143]

Proclus' description of being wholly perfect in this passage recalls the first kind of perfection, i.e., the perfection before the parts, which was established in the third intelligible-intellective triad. Although Proclus himself does not mention this threefold division of the kinds of perfection here, it seems logical to assume that the perfection of Athena's figurative armour is a perfection before the parts. In the fourth book, Proclus defined the perfection before the parts as the perfection that belongs to a henad which exists self-perfectly (αὐτοτελῶς) before the multiplicity which participates in it. In the passage cited above, Proclus explicitly refers to Athena as the henad (ἑνάς) of the immaculate gods. Coupled with the previous examples, this passage suggests that 'παντελής' can not only be used to describe the absolute first perfection of the Paradigm, but also the highest form of any subsequent level of reality, i.e., the transcendent henad from which that level originates. In other words, just as the term 'whole before the parts' refers *stricto sensu* to the intelligible Wholeness of Eternity, but also more generally to any specific unity which precedes a composition, so does 'παντελής' refer both to the absolute zenith of perfection and to the most perfect instance of any specific distinctive character.

---

142 Plato, *Leg.* VII, 796b6–c2; cf. Proclus, *TP* V.35, 128.21–129.4.
143 Proclus, *TP* V.35, 129.19–130.2.

5.7 The Indivisible Divided

Overall, Proclus' immensely complex exposition on the incorporeal intellect reveals three new insights into his mereological views. First, Proclus not only links wholeness to perfection, but he also envisions a complex ontological hierarchy, in which concepts such as 'whole', 'perfect', 'part', and 'division' have unique characteristics and arise at different levels in the causal procession from the One to the corporeal realm. Second, because of the nature of this procession, Proclus ends up conceiving of intelligible principles that are clearly distinct from one another and yet defined in relation to each other. Lastly, the fact that Proclus connects being whole to being perfect is a result of the fact that his entire mereology is axiological, as a consequence of fact that the metaphysical concept of unity equates to the concept of goodness.

5.7.1 The Concepts 'Whole', 'Perfect', 'Part', and 'Division' in Proclean Theology

As I have made clear, we should amend, but not reject, Baltzly's suggestion that wholeness and perfection are exactly parallel in structure. Baltzly is absolutely correct in stating that the threefold division of perfection (before the part, of parts, and in the part) is lifted wholesale from its ontological sibling, wholeness. However, this statement might be mistaken for one which implies that wholeness and perfection are of equal status in the hierarchy of beings. This is incorrect: Proclus always characterises perfection as *posterior* to wholeness in his theological writings. There are two reasons for this. First, Proclus distinguishes the concept of being whole *qua* being one from being whole *qua* possessing a totality of parts, as we have seen both in this chapter and in the previous one. The first whole is the whole *before* the parts, Eternity is a uniform principle which precedes the first intelligible plurality, and so on. Second, Proclus derives his concept of perfection from Plato's *Timaeus*, where it is linked to the concept of a totality through the adjective παντελής. As a result, perfection cannot be connected to the whole, since it is already indisputably linked to the totality by the Platonic revelations. Indeed, Proclean mereology owes many of its central points to Plato's cosmological treatise.

Although perfection shares in the threefold nature of wholeness, it is not allotted this honour at the same time as its sister concept is, i.e., within the second intelligible triad. In the previous chapter, we discussed the three kinds of wholes and discovered that Proclus locates their point of origin in Eternity. However, Eternity cannot also possess the three kinds of perfection, given that its superior unity makes it so that the concept of perfection is not even applicable to it. After all, Proclus defines perfection as possessing the full sum of one's

DIVIDING THE INDIVISIBLE

essential constituents (συμπληρωτικά). Eternity does not yet distinguish any intelligible kinds of living beings within itself, and because of this there are no essential components that it could possess or miss.[144]

The actual intelligible principle of perfection is not the first Whole but the first Multiplicity, i.e., the Paradigm or Living Being itself. Through the four universal Platonic Forms it contains, this Paradigm is the first being in the procession from the One to distinguish a multitude of living beings, as revealed in the *Timaeus*. These four Forms are essentially the first essential components in existence.[145] This primal multiplicity makes the Paradigm the monad of all complete beings, or Perfection itself. As the monad of perfection, the Paradigm mirrors Eternity insofar as both contain the three manifestations of their distinctive character in a unified manner: three kinds of wholes as unified in Eternity, and three kinds of perfection as unified in the Paradigm. Interestingly, whereas Proclus implied that the dissemination of the three kinds of wholes throughout the hypostases starts below Eternity,[146] the unitary perfection of the Paradigm is not unfolded into its three variations until the procession has passed a few hypostases and reached the third intelligible-intellective triad.

This does not mean that Proclus' development of wholeness is itself vaguely sketched in contrast to his description of perfection. Although the unfolding of the three kinds of wholes is not explicitly located in any lower hypostasis (as far as I am aware, at least), Proclus takes great care to distinguish the ontological concept of the whole from the two concepts that naturally follow from it: the part and division. For example, Proclus takes two different arguments from Plato's *Parmenides*, both of which argued for the mereological composition of the one being, and uses them to fashion two distinct hypostases. The first is the unqualified whole (ἁπλῶς ὅλον), which is the aforementioned Eternity. The second is its intelligible-intellective counterpart, the heavenly arch from the *Phaedrus*, which not only gives existence to wholes, but defines the parts within it *qua* parts. Considered in this way, the part is different from the whole, and as such it is defined in a separate hypostasis. Yet even in the heavenly arch, the opposition between whole and part is only one between ontological concepts. The actual division of specific Forms, and hence, of specific kinds of wholes and parts, such as those that appear in our cosmos, comes yet later in the procession of being, namely in the intellective realm.

As a result, Proclean mereology is characterised by the fact that the ontological concepts of whole and part in the abstract sense are created as really

---

144   Oosthout, A. (2023a: 133–134); Proclus, *IT* IV, 13.15–14.5 (3.10.22–11.4 Diehl).
145   Oosthout, A. (2023a: 131).
146   See Proclus, *TP* III.25, 88.24–89.2 (as discussed in chapter 4, section 2).

distinct intelligible principles before they are applied to any other kinds of beings. In this way, Proclus makes for an interesting contrast to the mereological writings of modern scholars. For example, Koslicki suggested a formula for defining a mereological compound in the abstract sense, made up of formal and material constituents.[147] In Koslicki's mereology, the formal and material variables in the mereological definition were determined by the ontological kind of whatever really existent being one applied them to. In other words, the f-components and m-components of Koslicki's formula remain undefined until one determines what specific kind of being one is describing with them, such as a human being or a tree. These formal and material constituents have no independent existence and only come to be in any specific creature or thing, whereas the Proclean whole and part exist independently and simply, before they manifest themselves in any other being. In Proclus' view, the whole and the part are not determined by the beings to which they are applied, such as the human or the tree. Instead, they are themselves participated by and define these more specific kinds of beings. In modern mereology, the whole and the part often end up as abstract universals or logical variables waiting to be specified. In Proclean mereology, whole and part are really existent transcendent entities with their own distinctive character. They require nothing from the beings in our corporeal realm, but they grant them a share in their nature nevertheless.

As a result of this, Proclean mereology suffers from a potential issue. Proclus defines whole and part as really existent entities with a proper place in the procession of beings. Yet he uses mereological terminology to describe beings which transcend those designated hypostases and thus should not be describable in such terms. Take the Paradigm, for example. As we have seen, the distinction between whole and part has not yet arisen at that level of reality, for it is located in the second intelligible-intellective triad. However, Proclus' definition of the Paradigm as a being that is perfect because it contains the four universal Forms necessitates some mereological description. To give another example, Proclus argues that Eternity is the first Whole because it contains the one and being as its parts, as stated in the *Parmenides*. Yet was Eternity not the intelligible Wholeness, the ultimate whole before the parts, and thus simply whole? Similarly, Proclus distinguishes corporeal division (into spatiotemporal parts) from incorporeal division (existing all together or each apart). However, he uses the terminology of whole and part in both cases without clearly delineating the incorporeal from the corporeal part. A modern philosopher would

---

147   For the full formula, see chapter 2, section 5.2.

DIVIDING THE INDIVISIBLE

perhaps prefer to employ distinct terms, such as 'property' to refer to incorporeal constituents, and 'part' to refer to corporeal ones.

5.7.2 *Relative or Rigid?*

This brings us to our second insight into Proclus' theological mereology. Although Proclus employs his terminology somewhat loosely, the issues raised in the previous paragraph can be softened, though not entirely dismantled, by the fact that even a transcendent whole before the parts already implicitly and causally (κατ' αἰτίαν) possesses the multiplicity that is unfolded by the inferior hypostases it generates.[148] Similarly, although the Paradigm does possess a multiplicity of essential components, those components only exist within the totality and transcend the predicate of (potentially) separable parts. In contrast, my arm can participate in the full character of parthood as defined by the heavenly arch, inasmuch as it can be separately defined as a part and subsequently can be cut off (a frightening prospect), even if this separation will mean its degradation to just being a *thing*. The inverse of this is true as well. Not only do superior principles implicitly contain the characteristics they produce, but inferior principles also retain images of the characteristics of their creators.

This is true for both perfection and wholeness. Already in the previous chapter, it was concluded that the concept of a whole before the parts can be employed in two different ways: either to refer to the absolute Wholeness of Eternity, or to the transcendent unity of any specific kind of whole. Similarly, the predicate 'wholly perfect' is applicable both to the Paradigm and to the hypostases below it. In the first case, the adjective refers to the absolute first Perfection of the most divine of all totalities. In the second case, the adjective refers to the transcendent perfection of each monad over the participated images it generates.

Accepting a certain fluidity not just within Proclus' terminology but also within the divisibility of the intelligible principles is necessary in order to unite the multiple revelations about wholeness and perfection included in the *Platonic Theology*. After all, if we postulate that the Paradigm is nothing but a whole composed of parts in contrast to the whole before the parts that is Eternity, we explain the difference between being a wholly perfect composite and being transcendently whole, but we deny the Paradigm its role as the unitary source of all living beings and all perfection. Indeed, Proclus ascribes to the Paradigm not only the status of a tetrad (which makes it wholly perfect), but also the status of a dyad and, most importantly, the status of a monad.

---

148   For the phrase κατ' αἰτίαν, see chapter 4, section 1.

In its tetradic form, the Paradigm is wholly perfect and a whole composed of parts. In its unitary form, it is a whole *before* the parts, given that in that capacity it is the transcendent cause of the Forms and of the composite cosmos. The Paradigm can play this double role because it is not a separately defined theological concept, but rather part of a continually proceeding evolution from the one to the many. It is more pluralised than its predecessors, yet more unified than its offspring. This principle applies to all hypostases in the procession of beings and also explains how, for example, Eternity can be not yet pluralised in comparison to the Paradigm, but also a dyad of one and being in contrast to the One Being itself. As I argued at the start of this chapter, this relativity can be traced back to Proclus' extensional characterisation of the products of 'more whole' and 'more particular' principles, and in turn to Porphyry's notion of genera and species as a series of wholes and parts relative to one another.

However, there are limits to the relativity of intelligible principles. As I noted in a previous publication (and briefly pointed out at the start of this chapter), Proclus rejects the Porphyrian vision of a homogenous intellect in favour of one which clearly distinguished unparticipated intellect from its participated manifestations. There is no version of intellect that is truly semi-unified and semi-divided (though it seems unlikely that the student of Porphyry would go as far as Proclus fears). Either all things are as one in the one Intellect, or everything exists in each intellect specifically. Although the theological principles described in the *Platonic Theology* can exist in more ways than two, they do not subsequently exist in any way whatsoever. Incorporeal multiplicities are always discrete multiplicities. This results in a dichotomy we must navigate when we study the writings of our Neoplatonic thinker. Proclus mediates between the discrete multiplicity of distinctive characters such as wholeness or perfection and a fluid procession from one to many, in which the multiplicities of each hypostasis are defined in relation to those of its superior causes and its inferior products. As Proclus himself notes in the *Elements of Theology*:

> πᾶσαι δὲ αὖ αἱ ἀμέθεκτοι μονάδες εἰς τὸ ἓν ἀνάγονται, διότι πᾶσαι τῷ ἑνὶ ἀνά-λογον· ἢ οὖν ταὐτόν τι καὶ αὗται πεπόνθασι, τὴν πρὸς τὸ ἓν ἀναλογίαν, ταύτῃ εἰς τὸ ἓν αὐταῖς ἡ ἀναγωγὴ γίνεται. καὶ ἢ μὲν ἀπὸ τοῦ ἑνὸς πᾶσαι, οὐδεμία τούτων ἀρχή ἐστιν, ἀλλ᾽ ὡς ἀπ᾽ ἀρχῆς ἐκείνης· ἢ δὲ ἑκάστη ἀμέθεκτος, ταύτῃ ἀρχὴ ἑκάστη.
>
> PROCLUS, *ET* 100, 90.7–12

Again, all the unparticipated monads are referred to the One, because all are analogous to the One. Insofar as they too are affected by a common

DIVIDING THE INDIVISIBLE   159

character, namely their analogy to the One, they are granted their reference to the One. In respect of their common origin from the One none of
them is a first principle, but all have that [One] as their first principle. Yet
each *is* a first principle *qua* unparticipated.

> Tr. DODDS 1963 (modified)

In other words, we cannot view Proclean concepts of wholeness, perfection,
and the like in isolation. Any definition of the intelligible monad of Wholeness
must not only take into account the unique characteristics of the eternal
whole, but also Eternity's role as a manifestation of the One. Because of this
dichotomy, Proclus defines the many metaphysical principles he discusses in
the *Platonic Theology* by their relations to one another as often as he discusses
them *per se*.

5.7.3   *The Whole and the Good*

As a result of this, Proclus' mereological writings do not contain axiologically
neutral formulae for defining wholeness and parthood. All the ontological concepts that arise in the procession of beings derive from the One, and the One is
the Good. As a result, being whole is pre-eminently related to being good. This
is evidenced by the many ways in which Proclus coats his mereological writings with axiological language. The most important difference between the
eternal whole and the mortal creature is the latter's inability to safeguard its
share in the good. This corruptive particularisation of mortal creatures stands
in sharp contrast to the lawful particularisation of Platonic Forms by Cronus,
Rhea, and Zeus.

Ultimately, the connection between perfection and wholeness follows naturally from the fact that both principles derive from the Good. To be whole
in Proclean terms means not just to be a unity that prefigures a composition,
but also to possess one's share in the good in a stable and unchanging manner.
The whole contains the entirety of what it is supposed to be simultaneously in
its unity. The conceptualisation of being perfect *qua* being complete naturally
follows from this idea. If a being has parts and also possesses its share in the
good wholly and in a stable manner, then it naturally cannot be missing any
of the components which are essential for retaining this goodness. As such,
being complete means not just to possess all of one's parts, but also to possess
the full goodness that one has been granted by the One. The whole contains its
proper goodness in one, and although the perfect being is not as pure a unity
as the whole, it makes up for it by taking into its possession any and all of the
essential constituents it needs to be its best self.

160   CHAPTER 5

TABLE 5   Overview of the development of wholeness, perfection, and division in intellect

Hypostasis	Wholeness	Perfection	Division of ontological kinds
One Being 1st intelligible	–	–	–
Eternity 2nd intelligible	**Whole** **Three wholes**	–	–
Paradigm 3rd intelligible	Whole + **totality** Three wholes	**Wholly perfect**	–
Realm above heaven 1st intelligible-intellective	Whole + totality Three wholes	Wholly perfect	–
Heavenly arch 2nd intelligible-intellective	Whole + totality + **part** Three wholes	Wholly perfect	–
Subcelestial realm 3rd intelligible-intellective	Whole + totality + part Three wholes	Wholly perfect **Three perfections**	–
Cronus 1st intellective	Whole + totality + part Three wholes	Wholly perfect Three perfections	**Division of kinds** (Uniform)
Rhea 2nd intellective	Whole + totality + part Three wholes	Wholly perfect Three perfections	Division of kinds (Uniform and pluriform)
Zeus/Demiurge 3rd intellective	Whole + totality + part Three wholes	Wholly perfect Three perfections	Division of kinds (Pluriform)

TABLE 6   Overview of the mereological properties (ἰδιότητες) of the One, the intelligible realm, and the intelligible-intellective realm as distilled from Plato's *Parmenides*

The One	Unity/goodness					
One Being	Unity/goodness	Being				
Eternity	Unity/goodness	Being	Wholeness			
Paradigm	Unity/goodness	Being	Wholeness	Perfection		
Realm above heaven	Unity/goodness	Being	Wholeness	Perfection	Number	
Heavenly arch	Unity/goodness	Being	Wholeness	Perfection	Number	Parts
Subcelestial realm	Unity/goodness	Being	Wholeness	Perfection	Number	Parts Shape

CHAPTER 6

Uniting the Imperfect

Any student of mereology who prefers a physiological approach over a logical one—in other words, anyone who accepts that, in our understanding of natural phenomena, there is a distinction to be made between heaps of things and compositions that truly form a singular entity—is eventually forced to face the challenge posed by Lewis. How is one supposed to fortify their support for a theory of restricted composition? One could declare a singular natural phenomenon to be the ultimate mereological criterion, as Van Inwagen did with his theorem of life-as-composition, but this inevitably results in the jettisoning of an unnecessarily large number of composite entities from our ontology. One could attempt to drop the issue on the lawn of ontology proper (or even other sciences entirely), as Koslicki proposes, but one might argue that this is merely an attempt to ignore the problem rather than to solve it.

It should be clear by now that Proclus is not a proto-Lewesian philosopher. His metaphysics does not revolve around abstract logical concepts such as the trout-turkey, whose representation or lack thereof in nature has no bearing on the truth of its existence. Proclus deals in entities which exist. He describes even the One itself, which transcends reality entirely, with the term 'ὕπαρξις,' which indicates that he considers it to be a principality.[1] Furthermore, the intelligible realm contains a discrete multiplicity of beings rather than a continual one, as we have noted before. In other words, there is a finite number of ontological kinds in the Proclean universe. Lastly, the rule of Proclus requires that composition be restricted, since Wholeness itself is inferior to Being and thus has a shorter causal reach. All of this prohibits the Proclean scholar from positing fusions such as the trout-turkey, logically sound as they might be.

The primary restriction on Proclus' view of composition is his equation of wholeness with eternity, as we discussed in the previous chapter. If only eternal beings can truly be called wholes, a lot of composite entities may be rejected from our Neoplatonic ontology. A mortal creature inherently possesses a merely temporal existence, for example. However, we have already seen that Proclus attempts to avoid such a drastic jettisoning of mortal creatures from the list of wholes, since he describes them as 'wholes in a partial manner'. This

---

1   See chapter 4, section 2.

© ARTHUR OOSTHOUT, 2025 | DOI:10.1163/9789004721760_007

raises the obvious question of how a partial being can still be considered a whole, especially if this partial being appears to lack the distinctive character of wholeness that would otherwise be bestowed upon it by Eternity. It is an answer we cannot distil from Proclus' theological writings alone, for in those he devotes his attention primarily to charting the development of being whole and being a part as ontological entities rather than enumerating all the kinds of beings which participate in wholeness.

Instead, we must investigate Proclus' cosmology to discern which kinds of beings the Demiurge and the younger gods instantiate as wholes within the sensible cosmos. It should come as no surprise that Proclus' *Timaeus*-commentary will be our primary source for information in this chapter. In reading this text, our focus shall lie on three aspects. First, we must devote our attention to Proclus' concept of time and its role in shaping material existence. It stands to reason that the metaphysical concept which mirrors eternity should influence Proclus' mereology in some way as well.

Second, a number of passages from the second through fifth books of the *Timaeus*-commentary will be analysed, specifically those passages in which Proclus categorises the wholes and parts of the cosmos in different ways. The primary goal of this analysis is not to provide a dry summary of all the various kinds of parts and wholes in the cosmos. One could very well reconstruct such a summary merely by reading the various scholarly articles which deal with these passages individually, each of which we shall refer to when the respective passage is brought forward. However, bringing these various categorisations of the parts of the cosmos together will give us an idea of the way in which Proclus distinguishes eternal wholes from partial wholes and, more importantly, to which entities we cannot apply the term 'whole' any longer. Once we have acquired this knowledge, the next item on our list will be a passage from the fifth book in which Proclus compares the gods who exist within the cosmos to mortal creatures, which will lead into a brief discussion of the special place of human beings in the Proclean universe and the way in which we, mortal as we are, might still be whole.

Having discussed all this, we shall end by reflecting on the way in which Proclus' union of metaphysics and Platonic axiology, which already shone through in his mereology of the gods in the previous chapter, informs the ideas presented in his *Timaeus*-commentary. We have discovered how Proclus distinguishes internal complexity from internal multiplicity, how he defines the whole as a transcendent unity over the parts, and at what point in the causal procession of beings wholeness begins. Now, what is left to discover is at what point in the procession wholeness reaches its end.

UNITING THE IMPERFECT 163

6.1 The Mereological Role of Time

Before we delve into the mereological composition of the sensible cosmos itself, we must determine how the concept of time slots into Proclus' mereology. The mereology of the intelligible gods revolved around the concept of eternity. As Kutash has shown, time plays a similar role in shaping the wholes and parts of the sensible realm. In order to avoid regurgitating her findings or those of other scholars, I shall give only a brief summary of Proclus' views on the nature of time.[2] For Proclus, time is not simply a dimension through which things move, but instead an active principle which bestows a measure of temporal existence upon the beings in the cosmos. In this sense, Time is the monad of all temporal beings just as Eternity is the monad which bestows unchangeable existence upon all eternal beings. This also means that it transcendently measures all wholes in the cosmos, just as Eternity instantiated the wholeness of the intelligible beings.[3]

Furthermore, Proclus follows Iamblichus in postulating that Time itself transcends the cosmos,[4] which logically follows from the fact that Eternity transcends the cosmic Paradigm. This also means that Time itself is primarily characterised by Proclus as transcendent principle of wholeness, i.e., a whole before the parts, just as Eternity was.[5] In this sense, Time *qua* unparticipated monad is more so an eternal being than a temporal one. In fact, following the suggestion of Siorvanes, Kutash notes that unparticipated Time must be situated within intellect and be symbolised by Zeus.[6] As a result, the

---

2 Unless stated otherwise, the analysis given in this paragraph and the following five is informed by that of Kutash (2009). Another overview of Proclus' concept of time can be found in O'Neill (1962), wherein Proclus' views are also compared to those of Aristotle and Plotinus. Additionally, Vargas (2021) has recently published a monograph which traces the various ancient sources for Proclus' theory of time, including Plato, Aristotle, the Stoics, and Plotinus. I do not focus here on the terminological issue of *Tim.* 37e, namely of how to understand the relation between the 'parts' of time (μέρη χρόνου), such as day and night, and the 'forms' of time (χρόνου εἴδη), such as 'was' and 'will be', in Plato's cosmology. Instead, I discuss time's role as an image of eternity, given the latter's link to wholeness. For Proclus' discussion of the parts and forms of time from *Tim.* 37e, see his *IT* IV, 44.11–47.15 (3.34.14–36.29 Diehl); cf. Martijn (2010: 205–206).

3 Proclus, *IT* IV, 39.18–20 (3.30.24–26 Diehl); cf. *IT* IV, 44.4–9 (3.34.7–13 Diehl).

4 This contrasts with Plotinus' theory, according to which time is situated in the soul; Kutash (2009: 44–45).

5 See, e.g., Proclus, *IT* IV, 51.16–24 (3.40.5–13 Diehl).

6 Siorvanes (1996: 134–135); Kutash (2009: 50 and 63 n. 14). Proclus considers time to be one of ten gifts which Zeus, the Demiurge, bestows upon the sensible cosmos, for which see section 2

relation between the cosmos and unparticipated Time also mirrors the relation between Eternity and the Paradigm. Proclus confirms that Time and the cosmos cooperate in their efforts to imitate their fathers, and in this respect, time also contributes to the process by which the cosmos becomes perfect (in the sense that it contains all things, just as the Paradigm does).[7]

Time's imitation of Eternity is nicely summarised in the fourth book of the *Timaeus*-commentary. When discussing the nature of the Platonic Great Year, i.e., the span of time in which the cosmic sphere completes a full circumference,[8] Proclus reveals that Time brings the movement of the cosmic sphere full circle, like a monad which delimits the multitude of a determinate number. Time, however, is not any given number, such as a month or a year. These time spans are mere parts of yet longer time spans. Instead, Time delimits the time span of the entire cosmic circumference, the Platonic Great Year, and as such is a perfect number (ἀριθμὸς τέλειος) and a perfect time span (χρόνος τέλειος). Its product, the time span of the cosmic circumference in its entirety, is purely a whole and not part of something greater, and in this respect, Time mirrors its predecessor Eternity, which is Wholeness itself. Yet Time and Eternity are not whole in quite the same way: Eternity bestows wholeness upon eternal beings all at once (τὴν ὁλότητα ὁμοῦ πᾶσαν ἐπιφέρει), whereas Time bestows wholeness upon temporal things over a certain duration (μετὰ παρατάσεως). To conclude, Proclus again utilises the term 'unfolding' (ἀνέλιξις) to describe temporal wholeness as the pluralised counterpart to eternal wholeness.[9]

Time is not a linear phenomenon in Proclus' eyes. Instead, he characterises it through the Neoplatonic imagery of circles which goes back to Plotinus. If Eternity is the whole as a point, unitary, unchanging, and undivided, then Time is the whole as the circle which centres on this point. It is perfect, but it does not contain all its parts at once. Instead, Proclus characterises its wholeness as wholeness through continuity and reversion to its starting point.

In this respect, Time follows the same mechanics which informed the development of wholeness in the intelligible realm. Just as the intelligible heaven, which distinguished the ontological concepts of whole and part from one another, was a more pluralised instantiation of the wholeness inherent in

---

below. For a more extensive analysis of Time's role as a product of the Demiurge and the manner in which Proclus distils this notion from the *Timaeus*, see Vargas (2021: 22–30).

7   See, e.g., Proclus, *IT* IV, 67.2–6 (3.51.30–52.3 Diehl); cf. *IT* IV, 65.4–66.1 (3.50.21–51.7 Diehl).

8   Cf. Vargas (2021: 64–66); the Platonic lemma to which Proclus refers for this concept is Plato, *Tim.* 39d2–7.

9   Proclus, *IT* IV, 118.17–119.5 (3.92.13–23 Diehl). We already noted in chapter 5, section 5 that Proclus describes inferior triadic principles within the Intellect as 'unfoldings' of their superior antecedents.

UNITING THE IMPERFECT

Eternity, in the same way Time is a principle which unfolds the unitary and transcendent wholeness of eternity and enables sensible beings to change over time. Already in the second book of his *Timaeus*-commentary, Proclus emphasises this more pluralised wholeness of temporal beings compared to the unchangeable 'all in one'-wholeness of Eternity, when he states that 'what has neither its whole essence or activity at once, remaining in one, is called "generated"' and that 'it is clear that all movement exists per part and will not be whole at once.'[10] In other words, wholes in the sensible realm are capable of undergoing change, in contrast to the stable wholes of the intelligible realm, because their principle of wholeness is one which bestows a more divided character than the intelligible Wholeness did.[11]

Whether the partial nature of temporal beings derives specifically from their changeability or more generally from their movement is not always clear. On the one hand, Proclus argues that the heavenly spheres undergo neither diminutions nor additions and states that the circumference of the cosmos is perfect, implying that the celestial bodies are whole because their movements are perfectly circular and thus stable. On the other hand, he establishes that all movement exists per part, which would include the circumference of the cosmos itself.[12] The obvious distinguishing factor between different kinds of temporal beings is their everlasting nature or lack thereof. The cosmos and the celestial bodies possess such everlastingness, whereas mortal bodies do not. Even if the celestial bodies change position, their circular movement overall is stable precisely because it never ceases. The movements and changes of the mortal creature are inherently partial because of their finiteness.[13]

The notion of change over time presents significant problems for scholars of mereology. Even today, scholars disagree on whether a whole which changes over time remains the same entity, just as the ancient philosophers did when they agonised over the nature of the ship of Theseus. Interestingly, though not

---

10   Proclus, *IT* II, 107.7–8 (1.227.27–28 Diehl): τὸ οὖν μὴ ὅλην ἅμα ἑστῶσαν ἐν ἑνὶ τὴν οὐσίαν ἢ τὴν ἐνέργειαν ἔχον γενητὸν ἐπονομάζεται; *loc. cit.* 13–14 (32–33 Diehl): ὅτι μὲν πᾶσα κίνησις κατὰ μέρος ὑφίσταται καὶ οὐχ ὅλη ἅμα ἔσται, δῆλον. Kutash (2009: 59) rightly points out that this does not mean that generation itself should be considered as a process with a definite point of origin (for then the cosmos itself would have been created at a certain point in time), but rather that 'there is a continuous converting process of a hypothetical disorder'. In contrast, eternal beings simply *are* ordered.

11   For a much more extensive discussion of Proclean Time as the principle of change in the sensible cosmos, see Vargas (2021: 46–110 *et al.*).

12   For the notion that the movements of the celestial bodies are stable, see Proclus, *IT* V, 97.8–16, cited below, and *IT* IV, 118.17–119.5, cited above. For the seemingly opposing notion that all cosmic movements are partial, cf. *IT* II, 107.13–14 and *IP* III, 823.25–824.2.

13   Cf. Proclus, *IT* V, 105.2–11, as discussed in section 2.4 below.

166 CHAPTER 6

surprisingly, Proclus is not bothered by such questions. In the fifth book of his *Timaeus*-commentary, when he comments on the additions of the young gods to the creations of the Demiurge,[14] Proclus raises a number of questions regarding the relation between the mortal/changeable and immortal/unchanging aspects of the soul. Among these is the following issue.

> ἀλλ᾽ ἆρα τοῦτο ὃ λέγουσί τινες, ὅτι μένει καὶ διαλύεται τὸ αὐτὸ διὰ τῆς ἀναστοιχειώσεως, καὶ διὰ τοῦτο θνητόν τε ἅμα καὶ οὐ θνητόν ἐστιν; ἀλλὰ τοῦτο καὶ καθ᾽ ἑαυτὸ μὲν ἄτοπον· τῆς γὰρ ἑνώσεως ἀπολομένης πῶς ἔτι τὸ αὐτὸ διαμένειν φήσομεν; οὐ γάρ ἐστι ζωῶν συμφόρησις ἡ ἄλογος, ἀλλὰ μία ζωὴ πολυειδής.
>
> PROCLUS, *IT* V, 97.8–16 (3.236.18–25 Diehl)

> But [should we affirm] what some say, that the same [living being] both remains and is dissolved on account of the dissolution [and renewal][15] of its elements, and that on this account it is at the same time both mortal and not mortal? But this is absurd in its own right, for once its unification is lost how shall we affirm that it still remains the same? Non-rational life is not an aggregation of lives, but a *single* multi-faceted life.
>
> Tr. TARRANT 2017 (modified)

Proclus' opponents appear to trace the duality of the mortal yet immortal soul back to the paradox of the Ship of Theseus. In other words, the soul continually undergoes change and is in this respect destroyed, just as one might claim that Theseus' ship is no longer the same once its planks have been systematically replaced. Yet, these opponents seem to claim, there is a shared identity between the various instances of this changing soul which renders it immortal.

Proclus' answer initially seems to be a pedantic attempt to avoid the argument. In what way, one might ask, is 'a single multi-faceted life' different from a collection of lives in one everchanging whole? The answer is obvious if one

---

14 Plato, *Tim.* 41d1–2.

15 Tarrant (2017: 120 and 120 n. 295) suspects that Proclus' opponents are referring to Plato, *Symposium* 207c9–208a7, where Socrates discusses how both the soul and the body remain the same despite the continual removal and renewal of their parts. His suggestion is supported by the fact that the phrase 'διὰ τῆς ἀναστοιχειώσεως' is linked to 'τὸ αὐτὸ' rather than 'διαλύεται,' and as such must refer both to the dissolution *and* to the remaining of the soul's life. As Tarrant explains, the term 'ἀναστοιχείωσις' is itself quite rare (most notably appearing once in Galenus and once in Alexander of Aphrodisias, as indicated by *LSJ* s.v. ἀναστοιχείωσις). However, Tarrant suggests that the theory outlined here might be associated with a Porphyrian conception of the psychic vehicle which is rejected by Iamblichus, for which see also Finamore (1985: 11); cf. Iamblichus, *Fr.* 84 Dillon and Dillon (1973: 380).

UNITING THE IMPERFECT

remembers Proclus' continued emphasis on the transcendence of the whole *qua* unity over its parts, but Proclus nevertheless restates this view in the following lines.

The pneumatic vehicle of the soul, like the soul itself, is created by the Demiurge and thus possesses 'the pinnacles of non-rational life' (τὰς μὲν ἀκρότητας τῆς ἀλόγου ζωῆς), according to Proclus. As a result, both these pinnacles of life and the soul-vehicle itself are everlasting (ἀΐδιοι). It is only when the younger gods weave individual lives onto this vehicle that it becomes mortal, for these lesser forms of life make the vehicle and its life-pinnacles extended and divided (ἐκτεινομένας καὶ μεριζομένας). It is this lesser life that the soul must be purified of in order to return to its proper place below Intellect.[16]

This distinction between a holistic and a divided kind of life shows that Proclus' mereology has little to fear from the paradox of the Ship of Theseus. Here again, he safeguards the unity of the whole by disconnecting it from the multiplicity of the parts. The soul *qua* immortal unity is instantiated by the Demiurge and logically precedes the soul *qua* ship-of-Theseusesque multiplicity, which does not come to be until the young gods take the immortal soul and weave a mortal, divided, and temporal life on to it—recall the way in which greater gifts from the gods serve as substrates for lesser gifts rather than vice versa.[17] In summary, Proclus does not need to answer the question how the hypothetical ship of Theseus, in this case the soul, can be considered a single composition out of everchanging parts, since the unitary and immortal essence of the soul is not logically composed out of and thus preceded by its temporal parts. In this way, we must understand Proclus' distinction between a 'collection of lives' and 'one pluriform life'. The former is primarily a multiplicity which must become one, whereas the latter is a unity which becomes pluralised.[18]

This is the mereological role of Time: to take the eternal and unchanging wholeness disseminated by the second intelligible triad, pluralise it, and then bestow this new divided and temporal existence upon the creatures of the sensible cosmos. We may then explain their unity by their reversion, through whatever means, upon the eternal unities of the intelligible realm. In this respect, Proclus' temporal wholes are similar to those described by the modern

---

16   Proclus, *IT* V, 97.20–98.3 (3.236.30–237.6 Diehl).
17   See chapter 3, section 1.
18   For a much more detailed discussion of Proclus' attempts to safeguard the identity of the soul from the continuous changes brought on by its descent into the material cosmos, see Steel (1978: 69–73).

theory of four-dimensionalism.[19] According to this theory the whole is not just a spatial compound (e.g., me existing out of bodily parts), but also a temporal compound (e.g., me existing out of the various instances of me across my life). Like Proclus' immortal unities, four-dimensional wholes are multi-faceted entities due to the changes their parts undergo over time, yet they retain a single identity *qua* whole throughout their existence.[20]

6.2   Between a Systematic and an Exegetical Mereology

Not all temporal beings are equal, however. In the previous chapter, we encountered passages in which Proclus insinuates that the wholeness of the everlasting cosmos transcended that of the mortal creature, but we have not yet discerned how the mortal creature is ranked exactly opposite the everlasting cosmos. Unfortunately, Proclus' answer to the question 'what kinds of wholes and parts exist within the cosmos?' tends to differ from passage to passage throughout books three through five of his *Timaeus*-commentary. However, even if the exegetical context of each lemma leads Proclus to shift the details of his mereology around, certain notions remain applicable throughout. These include not only the equation of wholeness with eternity, but also a more nuanced approach to the dividedness of the mortal creature. Since no full overview of these passages has yet been provided—though individual discussions of specific passages on cosmological mereology are available in the established literature— each of them is briefly analysed and discussed.

It is important to keep in mind that Proclus' account of the cosmogony is almost entirely derived from the cosmological concepts introduced in Plato's *Timaeus* (though the reader may have already suspected as much because of the name '*Timaeus*-commentary'). For the sake of clarity, the tenets of Proclus' views on demiurgy which are most important to follow the arguments he presents in his mereological discussions are summarised here.[21] First, Proclus distils from the *Timaeus* a list of ten gifts the Demiurge bestows upon his creation while fashioning it. These gifts stack upon each other, each being greater

---

19   For the distinction between four-dimensionalism and the rivalling theory of three-dimensionalism, see chapter 5, section 2.1.

20   The main distinction between Proclus and the four-dimensionalists is, of course, that four-dimensionalism does not presuppose reversion to or participation in a *transcendent* principle of unity.

21   Here too we find that Proclus gives no single overarching schema for the demiurgic process, but rather provides several alternative schemata in various passages, as Opsomer (2000a: 123) has already noted.

UNITING THE IMPERFECT 169

than the last.[22] This scheme of the ten gifts supposedly indicated by Plato informs the entirety of book three of the *Timaeus*-commentary and most of book four, and as such shapes the background of a number of passages we shall discuss.[23] Second, Proclus distinguishes between the acts of creation performed by the Demiurge himself and those of the younger gods whom he calls upon to finish his work. The former production processes are designated as the 'first demiurgy', whereas the latter are categorised under the 'second demiurgy' by Proclus.[24] Lastly, Proclus does not interpret Timaeus' creation story literally so as to envision a temporal creation process with clear starting and end points. Instead, any of the steps of the creation process must be understood as ordered not chronologically but according to logical priority.[25] With these contextual elements kept in the back of our minds, let us now trace the kinds of wholes and parts Proclus distinguishes in his exegesis of the Platonic cosmogony. To accomplish this, we shall discuss four select passages from the third, fourth, and fifth book of the *Timaeus*-commentary in detail.

6.2.1 *The Introduction to the Third Book of the Timaeus-Commentary*
The first relevant passage appears almost immediately at the start of the third book, within Proclus' introduction to the theory of the ten gifts of the Demiurge. After he discussed the general mechanics of demiurgy and the resemblance of the cosmos to the intelligible Paradigm in book two, Proclus now reveals how Plato supposedly envisioned the process of creation.

In the previous lines of the *Timaeus*, Proclus explains, Plato's titular character has shown us the cosmos's subsistence *qua* whole (τὴν καθ' ὁλότητα τοῦ παντὸς ὑπόστασιν), specifically when he called it 'ensouled and possessed of intellect' (ἔμψυχον καὶ ἔννουν) and indicated its resemblance to the 'wholly perfect living being' (παντελὲς ζῷον), i.e., the Paradigm.[26] In the lines to be discussed in the third book of the commentary, Timaeus will additionally show us the subsistence which divides the cosmos by wholes (τὴν καθ' ὅλα διαιροῦσαν τὸν κόσμον) and the production of the 'whole parts' (τὴν τῶν ὅλων ποίησιν μερῶν). These whole parts are the cosmic soul and the cosmic body. The

---

22 These ten gifts of the Demiurge are summarised and discussed in full in Kutash's (2011) aptly titled monograph.

23 For example, the previously discussed principle of Time is envisioned by Proclus as one of the last and greatest gifts bestowed upon the sensible universe.

24 See Opsomer (2000a, 2003, 2016, and 2021) for a more in-depth discussion of the many steps of the demiurgic process, which is only sketched in broad strokes here. For the Demiurge's address to the younger gods, see Plato, *Tim.* 40e5–41d3.

25 Proclus, *IT* III, 142.3 (2.102.7 Diehl); cf. Opsomer (2016: 143–144).

26 The two phrases are taken from Plato, *Tim.* 30b8 and 31b1, respectively.

170

aforementioned cosmic intellect also belongs among the 'whole parts', albeit as a part that is not in any way generated by the Demiurge (coming-to-be would diminish its total lack of extension, Proclus tells us), but simply flows forth from his providence. In a later passage, Timaeus will subsequently add the subsistence which 'cuts up the cosmos into parts' (κατὰ μέρη τέμνουσα τὸ πᾶν) when he contemplates the 'body-making activity' (ἡ σωματουργικὴ ἐνέργεια) of the Demiurge by describing the four elements. However, he does not discuss individual corporeal things but 'remains among the whole elements' (ἐν τοῖς ὅλοις μένει στοιχείοις). For the production by the Demiurge, Proclus explains, is a 'whole demiurgy of the wholes' (ὅλη δημιουργία τῶν ὅλων) which produces only 'whole parts'. The 'individuals and truly partial beings' (τὰ δὲ ἄτομα καὶ ὄντως μερικὰ) are passed on to the young gods for production, granting them the chance to mimic their father just as he mimics the intelligible Paradigm.[27]

This dense passage reveals a number of interesting facts. First, Proclus connects the previously mentioned framework of the first and second demiurgy to the distinction between eternal whole and divided temporal beings. Hence, the Demiurge's status as 'father of wholes' refers to the fact that he created all of the beings in the cosmos which Proclus considers truly whole, i.e., beings which participate in eternity in some regard. In contrast, our partial existence derives from the second phase of demiurgy.

Second, Proclus distinguishes the different kinds of true wholes in the cosmos, i.e., the products of the first demiurgy. The first rank belongs to the cosmos itself, which takes the shape of a unified (καθ' ὁλότητα) creature armed with a soul and a nongenerated intellect. The conceptual parts Proclus ascribes to the cosmos here, i.e., the World Soul and the participated intellect, are subsequently distinguished in the second rank alongside the cosmic body and designated individually as 'whole parts' (τὴν τῶν ὅλων ποίησιν μερῶν). This implies that the cosmos *qua* singular ensouled, corporeal, and intellective being is logically prior to the three whole parts *qua* parts (no surprise there). The third rank contains the parts which compose the cosmic body, one of the 'whole parts' from the previous rank.[28] These parts are the four basic elements: fire, air, earth, and water. In this case, one should not take the term 'elements' to refer to particular instances of earth-stuff or water-particles, but rather to the 'whole' elements (ὅλα στοιχεῖα). In other words, Proclus refers to the unitary

---

27   Proclus, *IT* III, 2.13–3.18 (2.2.9–3.8 Diehl).

28   Although Proclus does not confirm whether the parts of the World Soul also belong to this rank of cosmic parts, a daring interpreter might reasonably infer as much.

and monadic essence of each element, which is created by the Demiurge and subsequently divided into particular particles by the younger gods.[29]

6.2.2 The Third Gift of the Demiurge: the Whole of Wholes

Further on in the third book of the *Timaeus*-commentary, Proclus gives a different overview of the mereological composition of the cosmos. Here he discusses the supposed third gift of the Demiurge, revealed by Timaeus' statement that the Demiurge fashioned the cosmos as 'a living being as whole as possible and perfect, composed of perfect parts' and as 'one whole composed of all wholes'.[30] These descriptions, Proclus states, liken the cosmos to its wholly perfect Paradigm, since the wholes which compose the cosmos are discussed as parts of it, are referred back to the whole, and by themselves only possess the lesser type of perfection proper to parts instead of being purely (ἁπλῶς) perfect. Proclus then divides the cosmic whole and its parts across four categories.[31] The first is the 'whole holistically' (τὸ ὅλον ὁλικῶς), to which belongs the cosmos in its capacity as the aforementioned 'one whole composed of all wholes'. The second category is the 'part holistically' (τὸ μέρος ὁλικῶς), to which belongs each of the heavenly spheres. The third is the 'whole partially' (τὸ ὅλον μερικῶς), to which belong the divided beings (μερικά) or mortal individuals, for their wholeness is at all times accompanied by 'the distinctive character of a part' (μετὰ τῆς μερικῆς ἰδιότητος). The last category is the 'part partially' (τὸ μέρος μερικῶς), to which belong the parts of the aforementioned mortal creatures. These, Proclus concludes, are parts and *only* parts (μέρη γάρ ἐστι μόνον).[32]

This is perhaps Proclus' most famous mereological schema of the sensible cosmos, as evidenced by the fact that it has been cited by multiple scholars.[33] As such, only a short summary of this passage is required. The central opposition in this passage is the opposition between universal things which exist holistically (ὁλικῶς) and particular beings which exist partially (μερικῶς). As Opsomer and Van Riel have noted, all of the beings in the first category are products of the Demiurge himself, whereas the particular beings are created by the younger gods. This is, in effect, a clearer explanation of the same opposition we discerned in the previous passage.

---

29 For an example of this distinction between a particular element and the element *qua* monad, see Proclus, *IT* IV, 143.12–16 (3.111.13–17 Diehl).

30 Plato, *Tim.* 32c8–33b1 (as cited in the introduction to the book).

31 These same four categories are also discussed in the fifth book of the *Platonic Theology*, as we saw in chapter 5, section 8.

32 Proclus, *IT* III, 85.16–86.7 (2.61.26–62.8 Diehl).

33 Most notably, Baltzly (2008: 401–402), Van Riel (2009: 249), and Opsomer (2016: 144–148).

172   CHAPTER 6

The cosmos *qua* whole is once again distinguished from its parts, although its subsequent division into everlasting parts by the Demiurge is far less detailed than it was in the previous passage, with only the heavenly spheres being mentioned here. In contrast, the individual mortal creatures are discussed in more detail, as Proclus notes the intriguing duality of their being primarily divided (μετὰ τῆς μερικῆς ἰδιότητος) yet still whole to some extent. The parts of particular beings, i.e., things which can no longer be called whole in any way, complete the list.

6.2.3 *The Tenth Gift of the Demiurge: Resemblance to the Paradigm*

The next mereological schema appears in the fourth book of the *Timaeus*-commentary, specifically the section where Proclus discusses the tenth and final gift of the Demiurge to the cosmos: the fact that it contains all living beings which exist and, in doing so, mirrors its intelligible Paradigm.[34] If the cosmos contains all that pre-existed intelligibly in the Paradigm, Proclus argues, then it must also possess the three kinds of wholeness. The first type of wholeness, the whole before the parts, is present in the structure which the Demiurge imparts on the cosmos as a whole, namely that of the aforementioned 'ensouled living being in possession of intellect' (ζῷον ἔμψυχον ἔννουν).[35] To fashion this one whole, the Demiurge structured the disorderly moving material substrate (κοσμηθέντος μὲν τοῦ πλημμελῶς κινουμένου καὶ ἀτάκτως), while soul, intellect, and divine unification were added to it as well (ψυχῆς δὲ ἐπιγενομένης καὶ νοῦ καὶ θείας ἑνώσεως).[36] The account of the cosmogony then reveals how the cosmos constitutes a whole composed of parts: it shows that the Demiurge fashioned the two revolutions of the Same and the Different, the four corporeal elements, and the circles of the World Soul to function as essential constituents (συμπληρωτικά) of the cosmos, since it would not be the 'All' without them. The lines of the *Timaeus* currently under scrutiny, Proclus tells us, will reveal how the cosmos possesses the whole in the part too. Timaeus

---

34   Plato, *Tim.* 39e4–7.

35   Plato, *Tim.* 30b8.

36   *Pace* Baltzly (2013: 177), who translates the κοσμηθέντος μὲν ... ψυχῆς δὲ-construction so as to imply an arrangement according logical priority ('when ... then'), whereby the bestowal of soul, intellect, and divine unification follows (from) the ordering of the material receptacle. However, it seems more logical to presume that Proclus merely means to contrast the two aspects of the Demiurge's creation-process, i.e., shaping the material receptacle and granting the cosmos a share in the incorporeal principles respectively, without implying any strict order of priority. These two activities also constituted a single phase of the process of demiurgy when Proclus applied to it his rule of causality, for which see chapter 3, section 3.

reveals that the cosmos contains four regions, the heaven, the skies, the seas, and the earth, which together encompass all individual kinds of living beings which where seminally present in the four Forms of the intelligible Paradigm. All living things are present in each of these four regions in a proper manner, e.g., 'heavenly' (οὐρανίως) in the heavens, 'aerially' (ἀερίως) in the skies, and 'earthly' (χθονίως) on land. In other words, each region of the cosmos imitates the all-encompassing nature of that cosmos in a more specific way and is thus a whole in the part. These four regions are each completed by the presence of their individual inhabitants (τὰ μερικὰ ζῷα, δι' ὧν συμπεπλήρωται πᾶσα μερὶς τοῦ παντός), as a result of which they together encompass all individuals beings that could exist and so complete the cosmos's resemblance to the transcendently all-encompassing Paradigm.[37]

This passage is interesting for a number of reasons. Most striking is the fact that the three kinds of wholeness do not seem to be three manifestations of quite the same whole. The cosmos *qua* whole before the parts seemingly precedes the 'whole parts' mentioned earlier, i.e., soul, body, and nongenerated intellect. Yet none of these elements are represented by the whole in the part, which instead manifests in the four regions of the cosmos. D'Hoine has picked up on this intriguing aspect of the passage, noting that 'il ne s'agit donc pas d'une unique division du cosmos sensible, qui s'articulerait progressivement de l'implicite à l'explicite à travers les trois degrés de totalité. Ce sont davantage des considérations exégétiques qui semblent mener Proclus à cette tentative d'expliquer le sens des trois types de totalité à travers les différentes perspectives que Platon nous offre dans le *Timée* sur le cosmos visible.'[38] Here d'Hoine points out an essential aspect of Proclus' cosmogony: it derives not from a meticulously systematic philosophy, despite Proclus' best efforts to turn it into one, but rather from the complex and at times contingent mythology of Plato's *Timaeus*.

As d'Hoine noted, the three kinds of wholeness serve a specific function here, namely to indicate different mereological characterisations of the cosmos distilled by Proclus from Plato's *Timaeus*. The whole before the parts is represented by the cosmos *qua* ensouled and intellective living being (ζῷον ἔμψυχον ἔννουν). Baltzly infers that the cosmic soul and intellect '*supervened* (ἐπιγενομένης)', and thus concludes that Proclus calls the cosmos a transcendent whole to indicate that, 'although these features may suppose a certain arrangement, they are not *constituted by it*. They are prior.'[39] Although Baltzly

---

37   Proclus, *IT* IV, 125.12–127.1 (3.97.12–98.11 Diehl).

38   D'Hoine (2021: 197).

39   Baltzly (2013: 29–30).

174 CHAPTER 6

is correct in stating that soul and intellect transcend the material cosmos, Proclus is not referring to that specific form of transcendence here. Instead, the whole before the parts in this passage once again signifies the cosmos as *one* ensouled intellective living being and the same unity Proclus previously referred to as the cosmos according to wholeness (καθ' ὁλότητα) and as whole in a universal manner (ὅλον ὁλικῶς).

The whole composed of parts serves to represent the multitude of essential constituents (συμπληρωτικά) of the cosmos, as described at various points in Plato's *Timaeus*. These equate to the parts of the aforementioned soul and body of the cosmos, i.e., the circumferences of the World Soul, the monadic essences of the four elements, and so on, which Proclus already discussed in the first passage from book three. Notably, the distinction between true eternal wholes and partial beings remains present in the subtext of this passage. The examples Proclus gives of the cosmos's essential constituents all belong to the first demiurgy and are thus everlasting things. This concurs with Proclus' overall analysis of the term 'part' in the sixth book of his *Parmenides*-commentary, during which he notes that the demise of an individual mortal creature has no bearing on the completeness of the cosmos, and that this mortal creature is hence not an essential constituent of the cosmos as a whole.[40]

Interestingly, Proclus nuances this distinction somewhat at the end of our current passage. Although the mortal inhabitants of the cosmos cannot hope to complete the cosmos as one whole, they nevertheless constitute essential components of *parts* of the cosmos, namely the four regions. The implied argument here is that the aquatic regions of the cosmos, for example, would not truly be complete without individual aquatic creatures to inhabit them. The same holds for any other 'portion' (μερίς) of the cosmos. Thus, although any individual creature can die without diminishing the perfection of the cosmos, there must always exist at least a certain number of individual creatures in each region of the cosmos. The Proclean cosmos must concur with the description Timaeus gives of it, a description which prescribes that it contains *all* of the kinds of living beings.

The whole in the part plays a more general role in this passage. Instead of referring to a part of the cosmos which mimics it in a specific way, as the outermost sphere of heaven does, it represents the well-known 'all-in-all'-principle of Neoplatonic philosophy. Each region of the cosmos contains all of the cosmic ingredients, albeit in a manner particular to its distinctive character. As Baltzly rightly notes, this division of the cosmos is analogous to the division of the

---

40   Proclus, *IP* VI, 1113.3–7; cf. Oosthout, A. (2023a: 130).

UNITING THE IMPERFECT   175

World Soul, whereby every portion the Demiurge takes from the soul-mixture contains all of its metaphysical ingredients, albeit in a particular proportion.[41]

What is interesting about this passage on the whole is the fact that it actually does not provide a definitive overview of the three kinds of wholes as they appear in the material cosmos. Even if one grants Proclus that the three kinds of wholeness are connected to different cosmic parts in order to represent various perspectives on cosmogony distilled from the *Timaeus*, as d'Hoine indicated, Proclus makes no mention here of various other aspects of the cosmos which he links to kinds of wholeness, such as the aforementioned outermost sphere of heaven, or the cosmos's relation to the Paradigm as composite whole to transcendent whole.[42] The reason behind this move is made clear in the final lines of the passage. Proclus is specifically discussing the tenth gift of the Demiurge to the cosmos here, i.e., its resemblance to the universal Paradigm. As such, the three kinds of wholeness ascribed to the material universe represent not just any perspective on the Platonic cosmogony, but specifically those characteristics which can be used to prove its likeness to the Paradigm, whether that be the fact that both exist firstly as a monadic unity or the fact that the parts of both are images of their wholes in some way. The three kinds of wholeness possessed by the cosmos are once again three particular manifestations of a triad that is applicable in more ways than any one passage from Proclus' works can illustrate.

6.2.4   *The Demiurge's Speech to the Young Gods*
Our next passage comes from the fifth and final book of the *Timaeus*-commentary, a book which is especially relevant because it provides further nuances to the previously drawn distinction between true eternal wholes and partial wholes. In our next lemma, Proclus gives his final comments on the *Timaeus*-passage in which the Demiurge addresses his younger brethren and instructs them to create the mortal creatures in his stead.[43] To elucidate the distinction between the immortal products of the Demiurge and the mortal products of the younger gods, Proclus arranges the different types of immortal and mortal creations schematically.

First, the engendering of divine beings by the Demiurge (1) is distinguished from the engendering of mortal creatures by the young gods (2). The production of divine beings is then divided into (1.a) the production of the whole cosmos 'before the parts' (ὁ κόσμος ὁ πρὸ τῶν μερῶν) and (1.b) the production

---

41   Baltzly (2013: 29).
42   Cf. chapter 4, section 3.
43   See *Tim.* 41a7–d4.

176   CHAPTER 6

of its 'large and everlasting parts' (τῶν μεγάλων ἐν αὐτῷ καὶ ἀιδίων μερῶν). These universal parts in turn are divided into (1.b.i) the everlasting inhabitants of the heavens and (1.b.ii) the immortals living beneath the moon. Moving on to the production of the mortal creatures, Proclus explains that we should distinguish between (2.a) the engendering of their divine and immortal aspect and (2.b) the production of all that is mortal about them. These mortal aspects can then be distinguished into (2.b.i) the generation of souls and (2.b.ii) the generation of bodies. The latter generation in turn has several steps, namely (2.b.ii.1) the production of the bodies as wholes and (2.b.ii.2) the production of their bodily parts, such as their heads, their hearts, and their livers.[44]

A detailed dissection of this passage is not necessary, since an illuminating schema has already been devised for that very purpose by Opsomer.[45] Let us note instead how Proclus' categories in this passage overlap with those of earlier passages and what he adds to those earlier categorisations. The cosmos *qua* whole is described in the same terms as previously. Proclus also confirms what we logically inferred from the previous passages, namely that the division between the true wholes produced by the Demiurge and the divided individual beings equates to the distinction between everlasting immortality and a finite existence in time. Furthermore, Proclus has already provided an argument for the everlasting nature of the cosmos in the fourth book of his commentary.

In that fourth book, Proclus argues that the cosmos is produced by the Demiurge *alongside* time (μετὰ χρόνου), not *in* time (ἐν χρόνῳ). But all coming to be happens in time, i.e., at a certain moment in time, and as such the phenomenon of coming to be is 'younger than time' (μεταγενέστερον χρόνου). Yet the cosmos itself is not 'younger than time' (ὁ δ' οὐρανὸς οὐδαμῶς ἐστι χρόνου μεταγενέστερος), but coordinate with it, and thus does not come to be at some moment in time.[46] In the same vein, dissolution is a process which only occurs at some moment in time (ποτέ). Yet neither Time itself nor the cosmos

---

44   Proclus, *IT* V, 105.2–11 (3.242.9–19 Diehl).

45   See specifically Opsomer (2003: 7).

46   *Pace* Baltzly (2013: 109 n. 196), who suggests that Proclus utilises the 'semantic range' of 'μεταγενέστερος' to state that 'everything that has come to be is such as to be subsequent in time [itself]' (πᾶν τὸ γιγνόμενον μεταγενέστερον εἶναι χρόνου; tr. Baltzly 2013) in the one sentence, whereas his subsequent use of the term in the other means 'a younger sibling compared to time' (ὁ δ' οὐρανὸς οὐδαμῶς ἐστι χρόνου μεταγενέστερος; tr. Baltzly 2013). However, Proclus uses the exact same grammatical construction in both sentences (the comparative 'μεταγενέστερος' combined with the genitive 'χρόνου'). Hence, I see no direct indication in the text itself that this phrase should be read as signifying anything other than 'posterior to Time' in both cases, despite the fact that Baltzly's reading of the first phrase in principle fits well within Proclean metaphysics.

UNITING THE IMPERFECT 177

as a whole exist *in time*, and they never experience the moments in time at which their hypothetical corruption could occur. Hence, they can never be dissolved.[47]

In short, the cosmos is everlasting because it stands on equal grounds with Time and, as such, is not allotted a finite lifespan. We can infer that all of the cosmic parts which exist universally or holistically (ὁλικῶς) owe their wholeness to the fact that they all share in this everlasting nature of the cosmos. In this regard, the parts in a universal manner (μέρη ὁλικῶς) are all wholes in the part, since they imitate the cosmos through their immortality and perpetuity (ἀιδιότης), as Proclus indicated in the passage from the fifth book. This is a broader definition of the cosmological whole in the part than Proclus has given in some of the passages we discussed, but one that is fitting, nevertheless. It represents all of the cosmic parts which were designated as a whole in the part for various reasons, from the outermost heavenly sphere to the four regions of the cosmos.

On the other hand, the mortal creatures themselves are described in much greater detail in the fifth book than they were previously. Whereas beforehand, Proclus merely referred to them in general as the mortal creatures or simply distinguished the whole individual from its parts, we find a more complex schema of the mortal creature in our passage from book five. Incidentally, this new schema also gives us a glimpse at Proclus' solution for the aporia of how a mortal creature that can still be called whole if wholeness is intrinsically linked to eternity. Proclus not only distinguishes the body of a mortal being from its soul—ignoring for a moment its *nongenerated* aspect, intellect[48]—but he also adds a further aspect to the individual living being that is actually immortal. This immortal aspect of individuals is created not by the young gods, but by the Demiurge, as is made clear by Proclus' statement that 'while he again brought forth the immortal aspect of the second demiurgy himself, he assigned the many demiurges to the rest.'[49] Unfortunately, Proclus' language is somewhat obscure in this passage, for the aspect of the individual he refers to as its soul is actually the *irrational* soul. The immortal aspect, on the other hand, refers to the *rational* soul which only human beings possess.[50] This is corroborated by the sixth chapter of the third book of the *Platonic Theology*,

---

47 Proclus, *IT* IV, 64.9–16 (3.50.2–10 Diehl).

48 Opsomer (2003: 8). For the special status of intellect as a nongenerated aspect of cosmic being, see Proclus, *IT* III, 2.13–3.18 (as discussed in section 2.1 above).

49 Proclus, *IT* V, 105.13–15 (3.242.20–22 Diehl): τῆς δὲ δευτέρας τὸ ἀθάνατον πάλιν αὐτὸς παραγαγὼν ἐφίστησι τῇ λοιπῇ τοὺς πολλοὺς δημιουργούς.

50 Opsomer (2003: 8).

178 CHAPTER 6

wherein Proclus states that the true manifestation of the soul-hypostasis is the rational soul, which is immortal according to the *Phaedrus* and *Timaeus*.[51]

6.2.5 *The Mereological Lessons from the Four Passages*

A purely schematic overview of Proclean concepts is not a satisfactory end to this inquiry in itself, despite Proclus' own penchant for schematic overviews. It does, however, reveal how Proclus' Neoplatonic views on mereology inform his account of the cosmogony.[52] In the first place, the mereological theorems Proclus devised in his *Elements of Theology* and *Platonic Theology* (such as the three kinds of wholes) are once again purposefully generalised so as to fit in whatever exegetic context Proclus needs them to. As d'Hoine indicated, this approach allows Proclus to connect Plato's varied perspectives on the creation of the cosmos, even if it means that the terminology itself is somewhat loosely applied. Whether the whole in the part can be applied to every eternal part of the cosmos, or only to the outermost sphere in a very specific sense, for example, differs from passage to passage.

The first perspective on the cosmogony concerns the cosmos's status as a singular organism with a soul and an intellect. Despite its internal complexity and the myriad of creatures living within it, the cosmos is a whole according to Timaeus. Proclus characteristically distances the unity of this whole from the complexity within by describing it as a whole before the parts. In other words, within the logical order of the demiurgic process, Proclus suggests that the Demiurge first conceives a singular ensouled and intelligent living organism which imitates the monadic Living Being itself. Only after this unity has been established does the Demiurge proceed to pluralise and divide it internally.

The next step of creation, then, is to turn the whole into a whole *composed of wholes*. This is the cosmos as 'one many' (εἷς πολύς).[53] It is this manifestation of cosmic existence that one usually thinks of when one describes the concept of the universe, i.e., the ordered sum of all things which exist, albeit only sensibly in Proclus' universe, since purely intelligible beings transcend it. In this phase of describing the cosmogony, Proclus' strategy of loosely applied

---

51 Proclus, *TP* III.6, 23.16–21. A strange consequence of this argument is the fact that 'jede Form von Erkenntnis, also auch die γνωστικὴ δύμανις der irrationele Seele, ist dem Geist zu verdanken'; Opsomer (2006b: 139). In other words, the irrational soul derives not from the soul-hypostasis itself, but from the principle of *Intellect*. For a more detailed analysis of irrational souls in Proclus, see Opsomer (2006b).

52 Since the passages discussed above tend to vary in the complexity of the mereological schemata they present, all of the various concepts introduced in this section are arranged in table 7.

53 Proclus, *IT* II, 326.10–17 (cited in chapter 4, section 3).

TABLE 7 Schematic overview of the kinds of wholes and parts enumerated in the passages discussed in chapter 6, section 2

	Introduction to the third book (IT III, 2.13–3.18)	The third gift of the Demiurge (IT III, 85,16–86.7)	The tenth gift of the Demiurge (IT IV, 125,12–127.1)	The Demiurge speaks to the young gods (IT V, 105,2–11)
		FIRST DEMIURGY		
Cosmos qua unity	Existence 'according to wholeness' (καθ' ὁλότητα) An ensouled, intellective, and divine being	'The whole universally' (τὸ ὅλον ὁλικῶς) The one cosmos	Whole before the parts An ensouled and intellective living being	Production of the whole before the parts
Cosmos qua composite	Existence of 'the whole parts' (τῶν ὅλων μερῶν) A compound of soul, body, and nongenerated intellect		Whole composed of parts A compound of essential components (συμπληρωτικά), e.g., the circles of the World Soul, the four elements, etc.	
Parts which imitate the cosmic whole	Existence 'according to being cut into parts' (κατὰ μέρη τέμνουσα) Division of the cosmic body into monadic elements	'The part universally' (τὸ μέρος ὁλικῶς) Heavenly spheres	Whole in the part Regions of heaven, air, water, and earth, each of which contains all things in a manner proper to it	Production of the 'great and everlasting parts' (μεγάλων καὶ ἀιδίων μερῶν) The immortal inhabitants of the cosmos
Gift to the mortal creatures				Production of the immortal souls

TABLE 7   Schematic overview of the kinds of wholes and parts enumerated (*cont.*)

	Introduction to the third book (*IT* III, 2.13–3.18)	The third gift of the Demiurge (*IT* III, 85.16–86.7)	The tenth gift of the Demiurge (*IT* IV, 125.12–127.1)	The Demiurge speaks to the young gods (*IT* V, 105.2–11)
		SECOND DEMIURGY		
Mortal creatures		'The whole partially' (τὸ ὅλον μερικῶς) *Individual living beings*		Production of the irrational souls Production of the perishable bodies
Pure parts		'The part partially' (τὸ μέρος μερικῶς) *The parts of individual living beings*		Production of the bodily parts

terminology is in full effect. Proclus' description of the whole composed of parts in the *Elements of Theology* and *Platonic Theology* gives no indication which kinds of parts should be distinguished in particular kinds of wholes, and purposefully so. This strategy allows him to envision the cosmos both as a whole composed of soul, body, and intellect, explaining the inherent complexity of the aforementioned ensouled and intellective living being, and as a whole composed of more specific parts, incorporating concepts from the *Timaeus* such as the four elements or the circles of the World Soul.

The same principle applies to the characterisation of the parts themselves. Proclus' whole in the part is perhaps the least clearly defined of his three kinds of wholeness, with its only clear characteristics being its participation in the transcendent unity through its composition and the imitation inherent in such an act. This allows Proclus to apply the famous 'all-in-all'-principle to Plato's cosmogony, as we saw in his discussion of the four regions of the cosmos. At the same time, he is able to infer a more general relation between the cosmos and those parts which co-exist with it for all time, classifying both as things which exist holistically or in a universal manner (ὁλικῶς). On the other hand, the imitative nature of the whole in the part can be applied even to very specific parts, as exemplified by the way in which the cosmos and the outermost heavenly sphere are both stated to encompass everything in their own way.

Despite its wide applicability, however, the unfortunate consequence of using such loosely defined terminology is the fact that the limits of its use are less obvious. Proclus' paradoxical definition of the mortal creatures as 'wholes, albeit with the defining character of a part' is an example of this, as are the subtle changes in his designation of such individuals as essential or non-essential parts of the cosmos. For example, Proclus' most general definition of the term 'part' in his *Parmenides*-commentary involved the statement that the loss of a mortal creature does not diminish the cosmos whatsoever, firmly removing individual beings from the category of essential cosmic parts (i.e., συμπληρωτικά). Yet his description of the four regions of the cosmos in his *Timaeus*-commentary implied that the presence of mortal beings *is* essential for the cosmos to truly be considered a universe. Of course, Proclus has not left us entirely in the dark on this matter. On the contrary, he has given multiple potential solutions for the issue raised here: not only an implied distinction between mortal creatures as individuals and mortal creatures as a species of beings, but also the existence of an immortal part which the Demiurge himself bestows upon some of them (more specifically, upon mortal human beings).

A singular definition of the true essential parts of the cosmos is similarly unattainable from these passages alone. Based on Proclus' statements in the *Platonic Theology*, which revealed that the cosmos and the monadic elements are also called whole because of their indirect participation in Eternity, we may infer that the essential constituents of the cosmos are those beings which exist in a holistic manner, or in other words, those beings which are immortal and thus share in the cosmos's everlasting nature. This idea is supported by the distinction Proclus makes between first demiurgy and second demiurgy and by the link between true wholeness and eternity or immortality, which is again made explicit in the passage from the fifth book. Instead of tying all the various parts and wholes of the cosmos together, however, Proclus is content to focus on the specific ways in which individual kinds of cosmic parts relate to their whole.[54] Again, Proclus' reputation as a philosopher driven by a need to systematise needs to be nuanced slightly. Despite his systematic tendencies, he prioritises the variety inherent in Platonic exegesis, and thus chooses to discuss different mereological approaches to cosmogony. In doing so, Proclus adapts his mereological theorems to whatever context the *Timaeus* provides at any moment. On the other hand, the mereological theorems provide a solidly systematic background to the exegesis, no matter how loosely they may be applied in any individual lemma.

6.3   Material Existence and the Partial Wholeness of the Individual

The category of the partial part (μέρος μερικῶς) is bereft of such a changeable yet systematic framework, being discussed in much simpler terms. These pure parts are of little relevance to the context of the third and fourth books of the *Timaeus*-commentary, i.e., Timaeus' discussion of the everlasting body and soul of the cosmos. As a result, Proclus defines them only summarily. The things we think of when we speak of the partial part are 'just parts' (μέρη γάρ ἐστι μόνον). In other words, these are the entities in our world which are no longer capable of enjoying the generative power of Wholeness itself, since they are ranked too low in the causal hierarchy of being. Once he reaches the Demiurge's address to the young gods in the fifth book of his commentary, Proclus describes these pure parts in more detail. They are corporeal parts, such as the head or the heart of an animal. That such bodily parts cannot be considered whole of themselves is not a particularly strange conclusion for

---

54   Yet another example of such a relation between the cosmos and its everlasting parts can be found in Proclus, *IT* IV, 149.11–21 (3.115.27–116.6 Diehl). There Proclus adds another relation of imitation between the heavenly spheres and the cosmos as a whole when he reveals that they imitate its spherical shape. He does so on exegetical grounds as well, since Timaeus also states that the spheres imitate the universal sphere in Plato, *Tim.* 40a4.

UNITING THE IMPERFECT

Proclus to make. In his discussion of homonymy, Aristotle already emphasised the fact that such parts depend on their whole. A physical body part only functions within the larger whole. Cut it off from its body and it becomes a piece of dead meat, remaining an organ in name only.[55]

Indeed, the lack of a participatory relation to the principle of wholeness also deprives the pure parts of a whole before the parts to revert upon. When Proclus discusses the resemblance between the whole cosmos and the heavenly spheres in the fourth book of the *Timaeus*-commentary, he notes that certain parts have a twofold relation to wholeness: one to the compound which they compose, and one to the transcendent cause of that compound, i.e., the relation between the whole in the part and the other two forms of wholeness.[56] However, not all beings in the cosmos can claim to have such a twofold relation to wholeness. It is not right in every case, Proclus explains, for a part to imitate the essence of its whole.

> οὐδὲ γὰρ τῷ ὀφθαλμῷ τὸ ὁμοιοσχήμονι γενέσθαι πρὸς τὸ ὅλον ἄριστον, οὐδὲ ἐπὶ καρδίας οὐδὲ ἐπὶ κεφαλῆς ἀληθὴς ὁ λόγος, ἀλλ᾽ ὅταν μὲν ἡ ὁλότης πρὸ τῶν μερῶν ᾖ, δυνατὸν ὁμοιοῦσθαι τὰ μέρη πρὸς τὸ ὅλον καὶ τὸ ἀγαθὸν αὐτοῖς ὑπάρχει διὰ τῆς ἀφομοιώσεως ταύτης, ὅπου δὲ ἡ ὁλότης ἐκ τῶν μερῶν ἐστιν, ἐνταῦθα οὐκέτι τὸ μέρος ὁμοιούμενον πρὸς τὸ ὅλον ἔχει τὸ εὖ.
>
> PROCLUS, *IT* IV, 150.1–7 (3.116.10–16 Diehl)

> It is not the best for the eye to have taken the same shape as its whole, nor is this argument true in the case of the heart or the head. Instead, when the wholeness exists before the parts, it *is* possible for the parts to become like the whole, and [then] the good belongs to them through this resemblance, whereas wherever the wholeness is composed of the parts, there the part which becomes like its whole no longer possesses the good.
>
> Tr. BALTZLY 2013 (modified)

This passage is somewhat obscure, and one could erroneously interpret it to mean that no whole composed of parts can consist of wholes in the parts—this would, of course, contradict the *Elements of Theology*.[57] However, Proclus explicitly mentions bodily parts here as examples of parts which should not naturally imitate their whole (the implicit reasoning being that organs such

---

55   See, e.g., Aristotle, *Met.* Z.16, 1040b5–10; cf. Irwin (1981: 527–529) for a more extensive list of Aristotelian passages revolving around this particular notion of homonymy.

56   Cf. Chlup (2012: 103).

57   Specifically, Proclus, *ET* 68, 64.15; cf. Oosthout, A. (2022b: 10).

as the eyes would not be able to perform their natural functions without their distinctive shape and constitution). Furthermore, he discusses the heavenly spheres as parts which *can* imitate the cosmos in the lines immediately preceding this passage. As a result, we should interpret Proclus' claim here to mean that certain parts of the cosmos come forth from a whole before the parts, but others do not. The heavenly spheres are part of a compound (the cosmos) which in turn derives from a transcendent unity (either the cosmos *qua* unitary living being or the Paradigm, depending on the passage). In contrast, the corporeal compound has no transcendent unity to fall back on. The defining characteristic of Neoplatonic transcendence is its incorporeality, after all. Since the body itself has no whole before the parts, it cannot possess wholes in its parts either. The causal power of wholeness cannot reach such bodily parts, and as a result they have no transcendent wholeness to participate in.

Although the body of a mortal creature might not hold the key to the transcendent realms, it is clear that individual beings nevertheless share some connection with Wholeness itself. They are wholes after all, despite existing in a partial manner. At this point, we must return to the passage from the fifth book of Proclus' *Timaeus*-commentary which was discussed in the introduction of this study, i.e., the lemma where Proclus draws a line between what is dissoluble and what is indissoluble. The arguments presented there will give us a greater understanding of the precise nature of the mortal creatures and their lowest form of wholeness. In the introduction to this book, I discussed the distinction Proclus makes between 1) a pure unity, 2) a whole which is both one and many, and 3) a multitude of things which commingle to the extent that they become indistinguishable from one another.[58] In the lines directly following that passage, Proclus discusses the Platonic concepts of the dissoluble and indissoluble in more detail. Using the works of the Demiurge as an example, Proclus claims that the properties of being dissoluble and indissoluble are not mutually exclusive. After all, the works of the Demiurge, i.e., the everlasting inhabitants of the cosmos, are conceptually or potentially dissoluble in the sense that they possess distinguishable parts, yet they are also indissoluble in the sense that they will never actually come apart.[59] To further elucidate these concepts, Proclus enumerates the various ways in which a thing can be said to be dissoluble or indissoluble.

Similarly to the term 'self-constituted', the term 'indissoluble' (ἄλυτον) can be employed in two ways. First, it can be used in an absolute sense, i.e., to

---

58   See chapter 1, section 2.
59   Proclus, *IT* V, 64.5–10 (3.210.24–30 Diehl).

denote that which is *simply* (ἁπλοῦν) indissoluble (either by its own power or because of some external cause). Secondly, one might use it in a more qualified sense, i.e., to denote a thing which is indissoluble *in a certain way* (πῃ ἄλυτον). In opposition to these two terms, then, stand the correlated modes of being dissoluble: that which is dissoluble absolutely, and that which is dissoluble only in a certain way, by virtue of the fact that although it is composed out of discrete elements, those constitutive elements are nevertheless indissoluble because of the influence of their higher creative causes.[60]

The phrasing of the definitions is somewhat obtuse, especially when Proclus defines that which is dissoluble only in a certain way. However, given Proclus' earlier argument that the works of the Demiurge are dissoluble in a certain way only because they are merely conceptually divisible, we might infer that he presents a similar argument here. In other words, some beings are not dissolved in actuality, but the ontological distinctness of their parts nevertheless enables a conceptual dissolution into those parts. If one accepts this reading of the passage, the four ways of being (in)dissoluble are arranged as follows:

1. Simply indissoluble (whether by another or by itself).
2. Cannot be dissolved in some way (whether by another or by itself), i.e., *qua* perpetually persisting.
3. Can be dissolved in some way (whether by another or by itself), i.e., *qua* conceptually dissoluble.
4. Simply dissoluble (whether by another or by itself).

Having made this distinction, Proclus reveals which beings belong to which category. The intelligible beings belong to the first category, given the utter impossibility of subjecting them to composition of dissolution. In contrast, mortal creatures are solely dissoluble, for not only are they composite and internally pluriform, but they were also *made* to eventually come apart. In between these two extremes stand the 'works of the Father',[61] which are eternally bound together both by their own natures and by the power of their creator, and thus they are indissoluble. And yet, because the Demiurge contains within himself also the rational principles (λόγοι) which produce each of the parts of his works, the works themselves are also in some sense (i.e., conceptually) divisible and dissoluble.[62] The list above may then be supplemented as in table 8.

---

60 Proclus, *IT* V, 64.11–65.7 (3.210.30–211.14 Diehl).
61 Plato, *Tim.* 41a7–8.
62 Proclus, *IT* V, 65.8–66.2 (3.211.14–212.5 Diehl).

186   CHAPTER 6

TABLE 8   The intelligible and cosmic beings, ranked by dissolubility

1. Simply indissoluble.	Intelligible beings
2. Cannot be dissolved in some way, i.e., *qua* perpetually persisting.	Works of the Father, e.g.,
3. Can be dissolved in some way, i.e., *qua* conceptually dissoluble.	cosmic gods and souls
4. Simply dissoluble.	Mortal creatures

This categorisation should be familiar to us by now. Relative to the corporeal realm, the intelligible beings are fully indivisible and thus indissoluble. The corporeal beings are placed at the other end of this spectrum, defined once again by their mortality. More interesting are the two middle categories, which Proclus combines into the category of things which are indissoluble yet in some way dissoluble (or vice versa). Originally, he names only the gods in the cosmos, which logically follows from the context of this particular *Timaeus*-passage, i.e., the speech of the Demiurge to the young gods. However, the previous lemma established that the works of the Demiurge *in general* are to be categorised as indissoluble yet dissoluble beings. As such, souls too share in some degree of indissolubility, as do the monadic essences of the four elements. This resistance to decay is linked to their everlasting nature, for after a brief argument against a dualist reading of the *Timaeus*,[63] Proclus grounds the distinction between conceptually dissoluble things and actually dissoluble things in the divide between everlastingness and mortality.

Despite the fact that all composite things in the sensible cosmos are dissoluble, Proclus explains, everlasting (ἀΐδια) compounds are at the same time indissoluble, because they successfully participate without end in intelligible beauty, divine unification, and the harmony bestowed upon them by the Demiurge. The composite mortals, on the other hand, are infected by the disharmony of their material substrate. Whereas the everlasting compounds are granted a beautiful attunement from the one producer, the Demiurge, the

---

63   Proclus attributes to Severus, Atticus, and Plutarch (the latter as cited by Severus, as Tarrant (2017: 92 n. 197) points out) the view that the younger gods owe their dissolubility to their bodies, which existed in a disorderly state prior to the demiurgic process. Proclus argues that the young gods do not have two natures (indissoluble and ordered versus dissoluble and disordered), but rather one double nature which was bestowed upon them in its entirety by the Demiurge. In other words, they owe not just their indissolubility to their father, but also their dissolubility. For the full argument, see Proclus, *IT* V, 66.3–67.16 (3.212.5–213.12 Diehl).

mortal compounds are pulled in multiple directions by their multiple causes. The large amount of ingredients mixed up within them makes it so that they can only receive a lesser harmony from the Demiurge. Thus, Proclus tells us, when Timaeus states that 'all that was bound is dissoluble',[64] we should remember that some compounds in the sensible cosmos are as purely dissoluble as the intelligible is indissoluble, but that others are dissoluble yet also indissoluble.[65]

Here we find the same division of concepts we encountered in the *Platonic Theology*, i.e., a distinction between beings which participate in eternity and are thus everlasting on the one hand, and beings which are bereft of this participation and thus exist only temporarily on the other. From this, we can logically conclude that for Proclus, being indissoluble (whether absolutely or in some way) equates to being whole. Just as in the *Platonic Theology*, material weakness is named as a primary cause for the absolute dissolubility of the mortal creatures and, by extension, for their lack of true wholeness. Here too the distinction is axiologically charged, for in his analysis of the words used in the lemma from the *Timaeus* which is discussed here,[66] Proclus emphasises the goodness of the indissoluble works of the father.

> τὴν δὴ τοιαύτην σύστασιν, τὴν ἁρμοσθεῖσαν μὲν ὑπὸ τῆς μιᾶς δημιουργίας, κάλλους δὲ θείου πληρωθεῖσαν, ἑνώσεως δὲ ἀγαθοειδοῦς τυχοῦσαν, ἄλυτον ὑπάρχειν ἀναγκαῖον· τὸ γὰρ 'λύειν ἐθέλειν' αὐτὴν 'κακοῦ' φησιν αὐτός.
>
> PROCLUS, *IT* V, 68.15–19 (3.214.6–10 Diehl)

> For such a composition, one that is attuned through the one demiurgy, filled with divine beauty, and endowed with a boniform unification, it is necessary that it be fundamentally indissoluble. After all, [Plato] himself says that 'wanting to destroy' this is 'evil'.
>
> Tr. TARRANT 2017 (modified)

Although the works of the Demiurge are potentially and conceptually destructible, given that they exist in time and are composite material beings, their goodness keeps them whole. In this sense, this passage provides a mirror to the *Platonic Theology*, wherein Proclus argued that the wholeness of eternal beings, i.e., their resistance to change, kept them from losing their goodness.

---

64 Plato, *Tim.* 41a8–b1: τὸ μὲν οὖν δὴ δεθὲν πᾶν λυτόν, which Proclus cites as 'all that has been bound is dissoluble' (πᾶν τὸ δεδεμένον λυτόν).

65 Proclus, *IT* V, 67.22–68.6 (3.213.18–30 Diehl).

66 I.e., Plato, *Tim.* 41a8–b2.

188   CHAPTER 6

Here it is the goodness of the everlasting cosmic beings which prevents the Demiurge from ending their existence prematurely, lest he betray his own unchangingly good nature.[67] Thus, wholeness and goodness mutually sustain each other. If a cosmic being receives a superior share in goodness, beauty, and harmony from the Demiurge, it becomes whole and everlasting because its creator cannot bring himself to destroy it. At the same time, this everlasting wholeness allows the cosmic being to preserve its proper nature and avoid falling victim to the parasitic presence of evil.

The obvious implication of this passage is yet again that the mortal creature lacks such a value due to the overwhelming influence of the 'ill-formedness and disharmony of matter' (τῷ αἰσχρῷ καὶ τῷ ἀναρμόστῳ τῆς ὕλης). Throughout the previously discussed passages from Proclus' *Timaeus*-commentary, however, we have slowly collected the pieces necessary to construct a counter-argument to this fatalistic view of our mortal existence, and to explain why we might be considered wholes in some way. We have already noted that human beings are not designed solely by the young gods, since, as Opsomer pointed out, the Demiurge contributes to their creation by constituting the immortal rational soul. The current passage on dissolubility and indissolubility proves that Proclus considers the works of the father, which includes the rational soul, to be everlastingly good in a similar way to the true wholes he described in the *Platonic Theology*. In the subsequent lemma of his commentary,[68] Proclus does in fact rank the souls of individual beings among the immortal parts of creation. After emphasising the distinction between eternal immortality and everlasting immortality,[69] Proclus enumerates the kinds of cosmic beings which might be considered everlastingly immortal.

> καὶ ἔστι τὸ μὲν τῶν ἐγκοσμίων θεῶν ἴδιον, τὸ δὲ τῶν δαιμόνων τῶν τούτοις ἑπο-
> μένων. εἰ δὲ τὸ λοιπὸν καὶ λήθης ἀναπίμπλαται κατιόν, ἐγγυτάτω τῶν θνητῶν
> ἐστιν, ἀπολλύον πάντῃ τὴν ὡς ἀληθῶς ἐν αὐτῷ ζωὴν καὶ μόνην ἔχον τὴν οὐσι-
> ώδη. τοιοῦτον δὲ τὸ τῶν μερικῶν ψυχῶν ἀθάνατον· διὸ καὶ αὐτὸς 'ἀθανάτοις
> ὁμώνυμον' ἀποκαλέσει (*Tim.* 41c6) τὸ ἐν ταύταις ἀθάνατον. εἰ δέ τι μετὰ ταύτας
> καὶ τὴν οὐσιώδη ζωὴν ἀποβάλλοι, τοῦτο θνητὸν μόνως ἐστίν.
>
> PROCLUS, *IT* V, 73.19–74.1 (3.218.9–17 Diehl)

And one [kind of immortality in time] is characteristic of the gods in the cosmos, whereas the other is characteristic of the daimons that follow

---

67   Cf. d'Hoine (2011b).

68   I.e., the lemma focused on Plato, *Tim.* 41b2–6.

69   Proclus, *IT* V, 73.9–19 (3.217.31–218.9 Diehl); cf. chapter 5, section 2.1, and section 1 above.

these. And if hereafter they are affected with forgetfulness as they come down, they are very close to mortal, entirely losing the life which is truly within them, and having only the substantial kind. This is the immortality of individual souls, for which reason Plato himself will describe the immortality among them as 'homonymous with immortal beings' (*Tim.* 41c6). Should there be after these anything that discards even its substantial life, this is merely mortal.

Tr. TARRANT 2017 (slightly modified)

That the individual human soul is immortal and indissoluble (even if it comes dangerously close to mortality), and thus whole, does not contradict Proclus' earlier statements regarding the partial nature of individuals in general. After all, he took care to emphasise that it is the corporeal side of the individual which lacks in wholeness, both in the many passages wherein he attributes physiological and ethical decay to material weakness, and in the passages where he explicitly categorises *bodily* parts as those parts which cannot participate in any transcendent wholeness before the parts. An individual human being is thus at once truly whole and merely partial. One is partial in regard to one's body, which is destined to decay and whose weakness allows the parasitic nature of evil to prey upon the soul as well.[70] However, one is at the same time whole in regards to one's rational soul, which was devised by the Demiurge himself and which, in true Platonic fashion, transcends the body after death.

Unfortunately, this argument only explains the wholeness of a human being. The other mortal living beings within the cosmos, i.e., animals and plants, receive only an irrational soul. This irrational soul is not considered a true manifestation of the soul-hypostasis by Proclus and thus does not belong to the works of the Demiurge *stricto sensu*. Despite Proclus' dismissal of all animals as irrational,[71] however, there is nothing in his mereological schemata which suggests a strong distinction between human beings and animals as far as the wholeness of mortal creatures is concerned. He designates mortal creatures *in general* as wholes in a partial manner in the third book of the *Timaeus*-commentary, and he makes no distinction between human beings and animals in his overview of the products of the young gods in the fifth book either.

---

70 For the ways in which the human soul too can fall victim to corruption, see Chlup (2009 and 2012: 215–218).

71 As summarised by Opsomer (2006b: 158 n. 9), 'die Tiere (im Gegensatz zu den Menschen und den noch höheren Lebewesen) werden von Proklos in der Tat als vernunftlos betrachtet'; cf. Proclus, *IT* II, 348.18–349.5 (1.445.19–30 Diehl).

Fortunately, the immortal rational soul is not the only possible link between mortal creatures and the eternal wholeness of intelligible beings. A more general way of participating in it, and thus of becoming whole, is being shaped by a form. We have previously discussed the way in which material beings are informed and restricted by the Platonic Forms. To recap, Proclus linked the procession of Platonic Forms to the manifestations of the principles of limit and the unlimited from the *Philebus* in his *Parmenides*-commentary, ending at the level of reality where the unlimited divisibility and disorder of matter is limited and shaped by the so-called material form (ἔνυλον εἶδος), which passes onto its substrate the complex but immaterial compound of distinctive characters inherited from the intelligible principles.[72] However, despite their descent into matter, these forms are not the forms of individuals *stricto sensu*. We discussed the discrepancy between Baltzly's and d'Hoine's interpretation of the concept of a material form, whereby the former suggested that what Proclus calls an 'atomic form' equates to the form of a specific individual, whereas the latter argued that Proclus distinguished the form of a species such as the human being (ἔνυλον εἶδος) from the specific characteristics of individuals like Socrates (ἰδίως ποιόν). I came down on the latter side of the discussion, and concluded as d'Hoine did that the forms-in-matter are forms of species rather than specific individuals.[73]

Nevertheless, these forms exist within the matter of the beings which participate in them, and as such, they provide material creatures with a link to the transcendent realms. Proclus confirms as much in the fifth book of his *Timaeus*-commentary. In lines 41b7 through c3 of the *Timaeus*, the Demiurge claims that he cannot create the as of yet nongenerated mortal creatures, lest they become divine like all of his direct creations, but that their existence is nevertheless essential for the cosmos to be complete. Noting Timaeus' use of the term 'nongenerated' (ἀγέννητα) to describe the mortal creatures before their conception, Proclus asks how we must understand this predication. First, one must understand it as meaning 'not yet generated' (ὡς μήπω γενόμενα), so that Timaeus uses the term 'nongenerated' to indicate that at the current step of the Demiurgic process, we are not yet speaking of the production of mortal individuals. However, one may also take 'nongenerated' to imply that sensible individuals are both mortal *and* immortal.[74]

---

72   See chapter 3, section 3.

73   See chapter 4, section 4. Note, however, that Baltzly has since nuanced his suggestion slightly by stating that Forms of individuals exist 'in name only', for which see Baltzly (2009: 41–45).

74   Proclus, *IT* V, 80.25–81.3 (3.223.29–224.2 Diehl).

UNITING THE IMPERFECT

ὡς μὲν ἀπὸ τῆς δημιουργικῆς γιγνόμενα μονάδος καὶ τῆς ἀκινήτου καὶ αἰωνίου ποιήσεως ἀγένητα, ὡς δὲ ὑπὸ τῶν νέων θεῶν θνητά· μέτεστι γὰρ καὶ τούτοις ἀιδίου τινός, διότι κατ' εἶδος μέν ἐστιν ἄφθαρτα, κατὰ δὲ τὸ καθ' ἕκαστον φθαρτά· διῄρηται γὰρ ἐπὶ τούτων τὸ εἶδος τοῦ καθ' ἕκαστον καὶ οὐχ ὥσπερ ἐπὶ τῶν θείων καὶ μόνως ἀιδίων ζῴων ἕν ἐστι πᾶν τὴν ὅλην τῶν παραδειγμάτων πρόοδον ὑποδέξασθαι δεδυνημένον.

PROCLUS, *IT* V, 81.3–10 (3.224.2–9 Diehl)

To the extent that they come to be from the monad of the Demiurge and from his motionless and eternal creation they are nongenerated, but they are mortal insofar as they [are generated] by the young gods. These too possess a share in something everlasting, because they are indestructible as species, but destructible as individuals. In their case, the species has been distinguished from the individual, and there is no one totality capable of receiving the whole procession of paradigms as in the case of creatures that are uniformly divine and everlasting.

Tr. TARRANT 2017 (modified)

As we discussed previously,[75] Proclean causality consists in a continual unfolding of unity into multiplicity. Here Proclus applies that principle in order to explain Plato's remarks, which point to the presence of some eternal aspect within the mortal creatures. At our level of existence, the continuous division of beings has progressed to the point where our form, i.e., the human being, has been distinguished from our individual properties. Although Proclus makes no direct reference to the concept of the material form (ἔνυλον εἶδος), his use of the term 'εἶδος' to describe the species of mortal beings logically denominates the same concept. This means that, whereas any particular intellect is essentially the same as the one Intellect, albeit in a particular way, an individual human being contains two distinct sets of characteristics: the descended, material form of the human being, and those characteristics unique to his or her person. This means that the mortal creature is connected to the wholeness of the intelligible realm, but only through the form of its species. Proclus makes this distinction yet clearer in the subsequent lemma of his *Timaeus*-commentary.[76]

There Proclus explains that we should consider the cosmos's individual inhabitants neither to be wholly everlasting nor to be wholly perishable. On the first point, we should not make the mistake of searching for the Platonic Forms of the individuals Socrates and Plato (μηδὲ ἐπιζητῶμεν τὴν ἰδέαν Σωκράτους ἢ

---

75   See chapter 5, sections 3 through 5.
76   Cf. Plato, *Tim.* 41c3–5.

Πλάτωνος). Although the Demiurge creates the various *kinds* of mortal beings, he stops at 'universal intellections' (μέχρι τῶν ὁλικῶν ἵσταται νοήσεων) which transcendently encompass the partial beings. In this manner, he encompasses the individual in a universal or holistic manner (τὸ καθ' ἕκαστον ὁλικῶς προείληφεν). If we should say also that the Demiurge creates the individual mortals themselves, we must state that he does so through the young gods.[77]

On the other hand, we also should not make the mistake of saying that mortal things are not in some way also divine, for Proclus notes that:

> ἃ γὰρ προτείνει νῦν ὁ δημιουργὸς ἐν τοῖς λόγοις, ὑποστάσεις εἰσὶ περὶ τοὺς νέους θεούς, ἃς ὁ οὐρανὸς ὑπεδέξατο πρώτως, καθ' ἃς καὶ δημιουργοῦσιν οἱ νέοι θεοὶ τὰ θνητά· μονάδες γὰρ ἀπὸ τῶν νοητῶν εἰδῶν εἰς τὸν οὐρανὸν προῆλθον πάσης τῆς θνητοειδοῦς ζωῆς, ἀπὸ δὲ τούτων τῶν μονάδων θείων οὐσῶν πᾶν ἀπεγεννήθη τὸ πλῆθος τῶν ἐνύλων ζῴων· ἐὰν γὰρ τούτων ἀνεχώμεθα τῶν νοημάτων, τῷ τε Πλάτωνι συνακολουθήσομεν καὶ τῆς φύσεως οὐκ ἀπολειφθησόμεθα τῶν πραγμάτων.

> PROCLUS, *IT* V, 87.7–15 (3.228.29–229.5 Diehl)

For [the proclamations] which the Demiurge now extends in his words are real beings operating on the young gods, beings that the heaven first receives and in accordance with which the young gods create mortal creatures too. After all, from the intelligible Forms monads have come down to the heaven, monads of every mortal form of life, and from these monads, which are divine, the entire multitude of material living beings has been engendered. If we hold fast to these considerations, we shall be following Plato and we shall not be straying from the nature of things.

> Tr. TARRANT 2017 (slightly modified)

As he does in his *Parmenides*-commentary, Proclus affirms that there are no Platonic Forms of specific individuals.[78] The individual characteristics of a person are thus not the ones which make it whole, since they are solely mortal and dissoluble.[79] However, even if neither a human being called Socrates

---

77 Proclus, *IT* V, 86.23–87.7 (3.228.20–29 Diehl).

78 See d'Hoine (2010).

79 Think of the way in which Socrates' soul reincarnates upon his death without taking with it Socrates' famously bad looks or his tendency to annoy people with philosophical problems during their daily commute. Proclus also employs this argument in reverse, using the lack of perfection and universality inherent in individuals as a reason to claim that there are no Forms of individual characteristics in his *Parmenides*-commentary, for which see Proclus, *IP* III, 827.2–4 and d'Hoine (2011a: 165–167 and 180).

nor a guinea pig called Tygo are immortal *qua* individuals, they still carry within them something everlasting: the species of the human being and the guinea pig, respectively. In fact, Proclus explicitly states that the most specific kinds of intellective Forms are the forms of species of animals in his *Parmenides*-commentary, such as the Form of the Dog or the Form of Man. These Forms, Proclus explains, 'directly generate the monads in the individuals' (προσεχῶς ἀπογεννῶσι τὰς ἐν τοῖς ἀτόμοις μονάδας), such as the humanity in individual humans or the 'dog-ness' in individual dogs.[80]

Whereas Tygo and Socrates derive their individuality from the acts of the young gods, their species belong to the indissoluble works of the father.[81] Since their species are instantiated by eternal intellective principles, and everlasting-ness equates to wholeness for Proclus, we can distil from these passages that Socrates' and Tygo's existence as partial wholes derives from their combination of the unchangeable form of their species with a perishable individuality. In other words, within Tygo the form of a guinea pig is still present, but his snout is just a material part incapable of participating in 'guinea pig' or its superior genera. *Qua* representation of the species 'guinea pig', Tygo is whole. Unfortunately, in order to create the individual personality traits of Tygo (being more boisterous than his fellow guinea pig yet, when push comes to shove, also more cowardly) the intelligible form of the living being must descend and be divided to a point where the lifelessness of matter infects it, and thus poor Tygo is irreversibly susceptible to corruption or decay. This is how we should interpret Proclus' earlier remark that in the mortal creatures 'the third form of wholeness exists,' i.e., the wholeness of their species, 'albeit with the distinctive character of a part', i.e., their individuality.[82] Strange as this may sound to a

---

80   Proclus, *IP* II, 735.5–9.

81   Cf. Proclus, *IP* III, 824.3–4: ἕκαστον ἄρα εἶδος τῶν τε ζῴων καὶ τῶν φυτῶν ἐκεῖθεν κατά τι παράδειγμα νοερὸν ὑφέστηκε· The intellective paradigms naturally equate to the intellective Forms encompassed by the Demiurge.

82   As d'Hoine (2021: 217) states, ὅλον μερικῶς is an apt description for the ἔνυλον εἶδος of humanity within Socrates, since 'la forme est par nature un tout et quelque chose de complet, mais qui sera fragmenté dans la matière lors de sa participation.' What we conclude here also avoids another problem d'Hoine (2021: 210–212) raises against Baltzly's equation of the whole in the part with the individual characteristics of mortal creatures (for which see chapter 4, section 4). If the participated form *qua* whole composed of parts contains essential constituents (συμπληρωτικά), d'Hoine (2021: 211) rightly asks: 'Quelles sont les parties « constitutives » de l'ἔνυλον εἶδος?' The mortal creature as an individual obviously cannot be an essential constituent of its participated form, since its death has no bearing on the universe or its everlasting parts. The passages we discussed here show that d'Hoine's own candidate for the whole in the part, the species as represented by individuals, avoids this problem. The species of the guinea pig is perpetual, and thus Tygo

modern reader, such a negative judgement of individuality fits perfectly within the holistic worldview of the Neoplatonic philosophers.

Proclus' description of the descent of the Forms from the intelligible realm into the material one also fits relatively well with the analyses of the Forms and the three kinds of wholes in previous chapters. In the fifth book of the *Platonic Theology*, we encountered a threefold distinction between kinds of Platonic Forms, starting with purely indivisible Forms and ending at forms which are divided across bodies. Similarly, d'Hoine claimed that the three kinds of wholes could be applied to the Platonic Forms as well, in such as manner as to distinguish the transcendent Form *qua* unity, the participated form *qua* communal form of all of its participants, and the participated form *qua* represented in each individual participant.[83] In our passages from the *Parmenides*- and *Timaeus*-commentaries, we again encountered three manifestations of the Platonic Forms: the transcendent intelligible Forms, the monads of mortal creatures encompassed by heaven, and the species as represented within the individuals. Both the more general schemata of *Platonic Theology* and d'Hoine's union of the three wholes and the Platonic Forms can be applied to our current passages in order to create the schema of table 9.

TABLE 9   The parallel between the different kinds of forms as described in chapter 5 and the different manifestations of the Form of a mortal creature

Kinds of wholeness	*Manifestations of the Forms as described by d'Hoine (2021: 218)*	*Genera of Forms (TP V.30)*	*The Forms of mortal creatures (IT V and IP II)*
Whole before the parts	Unparticipated Form	Undivided and primary	Intellective Form
Whole composed of parts	Participated Form₁ ('forme commune')	Both undivided and divided at the same time	Monad of mortal life
Whole in the part	Participated Form ₂ ('forme particularisée')	Divided across bodies	Mortal creature which represents a species

---

can function as an essential constituent of the Platonic Forms *qua* representative of this species.

83   See chapter 4, section 4.

UNITING THE IMPERFECT

This connection between the exegetical arguments from the *Timaeus*-commentary and the more general schemata from the *Platonic Theology* remains implicit. Proclus does not explicate the schema above as I have done, which further supports the idea that Proclus' primary objective in the *Timaeus*-commentary is not to describe the entire Neoplatonic system, but rather to restrict himself to those arguments which are relevant for his exegesis of the text. This is not to say that Proclus' mereology is vague or ill-defined. The more general theorems of the *Platonic Theology* and *Elements of Theology*, such as the three kinds of wholeness or the equation of wholeness with eternity, are perfectly applicable to the passages we have discussed here. However, mereology is not the central theme of the *Timaeus*, and so it cannot be a central theme within the *Timaeus*-commentary either. This creates an interesting tension within Proclus' mereology: on the one hand, Proclus' capacity for systematic philosophy shines through in the recurrence of his most influential mereological propositions. On the other hand, the specific details of his mereology occasionally vary between works and even from passage to passage, since Proclus is ultimately bound to the whims of the Platonic texts he studies. If two different passages from the *Timaeus* require different mereological schemata to properly incorporate their philosophical concepts, Proclus does not hesitate to provide them. In the end, Proclus' discussions of the parts and wholes of the cosmogony are meant to form an exegetical mereology first and foremost, albeit with a systematic philosophy (not so) hidden in the background.

6.4   The Question of the Partial Good

Essential to Proclus' conception of the whole is the axiological side of his metaphysics, which in this case means the question of whether the whole's participation in the good is sufficiently safeguarded. As we discussed previously, in chapter eighteen of the first book of his *Platonic Theology* Proclus makes the distinction between beings which participate in the good eternally, without changing and thus without losing their share in goodness, and beings which are incapable of safeguarding their goodness. Beings of the former kind are truly whole because of their unchanging goodness; those of the latter kind are the partial beings (μερικά) we discussed in this chapter.[84] Following the distinction between eternal and temporal participants in the good, Proclus expands on the extent to which the divided beings are themselves good.

---

84   Proclus, *TP* I.18, 83.21–84.9, for which see chapter 5, section 2.1.

196   CHAPTER 6

Proclus notes first that not all divided beings are automatically susceptible to evil, and that of those that are, not all are susceptible to it to the same extent. To develop this argument, Proclus distinguishes between three levels of divided beings (no surprise there). At the highest level, there are the intellective (νοερά) kinds of partial beings, which are eternally boniform (διαιωνίως ἐστὶν ἀγαθοειδῆ). At the intermediate level, we find partial beings which 'exercise their activities in time' (τὰ δὲ μέσα καὶ κατὰ χρόνον ἐνεργοῦντα). Unlike the intellective kinds of partial beings, these temporally active partial beings possess an essence and powers which are not simple but composed 'out of opposites' (ἐξ ἐναντίων), as the Socrates of the *Phaedrus* says.[85] As a result of the temporal activity and mixed essences of these secondary partial beings, the unity and simplicity of the good in which they participate is mixed up with their temporal plurality and the multiformity of their essences. At the lowest level are situated the material (ἔνυλα) partial beings, which find themselves entirely at the mercy of the 'asymmetry and ugliness' (ἀσυμμετρία καὶ αἰσχρότης) inherent in their material substrate.[86] Their matter also fills them with much 'non-being' (πολλοῦ τοῦ μὴ ὄντος ἀναπεπλησμένα) and subjects them entirely to the unending changes and movements that come with a material and temporal existence. As a result of this, their participation in the good is disturbed to an even greater extent than that of the secondary partial beings. Proclus explains that those secondary partial beings were only corruptible in their activities, whereas these tertiary partial beings undergo an infection with 'material weakness' (ὑλικὴ ἀσθένεια) both of their activities and of their essences.[87]

The three types of partial beings distinguished in this passage concur with the various aspects of the mortal creature we distilled from the *Timaeus*- and *Parmenides*-commentaries. The intellective kinds of divided beings (νοερὰ γένη τῶν μερικῶν) correspond to the Forms of mortal species, such as the transcendent principle of humanity, as discussed in the *Parmenides*-commentary. These Forms are part of the incorporeal and timeless Intellect and thus cannot be robbed of their wholeness and, by extension, their natural goodness. The intellective Form from which I derive my humanity does not change regardless of my personal state of mind or body. No corruption of my personal nature, whether through unethical acts or through physical decay, influences the nature of the Human Being which transcends the material cosmos. The activity of this Form, i.e., creating the psychic and natural principles which shape the clump of matter

---

85   Proclus here cites Plato, *Phaedr.* 246b3.
86   The notions of ἀσυμμετρία and αἰσχρότης are taken from Plato, *Gorg.* 525a5.
87   Proclus, *TP* I.18, 85.6–86.4.

from which I am composed, is similarly undeterred by whatever those lower principles or their subordinate clumps of matter get up to.

At first glance, it seems strange that Proclus describes a transcendent eternal principle as a partial being (μερικόν), given the fact that, in the very same sentence, it is said to be eternal and thus truly whole. Recall, however, that intelligible wholeness is a relative principle, and thus we need not interpret the term 'intellective partial being' (νοερὸν μερικόν) *stricto sensu* as referring to a finitely temporal and changeable entity. After all, Proclus often employs the terms 'ὁλικός' and 'μερικός' to describe the hierarchical relation between two given intelligible principles.[88] And even when the context of this passage indicates a more strict interpretation of the term 'μερικόν,' such an interpretation is not out of place. According to Proclus' rule, the sensible realm mirrors the intelligible realm. Thus, if there exist partial creatures in the sensible realm which have some claim to true wholeness despite their individuality, there must also exist holistic principles in the intelligible realm which are characterised by a partial nature. Indeed, Proclus designated the intellective Forms which instantiate species of animals as the most specific (εἰδικώτατα). Since Proclus' distinction between whole and part overlaps with his distinction between universal and particular, it is not implausible to suggest that being the most specific of the intelligible principles is equal to being the most partial or divided of the intelligible principles. In this regard, the intelligible Human Being can be described as being whole yet also partial in a causal manner, just as the individual human being is partial yet whole by participation.

The second kind of divided being is that which exercises its activity in time, which is revealed to be the soul by Proclus' reference to the *Phaedrus*.[89] Indeed, Proclus previously stated that the immortality of the individual souls was ranked low on the scale of immortality in time, being closer to the actual mortality of material creatures than either the cosmic gods or daimons. Furthermore, Proclus establishes in the first book of his *Parmenides*-commentary that the intellective manifestations of divided beings (νοεροὶ μερικοί) mentioned above are participated by the individual souls.[90] The soul itself falls short in the sense that it can be seduced into committing unethical acts, as other scholars have already noted.[91] However, the rational soul remains a product of the Demiurge

---

88   See chapter 3, section 1.

89   For example, Proclus refers to the myth of the chariot and the two horses, and specifically to its role as a metaphor for the human soul in Plato, *Phaedr.* 246a6–b4.

90   Proclus, *IP* I, 628.1–21.

91   Chlup (2009 and 2012: 215–218); cf. Proclus, *DMS* 20–26.

himself, and as such it is an everlasting whole in essence and remains unchangingly good in this respect.

In contrast, the material individual is in every respect perishable. No evil act of mine would diminish the intellective Human Being to which I owe my humanity, and such acts would only unmake the wholeness of my soul's activity, but my individual existence *qua* author of this study would be entirely disrupted. It is this manifestation of the human being which cannot be whole in a true sense, since it is irrevocably destined to lose its proper goodness in the end and to ultimately pass away.[92] Schematically, these three aspects of the human being can be represented as in table 10.

It should be noted that it is one's individuality, *not* one's corporeality, which enables one's corruption. Proclus opposes the Plotinian thesis that matter is the root of all evil, as has been well established in scholarly literature.[93] Instead, as I indicated in my analysis of the partial intellective beings (νοερὰ μερικά), the distinction between good and evil is a distinction between universal and particular creatures. Proclus drives this distinction home in the same chapter of the *Platonic Theology*.

TABLE 10   The three kinds of divided beings enumerated in the *Platonic Theology*

Kinds of divided beings	Manifestation of the human being	Truly whole?
Intellective kind	The one Human Being (intellective Form)	Yes – Never loses its natural goodness in essence nor activity; Transcendently indissoluble
Intermediary kind with a temporal activity	The rational soul of the human being	Yes (essence) – Never loses its natural goodness No (activity) – May perform evil acts
Material kind	The corporeal Individual (e.g., Socrates)	No – Corruptible in its essence and in its activities; Finite lifespan

---

92   Cf. Proclus, *DMS* 27–29.

93   See, e.g., Opsomer (2001); cf. Proclus, *DMS* 30–37.

The realm of partial beings, Proclus explains, is not wholly devoid of goodness. Even if some evil befalls a material individual, this occurrence is a good thing within the cosmos as a whole. The cosmos itself is composed of perfect parts and as such is always fortunate. Unnatural, ugly, and asymmetrical properties can only affect partial beings. When they are damaged or corrupted, or when they perish, the 'parasitic existence' (παρυπόστασις) of evil affects them only insofar as they are individuals, not insofar as they are parts of the cosmic whole. The perishable is only perishable for itself; for the cosmos, it is indestructible. Hence, Proclus concludes, the individual creature which undergoes evil or acts in an evil manner can only ever pervert its individual nature, and never its status as part of a perfect cosmic whole.[94]

Although the suggestion that Proclus' concept of evil is limited to individual beings in the sensible realm is not revolutionary,[95] it is nevertheless an essential aspect of his mereology and so must be noted here. If a true whole is inherently defined by unchanging goodness, then the part is logically defined by its opposite: the possibility of evil. The passage above also reveals another important aspect of Proclus' axiologically charged mereology, namely that a thing cannot per se be judged to be good or evil. What we perceive as the evil in the cosmos is only of such a nature from our perspective as individuals with a finite and changeable existence. In other words, we as *parts* of the cosmos may be subject to the parasitic nature of evil. From the perspective of the one totality itself, however, there is no evil within it. On its own level, the cosmos exists only as a uniformly good and natural living being with a soul and an intellect. Even its parts are uniformly good from this perspective. After all, Proclus emphasised that even the mortal creatures contribute to the completeness of the 'all-complete' living being. The distinction he makes here between the partial being *qua* perishable and the partial being *qua* indestructible part of the cosmos also corresponds to the aforementioned distinction between the mortal creature as an individual (καθ' ἕκαστον) and the mortal creature as representing a species (κατ' εἶδος). In other words, the human being is unchangingly good when considered as one of the material species (ἔνυλον εἶδος) of mortal beings which make up the cosmos, but potentially evil when considered as a corporeal individual with a unique identity (ἰδίως ποιόν), since the weakness of his or her individuality creates the risk of bodily or spiritual corruption.

This axiological undercurrent of Proclus' mereology also informs his conflation of the distinction between part and whole with the distinction between

---

94   Proclus, *TP* I.18, 84.16–27.

95   See, e.g., Opsomer and Steel (2003: 20–24), d'Hoine (2011b), or Chlup (2012: 213).

particulars and universals. In contrast to most modern scholars of mereology, Proclus does not start with a predetermined set of parts to then describe how a whole is composed out of them. He starts at the primal principle of unity, i.e., the One, which is then increasingly *specified* as it remanifests in more pluralised ways. Proclus' overall view of causality consists in 'a sequence of specific levels of being, through which the procession is realised by gradually adding more specificity (and thus plurality) to being.'[96] In other words, the Neoplatonic universe starts with the Good or the One per se, which is then specified as the One Being or Good Being per se, and then as the One Whole or Good Whole. More specific kinds of wholes, such as the cosmos *qua* whole or the human being *qua* whole, do not arise until the unity of the Good has descended further and been pluralised to a greater extent. In this respect, *every* whole is a 'part' of the one Whole, because every whole derives from it. Similarly, both the individual and the species are part of the procession of beings which participate in the good. The species is a more universal phenomenon than the individual, but for Proclus it is also more 'whole' in the sense of being closer to the ultimate Good due to its greater resistance to change over time and, most importantly, to evil. After all, the good is subjected to greater pluralisation in its descent into the individual than in its descent into the species. In summary, Proclus' concept of a 'whole' is inherently loaded with an axiological subtext, as well as the implication of eternal existence. As a result, it comes to overlap with the concept of a universal, and by extension, the concepts of 'part' and 'particular' come to overlap as well.[97] As Proclus states in his *On the Existence of Evils*:

> The non-attainment [of a thing's appropriate good] is due to the weakness of the agent, since the agent has received a nature of such a kind that a part of it is better, a part worse, each part being separate from the other. For where the One is, there at the same time is the good. But evil is—and the One is not—present in a split nature. For incommensurability, disharmony and contrariety are in multitude; and from these weakness and indigence proceed.
>
> PROCLUS, *DMS* 50, 95, tr. Opsomer and Steel 2003

This does not mean that all parts are inherently evil. One could erroneously conclude from this passage that the pure bodily parts we discussed previously

---

96 Van Riel (2016: 87).

97 However, these arguments do not invalidate the criticisms of Baltzly and d'Hoine, for which see chapter 3, section 1. The fact remains that there are also passages in Proclus' oeuvre in which his concepts of the whole and the universal do not overlap.

UNITING THE IMPERFECT

are entirely devoid of wholeness and thus of goodness due to their division, but this is not the case. After all, wholeness is a specific form of goodness, i.e., unchanging goodness. It is not equal to the Good itself, and thus not the ultimate principle of all goodness. Indeed, in the first book of the *Platonic Theology*, Proclus emphasises that 'things which are absolutely devoid of the presence of the good cannot exist, nor can they even be conceived of.'[98] In the fifth book, he discusses the division of the intelligible principles into more specific intellective kinds of beings under the guidance of the divine Law.[99]

This confirms that division is not an inherently negative phenomenon. After all, the four universal Forms of living beings into which the one universal Paradigm is divided are themselves still whole and thus eternally good. To account for this fact, Proclus adds an essential nuance to his earlier statement in the treatise on evil.

> But if evil is also the cause of dissimilitude, division, and disorder, it is clearly necessary that it is deprived of assimilative goods, and of the indivisible providence of divisible beings, and of the order that exists in the divided beings.
>
> PROCLUS, *DMS* 51, 96, tr. Opsomer and Steel 2003

Even the divided beings possess some form of natural order. To state that they are inherently evil would be to imply that the One, which is the Good, is responsible for the production of a truly evil being, which is impossible (this is also Proclus' primary objection to Plotinus' designation of matter per se as the root of all evil). Thus, the mortal creatures fall short not simply because they are divided. Instead, the continual division of the one's unity required to reach their form of existence introduces concepts such as temporality and change into their nature. These concepts are opposed to the stability that grants the eternal wholes their unconditional goodness. The question Proclus asks us here is effectively: 'Can something *stay* whole?' In the logical order of cosmogony, the mortal creatures originate as true wholes when the Demiurge creates them as species, only to become vulnerable to change and, specifically, a change from their natural state to an unnatural (or unethical) one once those species are further divided to create individuals. In this sense, the cosmological side of Proclus' mereology revolves not around the question of what makes a whole, but around the question of what *un*makes a whole.

---

98   Proclus, *TP* I.18, 84.1–2: οὐδὲ γὰρ εἶναι δυνατὸν οὐδὲ τὴν πρώτην ὑποστῆναι τὰ παντελῶς ἄμοιρα τῆς τοῦ ἀγαθοῦ παρουσίας.

99   Proclus, *TP* V.9, 31.27–32.26 (as discussed in chapter 5, section 6).

202   CHAPTER 6

This does not mean that the individual mortal creatures are themselves born as perfect beings and lose their perfection over time. The main distinction between the intelligible realm and the sensible realm which mirrors it is the fact that intelligible causality proceeds from the perfect to the imperfect, whereas sensible beings are born imperfect and must then strive for perfection.[100]

> In general, everything that progresses through generation is born in an imperfect state and accomplishes its perfection in time. It is perfected by the addition of something. For each thing's end is [its] good.
>
> PROCLUS, *DMS* 26, 76, tr. Opsomer and Steel 2003

Thus, the corruption of a mortal individual comes down not to a loss of perfection, but to their *failure* (ἀπόπτωσις) to become perfect.[101] Evil is always defined in negative terms by Proclus, and the mortal creature is defined in the *Timaeus*-commentary by its *lack* of immortality.[102] It is prone to fail at both at becoming perfect and at subsequently staying perfect because it lacks both the unchanging stability and the infinite lifespan of eternal beings. Through this failure, the mortal creature blocks its own participation in the good, deprives itself of virtue, and perverts its own nature.[103]

The ultimate result of Proclus' combination of the concepts of eternity from the *Timaeus* and wholeness from the *Parmenides*, then, is that wholeness not only comes into being together with eternity, but also shares the exact same limit. If something falls outside of the definition of an eternal or everlasting being, it falls outside of the definition of 'being whole'. This longing for reversion to the transcendence of the intelligible realm permeates Proclus' discussions of partial wholes. Our individuality is a weakness. The only way out for us mortals is to transcend our finite individuality and become like god, as per the famous Platonic edict.[104] Only as representations of the one everlasting human being or the one everlasting living being may we claim to be truly whole.

---

100   See Proclus, *IT* III, 389.5–9 (cited in chapter 3, section 5).

101   Proclus, *IRP* I, 34.6–10; Steel (2016: 244–245); cf. d'Hoine (2011b).

102   As Opsomer (2001: 161) explains, were evil given a proper definition, it would necessarily be either an active principle derived from the ultimate Good, which is logically impossible, or an independent principle, which would introduce a type of dualism into the Neoplatonic system that Proclus wants to avoid.

103   Proclus, *DMS* 26, 76.

104   Plato, *Theat.* 176b1–2. For Proclus' interpretation of this Platonic edict, see Baltzly (2004: 306–319). Interestingly, the means Proclus recommends to escape this mortal realm are not solely philosophy, but also the ritualistic purification prescribed by the *Chaldean Oracles* and Eleusinian Mysteries, as Van den Berg (2003) shows.

PART 4

Bringing the Parts Together

∴

Οἷόν ἐστιν ἐν ἡνωμένοις τὰ μέλη τοῦ σώματος, τοῦτον ἔχει τὸν λόγον ἐν διεστῶσι τὰ λογικά, πρὸς μίαν τινὰ συνεργίαν κατεσκευασμένα. μᾶλλον δέ σοι ἡ τούτου νόησις προσπεσεῖται, ἐὰν πρὸς ἑαυτὸν πολλάκις λέγῃς, ὅτι μέλος εἰμὶ τοῦ ἐκ τῶν λογικῶν συστήματος.

MARCUS AURELIUS, *Meditations* VII, 13.1–5 ed. A.S.L. Farquharson, Oxford: Clarendon Press, 1944 (repr. 1968)

CHAPTER 7

The Best Kind of Whole (for a Neoplatonist)

The whole is something other than the sum of its parts for Proclus just as it is for Plato and Aristotle. It is only fitting, then, that we reflect on the entirety of this study in order to see the whole composed out of (and which perhaps even transcends?) its parts. The first section of this final chapter summarises the most important insights gained in the previous ones. The subsequent sections reflect on the tenets and merits of Proclean mereology overall, for a number of pertinent questions remain.

First, if one rejects the notion that Proclus' mereology is fundamentally inconsistent, one must explain how Proclus defines the concept of being whole, and whether this definition actually holds in the many contexts discussed previously. We must, in other words, ask what Proclus' ultimate definition of the concept of being whole is, and how this definition makes his mereology consistent. Secondly, a brief comparison between Proclus' late ancient approach to mereology and the contemporary union of logic and metaphysics is in order. There are a number of interesting parallels between the Proclean and modern kinds of mereology, and Proclus' view on parts and wholes holds certain advantages over its younger brethren. On the other hand, there are a number of irreconcilable differences brought about by the fact that Proclus practiced his philosophy in an entirely different era of history. One of the most important points of distinction is the intricate connection between mereology and axiology in Proclus' view. As we have seen in the discussion of the wholeness of mortal individuals in the previous chapter, this axiological connotation of wholeness even touches upon facets of Proclus' ethics, and as a result we must also ask to what extent Proclus' wholes can be considered to be ethical in nature. To close the study, I shall present a final critical review of Proclus' mereology.

7.1 Reflecting on the Sum of the Parts

7.1.1 Formalists versus Naturalists (Aka to Be Fuzzy or Not to Be Fuzzy)

In the first chapter following the introduction, we learned that the relation between the whole and the part can be conceived of in a variety of ways. Twentieth century logicians conceived of the whole as a simple set and, as such, as nothing above and beyond the members of that set. In fact, since the logical

© ARTHUR OOSTHOUT, 2025 | DOI:10.1163/9789004721760_008

whole is, in Lewis's words, 'ontologically innocent',[1] i.e., no different from its parts, formalistic theories of mereology are not restricted as to the kinds of wholes that can be postulated. Any two entities can be conceived of as members of a set and thus as a whole, including Lewis's trout-turkey. In contrast, naturalistic philosophers have argued that there is a distinction between the whole and its parts, even if it is only a numerical one. Although this more easily concurs with our subjective experience of the natural world (who has ever seen an actual fusion of trout and turkey?), naturalistic philosophers have to contend with Lewis's criticisms of their 'fuzzy' ontology. Whereas the formalistic philosopher provides a clear distinction between existence and non-existence (if the parts x, y, and z exist, the set {x, y, z} exists; if they do not, the set does not), the naturalistic philosopher must provide an additional criterion which determines when the entities x, y, and z form an ontologically distinct whole and when they do not. That such a criterion is not easily attainable is exemplified by Van Inwagen's theory of living wholes and non-living heaps of material simples, which involved the jettisoning of a great many compounds from our ontology, all of which the layman (as well as the physicist) would consider to be a single entity.

Some scholars took recourse to the writings of ancient philosophers in their quest to find the criterion for restricted composition, and specifically to the writings of Plato and Aristotle. These studies illustrate yet another fundamental dichotomy within the field of mereology: the question of whether one approaches a compound from a top-down perspective or from a bottom-up perspective. Harte's argument for the former, inspired primarily by Socrates' description of limit and unlimited in the *Philebus* and Timaeus' description of the elements in the *Timaeus*, was able to avoid the charge of fuzziness levelled by Lewis. If the whole logically precedes the parts instead of vice versa, one need not determine which parts can also become one whole and which cannot, for parts only exist within predetermined wholes. The downside of this theory, however, is that it does not account for the potential existence of parts apart from their whole. The bottom-up perspective taken by Koslicki avoids the latter problem but circles back to the original question of restricted composition: 'when is it true that the x'es compose y?'[2] Koslicki ultimately decides to leave this question to ontology proper and to the exact sciences, positing instead that the parts x, y, and z compose the whole W if they possess the formal constituents belonging to the ontological kind of whole W. In other words, x, y, and z compose whole W if they compose whole W, with the task of actually determining the variable 'W' remaining unfulfilled.

---

1   For the reference, see chapter 2, section 2.
2   For the reference to Van Inwagen, from whom the quote originates, see chapter 2, section 3.

THE BEST KIND OF WHOLE   207

7.1.2 *The Right Kind of Composition*

Proclus' approach to mereology is yet more complex, for he distinguishes between different applications of the concept of composition itself, as we saw in the subsequent chapter. In Proclus' axiomatic overview of Neoplatonic philosophy, the *Elements of Theology*, the concept of being composite (σύνθετον) is used in a *qualitative* sense rather than a *quantitative* one. The reason for this is a metaphysical theorem known as 'Proclus' rule'. Whereas Neoplatonic metaphysics traditionally revolves around a continuous multiplication of beings and ontological kinds as the One's influence extends downwards into reality, this Proclean rule states that the beings in the middle of the causal procession are the more composite, and that the extreme products, such as the Platonic receptacle, are just as simple as the One is. The reason for this is Proclus' belief that the superior intelligible principle has greater productive power, as a result of which its generative influence extends further down into reality than that of its subordinate brethren.

However, the two theories can coexist because Proclus explicitly ties the composition involved in his rule to the amount of distinctive characters (ἰδιότητες) a thing derives from the intelligible principles. In other words, this compositeness refers purely to a being's conceptual complexity. In contrast, the traditional Neoplatonic view of increasing multiplicity refers to divisibility in a *quantitative* sense. Proclus' rule in fact ensures that the lowest beings are the most divisible in this regard, because they lack any inherited characteristics to delimit them. As the *Parmenides*-commentary makes clear, the formal natures inherited from the intelligible realm serve as the limit imposed upon the unlimitedness of matter. As a result of this, the lowest being becomes the absolute continuum mentioned in the introduction, infinitely divisible because every part of it is homogenous in its indefiniteness (though it retains a single inherited character: unity). Yet Proclus' concept of composition is even more nuanced: not only does it have two different meanings in the forms of conceptual and quantitative composition, but the concept of conceptual composition has two meanings itself, depending on whether one applies it to the intelligible principles or to sensible beings. For the former, it implies a greater distance from the One and thus a lesser degree of perfection, but for the latter it implies a greater degree of participation in the transcendent principles and thus a higher degree of perfection.

7.1.3 *Expanding the Concept of Wholeness*

After having analysed Proclus' concept of composition, we discussed his definition of wholeness in the next chapter. Here the challenge was to unify the various scholarly analyses of Proclus' well-known division between three kinds of wholes: the whole before the parts, the whole composed of parts, and the whole in the part. Whereas the arguments Proclus gives in the *Elements of Theology* describe the three types of whole only in an abstract sense, the third book of the *Platonic Theology* grounds the tripartite wholeness in Proclus' metaphysical system. Furthermore, the *Platonic Theology* reveals the exegetical sources of the mereological triad. Although scholars have suggested the *Theaetetus* as a likely source of influence for the threefold wholeness presented in that work, and Proclus himself points to the *Statesman* and the *Timaeus*, I argued that the theory is in practice inspired mainly by Plato's *Parmenides*, *Philebus*, and *Timaeus*. From Proclus' exegesis of the second hypothesis of the *Parmenides*, the intelligible principle of all wholes derives its rank as the second intelligible being behind the One Being. Furthermore, like all intelligible principles, the intelligible Wholeness derives from the *Philebus* a triadic structure consisting of a transcendent henad, a participating being, and a power which serves as the mean term between the other two. Lastly, Proclus finds a description of the cosmos as whole composed of wholes in the *Timaeus*, leading him to conceive of the whole in the part.

Like all transcendent principles, the second intelligible triad irradiates the levels of reality below it with images of itself. Thus, Proclus explains, the many occurrences of wholeness in the Neoplatonic universe derive their threefold structure from the triad of transcendent henad, mediating power, and participating being present within the intelligible Wholeness. This is reflected in the *Elements of Theology*, where Proclus emphasises the simple wholeness (ἁπλῶς ὅλον) of the whole before the parts, ascribes an imitative nature to the whole in the part, and describes the whole composed of parts primarily with reference to its relation to the two other kinds of wholeness. Examples of mereology in Proclus' cosmological writings follow the same pattern: the World Soul is conceived of as a simple unity whose essence remains undisturbed at all times and yet is divided into portions which the Demiurge recombines to form a composite soul, in which each portion contains all of the metaphysical ingredients present in the original unitary Soul. With this theory, Proclus expands the concept of the whole in two directions. Not only is the whole both immanent in its parts, as in Aristotle's *Metaphysics*, and entirely prior to its parts instead of merely being distinct from them, but its influence also reaches down into the parts themselves, so that they too come to share in the whole's distinctive character.

7.1.4 *The Division of the Indivisible Whole*

Having charted the theoretical framework of Proclus' mereological views, we delved into the metaphysical system itself in the first chapter of part three in order to discern the nature of part-whole relations in the intelligible realm, where no spatiotemporal dimensions exist. First, we noted that Proclus'

THE BEST KIND OF WHOLE

209

description of Intellect as an indivisible whole rests on the idea that the Intellect is capable of reverting upon the entirety of itself. It owes this capacity to its non-extended nature. As a result of this utter lack of extension, the Intellect is in some sense composed of homogenous parts (ὁμοιομερῆς), since each 'part' of Intellect, e.g., any particular Platonic Form, is substantially identical to the whole of Intellect. This fluid border between the whole and the part fits well with Proclus' use of mereological terminology to describe grades of universality. Any given intelligible-intellective principle is 'more whole' (ὁλικώτερον) than an intellective principle, in the sense that it transcendently encompasses a greater number of participants. Yet by the same logic it is also 'more particular' (μερικώτερον) than an intelligible principle. Yet as well as this 'all-in-all' approach to the parts and wholes of Intellect may fit the sliding scale of universality, it is somewhat more difficult to reconcile with Proclus' emphasis on the emergence of strictly distinct distinctive characters (ἰδιότητες) at each new level of the Intellect or with the strict distinction between three different levels of wholeness as delineated by the tripartite model of the whole (before the parts, composed of parts, and in the part).

In fact, we noted that the concept of wholeness is itself one of the distinctive characters which arise within the Intellect. More specifically, it comes to be in the second intelligible triad, which is also the principle of Eternity (as a result of Proclus' combination of his insights from the *Timaeus* with his aforementioned reading of the *Parmenides* and *Philebus*). Given that this second intelligible triad constitutes the principle of all wholes in Proclus' Neoplatonic universe, all primary characteristics that belong to eternity must also automatically be shared by all wholes. These include such properties as being timelessly stable and being an immortal living being. As a result, all that exists in time and, more specifically, for a *finite* amount of time is excluded from the definition of being whole, being deemed 'partial' (μερικόν) instead. Furthermore, Proclus' equation of wholeness with eternity implies also an axiological connotation to the word 'whole', since Proclus argues that eternal beings enjoy a perfectly stable participation in their proper share of the good by virtue of their timelessness, whereas temporal beings can only claim a changeable, finite, and lacking participation of in their share of the good. From this axiological connotation to the notion of wholeness, a link between perfection and wholeness arises as well. Since the third intelligible triad is not only the totality (πᾶν) which follows logically from the whole (ὅλον)—in other words, the whole composed of parts which proceeds from the whole before the parts—but also the 'wholly perfect' (παντελής) totality from the *Timaeus*, the concept of being perfect or complete comes to be defined as encompassing a sum of parts from which no essential constituents (συμπληρωτικά) are missing.

Proclus does not stop there, however. The second and third intelligible triads both inhabit only the first of *three* main sublevels of intellectual reality. Since the distinctive character of each intelligible principle radiates downward through reality, the concepts of being whole and being perfect have further roles to play in the intelligible-intellective and intellective levels of intellect. Within the intelligible-intellective hypostases, the principles of wholeness and perfection are further specified: a second argument for the divisibility of the one being in the *Parmenides* allows Proclus to posit a second triad of wholeness, one which unfolds the singular concept of wholeness into the ontological distinction between the whole and its parts. The notion of perfection as a more specified form of wholeness (a full totality of essential constituents logically following from the idea of a unity prefiguring a multiplicity) returns as well, since in the third intelligible-intellective triad the concept of being perfect is granted the same structure as the concept of wholeness, namely a perfection before the parts, a perfection composed of parts, and a perfection in the part. Interestingly, all of these concepts (whole, part, perfection) transcend the ontological kinds we perceive in the sensible world. The production of such specified kinds of wholes does not commence until the intellective phase of the causal procession, where it is set in motion because of the intellection of Cronus, Rhea, and Zeus. Fittingly, the relations between these three gods mirror those of the three kinds of wholes, as do the manifestations of the Platonic Forms produced by the intellective gods. In this regard, the intelligible-intellective and intellective unfolding of the intelligible Wholeness reframes the priority of the whole over the parts as the priority of the concepts of wholeness, parthood, and division over the kinds of beings which appear in the sensible cosmos.

7.1.5 (A)Part Alone, Whole Together

The inhabitants of the sensible cosmos are not unequivocally expelled from Proclus' mereology, however. In fact, the time in which they exist is an image of eternity according to the Neoplatonic philosophers. Whereas eternity measures the multiplicity-in-unity of the nonextended intellectual beings, time bestows an extended form of wholeness upon its participants, i.e., the wholeness of a single entity whose parts change or are replaced over time. Such changes need not occur over a finite amount of time. As Proclus establishes time and again in the passages of his *Timaeus*-commentary concerned with the wholes and parts of the cosmos, a number of cosmic beings share in some way in the stability of eternal beings despite their temporality. The secret ingredient of their wholeness is their immortality. The cosmic spheres, for example, move around the earth, but their movement is nevertheless stable in the sense that

THE BEST KIND OF WHOLE

it is never disrupted or deformed, and the spheres themselves never decay or cease to be. Furthermore, each of these spheres is an essential constituent of the cosmos. Individuals such as Plato, Plotinus, and Proclus pass away, and the cosmos continues its circular movement undisturbed. The disappearance of a heavenly sphere, however, would fundamentally alter the constitution of the cosmos (and not in a positive way). These kinds of beings—which include the monads of the elements, the heavenly spheres, and other universal components established by the Demiurge after the creation of the one totality—are the purest wholes in the sensible realm, since their everlasting (ἀΐδιος) nature is a direct image of the eternal (αἰώνιος) nature of the transcendent wholes.

Although Proclus' aim in the passages discussed in the sixth chapter is mainly to adapt his general mereological framework to the various notions and ideas presented in the *Timaeus*, the distinction between changing, but everlasting cosmic wholes and partial mortals is not the only common element in these lemmas. Proclus nuances the distinction between immortal wholes and partial mortals throughout the passages we analysed, and he does this both in the *Timaeus*-commentary and in the *Platonic Theology*. What enables him to do so is his distinction between the species of any given kind of mortal creature and the individual manifestations of that kind. Following Plato's distinction between the works of the Demiurge and the works of the cosmic gods the Demiurge creates, Proclus allots the production of, e.g., humanity as a species to the Demiurge himself, but the creation of individual human beings to the younger gods. As a result of this, the species is whole and everlasting while the individual falters and decays. Furthermore, Proclus remains true to his threefold wholeness and allots a form of wholeness, albeit a partial one, to the individuals themselves. There is no Platonic Form of Socrates as an individual, but the man does possess within himself an image of the everlasting paradigm of humanity. He is thus the very last type of whole possible in the Proclean universe, the 'whole in a particular manner' (ὅλον μερικῶς).

7.2   What Is Proclus' Definition of the Whole(Some)?

The distinction between Socrates *qua* partial individual and his wholeness *qua* bearer of humanity exemplifies Proclus' overall approach to the relation between whole and part. In the introduction, we discussed a passage from Proclus' *Timaeus*-commentary in which the philosopher characterised the Neoplatonic universe as sandwiched between two extremes: pure and indivisible unity versus undetermined plurality. In between these two extremes exist beings which are manifold yet one, composed out of ontologically distinct parts yet constituting a singular entity. Fittingly for a Neoplatonic thinker, Proclus places this unity *above* its multiplicity. Socrates' wholeness, i.e., his humanity, transcends his bodily parts. However, the whole is not just something other than the sum of its parts in the sense of belonging to another ontological kind than its parts, e.g., being defined as a human being while the part is defined as a finger (this is true for Aristotle's immanent whole as well, after all). For a Neoplatonic philosopher like Proclus, 'whole' is not simply an ontological descriptor applicable to any given kind of unifying formal principle, but the name of a really existent intelligible entity with its own distinctive character. The various kinds of beings in the universe we call 'wholes' owe that designation to their participation in this distinctive character.

As stated, Proclus' definition of this distinctive character of the whole arises out of Plato's *Parmenides*, *Philebus*, and *Timaeus*. The Proclean whole derives its status as a more specific determination of unity and goodness from the first dialogue, its tripartite nature from the second, and its role as the measure of all eternal beings from the third. Taken together, Proclus' exegeses of these dialogues lead to the following definitions of wholeness and parthood.

> *1a—Proclean definition of the whole*: a being X is whole in an unparticipated manner if it is an eternal and transcendent causal principle which transforms an inferior multitude into a stable unity by transmitting its distinctive character into that multitude.
>
> *1b—Proclean definition of Wholeness itself*: the intelligible principle which possesses the characteristics described in *1a* not as gifts from superior principles but as its primary self-constituted character is Wholeness itself (this principle being the second intelligible triad, representing intelligible Life).
>
> *2a—Proclean definition of the part*: entities y_1, y_2 ... y_n are parts of compound z for so long as they collectively participate in the distinctive character of X (see *1a*).
>
> *2b—Proclean definition of the compound*: from *1a* and *2a* it follows that the compound z is whole in a participated manner.
>
> *3—Proclean definition of the whole part*: entities y_1, y_2 ... y_n are themselves whole in a participated manner if they participate in the distinctive character of X not just collectively (see *2a*), but also individually.

Through these definitions, Proclus essentially flips the central question of mereology on its head. Philosophers traditionally ask what kind of principle

THE BEST KIND OF WHOLE

is responsible for the transformation of a multiplicity of components into a single substance. As the first definition above indicates, Proclus instead asks when the unity flowing forth from the source of the Neoplatonic universe transforms into an actual multiplicity.

However, although the whole, taken on its own, transcends the multiplicity of its parts, it cannot be defined without reference to the multiplicity it produces. It is not sufficient to describe Proclean wholes simply as 'transcendent unities', since the description 'transcendent unity' can apply to yet superior principles (e.g., the One Being or the One itself) as well. What makes this particular transcendent unity whole is precisely the fact that it both prefigures a multiplicity and unifies that multiplicity at the latter's own level of reality.[3]

Furthermore, the relation between Proclus' wholes and the multiplicities they produce is not an unreciprocated one. The whole itself is described both as purely transcendent and as a productive principle, i.e., as something which both remains in itself and proceeds to lower levels of reality. The parts and the compound they form, on the other hand, are inherently defined by participation in the distinctive character of the transcendent whole and thus by reversion upon it. Whole and part are, in other words, mutually and inextricably attracted to one another. The whole cannot be whole without proceeding to parts, and the parts cannot be parts without reverting upon wholeness.

This mutual relation also protects Proclus from the absurdities that would follow from positing whole before part without any qualification. Within the sensible cosmos, for example, composite bodies tend to form out of parts rather than vice versa. Yet the forms these composites take once the parts come together are not created by the parts themselves, but rather by the incorporeal intellective Forms. Although the body of an individual person arises out of pre-existing material components, e.g., the four elements or the bodily parts, these components do not by themselves create the form of the human being. The form is instead imprinted upon the material compound by the intellective Form of the Human Being. In the grand scheme of things, the whole precedes the parts by virtue of the fact that the multiplicity of the parts is itself created by the whole. Yet the mutual attraction between whole and parts enables Proclus to account for parts which in some way precede wholeness in the realm of individual creatures.

> καὶ ἐπὶ μὲν τοῦ παντὸς προϋφίστατο τὸ ὅλον τῶν μερῶν καὶ τὸ ἓν τοῦ πλήθους, ἐπὶ δὲ τῶν θνητῶν τὰ πολλὰ πρὸ τοῦ ἑνὸς ἀπογεννᾶται, καὶ συντηκόμενα ταῦτα

---

3 As Kobusch (2000: 315) points out, this is the reason for Proclus' distinction between the concept of the whole and the concept of pure unity.

διὰ τῶν πυκνῶν γόμφων ἓν ἀποτελεῖ· σώματα μὲν γὰρ ἁπλᾶ συντήκεται, τὰ δὲ συντακέντα γομφοῦται, τὰ δὲ γομφωθέντα ζωοποιεῖται, τὰ δὲ ζωοποιηθέντα συναρμόζεται πρὸς τὴν ἀθάνατον ψυχήν.

PROCLUS, *IT* V, 211.4–10 (3.322.11–17 Diehl)

And in the case of the cosmos the whole was established before the parts and the one before the many, but in the case of mortals the many are engendered before the one, and when they are welded together by means of the frequent joining pieces they bring one thing to completion: simple bodies are welded together, the welded pieces are joined, the joined-up [bodies] are given life, and the creatures given life are harmonised with the immortal soul.

Tr. TARRANT 2017 (modified)

Regardless of the order of priority, however, Proclean parts are dependent on wholeness in some way. In the procession of beings that unfolds within the divine Intellect, the distinctive character of wholeness arises before the distinctive character of parthood, and per the rule of Proclus the former has a greater causal reach than the latter. Thus, there are no parts without wholeness. One might ask how the aforementioned bodily parts can exist prior to their composition, but Proclus' metaphysics accounts for this problem. The intelligible Wholeness is only the second intelligible principle after the primal Being and the third principle in total if one includes the One itself. Both of those superior principles naturally possess a greater causal reach than wholeness. As a result, there is nothing which prevents the components of bodies from pre-existing their compound *qua* beings and *qua* unities. Take the Aristotelian concept of homonymy as an example: cutting off my finger does not erase it from existence. The separated piece of flesh that drops to the floor is clearly a unitary (and gruesome) thing. It is, however, no longer *part* of me. Similarly, Proclus is able to avoid the problem raised by Harte—if the parts depend on the whole for their existence, what are they outside of the whole?—by distinguishing wholeness from both being and unity. A separated body part may not be whole, but it *is*, and it is a singular thing. Conversely, the distinctive character of parthood itself is entirely dependent on wholeness. Even when Proclus describes separate components as parts, as in the passage above, he does so by reference to the whole they are destined to compose.

Of all the characteristics of the Proclean whole, however, its kinship with the concept of eternity is undoubtedly its most distinctive one. For a Neoplatonist such as Proclus, equating these concepts is to be expected: he strives to reach the intelligible truths which transcend our ever-changing material reality.

THE BEST KIND OF WHOLE   215

It comes as no surprise then that he would seek to define the true whole as
that which is intelligible and eternal, existing timelessly and thus necessarily
possessing all of its parts (or aspects) at once. However, Proclus also seeks to
preserve the connection between our material existence and the coveted realm
of true wholes. This leads him to extend the definition of eternal wholeness.
Sticking to a concept of strict timelessness in defining the whole would result
in a more extensive expulsion of ontological kinds from our mereology than
even the one Van Inwagen's life-criterium brings about (nothing in the sensible
cosmos would be classifiable as a whole, after all). Instead, Proclus conceives
of lesser forms of eternity deriving from the true eternal whole. As Damascius
helpfully recapitulates in his own commentary on Plato's *Parmenides*:

Ἐκ δὲ αὖ τρίτων τὸ ὅλον ᾗ ὅλον ἀΐδιον, ἡ γὰρ φθορὰ σκεδασμός ἐστι τῶν μερῶν·
διὸ τὸ ἀληθῶς ὅλον πάντως ἀΐδιον· τὸ δὲ μέρος μᾶλλον ἢ ὅλον καὶ φαινόμενον
ὅλον ταύτῃ φθαρτόν ἢ οὐχ ὅλον· ταὐτὸν ἄρα καὶ ταύτῃ αἰὼν καὶ ὁλότης. Ἐπεὶ
καὶ τὸ μᾶλλον ὅλον μᾶλλον ἀΐδιον, ὡς τὸ πᾶν· τὸ δὲ ἧττον ⟨ἧττον⟩, ὡς τῶν πληρωμάτων ἕκαστον τῶν οὐρανίων· τὸ δὲ ἥκιστα ὅλον καὶ ἀΐδιον ἥκιστα, ὡς αἱ τῶν
ὑπὸ σελήνην στοιχείων ὁλότητες.

DAMASCIUS, *IP* I, 23.17–24.4

Thirdly [according to Proclus],[4] the whole *qua* whole is everlasting,
for corruption is a scattering of the parts. Hence, the truly whole is in
every respect everlasting. That which is more part than whole and [only]
appears to be whole, on the other hand, is perishable insofar as it is not
whole. Thus, eternity and wholeness are the same in this way as well.
For what is more whole is more everlasting, such as the universe, what
is less whole is less everlasting, such as each of the heavenly perfections
[i.e., the celestial bodies], and what is least whole is also least everlasting,
such as the wholes of the sublunary elements.

In other words, Proclus extends the definition of wholeness to include temporal everlastingness as well as timeless eternity, and this everlastingness is
granted to different material things to various degrees. As Westerink, Combès,
and Segonds note, 'dans la présentation de Damascius, l'argument de Proclus
introduit un dégradé dans la perpétuité en devenir, de l'univers aux plérômes

---

4   In this passage, Damascius presents a concise overview of Proclus' interpretation of the sec-
    ond hypothesis of the *Parmenides*—see Westerink, Combès, and Segonds (1997: 127). The two
    matters he discusses before these lines are Proclus' propositions that the first Whole is also
    the first Eternity and that an eternal being is the whole of itself at once.

célestes, et de ceux-ci aux totalités sublunaires.'[5] As a result of this, the wholeness of material beings is relative: the mortal creature is a whole with respect to its own bodily components, but merely a part with respect to the material cosmos itself. The cosmic beings are not the only ones whose wholeness is relative between one another, however, and our individual share in wholeness is the final step of a long procession of different kinds of wholes and parts going all the way back to the intelligible principle of Eternity. The intelligible beings too are whole in a relative manner, existing as transcendent principles or as participated and participating entities depending on their relations to inferior or superior principles. All immortal beings, whether they be timeless or temporal, are linked to one another through their respective participation in the distinctive character of being eternal.

The notion of a sliding scale of eternity lays bare a tension in Proclus' mereology, namely between a purely logical understanding of the whole as that which is composed out of (or, in Proclus' case, determines) its parts on the one hand, and the axiologically loaded sense of being complete or perfect—in other words, the sense that something is wholesome—on the other. The definitions which we settled on above are perfectly applicable to the various manifestations of wholeness in the logical sense, but they do not account for the axiological shift from truly whole eternal beings to their temporal participants, which are somehow 'less whole'. A complete overview of Proclus' understanding of the whole requires that we expand the definitions set out above in order to account for both the metaphysically neutral sense of the term 'whole' and the axiologically loaded one.

> The whole in a(n onto)logical sense.
>
> *1a—General definition of the whole*: a being X is whole in an unparticipated manner if it is an eternal and transcendent causal principle which transforms an inferior multitude into a composite unity by transmitting its distinctive character into that multitude.
>
> *1b—Definition of Wholeness itself*: the intelligible principle which possesses the characteristics described in *1a* not as gifts from superior principles but as its primary self-constituted character is Wholeness itself (this principle being the second intelligible triad, representing intelligible Life).

---

5 Westerink, Combès, and Segonds (1997: 128).

2a—Definition of the part: entities y_1, y_2 ... y_n are parts of compound z for so long as they collectively participate in the distinctive character of X (see *1a*).

2b—Definition of the compound: from *1a* and *2a* it follows that the compound z is whole in a participated manner.

3—Definition of the whole part: entities y_1, y_2 ... y_n are themselves whole in a participated manner if they participate in the distinctive character of X not just collectively (see *2a*) but also individually.

The whole in an axiological sense.

4a—Wholeness and eternity: all that participates in wholeness also participates in eternity.

4b—Distinction between the eternal and the temporal: a being X can participate in eternity either 1) in both its essence and its activity, 2) in its essence but not in its activity, or 3) in neither its essence nor its activity. Insofar as X participates in eternity, it is the whole of itself in a stable manner. Insofar as X does not participate in eternity, it is temporal and changeable.

4c—The nature of participated goodness: all things participate in the goodness flowing forth from the One Good, albeit each in the manner proper to its rank in the hierarchy of being.

4d—Eternity produces stable goodness: the proper mode of participation in the good for any given thing which is whole in an unparticipated manner or participates in eternal wholeness, is the stable preservation of its allotted share in the good. Hence, the extent to which a being X participates in eternal wholeness (*4b*) determines the extent to which it stably participates in the good.

5—Definition of wholesomeness: a being X is axiologically whole or 'wholesome' if it participates in eternal wholeness in all of its aspects (both essence and activity), as a result of which it also stably preserves its participation in the good (*4d*). This type of wholesomeness belongs to the intelligible, intelligible-intellective, and intellective beings.

6—Definition of unwholesomeness: a being X is axiologically partial or 'unwholesome' if it does not participate in eternal wholeness in any respect (neither essence, nor activity), as a result of which it becomes lifeless (see *1b* above) and utterly changeable, and as a further consequence

218   CHAPTER 7

of this it cannot preserve its participation in the good at all (*4d*). This type of unwholesomeness belongs to the lifeless objects in the sensible cosmos.

7a—Definition of mixed wholesomeness: a being X is a axiologically whole in a mixed manner or both 'wholesome' and 'unwholesome' if it participates in eternal wholeness only in its essence but not in its activity, as a result of which is always participates stably in the good in respect of its essence, but not always in respect of its temporal and changeable activity (*4d*). This type of mixed wholesomeness belongs to the rational souls.

7b—Definition of 'partial' wholesomeness: a being X is axiologically whole-in-a-partial-manner or 'partially wholesome' if one or more constituent properties of its essence participate(s) in eternal wholeness, but not its essence as a whole, as a result of which it is in principle temporal, changeable, and unwholesome, but retains on the other hand the capacity to become wholesome by reverting upon the part of itself which does constitute a stable goodness (*4d*). This type of partial wholesomeness belongs to individual animals, since they are 'whole parts' (*3*) insofar as they represent the whole(some) intellective form of their species (*5*), and individual human beings, since they not only represent the intellective form of their species (*5*) but also possess a rational soul (*7a*).

The second set of definitions is necessary for Proclus' mereology to function, insofar as it allows one to distinguish between different types of wholes which would be indistinguishable according to the first three definitions. For example, both a specific Platonic Idea and an individual human being are equally valid representatives of the 'whole part' of the third definition above. The specific Platonic Idea of Humanity participates in the unifying causal power of the principle of the Living Being itself not just together with other Platonic Forms, but individually as well (see *1a* and *3* above). The individual person likewise participates in the Platonic Idea of Humanity not just together with his or her human peers, but individually as well. And yet the Platonic Idea of Humanity is more 'whole' than the human individual is. The sliding scale of eternality and everlastingness described in the additional set of definitions allows us to explain this discrepancy and to show how both the Platonic Idea of Humanity and the human individual are comparable manifestations of wholeness on the one hand, but different manifestations of (un)wholesomeness on the other.

THE BEST KIND OF WHOLE

7.3   Is Proclus' Mereology Consistent?

One might wonder, however, whether this scale of eternal wholeness, ranging all the way from timeless Eternity to the mortal individual, is entirely perfect. In fact, Proclus' mereology rests on the rather questionable assumption that perpetuity is merely another form of eternity. In Proclus' view, the everlasting whole remains a stable unity just like the eternal whole, even if the parts of the former are spread out across time. However, the spatiotemporal division of the parts of everlasting wholes is not as natural an unfolding of the intelligible multiplicities as Proclus thinks it is. As we noted previously, Proclus characterises the everlasting wholes of the sensible cosmos in a manner akin to the modern theory of four-dimensionalism, a theory whose defining feature is the *extension* of parts across a span of time. In contrast, the eternal wholes of the internal realm are defined entirely by their lack of extension. The eternal being is the whole of itself *at once* (ἅμα ὅλον), whereas the exact opposite is the case for the everlasting whole: the total sum of its parts never exists all at once because of the parts' extension across time (and space).

As Damascius points out, we should distinguish the whole composed 'according to the concepts of earlier and later' (κατὰ τὸ πρότερον καὶ ὕστερον) from the whole composed 'according to the concepts of sameness and difference' (κατὰ τὸ ταὐτὸν καὶ θάτερον).[6] The Neoplatonic philosophers claim that the intelligible realm encompasses wholes of both kinds.[7] Yet in reality the parts of incorporeal intellect are ordered only according to logical priority. This logical order cannot be equated to some form of temporal extension whereby the one part of intellect exists at one point in time whereas the other does not, for no temporal extension exists in the intelligible realm. Regardless of the logical priority of the intelligible triads over the intellective ones, they all exist at once. In this respect, Proclus' mereology is faced with the same challenge Lewis levelled at the naturalistic philosophers. Although the (conceptual) parts of intellect are ontologically distinct from one another (sameness and difference), one cannot qualify their existence by claiming that one exists while the

---

6 Damascius, *IP* I, 62.10–13.

7 This includes Damascius himself: he too describes timeless eternity as the precursor to temporal extension (*ibidem*).

220 CHAPTER 7

other does not yet exist (earlier and later). As Lewis stated, 'once you've said "there is" your game is up.'[8] The totality of intellect either exists, or it does not.[9]

In fact, Proclus' resistance against the Porphyrian thesis of a homogenous soul and a homogenous intellect rests entirely on this fundamental distinction between sensible and intelligible multiplicities. Material mixtures are defined by the fact that their parts overlap one another. In contrast, immaterial mixtures retain their ingredients in a pure manner precisely because of the absence of any form of extension and, as a result, of continuity or overlap.[10] Because of this distinction between material and immaterial mixtures, the famous Neoplatonic edict that 'all things are in all things' likewise has a different meaning in the intelligible realm that it does in the sensible one. For sensible things, it implies that each temporal 'part' of the thing (e.g., each version of me at different points in my life) somehow retains its connection to the core essence of the whole (e.g., my identity as Arthur or, in Neoplatonic terms, my humanity). This core essence is, as Aristotle rightly points out, something *other* than the components, whether they be spatial or temporal ones. For intelligible principles, on the other hand, the statement 'all things are in all things' implies that any part of intellect remains substantially identical to the intellect as a whole—since it is the totality of intellect just as much as the whole intellect is—with the part(icular intellect)'s only distinguishing factor being the specific manner in which it encompasses the whole intellect.[11]

The difference between the sensible and the intelligible realm raises issues for Proclus' threefold division of wholeness as well. The most obvious is Proclus' attempt to apply the terms from this triad to his reframed version of the aforementioned Plotinian and Porphyrian notion of all intellect existing both in the Intellect and in an intellect. As I noted in a previous paper, the fact that this theorem places so much emphasis on the homogeneity of the intellectual essence's various manifestations makes it difficult to distinguish three separate intellectual entities to represent each form of wholeness.[12] In contrast, it is much easier to apply the three kinds of wholes in the more diversified sensible

---

8   For the respective reference, see chapter 2, section 2.

9   Proclus' arguments that the creation-story from the Timaeus describes an atemporal process would also threaten to crumble: if the conceptual division of the parts of intellect implies or prefigures some form of spatiotemporal extension, would the conceptual division of the works of the primal Demiurge not also prefigure some temporal order?

10 See the references to Oosthout, A. (2022b) in chapter 5, section 1.

11 For Damascius, this is reason enough to return to the Porphyrian terminology and describe the intelligible principles as beings that are more so homogenous than heterogenous; see Damascius, *IP* I, 60.6–11.

12 Oosthout, A. (2022b: 28–29).

realm, where the transcendent character of an intellective principle (e.g., the Human Being itself) is reflected not just in the immortal species (e.g., the supposedly everlasting human race) but in the mortal individuals as well (e.g., the humanity of an individual person).[13]

Within the intelligible realm, however, we are forced to conceptualise the three kinds of wholes as relative concepts in order for them to fully work. This is exemplified even by the definitions drawn up above. The definition of the whole (1a) suggests that any transcendent unity is whole in an unparticipated manner (supported by, e.g., Proclus' description of the intelligible Paradigm as the transcendent cause of the cosmic whole), whereas the definition of Wholeness itself (1b) suggests that only it can truly be whole in an unparticipated manner, since all other transcendent wholes possess their wholeness only as an image of its self-constituted characteristics. The loose application of these formulae of which Proclus has sometimes been accused is unfortunately necessary for these three terms to work at all in the realm of nonextended intelligible being(s).

The charge of a loose application of philosophical formulae unfortunately applies also to Proclus' use of terms such as 'whole', 'part', and 'composite' in general. We have well established by now that the term 'whole' denotes the ontologically determinate essence of a certain intelligible principle in Proclus' metaphysics, whose distinctive character is subsequently participated by lesser beings. Yet, as we also noted, Proclus follows Porphyry in equating wholeness and parthood with universality and particularity as well, and from this distils a distinction between higher principles which are 'more whole', i.e., more universal (ὁλικώτερον), than lesser principles, and lesser principles which are 'more particular' (μερικώτερον) than higher principles. This scale from more holistic to more particular principles does not depend on Proclus' ontological and axiological definition of the whole as the (partially) perfect and eternal thing. Instead, it appears to revolve around a much more broadly defined extensional understanding of the whole as the full sum of a given principle's products. In other words, what makes the Platonic Idea of Humanity more particular than the Living Being itself appears to be in principle no more than the fact that the Idea of Humanity produces a smaller set of participants (all of the human beings) than the Living Being itself does (all of the living beings). We pointed previously to Nicholas of Methone's criticism of this broader extensional understanding of wholeness-as-universality as well, which additionally points out that the intelligible principle of Being utterly transcends Wholeness itself

---

13   For which see d'Hoine (2021: 203–204), as noted previously.

in an ontological sense, but is still comparable to it in an extensional sense, insofar as it produces more participants than Wholeness itself and is thus a more 'holistic' principle than Wholeness itself within Proclus' scale of universality and particularity.[14]

The notion of wholeness as a marker for the total collection of participated manifestations of something stands in contrast not only to the axiological notion of wholesomeness, but also to the qualitative notion of essential composition out of a number of participated characteristics. The Idea of Humanity might be understood in an extensional sense as the transcendent unity which encompasses the sum total of all human individuals, but it is itself also a complex entity shaped by the distinctive characteristics of superior intelligible principles, such as being, life, sameness, difference, and so on.[15] When Proclus claimed that this made the Idea of Humanity 'more composite' than the intelligible principle of the Living Being itself, he referred to qualitative composition rather than quantitative composition. All of this means that one must adapt their understanding of the concept of being a whole slightly depending on the context in which Proclus the term, since in each case it indicates a different one (or more) of the following senses of being whole:

a broad logical sense (the whole which is either divisible into parts, if intelligible, or composed out of parts, if sensible),

a specific extensional sense (the whole which encompasses the sum total of its participated manifestations),

a qualitative sense (the whole which is essentially constituted out of distinctive characters derived from various transcendent principles),

or *an axiological sense* (the whole which participates in eternity in some way and thus possesses its proper goodness in a stable and unceasing manner).

---

14   See chapter 5, section 1.

15   In this regard the adjective 'extensional' is not entirely suitable to describe the Idea of Humanity as the sum of all human beings, since the extensional set of the Idea of Humanity, i.e., the set of *all* proper parts which it contains, would in fact consist of {received distinctive character$_1$, ... received distinctive character$_n$, participated manifestation$_1$, ... participated manifestation$_n$}. Although this is a perfectly acceptable way of describing the Proclean Idea from the perspective of Lewis or Varzi, Proclus himself would likely resist the gathering of the Idea's different types of parts in this manner. Note, however, that this issue can be avoided if one distinguishes between the Proclean principle in an extensional sense (i.e., the set of all its participated manifestations) and that principle in an *intensional* sense (e.g., the received characteristics that make humanity humanity), as, e.g., Muniz and Rudebusch (2018) have done in their analysis of Plato's greatest kinds.

And yet, despite these many variations in which the term 'whole' appears in Proclus' writings, the description 'inconsistent' does not do his mereology justice. Proclus is, after all, a Platonic commentator first and an original thinker second (in contrast to someone like Plotinus, despite the latter's rather modest description of himself). Take, for example, the three kinds of whole. When judged as exegetical tools, they constitute a remarkably effective framework for the Neoplatonic study of the Platonic writings. It is not without reason that Proclus introduces the three kinds of wholes by referring to Plato's discussions of kinds and species and of the nesting of wholes within the cosmic whole, nor that their primary role in the third book of the *Platonic Theology* is to represent the Phileban triad of limit, unlimited, and mixture.

Even when taken on their own, however, the definitions of the three kinds of wholes given in the *Elements of Theology* do a fine job of summarising the Neoplatonic approach to mereology. Given the Platonic emphasis on transcendent intelligible principles which are nevertheless approachable for material beings through the process of participation, it makes a great deal of sense that Proclus would want his mereological framework to represent not just the basic Aristotelian assumption that a whole is something other than the sum of its parts (the whole composed of parts), but also the transcendence of the intelligible principle (the whole before the parts) and its image in each of its participants (the whole in the part). A mereology based on the Neoplatonic interpretation of Plato would be incomplete without some form of transcendent wholeness, and Proclus' concept of wholeness in individual parts is a natural consequence of Plato's insistence in the *Timaeus* (one of the two most important dialogues in the Neoplatonic canon) that all whole organisms of the sensible cosmos are in actuality parts of one universal organism.[16]

Although these definitions of the three kinds of wholes remain relatively vague in the systematic summary of Neoplatonic philosophy that is the *Elements of Theology* (to the confusion of some of its interpreters), in Proclus' other works the fuzziness of the definitions turns out to be their greatest strength from an exegetical perspective. Even in individual lemmata of his commentaries, Proclus attempts to bring together a variety of concepts and ideas from the Platonic canon. As we saw in the fourth book of the *Timaeus*-commentary, for example, such an approach requires that the theoretical framework employed by the exegete is slightly malleable. The *Timaeus* touches on the idea of the

---

16   Such an idea is not unique to Platonic thought. Compare, for example, Marcus Aurelius' statement in his *Meditations* VII, 13.1–5 (for which see the opening citation to this part of the study) that we are parts of the greater rational order of the world just as our arms and legs are parts of us.

cosmos as one entity before it is divided, on the cosmos as an everlasting whole encompassing everlasting parts, and as a space divided into four regions. If Proclus wants to bring these different concepts together into one mereological system, he needs a theoretical framework whose terms are defined just loosely enough that they can be applied to all of these notions at once. It is in this light that we must judge the merits of triads like the threefold wholeness. Proclus' primary goal in reading the writings of Plato is to 'see the wholes for the parts' (ἐκ τῶν μερῶν τὰ ὅλα γινώσκειν).[17] Regardless of one's opinion of the validity of this Neoplatonic approach to philosophy, the mereological framework Proclus draws up in the *Elements of Theology* and *Platonic Theology* serves the goal of distilling a Neoplatonic whole out of the Platonic dialogues rather well.

7.4   Is the Proclean Whole Fuzzy or Fantastical?

Despite the vagueness of which Proclus is sometimes accused, his mereology is in actuality not all that fuzzy. Leaving aside the question of exactly which kind of whole any given being is supposed to be, it is generally quite clear which things are whole and which are not. The Platonic framework of top-down mereology helps in this regard. As we already noted in the chapter 'Dividing the indivisible', Proclus does not need to define his whole in a manner akin to Koslicki, according to whom things are whole if they encompass the material and formal components associated with ontological kind K while K itself remains undefined. Proclus' mereology is much simpler: either something participates in the distinctive character of eternity (whether as a timeless principle or as an everlasting material compound) or it does not.

Proclus' mereology seems more of a kind with Van Inwagen's instead, given the fact that both philosophers designate life to be the ultimate criterium for wholeness (recall that Proclus' second intelligible triad instantiates not just eternity and wholeness, but also life). However, Proclus' Neoplatonic background safeguards him from the most prominent issues faced by Van Inwagen. The most obvious problem for Van Inwagen is the rejection of an unnecessarily large amount of wholes from our ontology. In Van Inwagen's metaphysics, all non-organic compounds are reduced to heaps of material simples. This is not the case in the Proclean universe, for two reasons. Firstly, Proclus' concept of life is far broader than Van Inwagen's modern version of the notion. It is applicable to all the Platonic Forms, for example, which ensures their claim

---

17   The phrase derives from a discussion of the true interpretation of the *Philebus* in the *Platonic Theology*, specifically Proclus, *TP* II.4, 35.10–18; cf. Oosthout and Van Riel (2023: 388).

THE BEST KIND OF WHOLE   225

to wholeness. Secondly, a number of ancient schools of thought, the Platonic one included, conceive of the universe itself as an organism with its own soul. As a result, inorganic things in the sensible realm need not possess their own individual life in order to possess some relation to wholeness. Any rock in the cosmos is a part of the universal living being and, as we noted in the chapter 'Quantity versus complexity', it is thus connected to the World Soul. Although a rock is not a unitary whole, it is clearly identifiable as a *part* of the cosmic living being. Whereas the rock is undefinable *qua* singular thing in Van Inwagen's ontology, being classifiable only as a heap, Proclus is perfectly capable of defining the rock as a singular part of the cosmos.

Another issue with Van Inwagen's mereology is the subsequent classification of non-organic things. Given that we cannot designate the heap of material simples at which the reader is currently looking as a book, we must instead describe it with the rather unwieldy definition 'material simples arranged bookwise', whereby the nature of this 'bookwise' arrangement remains unclear. This is not so for Proclus. Wholeness is only one of the distinctive characters Proclus introduces into his ontology, and it is not even the most universal one. Regardless of this book's status as a physical part of the cosmic living being, it is individually identifiable as one qualified thing (ἓν ὄν) by virtue of its participation in the distinctive characters of the One and Being, respectively. In this respect, the book's status as a singular existence does not even depend on the concept of being whole.

The most obvious difference between these two life-as-wholeness-theories is the fact that the Proclean notion of a whole life implies immortality, whereas Van Inwagen's concept of life does not. The fact that Proclus' wholeness principally requires immortality might appear strange to contemporary philosophers, but in antiquity it was an entirely logical position to take. The ancient philosophers in general distinguish themselves from their contemporary counterparts by their insistence on the logical priority of essence over its changeable substrate.[18] In the eyes of someone like Proclus, the cosmos had always been the cosmos and would always be the cosmos, and humans had always been humans and would always be humans regardless of the physical condition of any individual person.

---

18   This is not a universal truth, of course. There were philosophers who questioned either the existence of stable essences beyond the changeable substrates, such as Heraclitus, or the human capacity to divine such universal truths from our phenomenological experiences, such as the Pyrrhonists. Nevertheless, most ancient philosophers showcase at least some affinity for the idea of stable essences hidden behind our ever-changing experience of the world around us.

226   CHAPTER 7

Because of this, Proclus would reject not only Van Inwagen's thesis of inorganic things as heaps, but his approach to mereology in general. Van Inwagen discusses composition from a bottom-up perspective, and he thus starts with qualified material simples and then establishes which simples can be said to constitute an ontologically distinct whole. For Proclus, on the other hand, the whole must come first. Indeed, what Van Inwagen calls material simples would in Proclus' mereology be the qualityless body, which depends entirely on the intelligible principles for its subsequent qualification. It is thus not even possible to state that this book exists as one qualified thing despite being a heap of material simples, since for Proclus there are no determinate material simples. Its matter is simply the indistinguishable multitude into which the book can be divided if one subtracts all formal aspects from it. From a Neoplatonic perspective, Van Inwagen mistakenly fixates on the material forms, neglecting the intelligible principles which make these material compounds what they are.[19]

Proclus could similarly claim to be able to safeguard his concept of the whole from the difficult challenge imposed upon modern naturalistic philosophers by Lewis. The reason Van Inwagen presumes such a restrictive ontology is the fact that, as Lewis indicates, it takes quite a strong philosophical commitment to posit the whole as something which is ontologically distinct from its parts, and a criterion which universally and consistently separates wholes from heaps is not easy to find. Proclus, on the other hand, approaches parts and wholes from the same top-down perspective Harte distilled from Plato (to the surprise, I expect, of absolutely no one), and is thus faced with a different question entirely. If one presumes the existence of a stable whole encompassing all of its essential characteristics at once, how does one then explain the rise of ontologically distinct parts within it? Proclus' answer rests on the rise of new distinctive characters at every level of the causal procession, which conceptually divide the whole in order to create more and more specific instances of wholeness, from intelligible principles such as the Living Being itself and intellective Forms such as the Human Being all the way to the individual person.[20] One could even argue that Proclus would consider Lewis's challenge to naturalistic philosophers on the

---

19 Proclus would likely dismiss Koslicki's Neo-Aristotelian mereology as a theory which 'only has eyes for' material compounds as well; see Proclus, *IP* VI, 1123.13–14 (as cited in the footnotes to chapter 3, section 3).

20 Whether one accepts this explanation depends entirely on one's opinion of Proclus' self-constituted monads in general, for which see, e.g., Proclus, *ET* 9–10, 10.14–12.8 and 40–47, 42.8–48.4. The question of their existence is undoubtedly one of the more interesting ones in Neoplatonic metaphysics: if all of reality constitutes a continuous causal procession flowing forth from the One, which is nothing other than one and good, what explains the Intellect's sudden possession of a new distinctive character (i.e., being not just one good thing, but *intellect*)?

THE BEST KIND OF WHOLE   227

basis of a simple distinction between 'the thing exists' and 'the thing does not exist' to be somewhat irrelevant for his mereology, given the fact that his metaphysics revolves around an ontology surrounded by non-beings at both ends of the causal procession (the supra-essential One and the absolutely indeterminate material substrate, respectively).[21]

7.5   Are Proclean Compounds Whole in an Ethical Sense?

Yet Proclus' Neoplatonic mereology differs from its modern counterparts to an even greater extent. For most contemporary philosophers (and this includes the naturalistic philosophers), mereology revolves around a combination of ontology and logic. For Proclus, mereology revolves around a combination of metaphysics—in the sense that the Neoplatonic system exchanges being for unity as its central object of study—and *ethics*. Proclus does not equate wholeness with eternity just to emphasise the Platonic belief in the existence of transcendent and stable essences. He also develops the notion of being whole at once into a definition of perfection as a full sum of essential constituents. The Platonic intelligible principle encompasses not just the idea of a thing (e.g., the one Human Being itself), but also the *ideal* form of this thing (e.g., what the human being should strive to be).

Central to this equation of unity with goodness are Plato's speculations on the nature of the Form of the Good in the sixth book of the *Republic*. There Socrates suggests that all good things in our lives are derived from the Form of the Good, which itself derives from the true Good which transcends all of being. Although the postulation of the latter notion is humorously nuanced by Plato himself—an incredulous Glauco can only respond to Socrates' suggestion with: 'By Apollo, that is quite a superlative!'[22]—the Neoplatonic philosophers took it deadly seriously and did not hesitate to draw a connection between this ultimate Good and the supposed revelations about the divine One in Plato's *Parmenides*.[23] As a more specified form of unity, wholeness is similarly linked to the Platonic Good. The whole is reframed as a compound from which no

---

21   Of course, the whole is something which must really exist in Proclus' metaphysics as well—it is the first manifestation of participated being, after all—but it nevertheless seems logical that Proclus' would be somewhat unfazed by Lewis's insistence on existence versus non-existence, given that the whole is primarily a more determined form of unity, the ultimate principle of which transcends all of being.

22   Plato, *Resp.* VI, 509c1–2: Καὶ ὁ Γλαύκων μάλα γελοίως, Ἄπολλον, ἔφη, δαιμονίας ὑπερβολῆς.

23   Similarly, both Plotinus and Proclus read Plato's discussion of the balance between intellect and pleasure required to lead the good life in the *Philebus* in light of the Good from the *Republic*; see, Plotinus, *Enn.* VI.7 [38], 22 ff. and Proclus, *TP* I.22.

essential constituent is missing, and whose share in goodness is thus never compromised.[24] In other words, the intellective Form of the Human Being is whole in the Proclean sense precisely because it is the ideal human being, suffering from no diminution or corruption whatsoever. Our claim to wholeness as individual mortals similarly rests on our innate tendency to revert to this ideal. Our body parts come together to form a whole human being precisely because of their innate drive towards the ultimate Good. That our wholeness is inferior to the kind enjoyed by the intellective Form is entirely down to our vulnerability to corruptive influences, which can disrupt both our natural physiological state and the righteousness of our actions.

One could ask whether the designation of Proclean wholes as things which are ethical in nature is, as Glauco implies, a bridge too far, and not without reason. The ultimate Good from Plato's *Republic* retains little in the way of connections to any actual ethics. It is the first principle of all things, but it can also only be that. In a similar vein, the eternal wholes of the intelligible realm are not good in a truly ethical sense, only good in the metaphysical sense of being undamaged or undisturbed. The fact that they simply *cannot* be disturbed removes them yet further from the realm of ethics, since there is no evil to oppose their supposed goodness. As my father has elegantly summarised:

> Man broadens his view of the world through ever widening concentric circles: from myself to my fellow men, from the individual to state and society, from the human scale to the enormously large and the unimaginably small. With each widening circle, the meaning becomes blurred of notions that apply quite well to the smallest ones. 'Good' and 'evil' fit the human realm and every-day life. We do not, however, gain a deeper understanding of life and history, the earth and the cosmos, simply by calling them good or bad.[25]

It is more prudent, then, to claim that Proclus' mereology is greatly inspired by Plato's attempt to raise ethical concepts to the level of metaphysics, in the sense that Proclus' understanding of what the whole is rests not just on passages in which Plato focuses purely on (meta)physical issues, but also on the result of Plato's attempt to extrapolate a metaphysical Good from ethical concepts such as goodness and justice. It is in this light that we should understand

---

24 Harte (2002a: 270–272 and 274) similarly discerns in Plato a 'normative' conceptualisation of the whole that appears to have some ethical dimension, though the exact nature of this dimension falls outside the scope of her inquiry.

25 Oosthout, H. (2019c).

THE BEST KIND OF WHOLE   229

notions such as the divine Law of Cronus which regulates the division of intellective Forms, namely as a metaphysical abstraction of an ethical process in
human life which has been transplanted onto the ontological structure of the
natural world. Given the questionable ethical status of the ultimate Good and
the top-down perspective inherent in Proclean mereology, it makes little sense
to describe the specification of Wholeness itself into ontological kinds and
then into material individuals and their parts as an ethical process.

Proclus himself would likely oppose such a dismissive description, and not
entirely without cause. The Neoplatonic worldview revolves not just around the
division and specification of the metaphysical Good, but also around the mortal's quest to return to this metaphysical birthplace. One must strive to attain
and retain one's natural state as much as possible in order to succeed in this
quest, but for Neoplatonists the natural state of man involves not just physical
health, but also ethical conduct. Through our ethical choices, such as the choice
to live a pious life and act righteously, we bring ourselves closer to the ideal states
encompassed by the eternal wholes. In this specific way, the Proclean whole can
be described as an ethical concept. For the partial individual, the intelligible or
intellective whole constitutes a *telos* which spurs him or her to act in a manner
that is ethically sound. Proclus' definition of the whole might not offer the modern reader much in the way of usable life advice. For the Neoplatonic thinkers
themselves, however, its ethical value was quite obvious.

7.6   Is Proclus' Mereology Actually Any Good?

This is ultimately the most distinctive characteristic of Proclus' mereology:
its tenets will elicit awe from those who are fond of Neoplatonic thought but
entice few outside of the intended audience. That is not to say that Proclus'
mereology is badly constructed. On the contrary, theorems like the triad
of wholes showcase not only a remarkable awareness of the central points of
Neoplatonic thought on Proclus' part, but also provide a sophisticated analysis
of the complex relation between part and whole. Similarly, the equation of different degrees of wholeness with different degrees of eternity allow Proclus to
incorporate the entire intelligible realm into his mereology without having
to sacrifice obvious natural occurrences of wholeness from his ontology like
Van Inwagen is forced to do. In fact, Proclus' meticulous distinction between
various ontological kinds, reframed in his metaphysics as intelligible principles, and his emphasis on the transcendence of the whole over its parts allow
him not only to sidestep the challenge raised by Lewis but also avoid the problems Harte raised in her analysis of the top-down approach to mereology.

230   CHAPTER 7

At the same time, it is almost impossible to reconcile Proclus' mereology with the mereological systems established by modern scholars. In order to wield the full power of Proclus' mereology, a contemporary philosopher must not only convert to Neoplatonic notions such as the existence of psychic, intelligible, *and* supra-existential levels of reality above the realm of empirical science, but also to the ancient way of looking at the universe, which includes rejecting any form of modern chemistry and conceiving of the cosmos as a teleological and inherently rational construct without beginning or end, in which species such as the *homo sapiens* have always existed and will always exist. Proclean mereology is, in short, too far removed from our current understanding of the world to provide the solutions to mereology's current problems, despite the fact that it offers a number of interesting arguments for the naturalistic approach of restricted composition.

Given the Neoplatonists' insistence that all things are in all things, it is fitting that the merits of Proclus' mereology are a microcosm of those of Proclus' general approach to philosophy. By this I mean that its greatest strengths are also its most glaring weaknesses. Proclus' insatiable appetite for system-building and unrivalled attention to detail result in an oeuvre that contains one of the most well-constructed and thorough syntheses of the ancient pagan tradition to be found in antiquity. Yet it also contains treatises that are genuinely inaccessible to all but the most well-versed experts on Neoplatonic thought.[26] In a similar vein, the quirks of his mereology, owing to its status as a child of the late ancient pagan worldview, ensure that it offers solutions to or simply avoids many of the issues plaguing current mereology and yet remains entirely unmarketable to modern scholars. Were one to ask me whether Proclus' mereology is actually any good, I would most likely reply with the same words which describe my overall impression of the philosopher: his systematic philosophy is awe-inspiring in its meticulousness, but it will probably fail to enthuse people outside of the circle of Neoplatonism-scholars. It is ultimately a philosophy by Neoplatonists, for Neoplatonists. Yet within the Neoplatonic framework, Proclus has managed to establish a mereology that undoubtedly offers a complete package.

---

26   The *Elements of Theology* shines brightly within Proclus' oeuvre as a work which is genuinely interesting in its construction (the *Elements of Physics*, although much less well-known, follows the same method of argumentation). In contrast to the exhausting barrage of arguments and exegeses that is the *Platonic Theology* or the voluminous yet incomplete commentaries on the *Timaeus* and *Parmenides*, the *Elements* is a text I would recommend to the interested layman without hesitation.

Bibliography

Primary Sources: Critical Editions

Angelou, A.D. (1984), *Nicholas of Methone. Refutation of Proclus' Elements of Theology*, Athens: Academy of Athens.

Boese, H. (1960), *Procli Diadoci tria opuscula*, Berlin: De Gruyter.

Bruns, I. (1887–1892), *Alexandri Aphrodisiensis praeter commentaria scripta minora*, 2 vols, Berlin: Reimer.

Burnet, J. (1900–1907, repr. 1967–1968), *Platonis opera*, 7 vols, Oxford: Clarendon Press.

Busse, A. (1887), *Porphyrii isagoge et in Aristotelis categorias commentarium*, Berlin: Reimer.

Diehl, E. (1965), *Procli Diadochi In Platonis Timaeum commentaria*, 3 vols, Amsterdam: Hakkert.

Diels, H. (1882), *Simplicii in Aristotelis physicorum libros quattor priores commentaria*, Berlin: Reimer.

Diels, H. and W. Kranz. (1952), *Die Fragmente der Vorsokratiker*, 3 vols, Berlin: Weidmann.

Dillon, J.M. (1973), *Iamblichi Chlacidensis in Platonis dialogos commentariorum fragmenta*, Leiden: Brill.

Dodds, E.R. (1963, repr. 2004), *Proclus. The Elements of Theology*, New York: Oxford University Press.

Giardina, G. (1999), *Giovanni Filopono matematico tra neopitagorismo e neoplatonismo*, Catania: University of Catania.

Friedlein, G. (1873), *Procli Diadochi in primum Euclidis elementorum librum commentarii*, Leipzig: Teubner.

Henry, P. and H.R. Schwyzer (1951–1973), *Plotini opera*, 3 vols, Leiden: Brill.

Henry, P. and H.R. Schwyzer (1964–1982), *Plotini opera*, 3 vols, Oxford: Oxford University Press.

Hicks, R.D. (1965), *Aristotle, De Anima; with translation, introduction, and notes*, Amsterdam: Hakkert.

Hoche, R. (1866), *Nicomachi Geraseni Pythagorei introductionis arithmeticae libri ii*, Leipzig: Teubner.

Jaeger, W. (1957, repr. 1969), *Aristotelis Metaphysica*, Oxford: Oxford University Press.

Kroll, W. (1899–1901, repr. 1965), *Procli Diadochi in Platonis rem publicam commentarii*, 2 vols, Leipzig: Teubner.

Kroll, W. 1902, *Syriani in metaphysica commentaria*, Berlin: Reimer.

Lamberz, E. (1975), *Porphyrii sententiae ad intelligibilia ducentes*, Leipzig: Teubner.

Louis, P. (1956), *Aristote. Les parties des animaux*, Paris: Les Belles Lettres.

Luna, C. and A.P. Segonds (2007–2021), *Proclus. Commentaire sur le Parménide de Platon*, 7 vols, Paris: Les Belles Lettres.

232 BIBLIOGRAPHY

Molesworth, W. (1839), *Thomae Hobbes. Elementorum philosophiae sectio prima de corpore*, London: John Bohn.

Onnasch, E.O. and B. Schomakers (2015), *Proclus: Theologische Grundlegung*, Hamburg: Meiner.

Pasquali, G. (1994), *Procli Diadochi in Platonis Cratylum Commentaria*, Stuttgart and Leipzig: Teubner.

Pistelli, H. and U. Klein (1975), *Iamblichi in Nicomachi arithmeticam introductionem*, Stuttgart: Teubner.

Rabe, H. (1892), *Syriani in Hermogenem commentaria. Vol. 1: commentarium in libros περὶ ἰδεῶν*, Leipzig: Teubner.

Rabe, H. (1985), *Hermogenis opera*, Stuttgart: Teubner.

Ritzenfeld, A. (1912), *Procli Diadochi institutio physica*, Leipzig: Teubner.

Ross, W.D. (1953, repr. 1970), *Aristotle's Metaphysics*, Oxford: Clarendon Press.

Ross, W.D. (1958), *Aristotelis Topica et Sophisti Elenchi*, Oxford: Oxford University Press.

Saffrey, H.D. and L.G. Westerink (1968–1997), *Proclus. Théologie platonicienne*, 6 vols, Paris: Les Belles Lettres.

Sodano, A.R. (1964), *Porphyrii in Platonis Timaeum commentariorum fragmenta*, Milan: Instituto Editoriale Cisalpino.

Steel, C. (2007–2009), *Procli in Platonis Parmenidem Commentaria*, 3 vols, Oxford: Oxford University Press.

Tricot, J. (1957), *Aristote. Histoire des animaux, tome 1*, Paris: Les Belles Lettres.

Van Riel, G. (2022), *Procli Diadochi in Platonis Timaeum Commentaria*, 5 vols, Oxford: Oxford University Press.

Vanhaelen, M. (2012), *Marsilio Ficino. Commentaries on Plato. Volume 2: Parmenides, Part II*, Cambridge, MA and London: Harvard University Press.

Westerink, L.G. (1956), *Olympiodorus. Commentary on the first Alcibiades of Plato*, Amsterdam: North Holland Publishing Company.

Westerink, L.G. and J. Combès (1986–1989), *Damascius. Traité des premiers principes*, 2 vols, Paris: Les Belles Lettres.

Westerink, L.G., J. Combès, and A.P. Segonds (1997), *Damascius. Commentaire du Parménide de Platon. Tome I*, Paris: Les Belles Lettres.

Ziegler, K. and H. Gärtner (2000), *Plutarchi vitae parallelae. Vol. 1 Fasc. 1*, München and Leipzig: K.G. Saur Verlag.

Primary Sources: Translations

Armstrong, A.H. (1966–1988), *Plotinus*, 7 vols, Cambridge, MA: Harvard University Press.

Baltzly, D. (2007), *Proclus: Commentary on Plato's Timaeus. Volume 3. Book 3 Part 1: Proclus on the World's Body*, Cambridge: Cambridge University Press.

BIBLIOGRAPHY

Baltzly, D. (2009), *Proclus: Commentary on Plato's Timaeus. Volume 4. Book 3 Part 2: Proclus on the World Soul*, Cambridge: Cambridge University Press.

Baltzly, D. (2013), *Proclus: Commentary on Plato's Timaeus. Volume 5. Book 4: Proclus on Time and the Stars*, Cambridge: Cambridge University Press.

Baltzly, D., J.F. Finamore, and G. Miles (2018), *Proclus. Commentary on Plato's Republic. Volume 1. Essays 1–6*, Cambridge: Cambridge University Press.

Bostock, D. (1994), *Aristotle. Metaphysics Books Z and H*, Oxford: Clarendon Press.

Bury, R.G. (1929), *Plato: Timaeus. Critias. Cleitophon. Menexenus. Epistles*, Harvard: Harvard University Press.

Dodds, E.R. (1963), see *Critical editions* above.

Ferwerda, R. (1984), *Plotinus: Enneaden. Porphyrius: Over het leven van Plotinus en de indeling van zijn traktaten*, Baarn and Amsterdam: Uitgeverij Ambo and Athenaeum-Polak & Van Gennep.

Festugière, A.J. (1966–1968, repr. 2006), *Proclus. Commentaire sur le Timée*, Paris: Libraire Philosophique J. Vrin.

Forster, E.S. and D.J. Furley (1955), *Aristotle. On Sophistical Refutations. On Coming-to-be and Passing Away. On the Cosmos*, Cambridge, MA: Harvard University Press.

Fowler, H.N. (1921), *Plato: Theaetetus, Sophist*, Cambridge, MA: Harvard University Press.

Fowler, H.N. (1925), *Plato: Statesman, Philebus, Ion*, Cambridge, MA: Harvard University Press.

Fowler, H.N. (1926), *Plato: Cratylus, Parmenides, Greater Hippias, Lesser Hippias*, Cambridge, MA: Harvard University Press.

Hicks, R.D. (1965), see *Critical editions* above.

Laks, A. and G.W. Most (2016), *Early Greek Philosophy, Volume v: Western Greek Thinkers, Part 2*, Cambridge, MA: Harvard University Press.

Lamb, W.R.M. (1924), *Plato: Laches, Protagoras, Meno, Euthydemus*, Cambridge, MA: Harvard University Press.

Luna, C. and A.P. Segonds (2007–2021), see *Critical editions* above.

Morrow, G.R. and J.M. Dillon (1987), *Proclus' Commentary on Plato's Parmenides*, Princeton: Princeton University Press.

Ogle, W. (1882, repr. 1987), *Aristotle on the Parts of Animals*, New York and London: Garland.

Onnasch, E.O. and B. Schomakers (2015), see *Critical editions* above.

Opsomer, J. and C. Steel (2003), *Proclus: On the Existence of Evils*, London and Ithaca, NY: Duckworth and Cornell University Press.

Peck, A.L. (1942), *Aristotle. Generation of Animals*, Cambridge, MA: Harvard University Press.

Peck, A.L. and E.S. Forster (1937), *Aristotle. Parts of Animals. Movement of Animals. Progression of Animals*, Cambridge, MA: Harvard University Press.

Perrin, B. (1914), *Plutarch: Lives, Volume 1: Theseus and Romulus, Lycurgus and Numa, Solon and Publicola*, Cambridge, MA: Harvard University Press.

Reeve, C.D.C. (2016), *Aristotle. Metaphysics*, Indianapolis: Hackett.

Runia, D. and M. Share (2008), *Proclus: Commentary on Plato's Timaeus. Volume 2. Book 2: Proclus on the Causes of the Cosmos and its Creation*, Cambridge: University Press.

Saffrey, H.D. and L.G. Westerink (1968–1997), see *Critical editions* above.

Shields, C. (2016), *Aristotle. De Anima. Translated with an Introduction and Commentary*, Oxford: Clarendon Press.

Surma, S.J., J.T. Srzednicki, D.I. Barnett, and V.F. Rickey (1992), *Stanisław Leśniewski: Collected Works. Volume 1*, Dordrecht: Kluwer.

Tarrant, H. (2007), *Proclus: Commentary on Plato's Timaeus. Volume 1, Book 1: Proclus on the Socratic State and Atlantis*, Cambridge: Cambridge University Press.

Tarrant, H. (2017), *Proclus: Commentary on Plato's Timaeus. Volume 6, Book 5: Proclus on the Gods of Generation and the Creation of Humans*, Cambridge: Cambridge University Press.

Taylor, T. (1816), *Six Books of Proclus, the Platonic Successor, on the Theology of Plato*, London: A.J. Valpy, accessed through *Wikisource* at https://en.wikisource.org/wiki/The_Six_Books_of_Proclus,_the_Platonic_Successor,_on_the_Theology_of_Plato.

Taylor, T. (1820, repr. 1998), *Proclus' commentary on the Timaeus of Plato. Vol 1*, Wiltshire: Anthony Rowe.

Trouillard, J. (1965), *Proclos: Éléments de théologie*, Paris: Aubier Montaigne.

Vanhaelen, M. (2012), see *Critical editions* above.

Vansteenkiste, C. (1951–1952), 'Procli *Elementatio Theologica* translata a Guilelmo de Moerbeke', 3 vols, *Tijdschrift voor Filosofie*, 13/2, pp. 263–302, 13/3, pp. 491–531, and 14/3, pp. 503–546.

Westerink, L.G. and J. Combès (1986–1989), see *Critical editions* above.

Westerink, L.G., J. Combès, and A.P. Segonds (1997), see *Critical editions* above.

Wicksteed, P.H. and F.M. Cornford (1957), *Aristotle. Physics, Volume 1: Books 1–4*, Cambridge, MA: Harvard University.

Secondary Sources: Edited Volumes

For the individual book chapters, see the subsequent section.

D'Hoine, P. and M. Martijn (2016), *All from One. A guide to Proclus*, Oxford: Oxford University Press.

Layne, D.A. and D.D. Butorac (2017), *Proclus and his Legacy*, Berlin and Boston: De Gruyter.

Perkams, M. and R.M. Piccione (2006), *Proklos. Methode, Seelenlehre, Metaphysik. Akten der Konferenz in Jena am 18.–20. September 2003*, Leiden and Boston: Brill.

Romano, F. and D.P. Taormina (1994), *Hyparxis e Hypostasis nel Neoplatonismo*, Florence: Leo S. Olschki.

BIBLIOGRAPHY

Segonds, A.P. and C. Steel (2000), *Proclus et la Théologie Platonicienne. Actes du Colloque International de Louvain (13–16 mai 1998). En l'honneur de H.D. Saffrey et L.G. Westerink*, Leuven and Paris: Leuven University Press and Les Belles Lettres.

Secondary Sources: Individual Publications

For any book chapters taken from an edited volume referenced in the previous section, only the title of the volume and relevant page numbers are given in the references.

Ainsworth, T. (2020), 'Form vs. Matter', in *The Stanford Encyclopedia of Philosophy* (Summer 2020 Edition), edited by E.N. Zalta, https://plato.stanford.edu/archives /sum2020/entries/form-matter/ (accessed January 2022).

Baltzly, D. (2004), 'The Virtues and "Becoming Like God": Alcinous to Proclus', *Oxford Studies in Ancient Philosophy* 26, pp. 297–321.

Baltzly, D. (2008), 'Mereological Modes of Being in Proclus', *Ancient Philosophy* 28/2, pp. 395–411.

Baltzly, D. (2009), see *Translations* above.

Baltzly, D. (2011), 'Review: Emilie Kutash, Ten Gifts of the Demiurge: Proclus on Plato's *Timaeus*', *Bryn Mawr Classical Review*, http://bmcr.brynmawr.edu/2011/2011-08-16 .html (accessed October 2019).

Baltzly, D. (2013), see *Translations* above.

Baltzly, D. (2020), 'The World Soul in Proclus' *Timaeus Commentary*', in *World Soul— Anima Mundi. On the Origins and Fortunes of a Fundamental Idea*, edited by C. Helmig, Berlin: De Gruyter, pp. 289–308.

Baxter, D.L.M. (1988), 'Identity in the Loose and Popular Sense', *Mind* 97/388, pp. 575–582.

Beierwaltes, W. (1985), *Denken des Einen*, Frankfurt: Klostermann.

Brisson, L. (2000), 'La place des *Oracles Chaldaïques* dans la *Théologie Platonicienne*', in *Proclus et la Théologie Platonicienne* (see *Edited volumes* above), pp. 109–162.

Brumbaugh, R.S. (1982), 'Cantor's Sets and Proclus' Wholes', in *The Structure of Being: A Neoplatonic approach*, edited by R.B. Harris, Norfolk: International society for Neoplatonic studies, pp. 104–113.

Butler, E.P. (2008a), 'The Gods and Being in Proclus', *Dionysius* 26, pp. 93–114.

Butler, E.P. (2008b), 'The Intelligible Gods in the *Platonic Theology* of Proclus', *Méthexis* 21/1, pp. 131–143.

Butler, E.P. (2010), 'The Second Intelligible Triad and the Intelligible-Intellective Gods', *Méthexis* 23/1, pp. 137–155.

Butler, E.P. (2012), 'The Third Intelligible Triad and the Intellective Gods', *Méthexis* 25/1, pp. 131–150.

236   BIBLIOGRAPHY

Charles-Saget, A. (1982), *L'architecture du divin. Mathématique et philosophie chez Plotin et Proclus*, Paris: Les Belles Lettres.

Chiaradonna, R. and A. Lecerf (2019), 'Iamblichus', in *The Stanford Encyclopedia of Philosophy* (Fall 2019 edition), edited by E.N. Zalta, https://plato.stanford.edu/archives/fall2019/entries/iamblichus/ (accessed June 2020).

Chlup, R. (2009), 'Proclus' Theory of Evil: An Ethical Perspective', *The International Journal of the Platonic Tradition* 3/1, pp. 26–57.

Chlup, R. (2012), *Proclus: an introduction*, Cambridge: Cambridge University Press.

Corcilius, K. and P. Gregoric (2010), 'Separability vs. Difference: Parts and Capacities of the Soul in Aristotle', *Oxford Studies in Ancient Philosophy* 39, pp. 81–119.

Corrigan, K. and L.M. Harrington (2019), 'Pseudo-Dionysius the Areopagite', in *The Stanford Encyclopedia of Philosophy* (Winter 2019 Edition), edited by E.N. Zalta, https://plato.stanford.edu/-archives/win2019/entries/pseudo-dionysius-areopagite/ (accessed March 2021).

De Rijk, L.M. (1986), *Plato's Sophist: a Philosophical Commentary*, Amsterdam: North-Holland Publishing Company.

D'Hoine, P. (2006a), 'The Status of the Arts. Proclus' Theory of Artefacts', *Elenchos. Rivista di studi sul pensiero antico* 27/2, pp. 305–344.

D'Hoine, P. (2006b), 'Proclus and Syrianus on Ideas of Artefacts. A Test Case for Neoplatonic Hermeneutics', in *Proklos. Methode, Seelenlehre, Metaphysik* (see *Edited volumes* above), pp. 279–302.

D'Hoine, P. (2010), '« Ceux qui acceptent des Idées de toutes choses » : sur l'interprétation de *Parménide* 130b3–e4 dans l'Antiquité tardive', *Philosophie Antique* 10, pp. 227–254.

D'Hoine, P. (2011a), 'Forms of *sumbebèkota* in the Neoplatonic Commentaries on Plato and Aristotle', in *Plato, Aristotle, or both? Dialogues between Platonism and Aristotelianism in Antiquity*, edited by T. Bénatouïl, E. Maffi, and F. Trabattoni, Hildesheim: Georg Olms Verlag, pp. 161–187.

D'Hoine, P. (2011b), 'Les arguments de Proclus contre l'existence d'Idées des maux', *Études Platoniciennes* 8, pp. 75–103.

D'Hoine, P. (2016), 'Platonic Forms and the Triad of Being, Life, and Intellect', in *All from One. A guide to Proclus* (see *Edited volumes* above), pp. 98–121.

D'Hoine, P. (2021), 'Totalité et participation dans les *Éléments de Théologie*', in *Les Éléments de théologie de Proclus: Interprétations, réceptions antiques et modernes*, edited by G. Aubry, L. Brisson, P. Hoffman, and L. Lavaud, Paris: Hermann, pp. 177–219.

Dodds, E.R. (1928), 'The *Parmenides* of Plato and the Origin of the Neoplatonic "One"', *The Classical Quarterly* 22/3–4, pp. 129–142.

Dodds, E.R. (1963), see *Critical editions* above.

Donnelly, M. (2011), 'Using Mereological Principles to Support Metaphysics', *The Philosophical Quarterly* 61/243, pp. 223–246.

BIBLIOGRAPHY

Ferreirós, J. (2019), 'The Early Development of Set Theory', in *The Stanford Encyclopedia of Philosophy* (Summer 2019 Edition), edited by E.N. Zalta, https://plato.stanford.edu/archives/sum2019/entries/settheory-early/ (accessed September 2019).

Finamore, J.F. (1985), *Iamblichus and the Theory of the Vehicle of the Soul*, Chico, California: Scholars Press.

Finamore, J.F. and E. Kutash (2016), 'Proclus on the Psyche: World Soul and Individual Soul', in *All from One. A guide to Proclus* (see *Edited volumes* above), pp. 122–138.

Gersh, S. 'Universals, Wholes, *Logoi*: Eustratios of Nicaea's Response to Proclus' *Elements of Theology*', in *Reading Proclus and the Book of Causes, Volume 2: Translations and Accumulations*, edited by D. Calma, Leiden: Brill, pp. 32–55.

Gerson, L.P. (2011), 'Proclus and the Third Man', *Études Platoniciennes* 8, pp. 105–118.

Gerson, L.P. (2016), 'The "Neoplatonic" Interpretation of Plato's *Parmenides*', *The International Journal of the Platonic Tradition* 10/1, pp. 65–94.

Gerson, L.P. (2018), 'Plotinus', in *The Stanford Encyclopedia of Philosophy* (Fall 2018 Edition), edited by E.N. Zalta, https://plato.stanford.edu/-archives/fall2018/entries/plotinus/ (accessed December 2018).

Glasner, R. (1992), 'The Problem of Beginning, Middle and End in Proclus' Commentary on Plato's *Parmenides* 137d', *Hermes* 120/1, pp. 194–204.

Glucker, J. (1994), 'The origin of ὑπάρχω and ὕπαρξις as philosophical terms', in *Hyparxis e Hypostasis nel Neoplatonismo* (see *Edited volumes* above), pp. 1–23.

Granieri, R. (2022), 'Is Being a Genus? Syrianus' Criticism of Aristotle', *Phronesis* 67/2, pp. 216–251.

Gray, J. (2017), 'Epistemology of Geometry', in *The Stanford Encyclopedia of Philosophy* (Fall 2017 Edition), edited by E.N. Zalta, https://plato.stanford.edu/archives/fall2017/entries/epistemology-geometry/ (accessed January 2019).

Greig, J. (2020), 'Proclus on the Two Causal Models for the One's Production of Being: Reconciling the Relation of the Henads and the Limit/Unlimited', *The International Journal of the Platonic Tradition* 14/1, pp. 23–48.

Greig, J. (2021), *The First Principle in Late Neoplatonism. A Study of the One's Causality in Proclus and Damascius*, Leiden: Brill.

Harte, V. (2002a), *Plato on Parts and Wholes. The Metaphysics of Structure*, New York: Oxford University Press.

Harte, V. (2002b), 'Plato's Problem of Composition', in *Proceedings of the Boston Area Colloquium in Ancient Philosophy Volume XVII, 2001*, edited by J.J. Cleary and G.M. Gurtler, Leiden: Brill, pp. 1–17.

Helmig, C. (2006), 'Die Atmende Form in der Materie. Einige Überlegungen zum ἔνυλον εἶδος in der Philosophie des Proklos', in *Proklos. Methode, Seelenlehre, Metaphysik* (see *Edited volumes* above), pp. 259–278.

Helmig, C. (2014), 'Iamblichus, Proclus and Philoponus on Parts, Capacities and *ousiai* of the Soul and the Notion of Life', in *Partitioning the Soul. Debates from Plato to Leibniz*, edited by K. Corcilius and D. Perler, Berlin: De Gruyter, pp. 149–177.

Hovda, P. (2009a), 'What is Classical Mereology?', *Journal of Philosophical Logic* 38/1, pp. 55–92.

Hovda, P. (2009b), 'Review: Kathrin Koslicki, The Structure of Objects', *Notre Dame Philosophical Reviews*, 26-04-2009, https://ndpr.nd.edu/news/the-structure-of-objects/ (accessed January 2019).

Hovda, P. (2014), 'Natural Mereology and Classical Mereology', in *Mereology and the Sciences. Parts and Wholes in the Contemporary Scientific Context*, edited by C. Caliso and P. Graziani, Berlin: Springer, pp. 141–159.

Hugget, N. (2019), 'Zeno's Paradoxes', in *The Stanford Encyclopedia of Philosophy* (Spring 2019 Edition), edited by E.N. Zalta, https://plato.stanford.edu/archives/spr2019/entries/paradox-zeno/ (accessed March 2019).

Irwin, T.H. (1981), 'Homonymy in Aristotle', *The Review of Metaphysics* 34/3, pp. 523–544.

Jackson, B.J. (1967), 'Plotinus and the *Parmenides*', *Journal of the History of Philosophy* 5/4, pp. 315–327.

King, H.R. (1949), 'Aristotle and the Paradoxes of Zeno', *The Journal of Philosophy* 46/1, pp. 657–670.

Klitenic-Wear, S. (2017), 'Pseudo-Dionysius and Proclus on *Parmenides* 137d: On Parts and Wholes', in *Proclus and his Legacy* (see *Edited volumes* above), pp. 219–232.

Kobusch, Th. (2000), 'Das Eine ist nicht das Ganze. Die Idee der Totalität im Werk des Proklos, besonders in der *Platonischen Theologie*', in *Proclus et la Théologie Platonicienne* (see *Edited volumes* above), pp. 311–324.

Koslicki, K. (2004), 'Review: Verity Harte, Plato on Parts and Wholes. The Metaphysics of Structure', *The Journal of Philosophy* 101/9, pp. 492–496.

Koslicki, K. (2006), 'Aristotle's Mereology and the Status of Form', *The Journal of Philosophy* 103/12, pp. 715–736.

Koslicki, K. (2008), *The Structure of Objects*, Oxford: Oxford University Press.

Kristeller, P.O. (1987), 'Proclus as a Reader of Plato and Plotinus, and his Influence in the Middle Ages and the Renaissance', in *Proclus. Lecteur et interprète des Anciens. Actes du colloque international du CNRS, Paris (2–4 octobre 1985)*, edited by J. Pépin and H.D. Saffrey, Paris: Éditions du centre national de la recherche scientifique, pp. 191–211.

Kutash, E.F. (2009), 'Eternal Time and Temporal Expansion: Proclus' Golden Ratio', in *Late Antique Epistemology*, edited by P. Vassilopoulo and S.R.L. Clark, London: Palgrave Macmillan, pp. 44–66.

Kutash, E.F. (2011), *The Ten Gifts of the Demiurge: Proclus on Plato's Timaeus*, London: Bristol Classical Press.

Lang, H.S. (2017), 'The Status of Body in Proclus', in *Proclus and his Legacy* (see *Edited volumes* above), pp. 69–82.

Leonard, H.S. and N. Goodman (1940), 'The Calculus of Individuals and Its Uses', *The Journal of Symbolic Logic* 5/2, pp. 45–55.

BIBLIOGRAPHY

Lernould, A. (2000), 'Mathématiques et physique chez Proclus: L'interpretation proclienne de la notion de "lien" en *Timée* 31b–32c', in *La philosophie des mathématiques de l'Antiquité tardive*, edited by G. Bechtle and D.J. O'Meara, Fribourg: Imprimerie Saint-Paul, pp. 129–147.

Lernould, A. (2011), 'Le statut ontologique des objets géométriques dans l'*In Euclidem* de Proclus', *Études platoniciennes* 8, pp. 119–144.

Leśniewski, S. (1916), 'Podstawy ogólnej teorii mnogości I [Foundations of the General Theory of Sets I]', in Surma, Srzednicki, Barnett, and Rickey, *Collected Works* (see *Translations* above), vol. 1, pp. 129–173.

Leśniewski, S. (1927–1931), 'O podstawach matematyki [On the Foundations of Mathematics]', in Surma, Srzednicki, Barnett, and Rickey, *Collected Works* (see *Translations* above), vol. 1, pp. 174–382.

Lewis, D. (1986), *On the Plurality of Worlds*, Oxford: Blackwell.

Lewis, D. (1991), *Parts of Classes*, Oxford: Blackwell.

Liddell, H.G., R. Scott, and H.S. Jones (1940), *A Greek-English Lexicon*, Oxford: Clarendon Press, accessed through the *Perseus Digital Library* at https://www.perseus.tufts.edu/hopper/text?doc=Perseus%3atext%3a1999.04.0057.

Liddell, H.G. and R. Scott (2007), *Abridged Greek-English Lexicon*, London: Simon Wallenberg Press.

Lloyd, A.C. (1998), *The Anatomy of Neoplatonism*, Oxford: Clarendon Press.

Longo, A. (2005), *Siriano e I principi della scienza*, Napels: Bibliopolis.

Luna, C. and A.P. Segonds (2007), see *Critical editions* above.

Markosian, N. (2004), 'Two Arguments from Sider's *Four-Dimensionalism*', *Philosophy and Phenomenological Research* 68/3, pp. 665–673.

Marmodoro, A. (2013), 'Aristotle's hylomorphism without reconditioning', *Philosophical Inquiry* 36/1–2, pp. 5–22.

Marmodoro, A. (2021), *Forms and Structure in Plato's Metaphysics*, New York: Oxford University Press.

Martijn, M. (2010), *Proclus on Nature: Philosophy of Nature and its Methods in Proclus' Commentary on Plato's Timaeus*, Leiden: Brill.

Martijn, M. and L.P. Gerson (2016), 'Proclus' System', in *All from One. A guide to Proclus* (see *Edited volumes* above), pp. 45–72.

Martini, C. (2024), 'A Functionalist Account of Epicurus' *Minima*', *Méthexis* 36/1, pp. 73–94.

Matula, J. (2020), 'Nicholas of Methone', in *Encyclopedia of Medieval Philosophy*, edited by H. Lagerlund, Dordrecht: Springer, pp. 1331–1334.

Mignucci, M. (1993), 'The Stoic Analysis of the Sorites', *Proceedings of the Aristotelian Society* 93, pp. 231–245.

Monaghan, P. (2016), 'The Largest Proper Parts of a Mereological Whole: A Refutation of Classical Extensional Mereology', *Metaphysica: International Journal for Ontology and Metaphysics* 17/1, pp. 19–26.

Moravcsik, J.M. (1979), 'Forms, Nature, and the Good in the *Philebus*', *Phronesis* 24/1, pp. 81–104.

Motta, A. (2018), 'Demiurgy in Heavens. An Ancient Account in Plato's *Statesman*', in *Plato's Statesman Revisited*, edited by B. Bossi and T.M. Robinson, Berlin: De Gruyter, pp. 141–156.

Moutsopoulos, E. (1997), 'L'idée de multiplicité croissante dans la *Théologie Platonicienne de Proclus*', in *Néoplatonisme et philosophie médiévale: Actes du Colloque international de Corfou, 6–8 octobre 1995*, edited by L.G. Benakis, Turnhout: Brepols, pp. 59–65.

Muniz, F. and G. Rudebusch (2018), 'Dividing Plato's Kinds', *Phronesis* 63/4, pp. 392–407.

Nikulin, D. (1998), 'The One and the Many in Plotinus', *Hermes* 126, pp. 326–340.

O'Meara, D.J. (1989), *Pythagoras revived*, Oxford: Clarendon Press.

O'Meara, D.J. and J. Dillon (2008), *Syrianus on Aristotle Metaphysics 3–4*, London: Duckworth.

Onnasch, E.O. and B. Schomakers (2015), see *Critical editions* above.

O'Neill, W. (1962), 'Time and Eternity in Proclus', *Phronesis* 7/2, pp. 161–165.

Oosthout, A. (2022a), 'A Wholesome Trinity. Proclus on the transcendence of whole over part', *Ancient Philosophy* 42/2, pp. 515–536.

Oosthout, A. (2022b), 'The problem of (in)divisible intellect in Proclus' *El. Theol.* 180. Proclus and Porphyry on the relativity of the incorporeal whole', *Études platoniciennes* 17, https://doi.org/10.4000/etudesplatoniciennes.2653 (accessed June 2022).

Oosthout, A. (2023a), 'More than perfect? The distinction between "completely perfect" (παντελής) and "more than perfect" (ὑπερτέλειος) in Proclus' description of the intelligible gods', in *Longing for Perfection in Late Antiquity. Studies on Journeys between Ideal and Reality in Pagan and Christian Literature*, edited by J. Leemans, G. Roskam, and P. Van Deun, Leiden: Brill, pp. 115–139.

Oosthout, A. (2023b), *De anatomie van de filosofische mythe*, https://anhypotheton.eu/txt/aho/anatomie.php (accessed April 2023).

Oosthout, A. (forthcoming), 'A Relativistic Approach to Proclus. Nicholas of Methone's Critique of *Elements of Theology* §67–74 (on Parts and Wholes)', in *Nicholas of Methone, Reader of Proclus in Byzantium: Context and Legacy*, edited by D. Calma, J. Greig, and J. Robinson, Leiden: Brill.

Oosthout, A. and G. Van Riel (2023), 'Three Instances of the Good in Proclus', *Apeiron* 56/2, pp. 371–393.

Oosthout, A., S.A. Kiosoglou, and T. Lejeune (2024), 'Introduction: Part and Whole in Antiquity', *Méthexis* 36/1, pp. 3–6.

Oosthout, H. (2015), *Kritische geschiedenis van de westerse wijsbegeerte. Deel 1: Oudheid, patristiek, vroege Middeleeuwen*, Utrecht: Uitgeverij Klement.

Oosthout, H. (2019a), *Paradoxen van het wijsgerig denken: de som meer dan de delen*, https://anhypotheton.eu/txt/par/56.php (accessed December 2021).

BIBLIOGRAPHY

Oosthout, H. (2019b), *Aphorisms: The metaphysical circle*, https://anhypotheton.eu/aforismen.php?lang=en (accessed December 2021).

Oosthout, H. (2019c), *Aphorisms: Circles*, https://anhypotheton.eu/en/02c1 (accessed January 2022).

Oosthout, H. (2021), *The passage of time and the mathematical universe*, Lecture for the Studentenvereniging voor internationale betrekkingen (SIB), Utrecht, Dec. 7, 2021, transcript retrieved from https://anhypotheton.eu/passtimemathuniv.php (accessed January 2022).

Opsomer, J. (2000a), 'Proclus on Demiurgy and Procession: a Neoplatonic Reading of the *Timaeus*,' in *Reason and Necessity. Essays on Plato's Timaeus*, edited by M.R. Wright, London: Duckworth, pp. 113–43.

Opsomer, J. (2000b), 'Deriving the three intelligible triads from the *Timaeus*', in *Proclus et la Théologie Platonicienne* (see *Edited volumes* above), pp. 351–72.

Opsomer, J. (2001), 'Proclus vs. Plotinus on Matter (*De mal. subs.* 30–7)', *Phronesis* 26/2, pp. 154–188.

Opsomer, J. (2003), 'La Démiurgie des Jeunes Dieux Selon Proclus.' *Études Classiques* 71/1, pp. 5–49.

Opsomer, J. (2004), 'Plutarch's *De animae procreatione in Timaeo*: Manipulation or Search for Consistency?', in *Philosophy, science, and exegesis in Greek, Arabic, and Latin commentaries 1*, edited by P. Adamson, J.N.M. Baltussen, and M.W.F. Stone, London: Institute of Classical Studies, pp. 137–162.

Opsomer, J. (2006a), 'To find the maker and the father: Proclus' Exegesis of Plato, *Tim.* 28c3–5', *Études Platoniciennes* 2, pp. 121–137.

Opsomer, J. (2006b), 'Was sind irrationale Seelen?', in *Proklos. Methode, Seelenlehre, Metaphysik* (see *Edited volumes* above), pp. 136–166.

Opsomer, J. (2014), 'Syrianus, Proclus, and Damascius', in *The Routlegde Companion to Ancient Philosophy*, edited by J. Warren and F. Sheffield, New York: Routledge, pp. 626–642.

Opsomer, J. (2015), 'A much misread Proposition from Proclus' *Elements of Theology* (prop. 28)', *The Classical Quarterly* 65/1, pp. 433–438.

Opsomer, J. (2016), 'The Natural World', in *All from One. A guide to Proclus* (see *Edited volumes* above), pp. 139–166.

Opsomer, J. (2021), 'Productive Knowledge in Proclus', in *Productive Knowledge in Ancient Philosophy: The Concept of Technê*, edited by T.K. Johansen, Cambridge: Cambridge University Press, pp. 263–282.

Opsomer, J. and C. Steel (2003), see *Translations* above.

Panayides, C. (2023), 'The Dispute Over the Part-Whole Puzzle in Aristotelian Hylomorphism and Ackrill's Problem: The Argument in *Metaphysics* Z 17, 1041b11–33', *Apeiron* 56/2, pp. 235–260.

Pantelia, M.C. (1972–2024), *Thesaurus Linguae Graecae Digital Library*, Irvine: University of California, http://www.tlg.uci.edu.

Perkams, M. (2006), 'An Innovation by Proclus. The Theory of the Substantial Diversity of the Human Soul', in *Proklos. Methode, Seelenlehre, Metaphysik* (see *Edited volumes* above), pp. 167–185.

Pritchard, P.W. (1990), 'The Meaning of δύναμις at *Timaeus* 31c', *Phronesis* 35/2, pp. 182–193.

Robinson, H.M. (1974), 'Prime Matter in Aristotle', *Phronesis* 19/2, pp. 168–188.

Rotkale, L. (2018), 'The Form is Not a Proper Part in Aristotle's *Metaphysics* Z.17, 1041b11–33', *Metaphysics* 1, pp. 75–87.

Saffrey, H.D. (1976), 'Théologie et anthropologie d'après quelques préfaces de Proclus', in *Images of Man in Ancient and Medieval Thought. Studia Gerardo Verbeke ab amicis et collegis dictata*, edited by F. Bossier, F. De Wachter, J. IJsewijn, C. Laga, G. Maertens, W. Vanhamel, D. Verhelst, and A. Welkenhuysen, Leuven: Leuven University Press, pp. 199–212.

Saffrey, H.D. and L.G. Westerink (1978), see *Critical editions* above.

Saffrey, H.D. and L.G. Westerink (1981), see *Critical editions* above.

Saffrey, H.D. and L.G. Westerink (1987), see *Critical editions* above.

Sambursky, S. (1968), 'The Theory of Forms: A Problem and Four Neoplatonic Solutions', *Journal of the History of Philosophy* 6/4, pp. 327–339.

Sheppard, A. (2000), 'Plato's *Phaedrus* in the *Theologica Platonica*', in *Proclus et la Théologie Platonicienne* (see *Edited volumes* above), pp. 415–424.

Sider, T. (1997), 'Four-Dimensionalism', *Philosophical Review* 106/2, pp. 197–231.

Sider, T. (2013), 'Against Parthood', in *Oxford Studies in Metaphysics* 8, edited by K. Bennett and D.W. Zimmerman, Oxford: Oxford University Press, pp. 237–93.

Simons, P. (1987), *Parts: a Study in Ontology*, Oxford: Clarendon Press.

Simons, P. (2003), 'The Universe', *Ratio* 16/3, pp. 236–250.

Simons, P. (2015), 'Stanisław Leśniewski', in *The Stanford Encyclopedia of Philosophy* (Winter 2015 Edition), edited by E.N. Zalta, https://plato.stanford.edu/archives/win2015/entries/lesniewski/ (accessed April 2019).

Silverman, A. (2005), 'Rezensionen. Harte, Verity: Plato on Parts and Wholes', *Archiv für Geschichte der Philosophie* 87/2, pp. 211–225, https://doi.org/10.1515/agph.2005.87.2.211 (accessed March 2019).

Siorvanes, L. (1996), *Proclus. Neo-Platonic Philosophy and Science*, Edinburgh: Edinburgh University Press.

Siorvanes, L. (1998a), 'Proclus', in *The Routledge Encyclopedia of Philosophy*, edited by E. Craig, London and New York: Routledge, https://www.rep.routledge.com/articles/biographical/proclus-c-ad-411-85/v-1 (accessed May 2020).

Siorvanes, L. (1998b), 'Proclus on Transcendence', *Documenti e studi sulla tradizione filosofica Medievale* 9, pp. 1–19.

Spade, P.V. (2018), 'Medieval Philosophy', in *The Stanford Encyclopedia of Philosophy* (Summer 2018 Edition), edited by E.N. Zalta, https://plato.stanford.edu/archives/sum2018/entries/medieval-philosophy/ (accessed March 2021).

BIBLIOGRAPHY

Steel, C. (1978), *The Changing Self. A study on the soul in later Neoplatonism: Iamblichus, Damascius, and Priscianus*, Brussels: Koninklijke academie voor wetenschappen, letteren en schone kunsten van België.

Steel, C. (1987), 'L'analogie par les apories', in *Proclus et son influence*, edited by G. Boss and G. Seel, Zürich: Éditions du Grand Midi, pp. 101–128.

Steel, C. (1994), "Ὕπαρξις chez Proclus', in *Hyparxis e Hypostasis nel Neoplatonismo* (see *Edited volumes* above), pp. 79–100.

Steel, C. (1996), 'Puissance active et receptive chez Proclus', in *Dunamis nel Neoplatonismo*, edited by F. Romano and R.L. Cardullo, Florence: La Nuova Italia, pp. 121–157.

Steel, C. (1997), 'Breathing Thought: Proclus on the Innate Knowledge of the Soul', in *The Perennial Tradition of Neoplatonism*, edited by J.J. Cleary, Leuven: Leuven University Press, pp. 293–309.

Steel, C. (2000), 'Le *Parménide* est-il le fondement de la *Théologie Platonicienne?*', in *Proclus et la Théologie Platonicienne* (see *Edited volumes* above), pp. 373–398.

Steel, C. (2001), 'The Moral Purpose of the Human Body: a reading of *Timaeus* 69–72', *Phronesis* 46/2, pp. 105–128.

Steel, C. (2016), 'Providence and Evil', in *All From One. A guide to Proclus* (see *Edited volumes* above), pp. 240–257.

Tarrant, H. (2017), see *Translations* above.

Taylor, A.E. (1926, repr. 1960), *Plato. The man and his work*, London: Methuen.

Taylor, A.E. (1928), *A commentary on Plato's Timaeus*, Oxford: Clarendon Press.

Thomson, J.J. (1983), 'Parthood and Identity Across Time', *Journal of Philosophy* 80/4, pp. 201–220.

Trouillard, J. (1959), 'La Monadologie de Proclus', *Revue Philosophique de Louvain* 57/55, pp. 309–320.

Trouillard, J. (1965), see *Translations* above.

Van den Berg, R.M. (2000), 'Towards the Paternal Harbour. Proclean theurgy and the contemplation of the Forms', in *Proclus et la Théologie Platonicienne* (see *Edited volumes* above), pp. 425–438.

Van den Berg, R.M. (2003), '"Becoming Like God" according to Proclus' Interpretations of the *Timaeus*, the Eleusinian Mysteries, and the *Chaldaean Oracles*', in *Ancient Approaches to Plato's Timaeus*, edited by R.W. Sharples and A. Sheppard, London: Institute of Classical Studies, pp. 189–202.

Van den Berg, R.M. (2008), *Proclus' Commentary on the Cratylus in Context. Ancient Theories of Language and Naming*, Leiden: Brill.

Van Inwagen, P. (1990), *Material Beings*, Ithaca, New York: Cornell University Press.

Van Inwagen, P. (1994), 'Composition as Identity', *Philosophical Perspectives* 8, pp. 207–220.

Van Riel, G. (2000), 'Ontologie et théologie. Le *Philèbe* dans le troisième livre de la *Théologie Platonicienne* de Proclus', in *Proclus et la Théologie Platonicienne* (see *Edited volumes* above), pp. 399–414.

Van Riel, G. (2001), 'Les hénades de Proclus sont-elles composées de limite et d'illimité?', *Revue de sciences philosophiques et théologiques* 85/3, pp. 417–432.

Van Riel, G. (2009), 'Proclus on Matter and Physical Necessity', in *Physics and Philosophy of Nature in Greek Neoplatonism*, edited by R. Chiaradonna and F. Trabattoni, Leiden: Brill, pp. 231–257.

Van Riel, G. (2010), 'Damascius', in *The Cambridge History of Philosophy in Late Antiquity. Volume II*, edited by L.P. Gerson, Cambridge: Cambridge University Press, pp. 667–696.

Van Riel, G. (2016), 'The One, the Henads, and the Principles', in *All from One. A guide to Proclus* (see *Edited volumes* above), pp. 73–97.

Van Riel, G. (2019), 'Proclus, Porphyrius, Atticus, and the Maker? Remarks on Proclus, *In Ti.* II, 1.393.31–394.5 Diehl (Atticus fr. 28)', *The Classical Quarterly* 68/2, pp. 681–688.

Van Riel, G. (2021), 'Matter Doesn't Matter: On the Status of Bodies in the *Timaeus* (30a–32b and 53c–61c)', in *Plato's Timaeus. Proceedings of the Tenth Symposium Platonicum Pragense*, edited by C. Jorgenson, F. Karfík, and Š. Špinka, Leiden: Brill, pp. 169–186.

Vargas, A. (2021), *Time's Causal Power. Proclus on the Natural Theology of Time*, Leiden: Brill.

Varzi, A. (2000), 'Mereological Commitments', *Dialectica* 54/4, pp. 283–305.

Varzi, A. (2006), 'The Universe Among Other Things', *Ratio* 19/1, pp. 107–120.

Varzi, A. (2008), 'The Extensionality of Parthood and Composition', *The Philosophical Quarterly* 58/230, pp. 108–133.

Varzi, A. (2009), 'Universalism entails Extensionalism', *Analysis* 69/4, pp. 599–604.

Varzi, A. (2010), 'On the Boundary Between Material and Formal Ontology', in *Interdisciplinary Ontology, Vol. 3: Proceedings of the Third Interdisciplinary Ontology Meeting*, edited by B. Smith, R. Mizoguchi, and S. Nakagawa, Tokyo: Keio University, pp. 3–8.

Varzi, A. (2016), 'Mereology', in *The Stanford Encyclopedia of Philosophy* (Winter 2016 Edition), edited by E.N. Zalta, https://plato.stanford.edu/archives/win2016/entries/mereology/ (accessed November 2018).

Verde, F. (2021), 'Atoms and minimal "Parts". The originality of Epicurean atomism,' in *Atomism in Philosophy. A History from Antiquity to the Present*, edited by U. Zilioli, London: Bloomsbury Academic, pp. 76–92.

Vlastos, G. (1965), 'Minimal Parts in Epicurean Atomism', *Isis* 56/2, pp. 121–147.

Wallis, R.T. (1972), *Neoplatonism*, London: Duckworth.

Wildberg, C. (2016), 'Neoplatonism,' in *The Stanford Encyclopedia of Philosophy* (Spring 2016 Edition), edited by E.N. Zalta, https://plato.stanford.edu/archives/spr2016/entries/neoplatonism/ (accessed January 2019).

Index locorum

The works of Plato and Aristotle are indexed by Stephanus- and Bekker-page, respectively. Marcus Aurelius, Plotinus and Thomas Hobbes are indexed by caput, Proclus' Elements of Theology and Nicholas of Methone's refutation of that same work by proposition, and fragmentary works by fragment number. All other sources are indexed by the page numbers of the critical edition used in the monograph (for an overview of which see chapter 1, section 5).

Anaxagoras
Fr. B6 DK   89n39

Aristotle
History of Animals
  1.486a   76n90, 120n19
Metaphysics
  Δ.18, 1022a   44n115
  Δ.25, 1023b   44–46
  Δ.26.1023b   61
  Z.7, 1032b   44n115
  Z.8, 1033b   44n115
  Z.10, 1035b   109
  Z.16, 1040b   183
  Z.17, 1041b   9, 42–46, 68, 109
  H.6, 1045a   41n100
On the Heavens
  279a   126–127
Parts of Animals
  II, 646a–647b   76n90, 120n19
Topics
  V.5, 135a–b   120n20

Damascius
Commentary on Plato's Parmenides
  I, pp. 23–25   127, 127n49, 215
  I, pp. 34–37   127n48
  I, p. 60   220n11
  I, p. 62   219
On First Principles
  II, pp. 175–176   105n86

Ficino, Marsilio
Commentary on Plato's Parmenides
  XCV.2, p. 244   136n89

Hobbes, Thomas
De Corpore
  II cap. 11   21n1

Iamblichus
Fragments of the Platonic Commentaries
  Fr. 84 Dillon   166n15

Marcus Aurelius
Meditations
  VII, cap. 13   223n6

Nicholas Of Methone
Refutation of Proclus' Elements of Theology
  Prop. 73   122
  Prop. 180   118n11

Olympiodorus
Commentary on Plato's Alcibiades
  pp. 109–111   55–56

Plato
Cratylus
  396a–b   143, 150n131
  402b–d   143
Critias
  121b–c   143
Gorgias
  525a   196
Laws
  VII, 796b–c   153
Parmenides
  131a–c   32
  132a–b   84n6
  132d–e   146

137c–142a	93
142b–155e	93, 133
142c–143a	94–95, 136
143d	133
144b–e	133, 136
144d–145b	133
145b–147b	143

Phaedo

106d	126–127

Phaedrus

246a–b	196, 197n89
247a–d	132–133

Philebus

16c	75
23c–26d	38–40, 39n88
23c–27c	94n54
30d	143

Protagoras

320c–322d	143

Republic

VI, 509c	227

Sophist

244b–245e	32
251d–e	32–33
252e–253a	32–33
261d–262e	37

Statesman

145e–146a	143
262a8–263b10	62n37, 93
268d–274e	143

Symposium

207c–208a	166n15

Theaetetus

176b	202
201d–205e	33–35

Timaeus

27d5–29d3	123
28a–c	70, 130n61
30a	72
30b	169, 172
30c–d	70, 102
31a–b	72, 130
31b–32c	40–42, 169
32c–33b	2, 171
32d	139
33a	41n97, 93, 101n73, 139
34b–c	99, 101n73

36d	143n113
36e	81
37d	123
37e	163n2
39d	164n8
39e	172
39e–40a	128
40a	182n54
40e–41d	169n24, 175
41a	185
41a–c	8, 187, 188n68, 190
41c	70, 188–189, 191n76
41d	166
51a	72
52d	41n98
53b	72
53c–61c	41

Plotinus

V.1 [10], cap. 7	55
V.8 [31], cap. 4	89n39
VI.2 [43], cap. 2	61
VI.2 [43], cap. 3	61, 118
VI.7 [38], cap. 22 ff.	227n23
VI.9 [9], cap. 5	118

Plutarch

Parallel Lives

23.1 (*Theseus*), p. 20	21

Porphyry

Isagoge

p. 7	106
p. 8	61

Sentences

10, p. 4	89
22, p. 13	119, 129n57

Proclus

Commentary on Euclid's Elements

pp. 50–51	111

Commentary on Plato's Cratylus

107, p. 56	150n131

Commentary on Plato's Parmenides

I, p. 628	146n121
II, pp. 734–735 and III, pp. 823–824	147n125

INDEX LOCORUM   247

II, p. 735	193
III, pp. 823–825	106, 165*n*12, 193*n*81
III, p. 827	192*n*79
III, pp. 833–834	111*n*105
IV, pp. 844–845	71–73
IV, p. 890	84*n*6
IV, pp. 912–914	146, 70*n*69
IV, p. 970	106
V, p. 981	106
VI, pp. 1112–1113	74*n*82, 104, 130, 174
VI, pp. 1119–1123	63*n*43, 75–76
VI, p. 1123	76, 226*n*19

Commentary on Plato's Republic

I, p. 34	202
I, p. 260	111*n*105
I, pp. 269–270	125*n*39
II, p. 307	150*n*133

Commentary on Plato's Timaeus

II, pp. 49–50 and 235 (1.239 and 1.366 Diehl)	126*n*42
II, p. 107 (1.227 Diehl)	165
II, p. 153 (1.310 Diehl)	71*n*73
II, pp. 310–313 (1.418–420 Diehl)	71, 78
II, pp. 321–322 (1.426 Diehl)	102
II, p. 326 (1.429 Diehl)	103, 129*n*56, 178
II, pp. 348–349 (1.445–446 Diehl)	74*n*81, 189*n*71
III, pp. 2–3 (2.2–3 Diehl)	101*n*76, 169–170, 177*n*48, 179
III, pp. 85–86 (2.61–62 Diehl)	71*n*73, 101*n*76, 138, 151, 171, 179
III, p. 142 (2.102 Diehl)	169
III, pp. 206–207 and 222–223 (2.151–152 and 163–164 Diehl)	64*n*46
III, pp. 264–265 (2.195–196 Diehl)	99–101
III, p. 344–345 (2.253–254 Diehl)	120
III, p. 389 (2.287 Diehl)	81, 202
III, p. 392 (2.290 Diehl)	67
III, p. 394 (2.291 Diehl)	67

IV, pp. 10–44 (3.8–34 Diehl)	126
IV, pp. 13–14 (3.10–11 Diehl)	154–155
IV, p. 39 (3.30 Diehl)	163
IV, pp. 44–47 (3.34–36 Diehl)	163*n*2
IV, p. 51 (3.40 Diehl)	163
IV, pp. 64–67 (3.50–52 Diehl)	164, 164*n*7, 176–177
IV, pp. 118–119 (3.92 Diehl)	164, 165*n*12
IV, pp. 125–127 (3.97–98 Diehl)	101*n*76, 102*n*78, 172–173, 179
IV, pp. 136–138 (3.105–106 Diehl)	128–129
IV, p. 143 (3.111 Diehl)	171*n*29
IV, pp. 149–150 (3.115–116 Diehl)	61, 106*n*88, 182*n*54, 183
V, p. 63 (3.210 Diehl)	8–9
V, pp. 64–68 (3.210–214 Diehl)	117, 184–187
V, pp. 73–74 (3.217–218 Diehl)	188–189
V, pp. 80–81 (3.223–224 Diehl)	190–191
V, pp. 86–87 (3.228–229 Diehl)	191–192
V, pp. 97–98 (3.236–237 Diehl)	165*n*12, 166–167
V, p. 105 (3.242 Diehl)	71*n*73, 74*n*81, 101*n*76, 165*n*13, 175–177, 179
V, p. 195 (3.311 Diehl)	71*n*73
V, p. 211 (3.322 Diehl)	213–214

Elements of Theology

Prop. 1	109*n*101
Prop. 7, 18, 26, and 31	88*n*31
Prop. 7	57*n*12, 88, 149*n*130
Prop. 9–10 and 40–47	226*n*20
Prop. 15	117–118
Prop. 23	84*n*90
Prop. 25–39	117

Prop. 25	65n55	II.3, p. 25	94n53
Prop. 28	88	II.4, p. 35	224
Prop. 45	81n103	III.6, p. 21	66n56
Prop. 52	68n63, 124	III.6, pp. 23–26	64–68, 67n60, 177–178
Prop. 57	57–58	III.14 and III.18	71
Prop. 58	58	III.15, pp. 53–54	130
Prop. 59	62–63, 65n55	III.16, pp. 55–56	125n40, 126–127,
Prop. 60	59, 79		127n45
Prop. 62	55, 79–80	III.24, p. 84	94n54
Prop. 65	88–89	III.25, pp. 86–89	93, 94n54, 95–98,
Prop. 67	83, 87–90, 97n63,		130n63, 140n103, 141,
	130n59		155
Prop. 68	68n63, 90, 183	III.26, p. 92	128n50
Prop. 69	90–91	III.27	95
Prop. 70	68–69, 122n25	III. 27, pp. 94–95	85, 107–108, 125
Prop. 71	59–60	IV.1, pp. 8–9	132, 135n86
Prop. 72	60, 60n26	IV.5, p. 20	133
Prop. 73	62, 122n25, 138	IV.19, p. 56	91n45
Prop. 74	62, 86n21	IV.23, pp. 68–69	134n82
Prop. 78	55n4	IV.25, pp. 74–76	3n4, 135, 139–141,
Prop. 80	63		139n102
Prop. 82–83	117	IV.27, pp. 78–79	135–136
Prop. 86	63	IV.35, p. 104	137
Prop. 89	75	V.1 and V.12	71n72
Prop. 97 and 99	66–67	V.1, p. 8	142
Prop. 100	158–159	V.1, p. 10	142
Prop. 103	64n46, 68n63, 77,	V.2, pp. 10–12	142–143
	89n39, 108n99, 127n46	V.3, p. 16	71
Prop. 105	127n48	V.4, p. 19	143n113
Prop. 108	85	V.9, p. 31–33	150, 152, 201
Prop. 135		V.11, p. 38	145
and 162–165	86	V.12 and VI.9	71n73
Prop. 167	117	V.12, pp. 40–41	142, 144–146
Prop. 168	132	V.13, p. 42	151–152
Prop. 171	118	V.16, p. 53	72
Prop. 180	119	V.16, p. 55	72
On the Existence of Evils		V.16, p. 57	72
cap. 20–26	197n91	V.30	149, 194
26, p. 76	202	V.30, p. 111	147–148, 148n126
cap. 27–29	198n92	V.35, pp. 128–130	153, 153n142
cap. 30–37	198n93	V.37–39	143–144
50, p. 95	200		
51, p. 96	201	**Simplicius**	
Platonic Theology		*Commentary on Aristotle's Physics*	
I.5, p. 25	93n49	I.3, p. 140	21n2
I.18, pp. 83–86	125, 195–196, 199, 201		
I.22	227n23		

Index rerum

Adrastia   134, 150
All, the (τὸ πᾶν, the universe)   14, 40–42,
    70–76, 91, 93, 123, 126n42, 126n44,
    127n47, 133, 143, 147, 150, 152, 155,
    163–165, 167–168, 175–177, 186–187,
    210–211, 216, 223–224, 225, 228,
    230
    as perfect totality   2–3, 125, 139, 163–165,
      172–175, 181–182 190, 199–200
    as whole before the parts   121, 169–175,
      178–179, 213–214
    as whole composed of parts   101–105,
      109–110, 116, 121, 129, 140, 158, 169–175,
      178–179, 208
Anaxagoras   89n39
Aristotle   9–10, 15, 21n2, 32, 36, 41–48, 51,
    61, 68n64, 76n90, 83n1, 87n28, 89n36,
    109–110, 120, 126–127, 163n2, 183,
    205–206, 208, 212, 220
asymmetry, axiom of   23
atomic form (ἄτομον εἶδος). *See* form, in
    matter

Baxter, D.   26–27, 48
becoming versus being   70–71, 81, 116, 146
being (τὸ ὄν)
    as Neoplatonic principle. *See* One
      Being
    Being-Life-Intellect, triad of   64, 77–78,
      122, 127n46, 143
    Being-Sameness-Difference
      (*Timaeus*)   99–101
Brentano, F.   4n7

Calculus of Individuals   23
Cantor, G.   84, 90
causality   42–43, 57–61, 62–74, 77–78,
    88–89
    existing according to a cause (κατ' αἰτίαν,
      mode of being)   87–89, 103–105,
      157
change over time   21, 30, 124–126, 164–168,
    187, 193–194, 196–197, 199–200–201,
    209–211, 217–218, 225

Classical Extensional Mereology   22–25,
    28–29
composition
    as identity   25–28
    in a qualitative sense   58–62, 67–76,
      78–82, 207
    in a quantitative sense   63, 69, 74–76,
      80–82, 207
cosmos. *See* All, the
Cronus. *See* intellective triads,
    Cronus-Rhea-Zeus

Damascius   14, 16, 105n86, 127, 132n70, 215,
    219, 220n11
Demiurge, the   2–3, 70–74, 78
    as Maker and Father. *See* Fathers and
      Makers
    as Zeus   143–145, 151–153, 160, 193n81
demiurgy
    generation by the Demiurge   14, 40,
      41n97, 70–74, 79, 99–100, 109–110, 123,
      151–152, 167, 169–172, 174–182, 184–192,
      197–198, 201, 211, 220n9
    generation by the young gods   71–75,
      80, 166–167, 169–170, 175–176, 179–182,
      188–189, 191–193, 211
    ten gifts of the Demiurge   163n6,
      168–169, 171–172, 175, 179–180
Difference (τὸ θάτερον, Platonic principle)
    99–101, 143n113, 147–148, 172, 219
dissolubility   42, 117, 165–168, 176–177,
    184–189, 192–193, 198
distinctive character (ἰδιότης)   9, 66–70,
    74–76, 78–82, 97, 104, 116–117, 112, 129,
    135, 138, 152–153, 158, 171, 174, 190, 193,
    207, 209–210, 216, 222, 225–226
    existing καθ' ὕπαρξιν (mode of
      being). *See* hyparxis, as mode of being
    of wholeness   98, 103, 109–110, 122–127,
      155–156, 161–162, 208, 212–214, 216–217,
      221, 225
division (διάκρισις) of Platonic Forms. *See*
    Platonic Forms, in the intellective
    Intellect

250 INDEX RERUM

Epicureanism   21
essence versus activity   131–132, 165, 196–198, 217–218
Eternity (ὁ αἰών, Neoplatonic principle)   78, 95, 107–108, 123, 129–131, 135, 158–160
  and time   123, 163–165, 210
  and wholeness   68n63, 116, 124–127, 136–137, 139n102, 141–142, 150–151, 153–157, 168, 170, 177, 181–182, 187, 195, 202, 209, 214–217, 219, 222, 224, 227, 229
eternity versus perpetuity   126, 219–220
Eustratius of Nicaea   111n107
evil   100n71, 102n80, 187, 198, 228
  as parasitic existence (παρυπόστασις)   188–189, 199, 202
  as result of a particularised existence   125, 196–202
  of the soul   189, 197–198
extension (in logical terms). See Classical Extensional Mereology and set theory
  versus intension   222n15
extension (in spatiotemporal terms)   117–118, 170, 209, 219–220

Fathers and Makers   71–73, 128n51
form
  as mereological criterion   42–47, 48–50
  as Platonic Idea. See Platonic Forms
  formal parts   44, 46–47, 48–50
  in matter   42–46, 76–77, 81–82, 85, 106–107, 125, 148–149, 190–194, 196, 199, 211, 226
four-dimensionalism   124, 126, 167–168, 219
four elements (fire, air, water, earth)   40–41, 64, 70, 71n73, 74n81, 75, 125, 170–172, 174, 179, 181–182, 186, 206, 211, 213, 215

General Extensional Mereology   23n10
General Sum Principle   24
Good, the (τὸ ἀγαθόν)
  as intelligible Form   125, 227
  as the One   41n97, 125, 131, 159, 200–201
  participation in the Good   57, 125, 131, 159, 183, 187–188, 195–196, 200, 202, 209, 217–218

the Good in Plato   227–228
the good in us   125
Goodman, N.   23

Harte, V.   10–11, 26–27, 32–43, 45, 46, 50, 61, 206, 214, 226, 229
henads (ἑνάδες)   85–86, 105, 107–108, 109n101, 128, 137, 153
  as members of intelligible triads   94, 108, 132, 137n94, 138–140, 208
  Limit and the Unlimited (τὸ πέρας, τὸ ἄπειρον)   75–76, 129n53
heaven (οὐρανός)   132–133
  as synonym for 'cosmos'   102. See also All, the
  cosmic heaven   104–105, 128, 172–173, 174–176, 179, 181, 192, 194
  heavenly bodies   70, 71n73, 74–75, 74n81, 74n82, 125, 165, 171–172, 179, 182n54, 183–184, 211, 215
  intelligible heaven   132–134, 136–138, 139n102, 140–142, 155, 157, 160, 164
Hobbes, Th.   22n1
Husserl, E.   4n7
hylomorphism. See form in matter
hyparxis (ὕπαρξις)   89n36
  as mode of being   87–92, 100
  as principality   94, 97, 140–141, 150, 162
hypostases of reality   55, 70–71, 85, 92–93, 94n54, 95, 106, 123–124, 125n40, 131–132, 134–137, 141–143, 145–149, 151–152, 155, 160, 210

Iamblichus   14, 16, 55, 134n82, 163, 166n15
Ideas. See Platonic Forms
Identity view. See composition as identity
immortality   80, 126–127, 165–168, 175–179, 181–182, 188–190, 197–198, 209–211, 213–214, 216, 220–221, 225
indissolubility of the works of the Demiurge. See dissolubility
individuality. See Platonic Forms, of individuals
indivisibility   33, 35
  of atoms   21
  of intelligible beings   117–118, 145, 147–149, 194, 208–209, 211

INDEX RERUM

Intellect, the (ὁ νοῦς)
  Being-Life-Intellect, triad of. *See* being
  in Plotinus   55, 118, 220
  in Porphyry   119–121, 122n24, 151n134, 158,
    220–221
  in Proclus   55, 57–58, 64–71, 77–78,
    82n106, 85, 104, 115, 117–123, 131–132,
    155–156, 158, 160, 163, 164n9, 167, 191,
    208–209, 214, 219–221, 226n20
  in the cosmos   169–170, 172–174, 177–179,
    181, 199
intellective triads (νοερά)   129, 138n95,
  142–144, 210, 217
  as origin of the Platonic Forms. *See*
    Platonic Forms, in the intellective
    Intellect
  Cronus-Rhea-Zeus   144–153
intelligible-intellective triads (νοητὰ καὶ
  νοερά)   94n54, 131–135, 140–141, 210, 217
  triad of perfection   134–135, 138–141, 145,
    155
  triad of whole and part   135–138, 141,
    156
intelligible triads (νοητά)   93–98, 93n47,
  123–124, 127–128, 131–132, 209, 217
  principle of Being. *See* One Being
  principle of Multiplicity. *See* Paradigm,
    the (Neoplatonic principle)
  principle of Wholeness. *See*
    Wholeness-itself

Koslicki, K.   11, 32, 36, 40, 42–51, 156, 161,
  206, 224

Leonard, H.S.   23
Leśniewski, S.   4, 22–23
Lewis, D.   11, 24–30, 32, 34, 36–37, 42, 46–48,
  50–51, 161, 206, 219–220, 226, 229
life
  as mereological criterion   29–31, 37,
    46–51, 127, 161, 215, 224–225
  as property of living beings   64–70,
    79–80, 82n106, 128, 166–168, 188–189,
    192, 194, 198, 202, 213–214, 222, 225
  contemplative life versus pleasurable
    life   38, 75n85, 227n23
  lifelessness   49, 58, 64–69, 75, 77, 80, 127,
    193, 217–218

Life (ἡ ζωή, Neoplatonic principle)   64–70,
  126–127, 212, 216
  Being-Life-Intellect, triad of. *See* being
limit and unlimited
  as mereological principles   38–40
  in Plato's *Philebus*   38–40, 75, 94, 206
Limit and Unlimited (τὸ πέρας and τὸ ἄπειρον,
  Proclean principles). *See also* henads
  in hylomorphic compounds   75–76, 190,
    207
  in intelligible beings   94, 129, 137–138,
    223
Living Being itself, the (τὸ αὐτοζῷον, Proclean
  principle). *See* Paradigm, the
    (Neoplatonic principle)

mathematical proportion   40–41
matter
  as infinitely divisible   63, 69, 80, 82
  in Aristotle   9, 41–47, 49, 68
  in Plato. *See* receptacle
  in Plotinus   198, 201
  in Proclus   8–9, 58, 60n26, 65n55, 72–73,
    75–77, 79–81, 186–188, 190, 193, 196–198,
    201, 207, 213, 226. *See also* matter, as
    infinitely divisible *and* substrate, of
    demiurgic production
  intelligible matter (ὕλη νοητή)   41–42
  material form (ἔνυλον εἶδος). *See* form, in
    matter
  material parts   42–47, 49–50, 68, 109,
    120n20, 156, 193, 213, 224
  material simples   29–31, 47–49, 206,
    225–226
materialism   48, 120
mereology
  formalistic versus naturalistic
    mereology   24, 47–51
  mereological atom   45
  mereological fuzziness   27–28, 48–49, 51,
    206, 223–224
  mereological regress   42–46
  mereological universalism. *See*
    unrestricted composition
mixture, the (τὸ μικτόν). *See* limit and
  unlimited, in Plato's *Philebus*
modes of being. *See* causality *and* hyparxis
  and participation

mortal beings (τὰ θνητά)   72, 74, 80, 127,
  150n133, 151n135, 159, 161–162, 165–168,
  171–172, 174–181, 184–194, 196–199,
  201–202, 205, 211, 213–214, 216, 219,
  220–221, 228–229. *See also* part(hood),
  particularised beings
movement   64, 142, 148n126, 165, 196
  of the heavenly bodies   164–165,
    210–211
multiplicity   3, 8, 55–56, 63, 69, 95, 97–98,
  103, 111–112, 118, 126n44, 133, 135–137,
  140–142, 145, 151n134, 158, 161, 210. *See
  also* procession *and* transcendence
  and unity, unfolding of unity
  as Neoplatonic principle. *See* Paradigm,
    the (Neoplatonic principle)
  as ultimate substrate   8–9, 227. *See also*
    substrate, in demiurgic production
myth of the winged chariot
  (*Phaedrus*)   132–133
  in Proclus   133–135, 155. *See also* heaven,
    intelligible heaven

Nicholas of Methone   16, 62n38, 118n11,
  120n17, 122, 221
Non-Identity view   26

Olympiodorus   11, 16, 55
One, the (τὸ ἕν)
  in Plato   93–96, 133, 136, 148n126, 210
  in Proclus   1, 8–9, 11, 14, 55–56, 58, 63, 65,
    69–70, 75, 77–80, 82, 86, 108n99, 125,
    138, 158–159, 161, 200–201, 207, 213–214,
    217, 225, 226n20. *See also* Good, the
One Being (τὸ ἓν ὄν)   72–74, 78–79, 94–96,
  102, 108, 123–124, 125n40, 127, 128n50,
  129–131, 133–138, 143–144, 150, 155, 158,
  160, 200, 208, 210, 213
one-power-being (ἕν, δύναμις, ὄν), triad
  of   94–98, 108, 132, 136, 140, 208
oneness. *See* unity
ontological innocence   30, 49, 115
  in Lewis   25–26, 205–206
  in Plato   32–35

paradigmatic cause   146, 191, 193n81, 211
Paradigm, the (Neoplatonic principle)   2,
  70–74, 78–79, 95, 105, 109, 120, 123–124,
  127, 133, 135, 149, 155, 160, 163–164, 184

as 'all-perfect' (παντελής)   130, 140–141,
  152–153, 155–158, 169–171
as composite thing   128–130, 142, 145, 155,
  157, 201
as whole before parts   102–105, 110, 129,
  145, 157, 172–173, 175, 221
part(hood)
  distinctive character of   213–214. *See also*
    intellective triads, triad of whole and
    part
  essential parts (συμπληρωτικά)   74n82
    130–131, 139, 154–155, 157, 159, 172, 174,
    179, 181–182, 193n82, 209–211, 222,
    227–228
  particularised beings (τὰ μερικά)   125,
    127, 146, 170–173, 180, 188–189, 195–198,
    209. *See also* mortal beings *and*
    participation, stability of
    participation *and* perfection,
    of mortal beings
  principle of. *See* intellective triads, triad of
    whole and part
  Proclus' definition of   103–104, 181, 212,
    217
  proper part(hood)   44–45, 49, 59, 80,
    116n2, 222n15
  pure parts   90, 138, 176, 180, 182–183
  whole in the part. *See* whole(ness), before
    the parts/composed of parts/in the
    part
  'whole parts' (ὅλα μέρη) of the
    cosmos   169–170, 173, 179, 218
participation   32, 56n6, 57, 60, 63–66, 92,
  168n20, 183–184, 193n82, 223
  and parthood   108n99
  between hypostases   85, 90, 106
  existing by participation (κατὰ μέθεξιν,
    mode of being)   87–80, 97–98, 197,
    225
  participation in the Good. *See* Good, the,
    participation in the Good
  stability of participation   125, 195–196,
    202, 209. *See also* Good, the,
    participation in the Good
  unparticipated versus participated.
    See Unparticipated, the
  problems of participation
    in Plato's *Parmenides*   82n105
    in Proclus   84n6, 146

INDEX RERUM 253

permanence (διαμονή)   126
perfection
  'all-perfect' (παντελής)   119, 130, 142,
    146, 152–154, 157–158, 209. *See also*
    Paradigm, the (Neoplatonic principle),
    as 'all-perfect' *and* part(hood),
    essential parts
  as completeness   2–3, 34, 116, 216.
    See also part(hood), essential parts
  before the parts/composed of parts/in the
    part   138–141, 147, 150, 153–154, 210
  beyond perfection (ὑπερτέλειος)   131*n*65,
    141
  of intelligible beings   57, 81–82, 116,
    123*n*26, 136, 146, 154–156, 160, 207, 209.
    See also intellective triads, triad of
    perfection
  of mortal beings   81–82, 192*n*97, 202, 207
  of Phileban mixtures   39–40
  of the cosmos. *See* All, the, as perfect
    totality
  of the whole   131, 159, 209–210, 221, 227.
    See also part(hood), essential parts
  perfect number. *See* Platonic Great Year
  principle of. *See* Paradigm, the
    (Neoplatonic principle), as 'all-perfect'
Plato   2–3, 32–42, 70, 94–95, 99, 123, 130,
    132–133, 227
Platonic Great Year   164
Platonic Forms (εἴδη)   35*n*70, 39*n*89, 62,
    77*n*92, 82*n*106, 84*n*6, 84–86, 98, 104,
    106, 111, 120, 218, 224–225
  in the intellective Intellect   142–152, 159,
    192–194, 196–197, 209–210, 213, 226,
    228–229
  in the Paradigm   70, 102–103, 128–129,
    155–156, 158, 173, 201
  of species. *See* form, in matter
  of individuals   85, 106–107, 190, 191–192,
    211
  traces of the Forms   72–74, 79
Plotinus   3*n*6, 7, 13, 16, 55, 61, 64, 89*n*39,
    93*n*51, 116, 118, 133*n*78, 163*n*2, 163*n*4, 164,
    201, 211, 223, 227*n*23
Plutarch   16, 21, 99*n*65, 186*n*63
Porphyry   7, 14, 16, 61–62, 89*n*39, 106, 118,
    119–121, 122*n*24, 129*n*57, 151*n*134, 158, 221
principality. *See* hyparxis, as principality

Proclus   *passim*
procession (πρόοδος)   55, 58, 60, 63–64,
    74–76, 80, 82, 108–109, 137, 142, 147, 149,
    150, 152, 158, 190–191, 200, 207, 216, 226
procession-reversion-remaining, triad
    of   55, 117

queer fusions   27–28

receptacle
  in Plato   41–42
  in Proclus. *See* matter, in Proclus *and*
    substrate, of demiurgic production
  in Van Inwagen   31, 47
relativity
  of intelligible principles   64, 107, 122,
    135, 186
  of whole and part   60*n*27, 79, 119–122,
    129, 146–147, 157–159, 197, 216, 221
remaining (μονή). *See* procession-reversion-
    remaining, triad of
remaining in one   123
Rest (στάσις, Platonic principle)   148*n*126
restricted composition   28–51, 161, 206,
    230
reversion (ἐπιστροφή)   114, 128, 164, 167,
    168*n*19, 183, 202, 213, 218, 228. *See also*
    procession-reversion-remaining,
    triad of
  self-reversion   117–118, 131–132, 208–209
Rhea. *See* intellective triads,
    Cronus-Rhea-Zeus
rule of Proclus   55–82, 127, 138, 161, 214
  and composition   58–62, 67–69
  and demiurgy   70–75
  and perfection   81–82

Sameness (τὸ ταὐτόν, Platonic
    principle)   99–101, 143*n*113, 148*n*126,
    172, 219
set theory   22–28, 47–48, 50, 84
Ship of Theseus-paradox   21, 29*n*38,
    165–167
Simplicius   16, 21*n*2
Special Composition Question   29, 31, 37
soul (ψυχή)   15, 55, 57–58, 64–69, 85, 127, 139,
    146–149, 163*n*4, 220
  and evil. *See* evil, of the soul

soul (ψυχή) (cont.)
  of the individual   60n26, 61, 67n60, 81,
    128, 132, 166–167, 176–180, 186, 188–190,
    192n79, 197–198, 213–214, 218
  vehicle (ὄχημα) of the soul   167
  World Soul   66, 99–101, 105, 109–110, 116,
    121, 143n113, 169–170, 172–175, 178–179,
    181, 208, 225
Stoicism   21
structure
  content versus structure   32–33, 48
  in Harte   36–43, 50
  in Koslicki   43–50
substrate   225
  as relation between participated
    characters   58, 60, 62, 68–69, 78–79,
    81–82, 167
  of demiurgic production   55n4, 63,
    71–75, 77–78, 82n106, 172, 186, 190, 227.
    See also matter, in Proclus
Syrianus   14, 16, 77n92, 111n106, 133n78

Tarski, A.   23n10
three-dimensionalism   124, 126
three-dimensional solids   40–41
three kinds of wholeness. See whole(ness),
    before the parts/composed of parts/
    in the part
third man-argument. See problems of
    participation
time. See also change over time
  and eternity. See Eternity
  as Neoplatonic principle (ὁ χρόνος)   163–
    165, 167–168, 169n23, 176–177
  forms (εἴδη) of time versus parts (μέρη) of
    time   163n2
totality   34, 130. See also All, the, as perfect
    totality
transcendence
  of being over wholeness   61–62, 122n25,
    130, 156, 221–222
  of form over matter   76, 84–85, 106–107,
    109, 194, 196–198, 212, 222
  of Intellect over the sensible cosmos. See
    extension (in spatiotemporal terms)
  of the Paradigm. See Paradigm, the
    (Neoplatonic principle), as whole
    before the parts
  of unity over plurality   14, 78, 82, 90,
    94n53, 109, 129, 142, 144–147, 150, 153,
    168n20, 192, 209–210, 213, 227. See also

Eternity, and time and henads and
    One, the, in Proclus and one-power-
    being, triad of
  of whole over part   34, 84, 91, 93, 98–104,
    109–110, 112, 115, 126, 135–138, 157–158,
    162, 166–167, 173–175, 181, 183–184,
    210–213, 216, 221, 223, 229. See also
    Wholeness itself
transitivity, axiom of   23–24, 59, 79
trout-turkey   25–27, 29, 32, 48, 161, 206

uniqueness of composition, axiom of   24,
    116n2
unity   3, 8–10, 25–26, 40, 42, 46, 69, 76,
    109–110, 112, 115, 118, 151, 154, 160, 184,
    201, 207, 211, 214. See also One, the
    and one-power-being, triad of and
    transcendence, of unity over plurality
  of the whole. See whole(ness), before the
    parts/composed of parts/in the part
    and transcendence, of whole over
    part
  unfolding (ἀνέλιξις) of unity   135–126,
    140–142, 155, 164–165, 210
universal-particular relation   14
  and whole-part relation (ὁλικῶς,
    μερικῶς)   59–62, 79–80, 119–122,
    171–172, 197, 199–200, 209, 221–222
  Aristotelean universal   84, 111
  as extensional set   61
  in Intellect   59, 64, 70n69, 79–80,
    85–86, 119, 129, 142, 145, 146–147,
    152, 155
  in the Proclean cosmos   71n73, 74,
    151–152, 171–172, 174–177, 179–181,
    182n54, 192, 198, 200
  three types of universal (antre rem, in
    rebus, post re)   111
unlimited, the. See limit and unlimited
    and Limit and Unlimited (Proclean
    principles)
unrestricted composition   24–28, 32, 47–48
Unparticipated, the (τὸ ἀμέθεκτον)   14,
    84–86, 91, 98, 111–122, 121, 129, 134, 140,
    148–149, 158–159, 163–164, 194, 212,
    216–218, 221–222
  unparticipated wholeness. See
    Wholeness-itself

Van Inwagen, P.   11, 28–32, 37, 46–51, 127, 162,
    206, 215, 224–226, 229

INDEX RERUM

Weak Supplementation Principle   23, 60*n*27

Whitehead, A.   23*n*10

whole(ness)
  and eternity. *See* Eternity
  and genus-species   61–62, 93, 119, 121
  and immortality. *See* immortality
  and Neoplatonic ethics   227–229
  and perfection. *See* perfection
  and the sum of its parts   1, 3, 22–28, 33–35, 42–44, 47–48, 51, 84, 109, 115, 130, 205, 212, 219, 223. *See also* transcendence, of whole over part
  and universality. *See* universal-particular relation
  as axiological term   116, 122, 123*n*26, 125, 130–131, 150–151, 159, 187, 195–202, 209, 216–218, 221–222
  as completeness. *See* perfection, as completeness
  as extensional term   22–28, 33–35, 61–62, 115, 116*n*2, 120–122, 158, 221–222
  as logical term   216, 221
  as relative term. *See* relativity, of whole and part
  as structure. *See* structure
  before the parts/composed of parts/in the part   1–2, 5, 61, 83–112, 116, 119, 121–123, 126*n*44, 129, 130*n*63, 133–134, 137, 139–141, 145, 147–150, 152–158, 163, 172–175, 177–181, 183–184, 189, 193*n*82, 194–195, 207–210, 213–214, 220–221, 223
  composed of wholes (ὅλον ὅλων)   41*n*97, 72, 74*n*81, 101, 103, 139, 171–172, 178–179, 208
  of intelligible beings. *See* Eternity, and wholeness *and* indivisibility, of intelligible beings
  of mortal beings. *See* mortal beings *and* perfection, of mortal beings
  Proclus' definition of   211–218, 222

Wholeness itself (ἡ αὐτοολότης)   62, 91–92, 95–98, 109, 121–123, 124–125, 131, 136, 141, 147, 153, 156, 161, 164–165, 182, 184, 208, 210, 212, 214, 216, 221–222, 229. *See also* Eternity

wholesome(ness). *See* whole(ness), as axiological term

young gods. *See* demiurgy, generation by the young gods

Zeno of Elea   21*n*2

Zeus. *See* Demiurge, the, as Zeus *and* intellective triads, Cronus-Rhea-Zeus

Printed in the United States
by Baker & Taylor Publisher Services